JOURNEYS IN
SOCIAL PSYCHOLOGY

JOURNEYS IN
SOCIAL PSYCHOLOGY

Looking Back to Inspire the Future

Edited by
Robert Levine • Aroldo Rodrigues
Lynnette Zelezny

Psychology Press
Taylor & Francis Group

New York   Hove

Psychology Press
Taylor & Francis Group
270 Madison Avenue
New York, NY 10016

Psychology Press
Taylor & Francis Group
27 Church Road
Hove, East Sussex BN3 2FA

Printed in the United States of America on acid-free paper
10 9 8 7 6 5 4 3 2 1

International Standard Book Number-13: 978-0-8058-6134-1 (Hardcover)
Library of Congress Control Number: 2007943029

**Visit the Taylor & Francis Web site at
http://www.taylorandfrancis.com**

**and the Psychology Press Web site at
http://www.psypress.com**

Contents

Preface   vii
Introduction   ix

One Happy Autobiography   1
    Ed Diener

Organizing for Surprise: A Career of Arranging to Be Captured   19
    Robert B. Cialdini

From Social Psychology to Neuroscience and Back   39
    Shelley E. Taylor

A Career on the Interdisciplinary Divide: Reflections on the Challenges of
    Bridging the Psychological and the Social   55
    Alice H. Eagly

Life Experiences and Their Legacies   69
    Bernard Weiner

The Journey from the Bronx to Stanford to Abu Ghraib   85
    Philip G. Zimbardo

The Full Cycle of an Interamerican Journey in Social Psychology   105
    Aroldo Rodrigues

Introduction, Methods, Results, Discussion: The Story of a Career   129
    Robert Rosenthal

An Autobiography: Why Did Culture Shape My Career?   145
    Harry C. Triandis

Toward Understanding Social Power: A Personal Odyssey   165

　　　Bertram H. Raven

A Social Psychologist Examines His Past and Looks to the Future   189

　　　Harold B. Gerard

Some Reflections on 50 Years in Social Psychology   211

　　　Harold H. Kelley

A Career That Spans the History of Modern Social Psychology   221

　　　Morton Deutsch

Conclusions: Looking Back to Inspire the Future   241

　　　Robert Levine and Lynnette Zelezny

Author Index   251

Subject Index   255

Preface

*T*he chapters that follow offer first-person accounts of the career journeys of 13 distinguished social psychologists. The authors describe their personal career journeys, the significant people and events that influenced their paths, the major turning points, the main decisions, the challenges, the opportunities and setbacks they experienced, and how the lessons they learned along the way may shine a beacon for future social psychologists. Taken together, these chapters chronicle the history of modern social psychology. Also, we believe they will serve as inspiration and counsel to students considering a career in social psychology.

This book grew out of two remarkable events, the Yosemite conferences of 1997 and 2006, both of which were sponsored by the Department of Psychology at California State University, Fresno. Both of these meetings took place in an idyllic setting on the edge of Yosemite National Park. The conferences followed the same general format: one- and one-half days of presentations from a small group of exceptional invited participants, along with ample time for formal and informal discussion between the participants and conference attendees.

In the first Yosemite conference, we brought together nine distinguished senior social psychologists to reflect on the history of the discipline that they were very much a part of creating. (The book *Reflections on One Hundred Years of Experimental Social Psychology* [Rodrigues & Levine, 1999] and a video from the conference were produced.) The second Yosemite conference, which took place in the spring of 2006, focused on a theme that was more about people. On this occasion, as in this book, we asked participants to describe the course of their own career journeys. Some participants from the first Yosemite conference attended as discussants.

Each of the eight presenters at Yosemite II have contributed chapters to this book: Robert Cialdini, Edward Diener, Alice Eagly, Aroldo Rodrigues, Robert Rosenthal, Shelley Taylor, Harry Triandis, and Bernard Weiner. Also in this book are chapters from five of the presenters at the first Yosemite conference: Morton Deutsch, Harold Gerard, Harold Kelley, Bertram Raven, and Philip Zimbardo. Some of the material in these latter chapters originally appeared in the first Yosemite book but, we believe, fits more properly into the current theme. We thank Joann Miller of Basic Books for permission to use this material. Harold Kelley and Harold Gerard died in early 2003. We modified their chapters for the present book with the input and the approval of their wives, Dorothy Kelley and Desy Gerard, respectively.

We owe thanks to many people. The Yosemite II conference was generously supported by Jeronima Echeverria, provost and vice president for academic affairs, and Kin Ping Wong, dean of the College of Science and Mathematics at California State University, Fresno. Thanks are also due to Sheri Osborn, Christine Thiboudeax, and Liliana Oceguera for their outstanding supportive roles in the organization of this endeavor. Many graduate and undergraduate students of California State University, Fresno dedicated hours of their time to the conference that led to the present book. Debra Riegert, our editor at Lawrence Erlbaum Associates, and Rebecca Larsen, her editorial assistant, were supportive and helpful in every phase of the production of this volume. Finally, we wish to express a special word of thanks to the anonymous reviewers who took time to read the manuscript and make many helpful suggestions. Without the concerted effort of many, this book could not have come to light.

Robert Levine
Aroldo Rodrigues
Lynnette Zelezny
Fresno, California

Introduction

*I*n this book, 13 prominent social psychologists reflect on their careers. You will read first-person accounts of the history and events that guided their career paths, the people and places that made a difference in their lives, the stepping-stones they took, the detours and bumps on their roads, and the choices they made along the way.

What makes for a successful social psychologist? Is there a social psychologist type—a personality or typical value system—that is drawn to the discipline? Or is the attraction mostly the result of happenstance and quirks of experience, perhaps a defining life event or an inspirational professor? Is there a path that personifies the great teachers? The best researchers? Can we predict or explain why one person's career takes a particular course while the next person's moves in another? Why do different people make different choices along the way? Why can the same decision have such different consequences for different people?

No people should be more qualified to answer questions like these than social psychologists. Charting the course of individuals through situations is, after all, what social psychology is about. Modern social psychology was founded on the belief that an interdisciplinary approach was needed to take on such broad, unwieldy questions about life. We are a hybrid of two older disciplines: personality psychology and sociology. The first of these tends to focus on the private, internal functioning of people; the latter focuses on their social groups. Social psychologists, at our best, take in the entire dynamic picture, across space and time. We study the give and take between individuals and the environments that guide their behavior, what our founding father Kurt Lewin called the "life space." Our flagship journal is aptly titled the *Journal of Personality and Social Psychology* (JPSP).

Social psychologists are used to studying the most personal of subject matters. Our bread-and-butter topics include questions about the self, persuasion, helping and altruism, aggression and violence, prejudice, and even the dynamics of liking and love. When social psychologists study the interaction of people in their environments, they are studying the living of life itself.

Thematically, then, the study of career paths fits neatly into the domain of social psychology. The chapters that follow, however, are hardly what we are used to reading from mainstream social psychologists. Although the content fits in the mainstream, the form does not. Social psychology, at least as it is practiced in today's world of academia, is among the most empirical and methodologically rigorous of disciplines. Look through practically any social psychological textbook and you will be hard pressed to find a theory or concept or even a comment that is not accompanied by empirical, scientifically derived research findings. Our flagship journals are almost totally composed of empirical studies or empirically grounded theories.

If social psychologists were asked to write an article about career paths for one of our academic journals, most of them would approach the problem via either or both of two tracks. Our personality side would assess dispositional traits and link these to peoples' career actions and choices. Our social side would identify the elements of the situations each of these individuals happened upon and how these situational forces guided their career paths. Finally, there would be the interaction between the person and the situation. Each of these approaches would be followed through meticulous scientific methodology: operationalizing and controlling independent and dependent variables, where time and place are portioned out, where sequences flow unidirectionally, usually linearly, and, most of all, where anything and everything we focus our scientific tools on can be quantified and, in the end, statistically analyzed.

But, as social psychologists are painfully aware, when it comes to big questions—and, by any definition, the course of our lives is a big one—the systematic, carefully controlled methods that so define our fields, and have led to so many of our greatest achievements, may lead to deeply unsatisfying answers. Capturing meaning in these paths requires a more flexible and spontaneous approach.

As a result, we gave the contributors to this book a very nonmainstream assignment: writing stories. As instructors—which each of the book contributors has been for many years—we are well aware of the power of storytelling. "Tell me a fact and I'll learn. Tell me the truth and I'll believe. But tell me a story and it will live in my heart forever," goes an Indian proverb. Good teachers understand the value of balancing systematic research with stories and anecdotes. When inserted effectively, the anecdotes don't water down the science; they bring it to life.

Academic writing, however, is virtually all science. There have been, to be sure, scattered attempts at personal storytelling, autobiographies by social psychologists and biographies about them. Perhaps the most notable of the former is Fritz Heider's classic *The Life of a Psychologist: An Autobiography* (Heider, 1983). A compelling example of the latter is the recent biography of Stanley Milgram by Thomas Blass, a social psychologist, titled *The Man Who Shocked the World: The Life and Legacy of Stanley Milgram* (Blass, 2004). For the most part, however, the storytelling that we embrace when giving lectures is not an acceptable mode of communication in our academic writing. Social psychologists may write articles in which they scientifically analyze samples of other peoples' stories. One does not, however, submit a personal narrative for publication to the JPSP. It is worth noting that the esteemed social psychologists who wrote the chapters in this book achieved their reputations through academic writing in journals such as JPSP.

For this book, then, we asked respected, mainstream social psychologists to step away from their usual academic writing style and instead write stories in a narrative style. (More cynical observers than we are might say we asked them to write in the English language.) Furthermore, we asked them to focus on a subject that is normally off limits in the academic world: themselves.

We think readers will be more than impressed with the results. For one thing, these distinguished scientists turn out to be first-rate writers. Who knew? More important, they each have rich and fascinating stories to tell. Like any good biography, these narratives teach us as much about ourselves as they do about the writers. They provoke fresh looks, mirrors of sorts, at our own paths, both those taken and those not taken. The chapters may be especially valuable to students who are wrestling with their own career decisions. To pursue a career in psychology? In teaching? Research? An applied specialty? Perhaps even a career in social psychology? For these students, we hope that these stories, as well as the implicit and explicit advice in these chapters, will provide worthy templates to consider.

These stories also contribute on another level. They not only describe particular idiosyncratic careers but, in a very real sense, record the story of modern social psychology.

The fact is that modern social psychology—the empirical, scientific discipline that is practiced in academia today—is a very young discipline. Its empirical roots are often traced back a little more than a century to Norman Triplett's 1898 study of bicycle racers (Triplett, 1897–1898). Of course, there were scholars who asked social psychology questions well before Triplett. In his classic chapter on the history of the discipline in the second edition of the *Handbook of Social Psychology*, Gordon Allport argued that a case can be made that the founder of social psychology was Plato, or perhaps Aristotle, or at least one of the later political philosophers such as Hobbes and Bentham (Allport, 1968). Or, he suggested, we could look in more recent times for our founding father, perhaps to one of the great thinkers of the 19th century—such as Hegel, Comte, Lazarus, and Steinthal—who wrote about social psychological issues. But these early scholars limited their social psychology to theory and philosophy. Social psychology in its contemporary, empirical form can be pretty safely traced to Triplett's experiment.

In reality, the field that most of today's social psychologists engage in is even younger than the 100 years since Triplett. The social psychology practiced for the next 30 to 40 years after Triplett's experiment was almost completely unrelated in both form and content to what we study today. Formwise, social psychology at the turn of the century mostly reverted to armchair theorizing. The field was dominated by theorists such as Cooley, Tarde, and McDougall, who offered programs that, as Morton Deutsch wrote, were "grandly ambitious but meager in detail." These are the roots from philosophy and sociology, not the empirical social psychology that defines the field today.

The true functional beginnings of modern empirical social psychology, it is generally agreed, are most closely traced to the work of Kurt Lewin and his Research Center for Group Dynamics (RCGD) in the late 1930s and 1940s. The RCGD revitalized the empirical approach and, more important, created one that was different from anything in the past and that still defines the best of the field today. Lewin brought about a boldly imaginative empiricism in which he and his students devised powerful social situations, both inside and outside the laboratory, that created big differences. The RCGD emphasized a balance between the pure and the applied, the laboratory and real-life field research, theory and application (a famous Lewin dictum is "There is nothing so practical as a good theory"). His field theory conceptualized the person and the situation as a dynamic unit. "Every psychological event depends upon the state of the person and at the same time on the environment, although their relative importance is different in different cases," Lewin (1936) wrote. The RCGD became the primary training ground for mainstream social psychology. It taught a spirit and model that defines the field today.

If asked, most senior social psychologists, including the present authors, could trace their professional lineage back one or two generations to Lewin's RCGD. Two of them, Morton Deutsch and Harold Kelley, were Lewin's actual students. Because the functional beginnings of social psychology essentially go back to Lewin, the career journeys in this book tell us much about the journey of modern social psychology. As Deutsch, the oldest of the authors, wrote, "My career almost spans the existence of modern social psychology."

In 1996, Robert Cialdini, as president of the Society for Personality and Social Psychology, began a symposium on Lewin with the proclamation, "I would like to declare personality and social psychology a mature discipline." If Cialdini's claim is justified, the authors of the following chapters are certainly among those most responsible for leading us through our adolescence. Taken together, these career stories are very much of the story of our young discipline.

A word about organization: The chapters are presented in reverse order of career experience. In other words, the book moves deeper into the history of social psychology as it progresses. We begin with Edward Diener, who began his first (and only) tenure-track job in 1974, and end with Morton Deutsch, who received his Ph.D. in 1948 and worked at the RCGD with Lewin.

The chapters that follow offer the richness of insiders' perspectives spanning a wide range of social psychology. These accounts chronicle the journeys of a group of scholars who, from the multitude of paths that were offered up to them, chose social psychology and became some of its most productive scholars. They began each of their careers with very different intentions and interests. They made choices leading in multiple new directions, eventually leading to the contributions we have come to know them by. Here, in their own words, are their professional travelogues.

Robert Levine

California State University, Fresno

REFERENCES

Allport, G. W. (1968). The historical background of modern social psychology. In G. Lindzey & E. Aronson (Eds.), *Handbook of social psychology* (Vol. 1, 2nd ed.). Reading, MA: Addison-Wesley.

Blass, T. (2004). *The man who shocked the world: The life and legacy of Stanley Milgram.* New York: Basic Books.

Heider, F. (1983). *The life of a psychologist: An autobiography*. Lawrence: University Press of Kansas.

Lewin, K. (1936). *A dynamic theory of personality* (p. 236). New York: McGraw-Hill.

Rodrigues, A., & Levine, R. (Eds.). (1999). *Reflections on one hundred years of experimental social psychology*. New York: Basic Books.

Triplett, N. (1897–1898). The dynamogenic factors in pacemaking and competition. *American Journal of Psychology*, 9, 507–533.

One Happy Autobiography

ED DIENER

Department of Psychology, University of Illinois

L ife looked bright in 1946 when I arrived in Glendale, California, the youngest of six children, several weeks overdue and a fat little guy at more than 9 pounds in weight. In the beginning, I knew very little about statistics and subjective well-being, but I had a loving family that produced subjective well-being in me. At my baptism, 2 weeks after my arrival, my older brother got his head stuck in the communion railing at the church and stole the show. After that unfortunate incident, I have had the wind at my back through the rest of my life. In this accounting I will present my life like a social psychology experiment: in a 3-by-3 design—three facets each for three major topics. The three overarching domains are (a) the three fun-filled stages of my professional career as a research psychologist, (b) the personality characteristics and resources that helped my success, and (c) the challenges I overcame. At age 60 I am hopeful that my life has another 30 or 40 years left to go, and therefore this report is a periodic update, not an autobiography per se, which will come much later.

CAREER STAGES

My father was a successful farmer, who wanted nothing more than to produce more successful farmers. So he sent me to Fresno State College to obtain a degree in agriculture. Unfortunately for my father, the study of seeds and weeds bored me to death. He did not seem to realize that plants do the same thing year after year, whereas I noticed this early on and was not enthusiastic about the repetitive character of Mother Nature. I was, however, drawn to anthropology and psychology, where the subject matter seemed less predictable.

My father was interested in concrete things such as tractors and tomatoes, not in something as ephemeral as the human mind. My father loved numbers, as I do, but he loved numbers applied to the physical world, not to human behavior. He thought the world needed more weathermen, not psychologists. For my dad, predictive validity meant accurately forecasting rain, not human behavior. He told me that we would not need psychologists if only people worked harder, because then their mental problems would disappear. Nonetheless, my parents allowed me to follow my own interests and were supportive once it was clear that psychology was my passion.

In the standard research methods course required of all psychology majors at Fresno State, each student had to conduct his or her own study, and I proposed to the professor that I assess the happiness of migrant farmworkers. After all, I had

1

grown up with farmworkers, and most of them appeared to me to be relatively happy, even though relatively poor. The professor was not pleased with my proposal. He said, "Mister Diener, you are not doing that research project for two reasons. First, I know that farmworkers are not happy, and second, there is no way to measure happiness." Ironically, I conducted my class project on conformity. Thus, I was temporarily diverted from studying happiness. It wouldn't be until 1981, when I received tenure at Illinois, that I would finally become free to study what I wanted: happiness. But in the interim, I needed a topic to fill the intervening 15 years; something to while away my time.

Stage 1: Deindividuation

After working in a psychiatric hospital for several years, I attended graduate school at the University of Washington. My wife, Carol, and I chose the university because Seattle was very green and pretty; we knew nothing about the school itself. When I see the effort students now put into choosing just the right graduate school, I am amazed at how nonchalant we were about this important decision. But this leads me to also wonder whether maybe finding the perfect graduate school is not as important as what you make of the experience once you arrive.

I was an eager beaver during those graduate school years; I even wrote a history book while working on my dissertation. I think the secret was that I did not waste time. I worked hard all day and a few evenings without interruption and, therefore, had the weekends free for my family. I came to grad school after being a hospital administrator, and so I was organized and efficient. While I was at Washington, the Department of Psychology moved to a new building, but I remained behind in the deserted Denny Hall because that allowed me to have an entire floor of the building to conduct my deindividuation studies. I had a small army of undergraduate assistants, up to 20 per semester, to help conduct studies and code data. We had a ball running those studies.

My major professors at the University of Washington were Irwin Sarason and Ronald E. Smith, who taught me the basics of personality psychology and the importance of multimethod measurement. Years later, I would edit a book on multimethod measurement, and I owe my interest in this area to my mentors in Seattle. An idea that I learned from my mentors at the home of the Huskies is that even when situations exert a powerful influence on behavior, personality can simultaneously produce strong effects. We published a review study that showed personality, on average, predicted as much variance as did experimentally manipulated situational variables.

Another one of my professors in Seattle was Scott Fraser, with whom I and other graduate students began a series of unusual studies on deindividuation, the loss of self-regulation in groups. Given the riots of the 1960s and the ongoing anti-Vietnam rallies, we were intrigued by crowd behavior. In one series of deindividuation studies, we observed thousands of trick-or-treaters as they came on Halloween to dozens of homes around Seattle. We experimentally manipulated factors such as anonymity, arousal, and responsibility and observed whether kids "stole" extra candy. In some situations, almost all trick-or-treaters made off with extra sweets, and in other conditions almost no children did so, thus demonstrating the power that situational factors sometimes exert on cute, costumed, rule-breaking children. These studies made the national news, often repeating each year just before Halloween. These studies were fun because I conducted them with fellow graduate students Art Beaman and Karen Endresen, with whom I became close friends. We worked hard for a common purpose and did not compete with each other. Notice to graduate students: Though you need to advance your own career, cooperation with your fellow graduate students, not competition, is the way to achieve this.

While in graduate school, I employed a method for studying group aggression called the "beat the pacifist" paradigm. Our participants were asked to help us test the training of pacifists, to ensure that they would remain nonaggressive when faced with challenges to their beliefs. The participants could do so by discussing pacifism with the target, by harassing him to see how he would react, or even by attacking the victim with various implements. We manipulated factors such as arousal, anonymity, and responsibility. The differences in aggression between conditions were dramatic. In some conditions, many participants used rubber bats to hit the target hundreds of times in a short period. In some instances, the study had to be halted because the participants were attacking the pacifist (often played bravely by me to spare my assistants from this unpleasant role) in a way that would injure him.

It may surprise some readers that we did not encounter problems in receiving ethics approval for these studies. However, as I recall, the psychology department in those times was overshadowed by much more scandalous affairs. One professor was fired for selling cocaine, and he justified his stash of drugs by claiming it was part of a psychology experiment. A second young professor turned out not to actually have a Ph.D., because he attended graduate school without being enrolled as a student. Another professor was found to be having sex with the undergraduates in his class and used the defense that he was helping the women by moving them to a higher spiritual level by putting them in moral conflict. Once, a female professor asked me whether I had an "open marriage," and I naively responded "yes." Only later did I realize that her inquiry was an invitation to sex rather than an inquiry about the honesty of my marriage. Once I understood the real question, I had to admit that my marriage was not open. Thus, although not many Institutional Review Boards today would approve the "beat the pacifist" studies, in the context of the 1970s, they seemed unremarkable.

In the 1980s, I traveled to South Africa to serve as an expert witness, based on my deindividuation research, in a murder trial in which a crowd had murdered a woman. An angry crowd of more than ten thousand beat and killed a woman who was believed to be a police informant. The entire incident was captured by a television network, and fourteen of those involved in the murder were apprehended by the police. My role for the defense was to convince the judges that the crowd situation provided mitigating circumstances; without this defense, the defendants would all be hanged, because the death sentence was automatically imposed unless mitigating circumstances could be proved. Most of the defendants were found guilty, but none were hanged. My work with deindividuation ended on a high note.

The deindividuation studies were fun, but I was anxious to move on to new territory. Because I was granted tenure at Illinois in 1980, I was finally free to begin studying happiness.

Stage 2: Subjective Well-Being

In 1980, Carol and I spent our sabbatical year in the Virgin Islands. While Carol taught nine psychology courses at the College of the Virgin Islands, I spent the year on the beach, reading the 18 books and 220 articles I could find that were related to subjective well-being. One might think that the island setting was conducive to happiness, but a surprising thing we noticed was that many people who moved to this tropical setting did not find the happiness they sought. Instead, their alcoholism, bad social skills, and chronic discontent often followed them to paradise. Living in paradise apparently does not guarantee high subjective well-being, and so I wondered, what does? That year I wrote a basic introduction for psychologists to the field of subjective well-being, which appeared in the *Psychological Bulletin* in 1984. That early paper has been cited more than 1,200 times.

Journalists ask why I decided to study happiness in those days, when it was a topic far from the beaten track. Although the works of the humanistic psychologists, such as Maslow, stimulated my interest in the ingredients of the good life, my parents also had a profound influence on me. They were happy people and believed in looking at the bright side of events. My mother presented me with books such as Norman Vincent Peale's *The Power of Positive Thinking*, and this piqued my interest. My mother told me that even criticism could be framed in a positive way. No wonder I was drawn to happiness.

When I began to read the literature on subjective well-being, I realized that this was relatively unstudied terrain. Yes, there were pioneers—such as Norman Bradburn and Marie Jahoda—but most topics in this area had not been analyzed in depth. Not only did the topic seem very important but it also seemed relatively easy to explore, because so little research had been done. What a happy decision for me.

In the 25 years since I entered this field, my laboratory has concentrated on several topics, including measurement. Although measurement is boring to many, I believe that it is pivotal, forming the foundation of scientific work. Thus, I have worked to create new measures, validate measures, examine the structure of well-being, and analyze the relations between various types of assessment. Measurement issues are still understudied, and issues about defining and measuring well-being are among the most important questions in this area of study. Besides measurement, research from my laboratory has spanned topics from the influence personality and culture have on happiness to the effects of income and materialism.

Recently, as an extension of my measurement work, I have been exploring the idea of national indicators of well-being to aid policy makers. The idea is that national accounts of subjective well-being can be useful to policy makers by providing them with a metric for societal betterment that includes information beyond that obtained by economic indicators. I argue that we need a "Dow Jones of Happiness" that tells us how our nation is doing in terms of engagement at work, trust in our neighbors, life satisfaction, and positive emotions. The proposed national accounts of well-being have been greeted by more acceptance than would have been possible a decade ago. For example, the government of the United Kingdom is considering what well-being measures might be used on a systematic basis to inform policy, and the biennial survey of the European Union already includes a large number of questions about subjective well-being.

Another interest of mine is the outcomes of well-being: How does the experience of happiness and life satisfaction influence people's behavior and success? Sonja Lyubomirsky, Laura King, and I argue that happy people are likely to be successful people in all sorts of realms, such as on the job, in relationships, and in longevity and health. On the basis of this work, my son, Robert, and I are developing a book for the public, in which we present the case that happiness means more than feeling good—it is one ingredient in the recipe for success.

When I entered the field of subjective well-being, a few facts were already known. Nonetheless, most of the territory was uncharted. Looking at the area, I felt that the first priority after the development of good measures was to discover some basic, replicable facts, to map the topography of who is happy and who is unhappy. My role models were not the great theorists of science such as Newton, Darwin, and Einstein. I felt the field was much too primitive for even rudimentary theories. Instead, I looked to Karl von Frisch and Tycho Brahe as my two models for scientific work on subjective well-being. I read von Frisch's *Dance of the Bees* at age 14 and was awestruck by the genius of his simple experiments with bees. I had grown up on a farm where millions of domesticated honeybees were used for pollinating crops, and yet their behavior was inexplicable to me—they were a swarm of dangerous madness with a queen at the middle. But von Frisch discovered so much about bees' frenetic behavior from his experiments, demonstrating that powerful observation and experimentation can lead to true advances in human knowledge even without elaborate theories. Brahe, who wore an artificial silver nose because of a sword-fight mishap, carefully mapped the heavens, and his maps provided the basis of the theoretical advances by Copernicus and Keppler. Just as Brahe spent years of nights ensconced on a dark island recording the movements of the stars, I hoped to carefully chart who is happy and who is not, so that some later geniuses could produce Newtonian laws of happiness.

One of my goals for the field of subjective well-being was to develop other measures besides broad self-report scales, which suffer from certain limitations such as self-presentational differences between people. One method we began using in our earliest studies in 1981 was the experience-sampling method, in which we used alarm watches to signal people at random moments through the day. When their alarms sounded, participants rated their moods. If they were involved in sex or some other absorbing activity where interruption might ruin the mood, they could wait up to 30 minutes to complete the mood scales. We also developed informant report measures and memory measures of happiness.

Although I worked in relative obscurity in the early years, the topic has recently become popular. Happiness has become a hot topic among television and documentary artists as well as newspaper and magazine writers. A problem is that many journalists have a message they wish to convey and are merely looking for experts to confirm their opinion. The media reports are sometimes barely recognizable from what I said to the journalist. Although it is exciting to be featured in prominent outlets such as *Time* magazine and documentary films, my feeling is that very often now the reporting is outstripping our knowledge. As the field develops, the dance with the media will be a continuing struggle between providing helpful information to the public and not getting caught in a trap of telling more than we know.

One question that journalists frequently ask is what have I learned from my studies about happiness that I can use in my own life. Many people think of me as the happiest person they know. My own assessment is that I am extremely high in life satisfaction, but I am only average in levels of positive moods. Studying happiness is not a guarantee of being happy, any more than being a biologist will necessarily make one healthier. One thing that is quite clear to me is that happiness is a process, not a place. No set of good circumstances will guarantee happiness. Although such circumstances (a good job, a good spouse, and so forth) are helpful, happiness requires fresh involvement with new activities and goals—even perfect life circumstances will not create happiness. For me this meant that I should not worry about getting to a sweet spot in my career where everything would be lined up just right. I realized that eminence, awards, a desirable teaching load, a larger office, or whatever other thing I might want not guarantee happiness, although these things might help. Instead, I discovered that continuing to have goals that I enjoyed working toward was a key ingredient for happiness. People often think that once they obtain a lot of good things, they will thereafter be happy, without realizing they are, for the most part, likely to adapt to the circumstances. On the other hand, fresh involvement with new goals and activities can continue to produce happiness.

Another fact that has been evident in my life is that all people experience some negative life events, and yet many people are nevertheless still happy. I found that tragic events in my own life led to temporary unhappiness, but I bounced back. People do not necessarily bounce back completely from all negative events, but most humans are pretty resilient. The major sources of happiness often reside in a person's activities, social relationships, and attitudes toward life.

Stage 3: The Future

Some people believe they are entering the last phase of their life when they turn 60. I consider 60 to be the halfway point of my productive years (from 30 to 90). Thus, I am exploring new avenues for the second half of life. One project is a journal I founded for the Association of Psychological Science, called *Perspectives on Psychological Science*. For 4 years, I was the associate editor of the *Journal of Personality and Social Psychology*, and then I served as the editor of the personality section of that journal for 6 years. Alex Michalos, Ruut Veenhoven, and I founded the *Journal of Happiness Studies,* for which I was the chief editor for several years. The 12 years of previous editing was my warm-up for editing *Perspectives.* My goal is a lofty one—to make *Perspectives* the most interesting psychology journal in the world.

Another project for the next 30 years is to make Carol's life as happy as it can be. I must remind myself that living the good life is more than being a productive researcher; it includes being a good human as well. Early-career scientists should not forget this point. Although it may seem strange to mention Carol's happiness in a professional biography, I want to ensure that young, ambitious psychologists do not forget the point that they should not excel at their jobs at the expense of being decent human beings.

On the whole, except for a few health problems relating to aging, I expect the next 30 years to be as good as the past 30 years! Andrew Carnegie said that to die rich is to die disgraced. Thus, Carol and I have plans to use our money before we die on projects related to helping people and advancing psychology, which will require our money, time, and energy. This is yet another lesson for young readers: Life is not over at 50. Or 60. Or 70. Although I may slow down a bit after 60, scientists often continue productive careers into their 80s.

RESOURCES AND STRENGTHS

I believe that to understand people, we must consider their strengths and resources, not simply the problems they face. In my case, I have certain personality characteristics that have helped me succeed in the career path I chose, as well as abundant resources for which I am very grateful. I was fortunate to come from an affluent family, which allowed me fewer pressures when it came to money. I did not have to take added summer work if it interfered with my research, and I was able to fund much of my own research so that I did not have to spend time applying for grants. However, other resources were much more helpful than money.

Resource 1: Personality Characteristics

From an early age, I wondered about phenomena I observed. As a child, my curiosity sometimes got me in trouble. I once threw a rock at a swarm of bees to determine how they would react, and I found out the painful answer. I also recall frustrating my seventh-grade teacher with questions about math, such as how to compute cube roots. My head still hurts, at times, from wondering about so many things.

I was a sickly child, and so I spent a lot of time at home. I would roll dice for hours and record the outcomes, and eventually I figured out how to compute probabilities. I then turned to calculating the probabilities of poker and blackjack hands, a more challenging task for a sixth grader. I feel that curiosity is one of my biggest assets as a researcher; I always seemed to be fascinated more by what I did not know than by what I already knew. Engineering is probably a good field for those who like more certainties; psychology intrigues those who are drawn to uncertainties.

My intense curiosity about things has served me well. For example, I not only constantly wonder about what makes people happy (and it sometimes keeps me awake at nights) but also wonder how measures can be improved and what shortcomings there are in our current research. Many people think the core of a good scholar is intelligence; I think it is an intense sense of curiosity.

Although I was a high-achieving child, I was also always a sensation seeker and nonconformist. This sometimes resulted in danger seeking; for example, climbing the Golden Gate Bridge on several occasions. As a teenager I experimented quite a bit with gasoline, gunpowder, and fire. My parents gave me a car at age 12, for driving on dirt roads only, and I made good use of it with my friends—hunting birds from the windows as we drove. I did quite a few nonconformist things, perhaps even some illegal ones (which I will leave to your imagination). As an adult, I was known for parties at our house that featured events such as walking on broken glass, carving Spam into art, and seeing whose method worked best for removing red wine stains from our carpeting. Although I am embarrassed to provide more examples of my behaviors, I believe this playful attitude to life had positive effects on my scholarship. I was willing to take on new topics, even if they were not popular, and I was not much affected by what others thought, if I believed the topic was an interesting one. This tendency to be nonconforming led me to be attracted to topics that were not heavily worked by others, and it continues to lead me to challenge conventional wisdom.

Resource 2: My Upbringing and Family

I possess personality characteristics that have aided my career, but by far the biggest resource in my life has been the help I have received from others, starting with my parents. My parents gave me a sense of security and meaning in life. They were optimists, but they also transmitted the idea that we must all work to improve the world. My four older sisters lavished attention on me and made me think I was special. Because my parents almost never argued and never moved from their farm, the universe was a secure and benevolent place for me. Although I was no more special than anyone else, feeling secure and valued gave me a self-confidence that helped me take on new and big projects later in life.

I was the youngest of six children, but my siblings were much older and went away to high school, so I grew up much like an only child. Because I was often sick in my early years, my mother read to me for hours. As I grew older, my mom was intent on my being a high achiever. I won dozens of merit badges in Boy Scouts and many awards in 4-H. I also competed in many public speaking events even before I got to high school. While my mother focused on my accomplishments, my dad was a disciple of hard work. My 4-H projects were raising cattle, cotton, and sugar beets. I also did electrical and carpentry projects and did welding in the farm shop. In the summer, my dad directed me to drive a mammoth tractor, but I would do anything to escape that boring task. On the farm, I learned a high degree of self-reliance; I was expected to figure out how to do things and get them done. No mollycoddling from my dad. If I could have a car at age 12, I could figure out how to get things done too. Thus, I grew up in a world of hard work, self-reliance, and achievement. The things I learned growing up shaped the rest of my life, and many of the metaskills readily transferred to the research arena.

I attended Westside Elementary School, which was a farm school with many students who had recently emigrated from Mexico and had trouble with English. Because of the difficulty of attracting teachers to such a remote area, many of our instructors possessed only provisional teaching certificates. I had a teacher in fourth grade who showed a huge number of movies and then showed them again in reverse. I was never assigned even one minute of homework in my first nine years in school. Dissatisfied with this state of affairs, my parents sent me to a high-powered Jesuit boarding school for high school. The curriculum was tough, and because I had never had to do homework before, the three hours per day of study hall was traumatic for me. In addition, we were given library assignments, and I had never used a library. So I boarded a Greyhound bus and ran away. My parents told me I had to return to the school, but I refused, so I went to live with an older sister closer to home. I attended a Catholic school that did not have a study hall.

This was a fortunate turn of events for me, because it was in that high school that I met the love of my life, Carol. Although we encountered the police and a lady with a shotgun on our first two dates, our relationship flourished from the outset. We dated through 2 years of high school and 2 years of college, and we finally got married at the advanced age of 20 in our junior year at Fresno State. Carol was pregnant by our senior year in college, and we had our first children the fall after graduation. I still recall Carol throwing up from morning sickness before each of her final exams during that last year in college.

Carol and I have had a wonderful family life. Rather than interfering with my research, it has provided the security and positive moods that have allowed me to be more successful in my research. Carol gave birth to our twins, Marissa and Mary Beth, when we were 22. In those days before sonograms, our twins came totally unexpectedly. We had Robert while I was a graduate student. Thus, when we moved to my first job, at the University of Illinois, we had three children. As I began my tenure-track job and Carol began her Ph.D. program in clinical psychology, the twins began first grade and Robert was expelled from the Montessori school for being too nonconforming. My life proves that it is possible to combine an academic career with a family, although it is a lot of work.

Carol returned to school in 1994 to obtain a law degree. She had mastered her job as a professor of clinical psychology and sought a new challenge. What made her first year in law school more difficult than usual was that she continued to teach part-time in the psychology department, and four of our children were all wed in that overly full year. Most law students find the first year of law school to be quite challenging, but they usually don't also have to contend with working and organizing weddings. Carol went to law school essentially for fun, an unusual motivation for most law students who find the law school experience to be stressful. And she did have fun. However, law school also helped her in forensic psychology work. Carol has been teaching service-learning courses in the community with the police and the juvenile detention center, in which her law background is helpful.

Our experiences of parenting our three children were so rewarding that we decided to take in hard-to-place children when our biological children were in high school. We took in five foster children, all when they were about 10 years old, and we ultimately adopted Kia and Susan.

In 1985 my father died, and this resulted in my becoming president of our large family farm. We grow processing tomatoes, cotton, lettuce, and other crops, and we have more than 70 employees. We grow more than 100,000 tons of processing tomatoes each year, and so if you have ever eaten Mexican food, Italian food, tomato soup, or ketchup, you likely have partaken of some of our tomatoes. This is why I founded the Psychology of Tomatoes Club of America, but so far only Paul Rozin of the University of Pennsylvania has joined. Being president of the farm was a big job, requiring about 2 days a week of my time. Thus, I had to work very hard in those days, and there was little time for hobbies, television, or socializing with friends. The farm management was a nice break from academic work, and the farm provided income that meant we did not have any financial worries. At the same time, I was working days, nights, and weekends to keep up.

Resource 3: Colleagues and Students

On my curriculum vitae, I have more than 200 publications, but what I like about my publication record is that I have had more than 100 different coauthors. My C2 index for "collaboration" is 10, meaning that there are ten scientists with whom I have each produced ten or more publications. In other words, it is my good fortune to have worked intensively with a large number of very talented individuals. I have been blessed with some of the best graduate students in all of psychology, and to them I am so grateful. The students who have worked with me have gone on to win many awards and acclamations, but these do not fully capture their enthusiasm, hard work, and creativity! They have made my career successful.

My first Ph.D. student was Randy Larsen, who went on to win the early scientific career award from the American Psychological Association. Robert Emmons came to my laboratory a few years later, and he was one of the most productive graduate students I have ever seen. In our first years in the field of subjective well-being, we published 15 studies in 1984 and 1985 alone. Because of these outstanding students, I was off to a strong start. Over the years, my research has often moved in new directions because of the people working with me. Eunkook Suh and Shigehiro Oishi moved my work toward questions of culture and well-being, while Richard Lucas prompted greater exploration of the role of adaptation to well-being. Similarly, Ulrich Schimmack, Frank Fujita, and Bill Pavot explored the structure of well-being in my laboratory and then later on their own. In the most recent years, I have had a new round of very talented students—Will Tov, Weiting Ng, Christie Scollon, Chu Kim-Prieto, Maya Tamir, and Derrick Wirtz. I have published more than 130 papers and books with 55 students and former students, and I have three students with whom I have published more than 20 papers each. I once sat in an auditorium with this very talented group of former graduate students, and someone walking by said "genius row." They were referring not to me but to the enormously gifted students with whom I have been so fortunate to work. As I will describe, I have also been fortunate to have my wife and three psychologist children work with me, and I continue to collaborate with them on a number of projects. This, too, is a very talented group. My wife Carol has more insight into people than any psychologist I have ever met.

In my work on happiness, I also have been blessed with such impressive coauthors as David Myers, Martin Seligman, Laura King, Sonja Lyubomirsky, and Daniel Kahneman. As I mentioned previously, I have had many outstanding graduate students and postdocs working with me. There are so many that I can't name them all here, but I should say that this group is responsible for most of the specific topics of my research. Excellent graduate students move their mentor's research in new directions, and they influence their mentor as much as he or she influences them. I have been the president of several scientific societies and have received a distinguished scientist award. However, the award of which I am proudest is a teaching award that was bestowed on me for involving students in my research.

My advice to young people who are entering the field is as follows: Work with excellent mentors and fellow graduate students, and your career will be enormously enhanced. When you become a professor, do everything you can to attract the most outstanding students. Don't compete with your colleagues and students; collaborate with them instead.

The Psychology Department at the University of Illinois

When I earned my doctoral degree, my first job offer came from Harvard University, and it was difficult to turn down this position. My parents taught me not to care about prestige, but I failed to completely learn the lesson. However, Carol was admitted to the clinical psychology graduate program at Illinois, which made the decision easier, and so we headed to the Midwest. Although I really wanted to go to Harvard—everyone recognizes that prestigious institution—I did not realize at the time that the Department of Psychology at Illinois is truly outstanding. After 32 years at the University of Illinois, I realize that my parents were again correct—do not worry about prestige but choose the place where you can do your best work, which for me has been at Illinois. Although our department is not as high profile as Harvard's, it has the most productive colleagues and students, and I have learned more psychology as a faculty member there than I did as a student. We never thought we would stay on the prairie in Illinois, but we are still there because of the excellence of the department and because it is such a wonderful scholarly environment. In every phase of my life I have been blessed with so many resources; I wonder what I did in the previous life to have deserved my good fortune.

LIFE CHALLENGES

I have faced several challenges in my life, and wrestling with these issues has energized my life.

Challenge 1: Making Time for Family and Research

My family was very close when I was a child, and I wanted a similar family when I became an adult. Carol and I met in high school and fell in love. We decided to have eight children, because we both enjoyed kids. To be truthful, I wanted eight and Carol wanted only six. However, when I became a researcher and Carol became a clinical researcher with a university appointment, the issue was how to be good parents and also good psychologists. I recognized that to be outstanding at research required long hours—it is unlikely to make major contributions working normal 40-hour weeks. Eighty hours is required. How could I resolve the 24-hours-in-a-day limitation, wanting to be outstanding as a husband and as a father, as well as a researcher?

One part of the solution was to drop out superfluous activities from my life. I decided I would have to watch television and read novels after retirement. When friends mentioned popular television programs such as *Seinfeld* or *Cheers,* I would have to admit I had never seen them. I did regret not being able to read novels because I knew there was simply no time for hobbies. Of course one can be a good researcher without working night and day, but for those who hope to work at the forefront of science, sacrifices are usually needed. For me, these sacrifices were always worth it, because I can't imagine an episode of *Seinfeld* that is as good as analyzing data or as spending time with my kids. In a recent study, sex was the most rewarding activity for a group of Texas women. I believe that is because they have never analyzed data.

Another part of my solution to the family–research dilemma was to frequently involve my family in my work. I often took our kids to work and discussed psychology with them. This had the unintended benefit of leading our three biological children into careers in psychology. Because our two adopted daughters did not go into psychology, we often joke that it must be genetic. But an alternative explanation is that we adopted our two daughters when they were 10 years old, and so they missed some of that early exposure to the discipline. Marissa became a developmental psychologist and teaches at the University of Utah, and Mary Beth became a clinical psychologist and teaches at the University of Kentucky. I joke that genes are not destiny, because although our twin daughters have virtually identical genes, their careers took different paths.

On the weekend and evenings, we sometimes carried out psychology projects with our children. For example, Robert did his science fair project on the relation of mood and weather. When Robert was a baby, I trained him to "magically" turn the television on and off by waving his arms—just for fun (waving his arms actually completed a circuit for the electric eye above him). We all tried receiving shocks from the shock machine in my laboratory, and the kids helped me collect beer bottles to throw in deindividuation experiments. At the dinner table, we often discussed the activities of the day like any other family, but we also discussed issues related to human behavior. There was never any attempt to influence our children's career choices; psychology was just something they learned is very interesting.

We traveled with our children every summer. Some of our trips were to standard destinations such as the Grand Canyon, while other travel was to more exotic locations. When we traveled in a dugout canoe to visit the Yagua Indians deep in the Amazon rainforest, they gave our son, Robert, a blowgun with curare-tipped poison darts. Knowing that curare can induce respiratory failure and be fatal, Carol was a strict mom and would not let Robert keep the curare. But he did bring the blowgun and darts back from our travels; we hope he did not use them on his friends.

To this day, Robert loves traveling to exotic places, and he has been a wonderful resource for me in collecting data from difficult sites. Few of my graduate students would be willing to live with the Maasai and be branded by them in a rite of manhood. Similarly, few of my graduate students could travel to northern Greenland and live among the icebergs with Inuit to collect data. I am certain that none of my other assistants would want to collect data in the worst slums of Calcutta or among the homeless. Thus, as the Indiana Jones of psychology, Robert has been a tremendous asset to me.

Challenge 2: How to Help the World?

My parents were very religious and built a Catholic church on their farm for their employees. They contributed their time and energy extensively to charities and were generous philanthropists. My mom and dad inculcated in me the idea that the most important goal in life is to improve the world. My mother once told me that some people believe they will get to heaven by faith, but she believed you have to earn heaven through good works. Although my parents were wealthy, making a lot of money was never their goal in life.

Despite my evolving views on religion, the motive to improve the world has stuck with me. But the question was always how best to help the world. I thought of becoming a priest, but meeting Carol interfered with that idea. I thought of becoming a doctor and going to Africa like Albert Schweitzer, but my squeamishness seemed to be an impediment to a career in medicine. Finally, I settled on clinical psychology because that combined a topic I found to be fascinating with helping people in trouble. When a psychology professor asked me why I entered psychology, I replied, "To help the world." He was crestfallen because he had hoped I would say my motivation was an interest in psychology for its own sake. My major motivation in those days, however, was to find a vocation that would improve the world. Only later did I come to terms with the idea that helping the world might come from doing what I did best and what I enjoyed most.

After college graduation, I was called for the draft to go to Vietnam. I registered as a conscientious objector. My family was disappointed in this choice, but I persisted and was fortunate to be granted CO status by my draft board. When I told people I was a CO, they assumed I meant commissioned officer, and they were shocked when I told them the real meaning of the letters. The draft board assigned me to two years of alternative service working in a psychiatric hospital to take the place of military service. This was wonderful for me because I thought I would get the needed experience to be accepted to a top program in clinical psychology. Little did I know that the experience would be very educational in another way—revealing to me that I hated working with patients. I was perceptive enough to realize that if one hates working with clients, one is probably not cut out to be a therapist.

Through a number of promotions I became the administrator of a new, small psychiatric hospital in the system. This heavy responsibility at age 24 was a huge lesson in many aspects of life. What does not kill you will strengthen you. Because of this intense experience in which I had to burden the heavy responsibilities of administering a hospital, I went to graduate school with a maturity beyond my years. The hospital also educated me regarding a future choice—I would never enter university administration because it turned out that I loved research much more than being an administrator.

Upon entering graduate school, I was still troubled by the issue of how I was going to help the world. I thought I could perhaps accomplish this by teaching psychology in a small liberal arts college, but graduate school taught me that my first love is research, and that has been my life story since. What I came to realize is that most researchers do not change the world in a direct and concrete way and that the fruits of science have the potential for changing history in profound ways. The "hard" sciences, including chemistry and biology, have dramatically changed our world. However, it seemed to me that the behavioral sciences have lagged behind, so that most of the major problems now facing humanity are in fact problems in human behavior. The disproportionate advances in the physical sciences compared to the behavioral sciences have produced some major problems. Yet if the behavioral sciences were successful, we could potentially solve the most important problems facing humanity.

I also came to realize that people usually contribute to the world most in areas where they are talented and in activities that they love. When talent and passion are combined, we are most effective. My hope is that my research will in some ways benefit humanity so that my parents will smile when looking down from heaven. I am certain that research is not for everyone, but for me it is a vocation and a passion. So, readers, help the world by doing what you do best and love most.

Challenge 3: Overcoming Opposition to Subjective Well-Being Research

When I began conducting research on well-being, many scientists were skeptical, including a few older professors in my department. For one thing, they thought that it would be impossible to define and measure happiness. It always puzzled me that psychologists believed that depression and anxiety were measurable but that positive states were not. Because several high-status professors in my department thought that studying happiness was a flaky endeavor, they blocked my promotion to full professor for a year or two.

The skepticism within my own department was a microcosm of the skepticism in the wider world of scientific psychology. When researchers presented studies showing the difficulties with measures of well-being, the findings were greeted with enthusiasm, whereas my studies showing the relative validity of the measures were often ignored. However, whereas many economists were actively hostile to the field, many psychologists simply ignored it. Thus, for many years I worked with very capable graduate students and we published frequently, but the topic of subjective well-being was a research area well off the beaten path. In those early years of my research, the area was not given much attention in any of the core subdisciplines, such as personality or social psychology, and classes on it were virtually nonexistent.

Finally, in the late 1990s, interest in subjective well-being exploded. Part of this change was due to the attention it received from Daniel Kahneman, a renowned experimental psychologist who won the Nobel Prize in Economics. When Kahneman began to publish in the field, he helped the area gain respect. Similarly, when Martin Seligman raised the banner of "positive psychology," his stature in clinical psychology and the attention he brought to the field of happiness helped greatly. David Myers, one of the best writers in psychology, wrote a book on the science of happiness that further helped legitimize the field. In addition, some economists became increasingly disenchanted with the reigning behavioristic and materialistic paradigm in their discipline, and they did interesting studies using measures of well-being. It is hoped that the research that we and others conducted on subjective well-being helped to bring respect to the field; our aim was to use rigorous methods so that the field would gain credibility and become more than another self-help "pop" area.

It appears that in this first decade of the 21st century, subjective well-being has become firmly established as a science. My citation count has grown to more than 11,000, and I have a citation H score of 42. This means that 42 of my articles are cited 42 or more times, meaning that lots of researchers are citing lots of our articles. The total number of publications in this area has grown rapidly. The number of publications on well-being (including topics such as life satisfaction, happiness, and positive emotions) over the past several decades (with the figure for this decade based on a projection from the first 5 years) currently amounts to 2,000 publications per year in the area, and it is climbing quickly. I have contributed almost 200 articles and books to the scholarly literature on subjective well-being. In the references I list 10 broad theory and conceptual articles that I believe have made important contributions to the field. I also list 10 empirical articles that I believe represent significant advances in knowledge. Because I have published so many empirical articles, it was difficult to select those that are most important.

Recently, my former students and research associates, headed by Randy Larsen and Michael Eid, wanted to plan a "Festschrift" for me—a celebration of my career at age 60. My response was, "No Festschrift"—those events are for old people. So they hosted a celebration with wonderful talks and a book, and they called it a non-Festschrift. The non-Festschrift was one of the high points of my life, because it was so clear to me that important work was going on in the field and that excellent scholarship will continue when I retire from the field.

CONCLUSION

I am one of the luckiest individuals in the world, because I discovered work I love and found wonderful people with whom to share this work. On Fridays, I can say TGIF, because I look forward to spending a bit more time with my family, but on Mondays, I can say TGIM, "Thank goodness it is Monday," because I love to conduct research and analyze data. In truth, there is no difference for me between weekdays and weekends because both include time with family and students and both include research activities. Research is not a career for everyone, and not everyone need be a maniac researcher like I am. There is ample room in the field for scientists who work at a much less intense level. However, I am positive that the most fulfilling life, whatever the particulars may be, is one in which a person can use his or her skills in activities he or she enjoys and with supportive people with similar values and goals. May all of you find such a life!

Readers need one caveat in evaluating my autobiography. I know the results of the nun study that showed that Catholic sisters who wrote more positive autobiographies lived longer than less happy nuns. Sarah Pressman has now replicated this finding with the autobiographies of psychologists and found that the mention of activated positive feelings predicted a 6-year longer life. Therefore, I have written the most positive of autobiographies in hopes that I will live a very long life. However, writing such a positive autobiography has made me happy, and I hope others enjoy reading it, so they, too, can have a long and happy life.

SUGGESTED READINGS

Ten Broad Theory and Review Articles on Well-Being

Diener, E. (1984). Subjective well-being. *Psychological Bulletin, 95,* 542–575.

Diener, E., Lucas, R., & Scollon, C. N. (2006). Beyond the hedonic treadmill: Revising the adaptation theory of well-being. *American Psychologist, 61,* 305–314.

Diener, E., Sandvik, E., & Pavot, W. (1991). Happiness is the frequency, not the intensity, of positive versus negative affect. In F. Strack, M. Argyle, & N. Schwarz (Eds.), *Subjective well-being: An interdisciplinary perspective* (pp. 119–139). New York: Pergamon.

Diener, E., & Seligman, M. E. P. (2004). Beyond money: Toward an economy of well-being. *Psychological Science in the Public Interest, 5,* 1–31.

Diener, E., Suh, E. M., Lucas, R. E., & Smith, H. L. (1999). Subjective well-being: Three decades of progress. *Psychological Bulletin, 125,* 276–302.

Diener, E., & Tov, W. (in press). Culture and subjective well-being. In S. Kitayama & D. Cohen (Eds.), *Handbook of cultural psychology.* New York: Guilford.

Kahneman, D., Diener, E., & Schwarz, N. (Eds.). (1999). *Well-being: The foundations of hedonic psychology.* New York: Sage.

Larsen, R. J., & Diener, E. (1987). Affect intensity as an individual difference characteristic: A review. *Journal of Research in Personality, 21,* 1–39.

Lyubomirsky, S., King, L., & Diener, E. (2005). The benefits of frequent positive affect: Does happiness lead to success? *Psychological Bulletin, 131,* 803–855.

Pavot, W., & Diener, E. (1993). Review of the Satisfaction With Life Scale. *Psychological Assessment, 5,* 164–172.

Ten Significant Empirical Articles on Well-Being

Biswas-Diener, R., & Diener, E. (2006). The subjective well-being of the homeless, and lessons for happiness. *Social Indicators Research, 76,* 185–205.

Diener, E., & Diener, C. (1996). Most people are happy. *Psychological Science, 7,* 181–185.

Diener, E., & Diener, M. (1995). Cross-cultural correlates of life satisfaction and self-esteem. *Journal of Personality and Social Psychology, 68,* 653–663.

Diener, E., & Emmons, R. A. (1985). The independence of positive and negative affect. *Journal of Personality and Social Psychology, 47,* 1105–1117.

Eid, M., & Diener, E. (2001). Norms for experiencing emotions in different cultures: Inter- and intranational differences. *Journal of Personality and Social Psychology, 81,* 869–885.

Lucas, R. E., Clark, A. E., Georgellis, Y., & Diener, E. (2003). Reexamining adaptation and the set point model of happiness: Reactions to changes in marital status. *Journal of Personality and Social Psychology, 84,* 527–539.

Oishi, S., & Diener, E. (2001). Re-examining the general positivity model of subjective well-being: The discrepancy between specific and global domain satisfaction. *Journal of Personality, 69,* 641–666.

Sandvik, E., Diener, E., & Seidlitz, L. (1993). Subjective well-being: The convergence and stability of self-report and non-self-report measures. *Journal of Personality, 61,* 317–342.

Schimmack, U., Diener, E., & Oishi, S. (2002). Life-satisfaction is a momentary judgment and a stable personality characteristic: The use of chronically accessible and stable sources. *Journal of Personality, 70,* 345–384.

Wirtz, D., Kruger, J., Scollon, C. N., & Diener, E. (2003). What to do on spring break? The role of predicted, on-line, and remembered experience in future choice. *Psychological Science, 14,* 520–524.

Organizing for Surprise
A Career of Arranging to Be Captured

ROBERT B. CIALDINI

Department of Psychology, Arizona State University

I was raised in an entirely Italian family, in a predominantly Polish neighborhood, in a historically German city (Milwaukee), in an otherwise rural state. It is no wonder that I became interested, early on, in learning the *art* of social influence, as navigating each of those domains required a deft negotiation of their varying norms, customs, and codes of conduct.

But learning the *science* of social influence had to await formal training in experimental social psychology—first at the University of North Carolina at Chapel Hill (UNC) and then at Columbia University—where my approach to research was affected profoundly by three mentors: Chet Insko, John Thibaut, and Stan Schachter. Of course, there were others who influenced me greatly at these two institutions, faculty and fellow students included. Still it can be safely said that these three individuals delivered the greatest impact. They did so differently, though, and each deserves separate consideration.

THE THREE TENORS

It wasn't that Chet, John, and Stan held fundamentally different values regarding the discipline of social psychology or of the scientific enterprise more generally. However, they sought to realize those fundamental values in ways that stood apart from one another. I've cast about in my mind for the right term to characterize the variances in approach I observed. *Style* is too superficial, *context* too general, *preference* too narrow. *Tenor* may be best. The tenor of their research orientations differed significantly from one another.

Chet Insko's Influence

Chet Insko was my first and only major advisor during the 3 years I spent in Chapel Hill—3 golden years as I recall them. From the outset, he taught me how to track down important, researchable questions and the answers to those questions through precise logic. Together we distilled hypotheses from theories, we derived tests from those hypotheses, and we held the theories accountable from the results of those tests. No sloppy thinking was allowed, no superficial analysis was accepted, no glib argument was unchallenged. Chet got to the heart of things via inescapable deduction. From him, I acquired the tools of the logician's trade.

The implications of this kind of tutelage went beyond a deep understanding of the hypothetico-deductive method for uncovering testable ideas. Chet's lessons in stripping away the nonessential aspects of a thing have helped me in two professional domains: research implementation and teaching.

In the first of these provinces, the lessons have proved invaluable in the vital arena of operationalization. Getting one's operationalizations right is a tricky business. It means selecting one particular form of a variable from the many forms it could be made to take. And it means ensuring that the chosen form reflects the essence of the concept. Precision is the key. Miss the core meaning of the concept in your operationalization, and your experiment tests something other than you intended. Chet taught me how to bring the nature of an operationalization into keeping with the nature of the variable under investigation, rendering each true to the other. For instance, in my dissertation research, which he supervised, we wanted to determine the effect of simply advocating an attitudinal position on the advocate's own attitude. Rather than asking participants to develop an elaborate statement on the topic, we had them interview a passerby on campus and to say the lone word *good* to the passerby's responses to certain survey questions but not to comparable other items. Later we asked the interviewers for their own opinions on the same questions. We found that they changed their views in the direction they had advocated but only for the items on which they had uttered the word *good*. Other, comparable items on which they had not provided this most strict form of advocacy showed no effect (Cialdini, 1971). Developing this study with Chet provided an early lesson in how to operationalize a concept (in this case advocacy) into a true and pure form.

The benefit of learning to recognize or craft proper exemplars of a central concept has paid dividends in the teaching realm as well. Let's be honest: Frequently, the only thing students remember about the theories, studies, and data covered in our classes is the stories we've told to illustrate these elements. This seems especially true with the passage of time. The student who returns to my office to say he or she enjoyed a class (sometimes years after taking it) almost always tells the story of a story—a fond recollection of some anecdote or personal account I'd shared to make a point. After a few such experiences, it became clear to me that if I wanted to convey material likely to be retained much beyond the date of the final exam, I'd need to spend more time on the narrative examples I used to illustrate the empirical, procedural, and conceptual lessons of the course. It also became clear that those illustrations had to be *apt* illustrations to do the job optimally.

Because examples and stories are likely to be the only things students lastingly recall, their aptness becomes central to achieving our pedagogic goals for undergraduate classes. Cute anecdotes with multiple engaging features (e.g., personal disclosures, embarrassing incidents, racy components) may well serve to hold an audience's attention but may simultaneously make the wrong (i.e., irrelevant) aspects of the tale memorable. I once read a study analyzing the use of jokes in speeches. The conclusion was that jokes are likely to increase the acceptance and retention of the speaker's message only when the punch line or lesson of the joke matched that message. Jokes that were designed simply to amuse or attract attention served to distract the audience from the intended take-away information of the speech.

I think the same is true of the narrative examples we provide in class to illus-trate our points. It's a mistake to embellish an illustrative story with various atten-tion-grabbing details that are oblique to the core purpose of the account. It's an even bigger mistake to settle for stories that are only roughly related to the con-ceptual point we are trying to make. I now view the aptness of the illustrations I employ in the classroom as the single most important determinant of my overall teaching effectiveness. As with the process of developing the right operationaliza-tions in the research arena, precision is the key here, too. If we don't studiously craft and ruthlessly hone our classroom illustrations to reflect exactly the teaching point we are hoping to make, everyone loses—the student, the instructor, and the field. Although Chet never provided a word of counsel to me regarding teaching (as my research advisor, it wasn't his job), I know that, nonetheless, he trained me to do it better.

John Thibaut's Influence

Whereas Chet Insko showed me how to track down phenomena in logical, lin-ear ways, John Thibaut taught me how to circle in on them in concentric fashion. John was never my principal advisor, but, in classes and research meetings, I was impressed with the breadth of his knowledge, which he mined to provide uncom-mon but instructive starting points for a program of inquiry.

For instance, let's say the question at hand was "How do people bargain differ-ently when they are negotiating for themselves alone versus when they are repre-senting a constituency?" John might begin by asking what any of the great novelists of our time had said about this. After group members thought about and discussed insights to be gained from this angle, he might ask, "Well, what have the phi-losophers said about the question?" So we'd move from a consideration of Henry James to William James. After we had talked for a while about the philosophical underpinnings of the issue, he'd press us to think about what the perspectives of our sister disciplines in the social sciences—sociology, political science, anthropol-ogy—could add to our understanding. Finally, then, John would tighten down the circle of inquiry to the thinking of other social psychologists who had reported on their findings in the literature of our discipline. It struck me that this end point would have been my starting point without John's insistence that it was valuable to begin the search for answers with a more diverse store of information.

An upshot of my exposure to John's far-flung-circles approach was a desire to build a broad array of perspectives into a consideration of research questions, espe-cially at the early stages. One way I have tried to do so has been to accept gradu-ate students to work with me from a wide variety of backgrounds. I've tried to be especially receptive to non–North American students, to applicants who have been in the working world for a time, and to candidates whose undergraduate majors were not in psychology. It may take these students a bit longer to get their minds around the core of the discipline, but the value they bring has made the trade-off more than worth it.

On an entirely different dimension, I learned something else from John. He was not merely liked and respected by those around him, he was beloved. I can't claim my exposure to John taught me how to achieve *that* personally. But it did teach me something about how he accomplished it.

A pair of incidents illustrates what I observed. The first occurred during my initial semester in Chapel Hill. At the time, John was a major figure in social psychology, the founding editor of the *Journal of Experimental Social Psychology*, a major grant getter, and the author (with Harold Kelley) of the virtual Bible of group research in the discipline, *The Social Psychology of Groups* (1959), in addition to being the immediate past head of the psychology department and the current director of the social psychology program at UNC. For some reason I can't even recall anymore, I had to go see him in his office—a big, corner room with a large desk that faced an impressive set of windows. When I knocked timidly at his open door, I was so new to the program that I wasn't sure that he knew my name. But he responded to that knock by rising out of his chair, throwing open his arms, and exclaiming, "Rrrobert!"

A few years later, I was a young initiate of the Society of Experimental Social Psychology and an attendee at its annual meetings, where it was rumored that John was to be given its Distinguished Scientist Award. Although the award winner was to be a secret until the announcement at dinner, word had spread that John would be honored that night. As a consequence, when he walked into the banquet room, he was surrounded by a gaggle of friends and well-wishers. As he passed, he noticed me out of the corner of his eye. I offered a half-wave of acknowledgment. He, on the other hand, rose out of his personal moment of triumph—like he had out of his chair more than a decade before—threw open his arms, and exclaimed, "Rrrobert!" That's why the man was beloved.

Stan Schachter's Influence

If Chet Insko taught me how to snare effects, and John Thibaut taught me how to circle them, then Stan Schachter taught me how to chase them wherever they led. He let the data steer him, and he took their counsel like no one I'd ever worked with. For instance, his classic program of work on affiliation (Schachter, 1959) started as an investigation of human isolation. When I asked him about the shift in focus, he explained that he had quickly recognized that isolation—he waved his hand dismissively as he said the word—was too rare in the repertoire of human responding to warrant his concerted focus. Now *affiliation*, that was another story. We are an intensely affiliative species; that's where the power is, he assured me. And so that's where he went. I recall being taken with his willingness to get off the horse he was riding and to get on one going in the opposite direction—in midstream—because he would rather follow the data than his preconceptions.

Although my exposure to Stan's believe-your-data-first model was relatively short—involving a less than 2-year postdoctoral stint at Columbia University—the impact on me was considerable. It didn't just teach me to prepare to be steered by surprising effects; it taught me to seek them, indeed, to organize myself to register and be captured by them. Once that was accomplished, I could use the lessons of my earlier teachers to help me properly select and attack the resultant questions. Thus, within my developing orientation to research, the process of systematically arranging for surprise became the first step. Because I've not seen it treated before, I give it special consideration here.

ORGANIZING FOR SURPRISE I

Knowing What to Look For

How does one organize to encounter and to be swept by surprising phenomena? Let's use a metaphor. If we can think of the course of human behavior as a river, an observer searching for interesting, surprising aspects of that behavior would do well to look to the irregularities at its surface—the breaks, swirls, and rapids—that bespeak of significant and enduring features of the riverbed below (the bedrock of human nature). Fine. But, in less metaphorical terms, what kinds of surprises should we be looking for? I can suggest several.

Inordinate Levels of Power   We should take special note of phenomena that exhibit more force than would be expected from the circumstances that produced them. That inordinate power indicates that there is a truly significant feature of human responding that lies beneath the phenomena, feeding their potency.

Consider, for instance, the instructiveness of an important event in my professional life that occurred one day in Columbus, Ohio. It is quite fitting that it took place not on a traditional workday in the excellent Ohio State University library, in my office, or in the labs of the social psychology doctoral program where I was a visiting professor that year but instead on a Saturday afternoon in the stands of Ohio Stadium, where 83,000 people had gathered to delight as a powerful and unbeaten Ohio State football team chewed its way through a much weaker opponent. Actually, my day at the stadium had begun considerably earlier. At the time, the social psychology program at Ohio State was located in the football stadium. The stadium is truly immense, and the university was housing some academic units within its bowels. Thus, when I went to my office to do some work that morning, I went to the stadium with the intention of attending the game later in the day.

My principal purpose in going to the office was to puzzle over some data I had gotten from a laboratory study of attitude change. The data were promising enough in that the means were in the predicted direction, but the effect I was looking for was not statistically significant. I was getting about half a point of difference between the two crucial experimental groups on a 7-point scale when I needed a full point of difference to attain conventional levels of significance.

It appeared as though I had probably uncovered an influence on the attitude change process that had not been documented before. The problem was to demonstrate that the influence was real. I had been in similar positions before, and so I was familiar with the task that faced me. If the effect were there, my job was to catch it, to capture it. I knew already that it was a phenomenon that tracked lightly. It would be necessary, then, to build an especially sensitive trap. I had a number of options in this regard that I had long before learned to use. I could increase the strength of the experimental manipulations, even though they might thereby become less representative of real-world events. I could switch to an attitude issue that my experimental participants had virtually no opinions about and would therefore be easier to influence. I could increase the number of scales in my dependent measure to make a more reliable index of attitude toward the topic at hand. I could cut error variance by reducing from two to one the number of experimenters conducting the study. Or I could simply increase my sample size and, provided everything else stayed the same, increase commensurately the power of my statistical test.

As I considered how best to proceed, I noticed that it was nearly game time. My office was located so that I could walk through a few empty corridors, pass through a pair of little-used doors, and be out of the deserted academic section and into the richly peopled stands of the stadium. Although I made the physical journey easily, my thoughts remained back below the stands with my data, my nonsignificant statistical test, and my experimental trap. Thus engaged, I moved toward my seat, mostly oblivious to the behavior around me. Not for long, though, because the Ohio State team had left the dressing room and had begun to run onto the field, *merely* to run onto the field. All at once people began bounding about, waving banners, spilling beer on one another, and yelling encouragement to their favorites below. Arcs of tissue paper crossed overhead. The university fight song was being sung. A large group of fans repeatedly roared, "We're number one!" while thrusting index fingers upward. I recall quite clearly being jolted away from thoughts of that additional half point of movement on a 7-point scale and recognizing the undeniable and intriguing power of the tumult around me. "Cialdini," I said to myself, "I think you're studying the wrong thing." Stan Schachter wasn't there, of course, but I'm pretty sure it's what he, too, would have said to me at that moment.

In the space of less than a week, with the inordinate power that sports teams have over their fans still in my head, I noticed something unusual as I walked on campus to my office. An uncommonly high percentage of passersby were wearing red, nylon windbreaker jackets with OHIO STATE printed on the back. I thought this was odd, because the weather wasn't much different—no cooler or windier— than the day before. When I got to my office and opened the campus newspaper, I thought I understood why: The Ohio State football team had been ranked number one in the nation the day before; as a result, all kinds of people—who had never made a tackle or scored a point—were literally dressing themselves in the success of the team, *their* team. These observations led to a program of research into the psychology of the sports fan and, more generally, into the tendency of individuals to "bask in the reflected glory" of successful others with whom they are merely connected. For instance, we found that students at a set of schools with traditionally strong football teams were much more likely to wear school-identifying apparel on the Monday following a team victory than a team loss (Cialdini et al., 1976). In other studies, we found participants significantly more willing to announce a connection between themselves and a successful (versus unsuccessful) other when that connection was as trivial as a common birthday (Cialdini & DeNicholas, 1989; Cialdini, Finch, & DeNicholas, 1989).

Opposite Procedures That Produce Similar Effects   There is something worth understanding and investigating in similar effects that are elicited by

procedural opposites. This became clear to me as a result of a mistake a student made in class during a lecture I was giving on the foot-in-the-door tactic, in which a requester gains compliance with a large request by first getting compliance with a small request that is consistent with the larger one. For example, home owners are more willing to display a large sign advocating driver safety if, a week earlier, they had displayed a small sign favoring the issue (Freedman & Fraser, 1966). The student shared a story that she said illustrated how the tactic had recently worked on her. A male friend had asked her for a loan of $25, which she refused because her budget couldn't afford it. But when he reduced the request to $15, she complied, even though she claimed she couldn't really afford that amount either.

Of course, in my apparently not-very-clear lecture, the student had gotten the foot-in-the-door's request sequence reversed. I explained the difference to the class and continued on to another lecture topic. But her story stuck with me because I could imagine myself falling for the same tactic her friend had used. Could it be that starting with a large request that is rejected and then retreating to a smaller one would generate increased compliance just like its procedural opposite of starting with a small request that is accepted and then advancing to a larger one? If so, how could that be?

To try to find answers, my students and I performed a series of studies (e.g., Cialdini et al., 1975) and learned, first, that the start-large-then-retreat sequence (which we labeled the "door-in-the-face" technique) is just as effective as the start-small-then-advance sequence of the foot-in-the-door technique. As to the question of how procedural opposites could lead to similar effects, the answer seems to lie in the fact that the success of each tactic is fueled by a different psychological principle—reciprocation, on one hand, versus consistency, on the other. That is, the door-in-the-face effect seems to be due to a desire to reciprocate concessions, whereas the foot-in-the-door effect seems to be due to a desire to be consistent with earlier commitments (Cialdini & Goldstein, 2004).

Effects That Overwhelm an Individual's Traits and Proclivities   A few years ago, a new graduate student (who, by the way, had been an English major and had been working in the advertising world) was coming to study with me from California. He was traveling with his fiancée at the time, whom he described as the most honest person he'd ever known. He'd never seen her borrow a paper clip or rubber band that she hadn't returned. They'd decided to take a bit of a detour so as to visit the Petrified Forest National Park. Near the entrance, they encountered a large sign admonishing visitors against stealing petrified wood from the park grounds. It read, "Your national heritage is being vandalized every day by the theft losses of petrified wood of 14 tons a year, mostly a small piece at a time." As they stood before the sign, my student reported hearing his fiancée whisper, "We'd better get ours now."

What about that sign could have spurred this otherwise entirely honest young woman to want to become a thief and to deplete a national treasure in the process? This seemed a question worth answering. To that end, my students and I set about trying to identify and test potential causes (Cialdini et al., 2006). Our conclusions implicate the features of messages far more varied than the one at the park entrance. There is an understandable but misguided tendency of public officials to try to mobilize action against socially disapproved conduct by depicting it as regrettably frequent, thereby inadvertently installing a counterproductive descriptive norm in the minds of their audiences (Cialdini, 2003).

Examples abound. Teenage suicide prevention programs inform students of the alarming number of adolescent suicides; when publicizing cases of school violence, news outlets assemble accounts of incident after incident; and government information campaigns decry the frequency of everything from alcohol abuse to tax cheating. Although their claims may be both true and well intentioned, the creators of such campaigns have overlooked something basic about the communication process: Within the statement "Look at all the people who are doing this undesirable thing" lurks the powerful and undercutting normative message "Look at all the people who *are* doing it."

Could this everyone's-doing-it subtext message actually cause people reading the Petrified Forest National Park sign to become more likely to steal wood there? To test that possibility, we gained permission from park officials to place secretly marked pieces of petrified wood along visitor pathways in three park locations. During five consecutive weekends, at the entrance to each path, we displayed signage that either normalized the theft of petrified wood from the park or marginalized such behavior. The normalizing sign urged visitors not to take wood and depicted a scene showing three thieves in action. After passing that sign, visitors became more likely to steal than before. Our marginalizing sign also urged visitors not to take wood, but it depicted a lone thief. Visitors who passed it became less likely to steal than before.

It is worthy of note that our countereffective persuasive appeal simulated the sort of message that was regularly and officially sent to visitors at the park. Our results indicate that appeals of this type should be avoided by public service or health communicators in their persuasive undertakings. Unfortunately, this is not always the case, even when communicators are able to act in line with available scientific evidence.

For instance, after we reported the outcomes of our study to park administrators, they decided not to change the relevant aspects of their signage. This decision was based on evidence from park ranger interviews with visitors, who felt that information indicating that the theft problem at the park was sizable would not increase their likelihood of stealing wood but decrease it. We were disappointed—but, truth be told, not surprised—that park officials weighted visitors' subjective responses more than our empirical evidence in their signage decision, as it confirms what appears to be a lack of understanding of and confidence in social science research within the larger society (Cialdini, 1997, 2005).

ORGANIZING FOR SURPRISE II

Knowing Where and How to Look

So far we've addressed the question of how to organize for surprise by identifying what to look for; however, the question that remains is where to look. Returning to our previous river metaphor may offer some help with this one. If we can conceive of the course of human behavior as a river, we might also conceive of "in river" as the optimal place to examine its irregularities. That is, the best situated observer may not be the one who stands, dry on the shore, recording from a distance. Instead, it may be the one who wades in, hip deep, and observes close up. In this regard, I want to recommend a research methodology, *participant observation,* that has been employed much more frequently in disciplines (e.g., anthropology, sociology) outside of our own and requires that an investigator wade into a research setting to analyze it from the inside.

During my research career, I have employed two main varieties of systematic personal observation. First is a spontaneous kind, in which I have found myself exposed to a highly effective influence process and then decided to study the generality and mediation of the process. This is how I began to investigate certain phenomena that I have already described, such as basking in reflected glory, the door-in-the-face tactic, and the backfire effects of descriptive norms.

The second type of systematic personal observation is a more purposive kind and is akin to participant observation. It's fine to stand ready and waiting to be struck in the course of one's daily affairs by a phenomenon worthy of scientific pursuit, but there is no reason to be only reactive in these matters. This is especially the case in an area such as social influence, where there are all sorts of organizations dedicated to influencing us to comply with their requests. It is possible to interact actively with these agencies to observe from the inside the nature of the techniques they regularly and effectively employ.

This is a valuable sort of observation, because the effects that appear consistently across a range of different compliance practitioners are likely to be the most influential ones. That is, these organizations serve as natural proving grounds for procedures that work. They have to work—a rule not unlike natural selection ensures it. Therefore, when we examine them in controlled experimental settings to learn why they work, we can do so with the knowledge that these are genuinely powerful phenomena that we are studying. It is worthy of note, however, that this analysis applies primarily to *commercial* compliance professionals whose economic welfare is highly related to the success of the compliance practices they employ. We should not expect a body of adaptive procedures to develop and proliferate to the same degree among noncommercial compliance organizations, in which the "invisible hand of the market" does not sweep away inefficient practices over time.

For example, patient compliance with various medical regimens (medication, diet, exercise) is notoriously poor. One reason may be that, unlike the direct commercial compliance situation wherein a noncompliant target person departs from and impoverishes the practitioner, in a medical care system, a noncompliant person stays and enriches the practitioner. Thus, in seeking evidence as to the most regular and potent influences on the compliance process, we are well advised to pay principal attention to the compliance repertoires of long-standing commercial compliance professionals.

This is what I resolved to do, then—to observe from the inside the compliance practices of all of the influence organizations I could get access to whose principal goal it is to get us to say yes. In a nearly 3-year study, I became a spy of sorts, infiltrating the training programs of as many influence professions as I could get access to and learning from the inside how people can be led to say yes to requests in sales, fund-raising, marketing, and negotiation settings. Occasionally, I ventured outside of traditional business circles to find out how other influence professionals generated "yes." For example, I interviewed political lobbyists and cult recruiters to learn what they did to produce their own brand of powerful influence.

And through it all, I watched for commonalities, for parallels. I thought if I could identify which psychological principles were being used successfully by individuals selling insurance and industrial machinery and computer equipment and portrait photography and if these were the same principles being used successfully by negotiators and fund-raisers and recruiters and lobbyists, then I would know something very important. I would know that *these* must be the most powerful and flexible principles of influence available, because *these* are the principles that work across the widest range of influence professions, influence practitioners, and influence opportunities (see Cialdini, 2001, for a fuller description of the methods and outcomes of this participant observation study).

My initial intent in embarking upon this program of work was to find social influence practices that were clearly powerful yet unclearly grasped; that is, I was looking for strong effects for which possible explanations coexisted. It's important to recognize that even though compliance professionals know the procedures that work—that, after all, is their job—they don't necessarily know why they work. That is *my* job. So I set about the task with the purpose of identifying these potent practices and then bringing them back to my lab, where I could unpack their underlying causes. It wasn't long before I recognized that another, larger purpose could be achieved as well: There was a book to be written. It wasn't to be a book for the academic community, though. It was to be a book for the popular reader, who could learn what I'd learned and become better able to recognize and resist influence tactics that were employed in an unethical, undue, or unwelcome fashion.

The idea to write for a general readership sprung from a long-standing sense I had that social science as a profession and social psychology as a discipline were not holding up their end of an implicit contract with the larger society. The public was expected to fund social scientific research, and, in turn, researchers were expected to describe—in a much more elaborated and ongoing fashion than has ever been the case—what society had received for its money. On this point, I'd like to be blunt about the fact that although I have long been a fan of former APA president George Miller and of the spirit of his celebrated advice to "give psychology away" (Miller, 1969), I have never been a fan of the phrase itself. It implies that the psychological knowledge we have generated from our research is ours to dispense, gratis, to the public—when in fact it has always been at least as much theirs as ours because, in any meaningful sense, they have paid for it. We should think of the wide dissemination of that knowledge not as a gift bestowed but rather as an order filled or, better still, a promise kept. So far, although we have done a fine job of producing the societally useful goods, we have done a poor job of shipping them.

A small but crucial change in the phrase seems right. We should be devoting our efforts not so much to giving psychology away as to giving psychology a *way*—a *way* to communicate our science widely to the society and a *way* to do so in a professionally responsible fashion. That is something I attempted in the resultant book.

WRITING A POPULAR PRESS BOOK

It's altogether appropriate to begin a discussion of writing a book for a popular audience with a story, because storytelling is a major part of the process. The story comes from the old *Bob Newhart Show,* in which Bob plays a clinical psychologist. If you don't remember it, you can probably still catch episodes on "Nick at Night." This is the show, by the way, that is responsible for the way many of the members of my extended family view my job, despite my protestations: "No, Uncle Charlie, there's no dentist down the hall from my office. I'm not *that* kind of psychologist."

Anyway, here's the story. In one episode, Bob is visited by an old friend from graduate school who is touring the country promoting a book he had recently published. While promoting that book, he's finishing a second on the topic of psychosis in America. But, he tells Bob, he doesn't want to call it *Psychosis in America* because that's too dry and clinical sounding. So he's decided to title it *Fires of the Mind,* which he feels evokes the concept in a tastefully provocative fashion. Suddenly, an urgent call comes through from his publisher who has a great marketing idea: change the title from *Fires of the Mind* to *Blazing Brains.*

My point is that if your experience is like mine—and that of several other academics I've talked to—your popular press publisher is going to try to get you to write *Blazing Brains.* For example, at one point I was being urged to use for my book *Influence* the subtitle *Weapons of Social Seduction* because that would have sex and violence in the very same title.

This title business is no minor item, by the way. A big difference between professional and trade books is that people frequently buy the latter on the basis of little information except that conveyed in the title. My editor once said to me, "What is it about your title that will make people reach for it on a bookstore shelf?" I was dumbfounded. I had never considered the issue, expecting that the book would somehow sell itself on other grounds. That belief is simply not the reality—not for an unknown, first-time trade book author, anyway.

A second way you will be urged to write *Blazing Brains* is through the agenda you set for the book. Your publisher's agenda will be to sell the most books possible, even if it means sensationalizing the material or diluting it to appeal to a broader and ever broader audience. Be very careful here not to buy into that agenda, because it will run counter to the larger agenda of maintaining your reputation in the academic community in the process of communicating your message to the public. Your editor and publisher won't understand why you refuse to do things designed to sell more books and make more money for all of you. They'll accuse you of being too high minded and naïve. In my case, I don't think I was either. My decisions to resist some of their suggestions were quite pragmatic: I was going to return to the academic community for the rest of my professional life. Anything I did to poison that particular well would be self-destructive. A trade publisher's agenda for your book extends anywhere from six to nine months. Your agenda, of course, extends well, well beyond that.

You should also recognize how difficult it will be to keep from being swayed by your publisher's perspective in this regard. That perspective will be very salient to you as you write and rewrite material, because the publisher will be, in essence, standing over your shoulder during the process. Taking a hint from social cognition research, I found that one way to counteract that saliency advantage was to place a respected colleague over my other shoulder while I wrote. Have Marilyn Brewer or Dick Nisbett or Alice Eagly peer over your shoulder as you write. Woo, does that ever straighten your backbone.

Another way that you'll be asked to write *Blazing Brains* is in the level of discourse you apply to the work. I'll assume that if you are discussing social psychological research, you will speak academically and conceptually from time to time. This will necessarily truncate the potential audience, cutting off all those people who are uninterested in following academic language and conceptual analysis—a significant number of people. The thought of such a thing will make your editors dig their fingernails into their flesh, bite their lips until they bleed, and plead with you to change. My advice is to concede on the academic language but not the conceptual analysis.

In fact, if there are some things that you think might be too academic in form, but you're not sure, leave them in at first and be willing to give them up as concessions that can then be employed to preserve conceptual analysis. The bargaining and compliance literatures suggest that you'll be successful. In my case, footnotes that initially appeared at the bottom of the page were negotiated away to become endnotes at the back of the book. (In the classroom version of the book, they're footnotes at the bottom of the page again, because a more academic system is appropriate there.) Taking your cue from the research literature once more, you can persuade your editor in your direction by providing highly available, vivid examples of academic authors who have written successful popular books while not sacrificing sophistication. Another thing you might do is to be prepared to cite the circulation figures of some national magazines such as *Time* and *Newsweek*—which use fairly sophisticated communication forms—and argue that if only 10% of the readers of those two magazines bought your book, you'd all be rich. For your own purposes, you might want to use those two magazines as guidelines for issues of level of discourse and vocabulary. Their readerships are likely to well represent your projected audience.

Hints on How to Get Started

First, write a detailed prospectus and a couple of sample chapters to send off to potential publishers and/or agents. Take one of these chapters and write it over and over to get all of the "academeze" out of it. But don't try to do this in your university office, which is full of cues likely to prime a certain vocabulary, style, and way of communicating information that is inappropriate for a nonacademic audience. Instead, write it from a coffee shop or a place at home with a window overlooking a street with passersby. They're your intended audience after all. Let them prime the writing cues appropriate for them. When I made such a change, the first sentence in *Influence* went from "My home discipline, experimental social psychology, has as its domain the study of everyday human behavior" to "I can admit it freely now, all my life I've been a patsy." I think the difference is evident.

Second, in structuring your material for a popular audience, beware falling victim to one particularly troublesome form of the false consensus effect (Ross, Greene, & House, 1977), in which people assume that their own beliefs are held to a disproportionate extent by those around them. That is, like our academic brethren, we have to avoid the mistake of thinking that nonacademics will be as excited by questions, in general, as we are. The truth is that, as a profession, we are virtually alone in this regard. Almost everyone else is primarily interested in answers. While open questions fascinate, challenge, intrigue, motivate, and preoccupy us, they just frustrate the rest of the world. I think it is telling that while other professions honor those individuals who have wrapped up a problem area with a consummate solution (e.g., a cure for polio), we lionize thinkers/theorists who have launched a problem area with many, many questions waiting to be addressed (e.g., cognitive dissonance). This is partially the case because we are a curious lot. But—let's be honest now—it is also the case because we are rewarded in our research efforts by the availability of questions. Without those unanswered questions, where would our careers be? It is important that we not project this reverence for questions to the nonacademic community, which prefers certainty to uncertainty in all things. Be assured that I'm not suggesting that, in writing for the popular reader, we claim that we have answers where we do not. However, we should not be so naïve as to expect that our audience will find a lack of closure satisfying. We are well advised, then, to focus on material that allows us to make relatively confident statements and to draw relatively confident practical implications from them. This issue of practical implications for the reader strikes me as centrally important to a successful trade book. In another academics-versus-nonacademics distinction, our readers are much less likely to be concerned with the "hows," "whens," or "whys" in our material as by the "therefores" in it.[1]

Before writing the book and sample chapters, go to the library and get all of the books you can find written by academic authors for popular audiences. Read them and note those sections that you found most and least successful. Later analyze them for the common properties of the good and bad sections.

I did this, and here's what I found: The most successful sections frequently began with a puzzle. What is more, it was the physical scientists who used this technique the most—because often their material is not inherently interesting to a large audience. So when Carl Sagan asked what the rings of Saturn are made of and described the possibilities of dust, ice, or gas, he did it like a mystery story. He used the sweep of science as a detective story to bring his readers along with him to the conclusion. Those of us in behavioral science forget to use the draw of the detective story—which is a fitting metaphor for science—because we mistakenly expect that our material will be so interesting that our readers will follow our plodding arguments for their own sake. With this in mind, I structured my book *Influence* so that every major section begins with a mystery, a puzzle.

It is interesting that over the years since the book's publication, my use of this literary device has gone unrecognized. I can't think of one person who has commented to me about it. But why not? I certainly didn't try to hide it. My most confident answer to the puzzle has to do with one reason that the device is so effective. It grabs readers by the collar and pulls them in to the material. When structured properly, mysteries are so compelling that the reader cannot remain an aloof and neutral outside observer of the story's form and structure. In the throes of this particular piece of pedagogy, one is simply not thinking of pedagogy; one is focused on content.

A teaching implication. I first saw evidence of the ability of mysteries to keep an audience eager for content shortly after I began using them in my classroom lectures. I was still inexperienced enough that, on one particular day, I got the timing wrong, and the bell rang ending the class session before I'd revealed the solution to a puzzle I'd posed earlier. Normally, 5 to 10 minutes before the scheduled end time, some students start preparing to leave. We all know the signals—pencils are put away, notebooks folded, backpacks zipped. But in this instance, not only were there no such preparations, after the bell rang, no one moved. In fact, when I tried to end the lecture there, I was pelted with protests. They would not let me stop until I had given them closure on the mystery. I remember thinking that I'd stumbled onto dynamite.

Besides mystery stories being excellent devices for engaging and holding student interest, there is another reason to recommend the increased use of them in the classroom: They are pedagogically superior to other, more common forms of classroom presentation such as providing descriptions of course-relevant phenomena or asking questions about the phenomena. That is, whereas descriptions demand attention and questions demand answers, mysteries demand *explanations*. When we spur our students to engage in the process of providing explanation (rather than mere attention or answers), we offer them the best opportunity to understand psychological phenomena in a conceptual, meaningful, and enduring way.

Of course, there are various ways to set up and execute the mystery story sequence. Let me illustrate one that has worked especially well for me. Suppose we want to teach about the power of counterarguments in resisting a persuasive appeal. Before describing the research evidence, we might engage student attention by taking the following steps:

1. *Pose the mystery.* We are all familiar with cigarette advertising campaign successes featuring Joe Camel, the Marlboro Man, and "You've come a long way, baby." But perhaps the most effective marketing decision ever made by the tobacco companies lies buried and almost unknown in the industry's history: After a 3-year slide of 10% in tobacco consumption in the United States during the late 1960s, Big Tobacco did something that had the extraordinary effect of ending the decline, boosting consumption dramatically, and slashing advertising expenditures by a third. What was it?

2. *Deepen the mystery.* The answer seems equally extraordinary. On July 22, 1969, during U.S. congressional hearings, representatives of the major American tobacco companies strongly advocated a proposal to ban all of their *own* ads from television and radio, even though industry studies showed that the broadcast media provided the most effective routes to new sales. As a consequence of that unprecedented move, tobacco advertising has been absent from the airwaves in the United States since 1971.

3. *Home in on the proper explanation by considering (and offering evidence against) alternative explanations.* Could it be that American business interests, sobered by the surgeon general's report that detailed the deadly denouement of tobacco use, decided to forego some of their profits to improve the well-being of fellow citizens? That appears unlikely, because representatives of the other major U.S. business affected by the ban—the broadcast industry—filed suit in the Supreme Court to overturn the law one month after it was enacted. Thus, it was only the tobacco industry that supported the restriction on its ads. Could it have been the tobacco company officials, then, who suddenly became concerned with the health of the nation? Hardly. They didn't reduce their concentrated efforts to increase tobacco sales one whit. They merely shifted their routes for marketing their products—away from the broadcast media to print ads, sports sponsorships, promotional giveaways, and even movie product placements. For example, secret documents of one tobacco firm included a letter from movie actor/director Sylvester Stallone agreeing to use its cigarettes in several films in exchange for $500,000 (Massing, 1996).

4. *Provide a clue to the proper explanation.* So by tobacco executives' logic, magazines, newspapers, billboards, and films were fair game; only the airwaves should be off limits to their marketing efforts. Why? What was special about the broadcast media? Two years earlier, the U.S. Federal Communications Commission had ruled that its "fairness doctrine" applied to the issue of tobacco advertising. The fairness doctrine required that equal advertising space must be granted on radio and television— solely on radio and television—to all sides of important and controversial topics. If one side purchased broadcast time on these media, the opposing side must be given free time to counterargue.

5. *Resolve the mystery.* That decision had an immediate impact on the landscape of broadcast advertising. For the first time, antitobacco forces such as the American Cancer Society could afford to air counterarguments to the tobacco company messages. They did so via counterads that disputed the images created in tobacco company commercials. If a tobacco ad featured healthy, attractive, independent characters, the opposing ads would counterargue that, in truth, tobacco use led to diseased health, damaged attractiveness, and slavish dependence. During the 3 years that they ran, those antitobacco spots slashed tobacco consumption in the United States by a total of nearly 10% (Simonich, 1991). At first, the tobacco companies responded predictably, increasing their advertising budgets to try to meet the challenge. But by the rules of the fairness doctrine, for each

tobacco ad, equal time had to be provided for a counterad that would take another bite out of industry profits. When the logic of the situation finally hit them, the tobacco companies maneuvered masterfully. They worked politically to ban their own ads, solely on the air where the fairness doctrine applied, thereby ensuring that the antitobacco forces would no longer get free airtime to make their case. As a consequence, in the year following the elimination of tobacco commercials on the most effective advertising medium for producing new sales, the tobacco companies witnessed a significant jump in sales coupled with a significant reduction in advertising expenditures (Fritschler, 1975)—a nearly unheard-of combination.

6. *Draw the implication for the phenomenon under study.* Tobacco opponents found that they could use counterarguments to undercut tobacco ad effectiveness. But the tobacco executives learned (and profited from) a related lesson: One of the best ways to reduce resistance to a message is to reduce the availability of counterarguments to it.

Note that at this stage in the sequence, our teaching point about the impact and availability of counterarguments is neither a description nor an answer. It is an explanation.

I trust it goes without saying that this sequence is best approached *not* by providing it to students as a set of pronouncements. Instead, at appropriate intervals, students should be invited into the process. They should be given the opportunity to offer their own speculations and explanations. They should be asked to consider how these explanations could account for all of the evidence revealed to that point and for new pieces of evidence that you reveal. At the end of the sequence, they should be asked if they could develop an alternative explanation that fits all of the evidence, and so on. This is not something that deserves special emphasis in the present case. It's just good teaching. And good teaching—getting student participation, spurring critical thinking—applies to mystery stories, too.

There is a final reason for the instructional superiority of mystery stories. To best describe what it is, I first need to describe a little trick I learned to play on myself long ago to improve my teaching. After a few years in the classroom, I noticed that there were some lectures I dreaded giving because the students were bored by the material. There were other lectures that I loved to deliver because the students enjoyed the material. I'm sure that the self-fulfilling prophecy phenomenon played a role. On certain days, I expected to be uninteresting, and dispirited by the prospect, I was. On other days, I expected to be interesting, and enlivened by the prospect, I was.

Anyway, the trick was to reconfigure my lectures so that, into each one, I inserted something that I genuinely looked forward to presenting because students loved it—a humorous anecdote, a riveting example, an especially clever experiment, and so on. The key was to have at least one such high point per session. Sometimes this meant rearranging the material so that I'd remove a highlight from a lecture that had two and place it in a lecture that had none.

The intent was to motivate students to look forward to class by motivating *myself* to do the same. I found I was a much better teacher when I had a special reason to want to be in each class session. And the consequent boost in my performance was not restricted to the day's home run. It generalized to the other material I presented that day as well.

This is how mystery stories offer that final instructional advantage: They are ready-made high points. Students love them, which energizes both students and teachers to want to be in class. There's a lot to be said for thinking about ways to generate teacher excitement for the classroom, not just student excitement. After all, each kind of excitement feeds the other. And if we find something (such as mystery stories) that works both sides of the street simultaneously, we would do everyone a disservice not to use it.

CONCLUDING REMARKS

To bring things full circle, I'd like to end this piece in the way it started, by relating an account of an early experience with significant subsequent impact. While I was a first-year graduate student at UNC, Chapel Hill, it was occasionally the case that an eminent social psychologist would unexpectedly appear in the halls of the psychology building—perhaps Hal Kelley would be there to work with John Thibaut on their next project or Bibb Latane would stop in after visiting family in town. These events always generated great excitement among the graduate students, who would report sightings and spread related rumors: "I saw him coming out of John's office, but I think he's only here for a day." I even recall waiting in a corridor with my cohort member, Alan Chaikin, and positioning ourselves to be able to peer around a corner to catch a glimpse of Hal Kelley on his way to lunch with some of the faculty.

Thirty years later, I was invited back to UNC to get an award. Before my acceptance speech, I was asked to describe the biggest change I had noted in the place since I had left. I lied and, trying to be funny, made a comment about the "gentrification" of the town.[2] In truth, the biggest change I registered had occurred earlier in the day when, on my way to lunch with some of the faculty, I saw a pair of graduate students peering around a corner to catch a glimpse of me ... of *me*.

The moment took my breath away. Although I would have been ungracious to have said so to my hosts in my prespeech remarks, it meant more to me than the formal award of that day—or of any other day, for that matter. Because I have always considered graduate students to be expert at deciding what of the past to carry with them into the future, that moment offered a unique kind of forward validation to a long career.

After all, graduate students are the oracles of our discipline. I hope that one outcome of this chapter is that I have been able to look back to assist them in their crucial job of looking ahead.

ACKNOWLEDGMENTS

Thanks are due especially to my colleague Gregory Neidert and to my graduate students at the time, Petia Petrova, Noah Goldstein, Vladas Greskevicius, and Chad Mortensen, for astute comments on an earlier version of this chapter.

NOTES

1. As an outgrowth of having written a trade book on the topic of social influence, I am frequently asked to speak to nonacademic groups—practitioners in business, law, and public service. I regularly accept these invitations because, for one reason, they provide an opportunity to demonstrate the worth of social scientific (and especially social psychological) approaches beyond the borders of our discipline. It has been plain to me from the outset that the (sometimes lavish) compensation these groups provide—a second reason that I accept the invitations—is meant in return for the "therefores" of the presented material. Rather than feeling unduly constrained by this expectation, I've come to experience it as a welcome and proper expansion of my orientation to the issues at hand. It's made me consider the implications of my data for settings outside of the one where they were obtained. This has affected not just the way that I present my work after the fact but how I plan it in the first place as well—so that the settings, operationalizations, and populations I employ make potential practical implications much easier to draw, which has proved to be an unanticipated bonus for all concerned.
2. I think I said that the best way to describe the difference was in terms of the grits-to-biscotti ratio: When I arrived in Chapel Hill in 1967, there were no biscotti, only grits on downtown Franklin Street; by 1997, there were no grits, only biscotti. As an aside, I can report that coming from an entirely Italian family, in a predominantly Polish neighborhood, in a historically German city, in a very northern state had not prepared me for grits. In fact, when I first got to Chapel Hill, I didn't even know what grits were. That didn't last long, though, as they seemed to accompany everything—breakfast, lunch, and dinner. I remember buying a suit back then that came with an order of grits. OK, this last isn't true, but almost.

REFERENCES

Cialdini, R. B. (1971). Attitudinal advocacy in the verbal conditioner. *Journal of Personality and Social Psychology, 17*, 350–358.

Cialdini, R. B. (1997). Professionally responsible communication with the public: Giving psychology a way. *Personality and Social Psychology Bulletin, 23*, 675–683.

Cialdini, R. B. (2001). *Influence: Science and practice* (4th ed.). Boston: Allyn & Bacon.

Cialdini, R. B. (2003). Crafting normative messages to protect the environment. *Current Directions in Psychological Science, 12*, 105–109.

Cialdini, R. B. (2005). Basic social influence is underestimated. *Psychological Inquiry, 16*, 158–161.

Cialdini, R. B., Borden, R. J., Thorne, A., Walker, M., Freeman, S., & Sloan, L. (1976). Basking in reflected glory: Three (football) field studies. *Journal of Personality and Social Psychology, 34*, 366–375.

Cialdini, R. B., Demaine, L., Sagarin, B. J., Barrett, D. W., Rhoads, K., & Winter, P. L. (2006). Managing social norms for persuasive impact. *Social Influence, 1*, 3–15.

Cialdini, R. B., & DeNicholas, M. (1989). Self-presentation by association. *Journal of Personality and Social Psychology, 57*, 626–631.

Cialdini, R. B., Finch, J. F., & DeNicholas, M. (1989). Strategic self-presentation: The indirect route. In M. Cody & M. McLaughlin (Eds.), *The psychology of tactical communication*. London: Multilingual Matters, Ltd.

Cialdini, R. B., & Goldstein, N. J. (2004). Social influence: Compliance and conformity. In S. T. Fiske, D. L. Schacter, & C. Zahn-Waxler (Eds.), *Annual review of psychology* (Vol. 55, pp. 591–621). Palo Alto, CA. Annual Reviews, Inc.

Cialdini, R. B., Vincent, J. E., Lewis, S. K., Catalan, J., Wheeler, D., & Darby, B. L. (1975). Reciprocal concessions procedure for inducing compliance: The door-in-the-face technique. *Journal of Personality and Social Psychology, 31*, 206–215.

Freedman, J. L., & Fraser, S. C. (1966). Compliance without pressure: The foot-in-the-door technique. *Journal of Personality and Social Psychology, 4*, 195–203.

Fritschler, A. L. (1975). *Smoking and politics.* Englewood Cliffs, NJ: Prentice Hall.

Massing, M. (1996, July 11). How to win the tobacco war. *New York Review of Books*, pp. 32–36.

Miller, G. A. (1969). Psychology as a means of promoting human welfare. *American Psychologist, 24*, 1063–1075.

Ross, L., Greene, D., & House, P. (1977). The "false consensus effect": An egocentric bias in social perception and attributional processes. *Journal of Experimental Social Psychology, 13*, 279–301.

Schachter, S. (1959). *The psychology of affiliation: Experimental studies of the sources of gregariousness.* Stanford, CA: Stanford University Press.

Simonich, W. L. (1991). *Government antismoking policies.* New York: Peter Lang.

Thibaut, J., & Kelley, H. H. (1959). *The social psychology of groups.* New York: Wiley.

From Social Psychology to Neuroscience and Back

SHELLEY E. TAYLOR

Department of Psychology, University of California, Los Angeles

My journey from social psychology to neuroscience and back has, thus far, taken 40 years. It has involved stops in politics, health, endocrinology, psychoneuroimmunology, brain science, and even genetics. It does not yet feel as though it is winding down, and I am not altogether certain of the destination, but the trip has been invigorating, enlightening, sometimes even astonishing in its revelations.

The basic theme of my career has been the exploration of psychosocial resources as buffers against stressful experiences. To understand sources of resilience, I look at how people manage the stressful, traumatic, and challenging circumstances of their lives, namely, those factors that help people to cope and recover successfully, as well as vulnerability factors that may open a person up to the mental and physical ravages of stress.

EARLY HISTORY

The first person who influenced my career was my father. He was a high school history teacher and then a college counselor. But before he settled on his career path, he had an interesting early one as a psychiatric nurse. During World War II, he had been ineligible for military service because of polio, so he volunteered with the Society of Friends. He was sent to North Africa and ultimately to Eritrea, where he literally built the first mental hospital in that poor country. What I admired especially about my father was his utter fearlessness. For example, going to Eritrea and setting up a field mental hospital that ultimately served primarily Italian soldiers was, I think, a very brave thing to have done.

My father did his master's thesis on Stonewall Jackson, and I often felt that Jackson was a member of our family. So colorful and entertaining were my father's descriptions of historical adventures that I leaned in the direction of history as a career. But it was always the personalities who had dominated it—Stonewall Jackson, Teddy Roosevelt, FDR, and other heroes from my father's vivid portrayals—that most captivated my attention.

My mother was a pop and jazz pianist who played in clubs in New York before my parents moved out to the suburbs of Chappaqua, New York, where she became a piano teacher. One of the most important lessons I learned from her was the value of improvisation. In jazz, once a melody line is established, the musicians can pass it around to different instruments, change the rhythm, embellish the melody line, and go far afield before bringing the melody home to wind up the song. Improvisation is exciting because it enables you to see many dimensions of a melody that you would not otherwise see. Substitute the word *theory* or *concept* for *melody* and you can see how important improvisation can also be in science.

I went to Horace Greeley High School, a high school with amazing resources. One of the history teachers, Alice Barry, received a grant from the school to study psychology in the summer, and when she came back, she was very excited by what she had learned. Instead of teaching her history course, she taught a psychology course to many of us who were juniors and seniors. I recently attended my 40th high school reunion and was stunned by how many in our class had made their careers in psychology, psychiatry, social work, and related fields because of this high school experience.

BECOMING A PSYCHOLOGIST

When I got to college, I enrolled in both history and psychology classes. Although I was headed for history, I was quite literally abducted into psychology. The instructor in the introductory psychology course, Robert Rhine, was a much-feared and stern professor who gave out high grades with reluctance. At the end of class one day, he announced that he wished to see three people in this class of 55 in his office immediately, and I was one. The three of us went with great trepidation, unclear as to what we could possibly have done to incur his wrath. The first student went in and came out about 15 minutes later, smiling. When we asked her what was up, she said, "You'll see." When my time came, Professor Rhine informed me that my performance in class indicated that I had talent in the area of psychology, and he had determined that this would need to be my choice of major. When I protested and explained my enduring interest in history, he waved my objections aside ("You'd be a terrible historian."). A psychology major I became.

It wasn't long before I discovered the wisdom of his advice. In the very first experiment that I conducted, which examined women's evaluations of other women who had chosen to go into careers instead of having traditional family roles, I obtained highly significant effects. The findings are no longer particularly interesting, but seeing those significant F ratios simply transported me. The idea that I could produce knowledge that no one had seen before was simply captivating, and from that point on, there was no question that I would continue in psychology. I worked on a number of projects in college, first with Otello Desiderato and then with Sara Kiesler as my advisor. An inspiring advisor, she crystallized my interest in the field and ensured that I would go on to get a Ph.D. When it came time to apply to graduate school, she felt that I should go either to the University of Rochester to work with Elaine Walster or to Yale to work with David Mettee.

GRADUATE SCHOOL AT YALE

I decided to go to Yale and did work briefly with Mettee, although our interests and personal styles were not well matched. I floundered a bit in graduate school, not finding anyone with whom I had an obvious affiliation. I most admired the work of Dick Nisbett, but his lab was already full.

Ultimately, I did my dissertation research on attribution theory with John McConahay, a political scientist/psychologist who had worked with David Sears as a graduate student at UCLA. He knew a great deal about attribution theory from his UCLA experience, and so he gave me good advice. My dissertation explored the limits of Bem's self-perception theory, addressing the question, When do people infer their attitudes from their behavior? My findings suggested that (even false) feedback of one's behavior is accepted as a basis for one's attitudes if it is consistent with preexisting attitudes. These findings were subsequently upheld in other research as well.

At the time that I was at Yale, other students who would prove to be among the leaders in the psychology of the future were also there. Lists are always risky, but my cohort included Mark Zanna, Michael Storms, Ellen Langer, Carol Dweck, James Cutting, Henry Roediger, and Robert Kraut, among other stellar scientists. Although my contacts with some of them were primarily through courses or casual conservations, my peers influenced my development as a scientist as well. Indeed, there seems to be remarkable cohort effects whereby the simultaneous presence of peer leaders in graduate school leads to emerging leadership across a broad array of areas within psychology. Similar cohort effects may be seen in the attribution research of the 1970s at UCLA and the personality/social researchers who came out of the Texas program in the mid-1970s. My first bit of advice to graduate students, then, is to pick your cohort carefully!

A pivotal person in my development as a scholar whose influence would become evident to me only much later was Kenneth Keniston, the psychiatrist who wrote *The Uncommitted* and *Young Radicals,* books that explored the political movements of the 1960s. As a psychiatrist in the medical school, Keniston did not typically work with psychology graduate students, but after much badgering, he was persuaded to take on four of us who sincerely wanted to learn his research methods and learn more about the radical movements he described. He taught us how to use interviewing as a hypothesis-generating and hypothesis-testing technique. I had always assumed that interviewing consisted of asking people a bunch of questions, and so the fact that it had an internal discipline as a methodology was enlightening.

Another profound influence on my development at this time was the radical movements of the 1960s, especially the women's movement. I joined New Haven Women's Liberation and helped organize demonstrations, sit-ins, protests, and conferences. It is remarkable that I was arrested only once, which was when we stormed Mory's, the bastion of decision making at Yale that was open only to men. Within months of our sit-in, Mory's changed its policy to admit women. It would be easy to chronicle the ways in which Yale discriminated against women, but what was most impressive to me was how quickly Yale changed when these patterns were pointed out. I loved being at Yale. It provided some of the most riveting and exciting intellectual experiences of my life. It also provided me with a husband, architect Mervyn Fernandes.

EARLY CAREER AT HARVARD

After Yale, we moved to Cambridge where I was a professor in the psychology and social relations department at Harvard. By this time, my interests had crystallized into social cognition, an emerging field that drew heavily on attribution theory for its origins but was largely developed from the profound insights, first by Kahneman and Tversky, that people solve complex problems by reducing them to manageable operations termed *heuristics*. These heuristics usually produce right answers, but the conditions under which they produce wrong ones are enlightening as to how the mind works. Kahneman and Tversky would be important influences on my intellectual development, as they were for so many.

I found social cognition to be fascinating in the way that one might find a giant puzzle fascinating. I was intrigued by how the human mind departs from rationality and the reasons that might underlie those departures. Early on, I began to think that many of these departures simply served other unrecognized needs.

The first is the need to be efficient. Normative models implicitly assume that one has the time to process all the information present, but given the buzzing confusion of the world, efficient methods are preferable, even if they are sometimes flawed. The second characteristic that marks many errors and biases in the social cognition process is that they are self-serving, in the sense that they make people feel better about their choices and decisions and also motivate them to persevere. These are kernels of truth that emerged early not only from my own work but from reading the work of other people, and they would form the basis of much of my work in the future.

One lucky day, a curly-headed undergraduate named Susan Fiske wandered into my office, and together we began a research program on salience; that is, the conditions that lead people to focus on part of the environment as opposed to another and the effects that salience has on the inferences that people draw. We found, for example, that point of view influences perceptions of causality, such that a person who engulfs your visual field is seen as more impactful in a situation (Taylor & Fiske, 1975). We found that imagining actions from the perspective of a particular character leads to empathetic inference and recall of information best learned from that person's perspective.

Perhaps the most important insight from this program of research concerns stereotyping and its cognitive bases. We found that if a person who engulfs your visual field is a token or solo member of a stereotyped group, he or she is more likely to be seen in stereotyped roles than if the person is in a group of similar others (Taylor, 1981). We found that when people observed a group of men and women talking, they organized their recall to a degree around gender, such that they were more likely to mix up the comments of women with other women and men with other men than to make cross-sex errors. We also showed that people who are stigmatized or unusual-appearing in any of several ways, including being pregnant or disabled, attract particular attention, leading to inferences about their personalities consistent with the particular stigma or unusual attribute they possess. This line of work was quite influential within social psychology and led to a paper in the

Advances series with Susan Fiske on "top-of-the-head" phenomena, which, to use present-day parlance, describes social heuristics (Taylor & Fiske, 1978).

MOVEMENT INTO HEALTH PSYCHOLOGY

Around 1976, my career took an abrupt turn. I was contacted by Judy Rodin and asked if I'd be willing to participate in a cancer conference to present what social psychology had to say about psychological responses to breast cancer. I admired Judy greatly and wanted to say yes, but I couldn't think of a single thing that social psychology could contribute to the issue. However, a close friend, Smadar Levin, a social psychologist who had breast cancer at the time, wanted very much to undertake the project. So together we began to explore links between social psychology and what would ultimately become health psychology.

Health psychology grew out of several sources, including behavioral medicine undertakings in clinical psychology that were especially focused around heart disease. From the outset, social psychologists had much to offer to the field as well. I took it upon myself to write several position papers about the potential contributions of social psychology to the emerging discipline of health psychology, and I subsequently wrote the first textbook in the field that defined its guidelines and topics (Taylor, 1986). I am particularly happy to have been a part of those very early endeavors and to be able to see what profound effects they have had on the topics that social psychologists now study.

It was difficult to pursue health psychology at Harvard, because the medical school is across the river and one takes a very long bus ride to get there. Nonetheless, I wrote a letter to Harvard's president, Derek Bok, asking him if he'd be willing to commit some funds to my developing health psychology at Harvard. His secretary called almost immediately and asked me how much it would take. I said about $3,000, and she called back within the hour to tell me there was a check waiting for me for $10,000 that I could use in any way I wanted to develop a health psychology interest in the psychology department.

MOVE TO UCLA

Ultimately, though, I did not get tenure at Harvard, and so I went to UCLA. The psychology department had a fledgling health psychology program under the direction of Bert Raven. He was extremely interested in building it up, and so I took that on as my charge when I arrived. My movement into health psychology necessitated a substantial reorientation in my career and additional training. To understand the underlying disease processes with which I needed to become familiar, I applied to the National Institutes of Health for a Research Scientist Development Award, and with their funding, I was able to complete coursework and readings that gave me a working understanding of the diseases I studied. This retooling process was invigorating personally and beneficial for my research program as well, because it enabled me to think about the impact of social cognition in ways that had not been possible before in my work. Retooling and extending one's horizons is a wonderful way of keeping one's scientific interest at fever pitch (Taylor & Martin, 2003). Our health psychology program, I am pleased to say, is one of the leading programs in the country and has been for the past 25 years. Currently, under the joint direction of Christine Dunkel-Schetter and Annette Stanton, we attract many of the best students in the country to this integrative training program.

The companion research endeavor that I undertook at this time involved empirical studies of cancer patients and understanding the role of personal control, attributions, and other cognitions for coping with the threat of cancer (e.g., Taylor, Lichtman, & Wood, 1984). Using the intensive interview techniques taught to me by Kenneth Keniston 10 years earlier, my collaborators Rosemary Lichtman and Joanne Wood and I interviewed breast cancer patients and their partners about their experiences.

Early on, we discovered that some of the beliefs these women held about their likelihood of recovering, their ability to control their cancer, and their perceptions of personal change were based to a degree on illusions. That is, many of the women with whom we spoke seemed to be thriving in the wake of their cancer but clearly held false beliefs about their abilities to rid themselves of the cancer and keep it from coming back. I consulted with a clinical psychology colleague about these findings and inquired if they were worrisome and if we should try to coax the women back into more realistic perceptions about the likely recurrence of their disease. Although she told me to not worry about them, I thought they were fascinating.

The notion that people can develop false beliefs that are protective of their mental health led me to realize that it is the construction of our world rather than accurate perceptions of reality that helps us negotiate the threatening and stressful events we encounter. This work led to a theoretical paper in 1983 on positive illusions and their role in helping cancer patients adjust to their revised circumstances (Taylor, 1983). In this paper, "Adjustment to Threatening Events: A Theory of Cognitive Adaptation," I suggested that meaning, mastery, and self-enhancement through social comparisons enable people to adjust successfully to threatening events. For the next several years, the empirical research my collaborators and I conducted would focus on positive illusions in medical populations and the ways in which they help people cope with threatening health events (e.g., Reed, Kemeny, Taylor, Wang, & Visscher, 1994).

RESEARCH ON POSITIVE ILLUSIONS

In 1988, Jonathon Brown and I published a paper in the *Psychological Bulletin* titled "Illusion and Well-Being: A Social Psychological Perspective on Mental Health" (Taylor & Brown, 1988). One of the most widely cited papers in social psychology (1,850 citations, by one recent count), this work built on the investigations we had conducted with medical populations and suggested that normal human cognition is also marked by positive illusions, including modest biases toward self-enhancement, unrealistic optimism, and personal control. These cognitions, we argued, foster the outcomes normally associated with mental health, namely, a positive sense of self; satisfying social relationships; the capacity for creative, productive work; the ability to set goals and sustain the motivation and persistence to achieve them; and the ability to cope effectively with setbacks and change. Until this time, scientists had regarded departures from rationality primarily as errors to be corrected. We showed that irrationality has its functions and can be adaptive.

This theoretical perspective generated several lines of empirical work. We uncovered how social comparison activities under threat are motivated to maximize information and positive self-perceptions (Taylor & Lobel, 1989). We identified the conditions under which positive illusions are most likely to be in evidence and their beneficial effects on motivation and performance (e.g., Armor & Taylor, 2003; Aspinwall & Taylor, 1992; Taylor & Gollwitzer, 1995). David Armor and I extended the work on unrealistic optimism (Armor & Taylor, 1998) to show that unrealistic optimism not only can be associated with positive outcomes but also can be reconciled with the need to monitor reality effectively. With Suzanne Segerstrom, we looked at the relations of optimism and causal attributions to health behaviors and explored how optimism is associated with immunologic responses to stress (Segerstrom, Taylor, Kemeny, & Fahey, 1998).

Nonetheless, this has been a highly controversial field that has produced some strong attacks (e.g., Colvin & Block, 1994). Some of these reactions have stemmed from misinterpretations, for example, the idea that more illusion is better, which is not the case. We argued that positive illusions typically stay within quite modest bounds largely because the feedback of the world is corrective, and the necessity of having useful information depends on at least relative accuracy. Thus, illusions that might spin out of control tend to be bumped back into more modest proportions by feedback from the world.

One particularly surprising paper (Shedler, Mayman, & Manis, 1993) reported evidence that people who have overly positive views of themselves are in fact maladjusted when clinical interviews are the adjustment criteria. The Shedler et al. (1993) findings also suggested that people with this "illusory mental health" have stronger biological responses to stressful tasks, suggesting potential health risks of these positive beliefs. This was surprising to me, because early in our program of cancer research, we had found evidence that people who held positive illusions about their ability to recover from cancer, in fact, lived longer, controlling for initial prognosis. Because the findings were enhanced by a few outliers, I did not publish these data, but the article by Shedler et al. (1993) made me want to return to this issue.

In a pair of articles, we rebutted the claims of Shedler et al. (1993) by showing that self-enhancers were evaluated as well adjusted and well liked by clinicians, peer judges, and friends (Taylor, Lerner, Sherman, Sage, & McDowell, 2003b) and that self-enhancing cognitions were associated with healthier biological responses to stress, including lower baseline heart rate and blood pressure and a lesser cortisol response to stress (Taylor, Lerner, Sherman, Sage, & McDowell, 2003a; see also Creswell et al., 2005).

I was able to further test these ideas in medical populations. Margaret Kemeny was just beginning a program of research with men diagnosed with AIDS or

HIV-seropositive status to identify factors that might prolong their lives. Her interests and mine complemented each other well, and as a consequence, with Geoffrey Reed, we were able to show that men who held unrealistically positive beliefs about their ability to overcome AIDS lived longer (Reed et al., 1994). Men who were seropositive and asymptomatic and who held unrealistically positive beliefs were less likely to develop symptoms of AIDS over time (Reed, Kemeny, Taylor, & Visscher, 1999). These findings extended our work on positive illusions into the arena of hard health outcomes (Taylor, Kemeny, Reed, Bower, & Gruenewald, 2000).

When we realized that the social cognitions of self-enhancement, feelings of mastery, and unrealistic optimism not only have psychological effects on well-being but actually influence biological processes to affect health, only then did we begin to fully realize the importance of beliefs. I made some efforts to extend these ideas to cardiovascular disorders as well (Helgeson & Taylor, 1993), a line of work that Vicki Helgeson subsequently has fruitfully pursued (e.g., Helgeson, 1992).

Even when my work focused heavily on health and underlying biological mechanisms, my interest in social cognition was never far away. As part of our interest in coping, my students and I undertook a program of research on mental simulation (Taylor & Schneider, 1989) and found that mentally rehearsing the processes needed to achieve a goal led to more effort and success in achieving the goal than mentally rehearsing the realization of the goal. We showed that people who undertook these process-oriented mental simulations coped better with stress and got better grades, among other beneficial outcomes (Taylor, Pham, Rivkin, & Armor, 1998). The significance of this work derived from its challenge to a long-standing but false tenet of the self-help literature, namely, that imagining yourself as having achieved a goal you desire will help you achieve it. We found, instead, that these outcome simulations actually interfere with progress toward one's goals.

MOVE TO SOCIAL NEUROSCIENCE

In the mid-1990s, my career took a new direction. As a result of participating in the MacArthur Network on Socioeconomic Status and Health and the consequent exposure to outstanding health psychologists including Nancy Adler, Sheldon Cohen, and Karen Matthews and to neuroscientists such as Bruce McEwen, I developed a deep interest in the mechanisms that link antecedent psychosocial conditions to health outcomes. Because not all of us in the network (especially me) were up to speed in the neuroendocrine processes underlying many of the processes we were studying, we were given lots of articles to read, and I devoured these with great curiosity and ultimately professional enrichment.

The first paper to result from this retooling was an *Annual Review* chapter titled "Health Psychology: What Is an Unhealthy Environment and How Does It Get Under the Skin?" (Taylor, Repetti, & Seeman, 1997). In this paper, we explored the processes by which environments marked by poverty, violence exposure, threat, and other chronically stressful events typically associated with low socioeconomic status (SES) lead to the extraordinary SES gradient in most health outcomes.

One of the striking findings to emerge from our review was the power of the early environment to shape health outcomes across the life span. Rena Repetti, Teresa Seeman, and I subsequently published a paper titled "Risky Families: Family Social Environments and the Mental and Physical Health of Offspring" (Repetti, Taylor, & Seeman, 2002) in which we reviewed the literature connecting risky childhood family experiences, marked by family conflict and/or cold, non-nurturant behavior, to adverse health outcomes in adulthood. We posited what some of the underlying physiological and neuroendocrine mechanisms might be that would help explain these lifelong effects (Repetti et al., 2002). We drew on McEwen's concept of allostatic load (McEwen, 1998), which provides a model for understanding how stressful events and their cumulative adverse effects on biological processes can lay the groundwork for health problems that may not be evident until decades later.

In our empirical work on these risky families, we showed that a risky early family environment predicts elevated blood pressure and heart rate (in men) and an elevated flat cortisol trajectory to stressful laboratory tasks (Taylor, Lerner, Sage, Lehman, & Seeman, 2004). In collaboration with the Coronary Artery Risk Development in Young Adults (CARDIA), we showed that a risky family environment links SES to psychosocial deficits, including negative emotions and poor social contacts, which in turn affects health-related outcomes, such as metabolic syndrome (Lehman, Taylor, Kiefe, & Seeman, 2005) and C-reactive protein (Taylor, Lehman, Kiefe, & Seeman, in press). In this work, we regarded psychosocial resources, which include the positive illusions described earlier, as key steps in pathways that link early environments to health outcomes via biological stress mechanisms involving cardiovascular physiology and the hypothalamic–pituitary–adrenocortical axis.

In recent years, my interests have also included social support and its biological underpinnings. Social support has long been thought of as a nice thing to have, but its impact on health is as strong in the positive direction as cigarette smoking and lipids are in the negative direction. Accordingly, social support is an important resource for ensuring good health (Taylor, 2007). We have looked at social support in several ways. We've explored cultural differences in the use of social support for coping and shown how social support efforts can adversely affect adjustment to stressful events if it violates cultural norms (e.g., Taylor, Sherman, et al., 2004). We've explored an intriguing gender difference: across the life span, girls and women are far more likely to seek out and provide social support for dealing with stressful events than men are. Although the difference is relatively modest in size, it is extremely robust, with virtually no reversals of this pattern (e.g., Tamres, Janicki, & Helgeson, 2002).

In a paper on biological responses to stress in females, we developed a theoretical model we termed "tend and befriend" (Taylor, Klein, et al., 2000). Adopting an evolutionary perspective, we maintained that females were historically responsible not only for their own safety but for that of offspring and thus would have developed responses to stress that ensured their joint survival. Neither fight nor flight, the traditional ways of looking at human stress responses, would qualify as responses to stress that could protect both the self and immature offspring.

The tend-and-befriend model maintains that people, especially women, evolved social means for dealing with stress that involved caring for offspring and protecting them from harm and turning to the social group for protection for the self and offspring. We suggested that the biological underpinnings of tending and befriending are likely to depend on oxytocin and endogenous opioid peptides, and we have been pursuing these issues empirically for the past several years (Taylor, Gonzaga, et al., 2006; Taylor, Klein, et al., 2000).

More generally, we have explored the biological processes whereby social support exerts effects on health. We have shown that people with more psychosocial resources have lesser cardiovascular and hypothalamic-pituitary-adrenal (HPA) responses to stress, leading to less wear and tear on these stress regulatory systems over time. The accumulation of allostatic load (i.e., the biological accumulation of stress [McEwen, 1998]) in people with strong social networks may be less, accounting at least in part for social support's beneficial effects (e.g., Lehman et al., 2005).

Together, these lines of work have helped turn me into a social neuroscientist, somewhat to my surprise. I did not choose to become a social neuroscientist so much as my research led me in directions that made it essential to understand the neural underpinnings of the phenomena we investigate. When you see that psychosocial resources have such an enormous impact on health not only immediately but across the life span, that observation cries out for understanding the mechanisms that underpin such relations. As a consequence, my retooling in this area continues.

Recently, our work has moved to the brain, as has the work of many social neuroscientists. I am fortunate to have as collaborators Matt Lieberman and Naomi Eisenberger, who use fMRI methodology to examine patterns of brain activation that may underlie socially meaningful phenomena. For example, we have shown that high levels of social support are associated with attenuated neuroendocrine responses to stress via (lesser) activation of the dorsal anterior cingulate cortex (dACC) and Brodmann's area 8 (BA8), regions of the brain that are usually especially active in response to social stress (Eisenberger, Taylor, Gable, Hilmert, & Lieberman, 2007). We have found that offspring from risky families have deficits in emotion regulation in response to stressful circumstances that are evident at the neural level (Taylor, Eisenberger, Saxbe, Lehman, & Lieberman, 2006). We have found that psychosocial resources moderate biological stress responses, such that these resources are associated with lesser dACC and greater prefrontal cortical responses to stressful circumstances. Thus, fMRI methodology has proved to be an exceptionally useful tool for understanding some of the neural mechanisms that help us to chart threat regulation pathways in general and the relation between psychosocial resources/risk factors and health outcomes more specifically.

Had you asked me at the beginning of my career what areas of science I would never explore, I would have answered confidently that genetics would be one of those areas. Clearly, I have little insight into the unfolding nature of science and my role in it, for genetic approaches represent an important direction in which our work has headed most recently. Specifically, we are exploring genetic polymorphisms related to the serotonin and dopamine systems as potential underpinnings of psychosocial risk factors and resources, respectively, for mental and physical health. Although this work is currently in its infancy, we have some findings to date. One reports a strong gene–environment interaction on the relation of the serotonin transporter polymorphism in interaction with early family environment or current adversity on risk for depression (Taylor, Way, et al., in press). Specifically, we find that the serotonin transporter polymorphism interacts with an early family environment (or current adversity), such that individuals with the s/s variant of the polymorphism are at significantly greater risk for depression if they are from a risky family background and at significantly less risk for depression if they are from a nurturant family background (Taylor et al., 2006). These kinds of crossover interactions are extremely intriguing because they indicate that the effects of a genotype may be completely reversed by the nature of the social environment. Such findings have led me to a renewed respect for the potency of the social environment.

In a second study (Eisenberger et al., 2007), we examined the MAO-A promoter VNTR and found that individuals with low expression of the MAO-A gene are more prone to negative emotional states, are especially sensitive to interpersonal threat cues, show stronger dACC reactivity to rejection in a virtual social exclusion task, and demonstrate a stronger cortisol response to a laboratory test involving social evaluative threat. Thus, our research to date suggests that polymorphisms relating to serotonin transport and to MAO-A are tied to psychosocial risk factors and resources in ways that are expressed in neural and neuroendocrine reactivity to stress.

LESSONS LEARNED

So, in conclusion, what have I learned during this 40-year-long strange trip? I've learned that how people construe the events that happen to them, particularly the challenging, stressful, and traumatic events they encounter, affects their psychological adjustment, their biological functioning, and their physical health. I've learned that these construals don't have to be true to have these beneficial effects. I've seen that construing events in positive ways is an ability, affected by genes, early family environment, and SES, among other factors. Perhaps the most astonishing thing I've learned is that we can actually chart these processes from genes and early environment to psychosocial resources and risk factors to neural mechanisms in the brain and neuroendocrine and immunologic systems in the body all the way to mental and physical health outcomes. We can actually see these processes unfolding over the life span. I've also learned that human vulnerability and resilience are reflected in data as rich as interviews and as precise as genes. As I've gotten older, I've been a bit panicked by the fear that I wouldn't live long enough to see the integrative biobehavioral science that would connect up all these levels of analysis, but science has moved so fast that I needn't have worried. The pieces are largely there, and the interconnections are made daily.

Let me return to the title of my talk, "From Social Psychology to Neuroscience and Back." In my empirical efforts to understand the powerful impact of the social environment on human thought, behavior, and psychological adjustment, my research endeavors have led me into health, neuroscience, and genetics.

The lessons I've learned tell me that the social environment profoundly affects human behavior, overriding or reversing even genetic contributions to behavior. Such findings foster a profound respect for the social psychological perspective on human behavior and the realization that the integrative science of the future that brings together biological and behavioral insights cannot succeed without recognition of social psychological contributors.

Woody Allen once said that 90% of life is just showing up. If you have the skills to do your job well, this quip is more true than you might realize. The trick, then, is to identify what makes you show up, year after year, sustaining interest and motivation to pursue a career for decades. I would say that, for me, the answers to this question have centered on constantly retooling to gain new methods and perspectives on the problems that are of enduring interest to me. In addition, my research program shows that I have been privileged to work with stunningly creative and insightful collaborators as well as brilliant students, many of whom who have gone on to stellar research careers of their own.

ADVICE TO YOUNG SCIENTISTS

What advice can I offer to young scholars entering the field of social psychology? There are a few lessons I've learned that I will pass on. First and most important, listen to data. Data may not come out the way you expect them to or the way you want them to, but data are never wrong. Theories and hypotheses, on the other hand, can be wrong. When the data are not showing what you expect, they will almost certainly be teaching you other lessons, and at least sometimes those lessons can be extremely valuable. Had I not been unnerved by the "positive illusions" uncovered in my interviews with cancer patients and paid attention to that evidence, one of my contributions to the field might never have come about.

Accept career advice judiciously. Many people are likely to offer you advice about what theories you should hold and what problems you should explore. Although virtually all this advice is well intentioned and some of it is valuable, some of it may come from an overly conservative bent in the field. Established scientists may perhaps unwittingly advise students to go into fields that are already well ploughed or that represent the current but perhaps not the future thrust of the field. Yet if you look at the social psychologists, or indeed to any scientific field's leaders, who have made the major contributions, you see that they tend to be set breaking. That is, rather than taking the well-trodden path, scientific leaders often move into arenas not yet trodden at all. They invent new fields, and they develop new problems to study. You may well be warned off a novel idea or research area by an advisor or colleague who feels you should play it safer. For example, I was once told by a well-meaning colleague to "stop doing this health stuff; it will be the end of your career." If the new ground is what you want to explore, then ignore this kind of advice.

A third lesson I have learned is to be fearless. For reasons I have never understood, social psychology is a discipline that is particularly critical of young and old scholars. As one anonymous head of a federal granting agency put it, "Social psychology is the only field that routinely eats its young." Because you are likely to get a lot of negative feedback anyway, you may as well be fearless and move into areas where it is virtually certain that you will get some negative feedback. The other part of my "fearlessness" advice is to not be afraid of new tools or developments in the field that may help you understand your phenomena better. If genes or gene-environment interactions are likely to be implicated in the problem you're studying, then by all means work with a geneticist and learn enough about genetics to know how to design the studies and make sense of the data when they come in. If fMRI methodology will be a useful tool for you, then by all means either learn it or get a collaborator who knows the brain and the tools for assessing brain activity well. If your social cognition research is taking you into behavioral economics, then learn enough economics to know whom your audience will be. In making these recommendations to my graduate students and postdocs, I often say, "Yes, it may be rocket science, but we're rocket scientists." This advice does not mean that you should become a neuroscientist or an economist but means that you should know enough about the fields to know with whom to collaborate and on what problems.

Improvise. Too often when one reads an article in the *Journal of Personality and Social Psychology,* one sees the same paradigm employed over and over again in a set of four or five studies that are essentially replications of each other. Improvisation means branching out and looking at the problem a new way. At the very least it entails conceptual replication, and at best it entails a completely new vantage point on an established problem. Try your ideas out in new content areas. If your ideas are supported in college students going through stressful events, will they also be supported among cancer patients undergoing treatment, for example? Change your subject population and the domains in which you test your theoretical ideas fairly often or you will never know whether your theories are broad and expansive, applying to a broad range of situations, or narrow and focused only on a specific type of situation.

Collaborate with well-chosen colleagues and talented students. Long-term collaborations, such as those enjoyed by Alice Eagley and Wendy Wood, Susan Fiske and me, Kahneman and Tversky, and Scheier and Carver can have much benefit if each person brings somewhat different interests, talents, and insights to the table. Alternatively, find colleagues whose interests are similar to your own but whose skills are quite different. Bringing together a diverse set of research skills by forming a team of scientists with only partially overlapping areas of expertise can make your empirical contributions far more profound and influential than they would otherwise be.

And finally, make your own luck. To paraphrase an old adage, scientific breakthroughs are a combination of mental preparedness and opportunities. Be mentally prepared by reading broadly in the field, and create your own opportunities by reaching out to others with interests and skills that will complement your own.

CONCLUSION

This is an amazing time to be in science. Who knew that in such a short period of time, we could put social behavior together with breakthroughs in genetics, brain science, and the latest developments in immunology and endocrinology? Social psychology used to be a relatively small field of scholars who talked primarily to each other, but now we have unprecedented opportunities to collaborate with the other sciences in ways that we could never have imagined even a few years ago. By acknowledging this scientific evolution and its intrinsic worth, we can build an integrative body of knowledge previously only imagined. It is an exciting time to be a scientist, and through today's talented students, we have an extraordinary future to anticipate.

AUTHOR'S NOTE

Preparation of this paper was supported by grants from the National Science Foundation (Grants 444040-ST-21549 and 0338631) and the National Institutes of Health (Grants MH56880-05 and MH071521).

REFERENCES

Armor, D. A., & Taylor, S. E. (1998). Situated optimism: Specific outcome expectancies and self-regulation. In M. P. Zanna (Ed.), *Advances in experimental social psychology*. New York: Academic Press.

Armor, D. A., & Taylor, S. E. (2003). The effects of mindset on behavior: Self-regulation in deliberative and implemental frames of mind. *Personality and Social Psychology Bulletin, 29*, 86–95.

Aspinwall, L. G., & Taylor, S. E. (1992). Modeling cognitive adaptation: A longitudinal investigation of the impact of individual differences and coping on college adjustment and performance. *Journal of Personality and Social Psychology, 63*, 989–1003.

Colvin, C. R., & Block, J. (1994). Do positive illusions foster mental health? An examination of the Taylor and Brown formulation. *Psychological Bulletin, 116*, 3–20.

Creswell, J. D., Welch, W. T., Taylor, S. E., Sherman, D. K., Gruenewald, T., & Mann, T. (2005). Affirmation of personal values buffers neuroendocrine and psychological stress responses. *Psychological Science, 16*, 846–851.

Eisenberger, N. I., Taylor, S. E., Gable, S. L., Hilmert, C. J., & Lieberman, M. D. (2007). *Neural pathways link social support to attenuated neuroendocrine stress responses.* Manuscript submitted for publication.

Helgeson, V. S. (1992). Moderators of the relation between perceived control and adjustment to chronic illness. *Journal of Personality and Social Psychology, 63*, 656–666.

Helgeson, V. S., & Taylor, S. E. (1993). Social comparisons and adjustment among cardiac patients. *Journal of Applied Social Psychology, 23*, 1171–1195.

Lehman, B. J., Taylor, S. E., Kiefe, C. I., & Seeman, T. E. (2005). Relation of childhood socioeconomic status and family environment to adult metabolic functioning in the CARDIA study. *Psychosomatic Medicine, 67*, 846–854.

McEwen, B. (1998). Seminars in medicine of the Beth Israel Deaconess Medical Center: Protective and damaging effects of stress mediators. *New England Journal of Medicine, 38*, 171–179.

Reed, G. M., Kemeny, M. E., Taylor, S. E., & Visscher, B. R. (1999). Negative HIV-specific expectancies and AIDS-related bereavement as predictors of symptom onset in asymptomatic HIV-positive gay men. *Health Psychology, 18*, 354–363.

Reed, G. M., Kemeny, M. E., Taylor, S. E., Wang, H.-Y. J., & Visscher, B. R. (1994). "Realistic acceptance" as a predictor of decreased survival time in gay men with AIDS. *Health Psychology, 13*, 299–307.

Repetti, R. L., Taylor, S. E., & Seeman, T. E. (2002). Risky families: Family social environments and the mental and physical health of offspring. *Psychological Bulletin, 128*, 330–366.

Segerstrom, S. C., Taylor, S. E., Kemeny, M. E., & Fahey, J. L. (1998). Optimism is associated with mood, coping, and immune change in response to stress. *Journal of Personality and Social Psychology, 74*, 1646–1655.

Shedler, J., Mayman, M., & Manis, M. (1993). The illusion of mental health. *American Psychologist, 48*(11), 1117–1128.

Tamres, L., Janicki, D., & Helgeson, V. S. (2002). Sex differences in coping behavior: A meta-analytic review. *Personality and Social Psychology Review, 6*, 2–30.

Taylor, S. E. (1981). A categorization approach to stereotyping. In D. L. Hamilton (Ed.), *Cognitive processes in stereotyping and intergroup behavior*. Hillsdale, NJ: Lawrence Erlbaum.

Taylor, S. E. (1983). Adjustment to threatening events: A theory of cognitive adaptation. *American Psychologist, 38*, 1161–1173.

Taylor, S. E. (1986). *Health psychology*. New York: Random House.

Taylor, S. E., Way, B. M., Welch, W. T., Hilmert, C. J., Lehman, B. J., & Eisenberger, N. I. (2006). Early family environment, current adversity, the serotonin transporter polymorphism, and depressive symptomatology. *Biological Psychiatry, 60*, 671–676.

Taylor, S. E. (2007). Social support. In H. S. Friedman and R. C. Silver (Eds.), *Foundations of health psychology* (pp. 145–171). New York: Oxford University Press.

Taylor, S. E., & Brown, J. (1988). Illusion and well-being: A social psychological perspective on mental health. *Psychological Bulletin, 103*, 193–210.

Taylor, S. E., Eisenberger, N. I., Saxbe, D., Lehman, B. J., & Lieberman, M. D. (2006). Neural responses to emotional stimuli are associated with childhood family stress. *Biological Psychiatry, 60*(3), 296–301.

Taylor, S. E., & Fiske, S. T. (1975). Point of view and perceptions of causality. *Journal of Personality and Social Psychology, 32*, 439–445.

Taylor, S. E., & Fiske, S. T. (1978). Salience, attention, and attribution: Top of the head phenomena. In L. Berkowitz (Ed.), *Advances in experimental social psychology*. New York: Academic Press.

Taylor, S. E., & Gollwitzer, P. M. (1995). The effects of mindset on positive illusions. *Journal of Personality and Social Psychology, 69*, 213–226.

Taylor, S. E., Gonzaga, G., Klein, L. C., Hu, P., Greendale, G. A., & Seeman, S. E. (2006). Relation of oxytocin to psychological and biological stress responses in older women. *Psychosomatic Medicine, 68*, 238–245.

Taylor, S. E., Kemeny, M. E., Reed, G. M., Bower, J. E., & Gruenewald, T. L. (2000). Psychological resources, positive illusions, and health. *American Psychologist, 55*, 99–109.

Taylor, S. E., Klein, L. C., Lewis, B. P., Gruenewald, T. L., Gurung, R. A. R., & Updegraff, J. A. (2000). Biobehavioral responses to stress in females: Tend-and-befriend, not fight-or-flight. *Psychological Review, 107*, 411–429.

Taylor, S. E., Lehman, B. J., Kiefe, C. I., & Seeman, T. E. (in press). Relationship of early life stress and psychological functioning to adult C-reactive protein in the CARDIA study. *Biological Psychiatry*.

Taylor, S. E., Lerner, J. S., Sage, R. M., Lehman, B. J., & Seeman, T. E. (2004). Early environment, emotions, responses to stress, and health [Special issue on personality and health]. *Journal of Personality, 72*, 1365–1393.

Taylor, S. E., Lerner, J. S., Sherman, D. K., Sage, R. M., & McDowell, N. K. (2003a). Are self-enhancing cognitions associated with healthy or unhealthy biological profiles? *Journal of Personality and Social Psychology, 85,* 605–615.

Taylor, S. E., Lerner, J. S., Sherman, D. K., Sage, R. M., & McDowell, N. K. (2003b). Portrait of the self-enhancer: Well-adjusted and well-liked or maladjusted and friendless? *Journal of Personality and Social Psychology, 84,* 165–176.

Taylor, S. E., Lichtman, R. R., & Wood, J. V. (1984). Attributions, beliefs about control, and adjustment to breast cancer. *Journal of Personality and Social Psychology, 46,* 489–502.

Taylor, S. E., & Lobel, M. (1989). Social comparison activity under threat: Downward evaluation and upward contacts. *Psychological Review, 96,* 569–575.

Taylor, S. E., & Martin, J. (2003). The academic marathon: Managing the academic career. In J. M. Darley, M. P. Zanna, & H. L. Roediger, III (Eds.), *The complete academic* (2nd ed.). New York: Random House.

Taylor, S. E., Pham, L. B., Rivkin, I., & Armor, D. A. (1998). Harnessing the imagination: Mental simulation and self-regulation of behavior. *American Psychologist, 53,* 429–439.

Taylor, S. E., Repetti, R. L., & Seeman, T. E. (1997). Health psychology: What is an unhealthy environment and how does it get under the skin? *Annual Review of Psychology, 48,* 411–447.

Taylor, S. E., & Schneider, S. K. (1989). Coping and the simulation of events. *Social Cognition, 7,* 176–196.

Taylor, S. E., Sherman, D. K., Kim, H. S., Jarcho, J., Takagi, K., & Dunagan, M. S. (2004). Culture and social support: Who seeks it and why? *Journal of Personality and Social Psychology, 87,* 354–362.

Taylor, S. E., Way, B. M., Welch, W. T., Hilmert, C. J., Lehman, B. J., & Eisenberger, N. I. (in press). Early family environment, current adversity, the serotonin transporter (5-HTTLPR) polymorphism, and depressive symptomatology. *Biological Psychiatry.*

A Career on the Interdisciplinary Divide

Reflections on the Challenges of Bridging the Psychological and the Social

ALICE H. EAGLY

Department of Psychology, Northwestern University

A faint glimmering of my eventual career journey emerged in eighth grade when I gave an oral report on the occupation of social scientist. The assignment was to report on an occupation, and I delivered an enthusiastic description of the work of social scientists. My information was very limited; it came from a magazine article, perhaps the *Reader's Digest*. This event seems important in retrospect because it was my first exposure to the idea that human behavior could be the subject of science. In those days, newspapers and magazines provided little coverage of psychology or the social sciences more generally. To my 13-year-old self, the idea that a person could be a social scientist was new, and such a career seemed to be attractive. So a seed was planted.

At that early point, I was already interested in science but had studied only physical and biological science. In high school, still lacking meaningful exposure to social science, I developed the idea that I might become a chemist because chemistry seemed interesting and accessible. At that point, my incipient interest in a scientific approach to human behavior lay dormant. I don't think that my public school education should be especially faulted for this lack of education in the social and behavioral sciences, because few American schools offered much in these areas, except for the occasional psychology course. The public schools that I attended, located in several cities in California and then in Seattle from seventh grade onward, were in fact relatively progressive for their era.

I did not encounter social science again until I was in college. Yearning to see a world beyond the West Coast, I had left Seattle for Radcliffe College, Harvard's associated women's college. My first-year program included some mathematics and chemistry courses, which were mildly interesting, but I soon gravitated to a major known as social relations. My eighth-grade insight proved correct: The social sciences were irresistibly attractive. Social relations, popularly labeled "soc rel," was an interdisciplinary major that incorporated social, developmental, personality, and clinical psychology and even some biologically oriented psychology, along with sociology and anthropology. It was a heady mix of disciplines, all of which I found utterly fascinating.

The social sciences were in a period of transition during my college years (1956–1960). Some grand theorizing was still alive. At Harvard, we still studied Freud in psychology, and Talcott Parsons was active with his big-picture sociology. David McClelland (1961) was well advanced in his tour de force in understanding achievement motivation. Gordon Allport's (1954) expansive book on prejudice had already appeared. Social psychology was identifiable in this mix and quickly gaining increased visibility with the beginnings of cognitive consistency theories. Critical events that shaped social psychology when I was an undergraduate included the publication of Festinger's (1957) *A Theory of Cognitive Dissonance* and Heider's (1958) *The Psychology of Interpersonal Relations* as well as some of the Yale series of books on attitudes (e.g., Rosenberg, Hovland, McGuire, Abelson, & Brehm, 1960). Clearly, social psychology was emerging from its early beginnings with interesting theories and high-profile experimental studies.

Despite the methodological diversity of the interdisciplinary mix that constituted Harvard's social relations major, it was becoming apparent that the experimental method was the wave of the future in social psychology. People began talking about experimental social psychology as a recognizable movement. My honors thesis, which was directed by Herbert Kelman, consisted of an experiment, and it helped define social psychology for me. I had many interests, however, and finished my undergraduate education knowing something about a lot of different kinds of social science. My undergraduate education was excellent in many respects and certainly very stimulating even though it lacked depth in some of the topics that were part of the psychology major in most departments of psychology.

GRADUATE EDUCATION

As a senior undergraduate, I decided to go to graduate school and faced making a decision about what kind of graduate program to pursue. It seemed that social psychology was right for me. The field seemed to be rising in importance. The area also impressed me as somehow central within the social sciences and potentially integrative, at least of psychology and sociology. Social psychology struck me as encompassing many different theories and methods and offering breadth and lots of different directions to pursue. Guided by my preference for interdisciplinarity, I applied to social psychology programs. But I really had it all wrong as far as the direction of social psychology in the coming years was concerned.

Choosing a graduate program in social psychology was not as difficult then as it is now: There were far fewer established programs. I settled on the University of Michigan, in part because it offered a program sponsored jointly by sociology and psychology. The program involved first obtaining a master's degree in psychology or sociology and then entering the social psychology program for the Ph.D. I chose to obtain the master's degree in psychology, largely because I believed that I needed much more background in psychology. After this 1-year program of courses and the completion of a first-year project, I entered the interdisciplinary program in social psychology. The breadth of this program did make it especially interesting for me. However, despite the efforts of outstanding senior faculty such as Theodore

Newcomb, Daniel Katz, and Helen Peak, it turned out that this joint program was in its dying days. Given the developments in social psychology, it had become much more difficult to integrate psychology and sociology in a single curriculum.

What were the problems? The issues were not specific to the University of Michigan but reflected broader intellectual trends. Social psychology was indeed rising in psychology departments. At the same time, theory and research were moving away from the broader social processes that interested sociologists and instead concentrating on individual processes. Research methods were becoming more exclusively experimental in psychology departments, despite some voices advocating methodological diversity. The students in this joint program at Michigan who intended to pursue careers in psychology departments found it increasingly irrelevant to their core interests to read Marx, Weber, Parsons, and other social theorists and to think broadly about individuals in the context of social structure and culture. These concerns seemed quite remote from the experiments that we were designing to test theories of attitudes and cognitive processes.

For these reasons, it was an unsettled period in the history of social psychology at Michigan. The strains were apparent. The faculty assembled a committee to talk about definitions of social psychology and to discuss its key concepts. But this effort failed to bring the psychologists and sociologists together. Quite a few of the faculty who were central to the interdisciplinary social psychology program took positions at other universities in the next few years, although the most senior faculty remained.

I was vaguely dissatisfied with my progress and felt that I had not really found a comfortable specialization as a researcher. I spent 4 years as a graduate student. Perhaps had I taken more time with my graduate education, I would have developed a clearer sense of my research direction. I did take a lot of courses during this period. The curriculum's broad interdisciplinary scope required this approach. In my fourth year, I carried out a dissertation on involvement and persuasion, a topic that was of some importance in attitude theory of the 1960s. Herbert Kelman directed my dissertation, and I had also completed some research with Melvin Manis earlier in my graduate program.

ALLURE OF THE PSYCHOLOGY OF ATTITUDES

With the dissertation completed and my Ph.D. in hand in 1965, I took an assistant professor position, first at Michigan State University for just 2 years and then at the University of Massachusetts in Amherst. As I look back on my publications from that first decade of my post-Ph.D. career, I see some tentative branching out from research on attitudes, but my main efforts centered on attitude research. There was of course the pressure to publish. The late 1960s was a period of unprecedented expansion in American universities, so obtaining tenure was not as difficult as it became in recent decades. Still, substantial productivity was required. So I mainly continued with the attitudes theme where I had already gained some experience. I settled into more persuasion studies in the 1970s and 1980s. Some of these projects pertained to reception processes in persuasion—the idea that some variables affect the persuasiveness of messages by influencing how well message recipients understand messages (e.g., Eagly, 1974). Other projects investigated attributions about why communicators take positions on issues and the effects of these attributions on the persuasiveness of messages (e.g., Eagly, Wood, & Chaiken, 1978). Some studies were precursors of the dual-process heuristic–systematic model that Shelly Chaiken developed in her dissertation for which I served as advisor (Chaiken, 1980). I fostered this theory at several points and thereby participated in the dual-process phase of theorizing in social psychology (e.g., Chaiken, Liberman, & Eagly, 1989).

My attraction to the attitudes area of social psychology went beyond persuasion research and dual-process theories. I found the research area appealing because of its centrality in social psychology and its intellectual breadth. Because people have attitudes about many things, including social and political issues, it seemed to me that attitude should serve as a core integrative concept linking individual and social processes and thus help me fulfill my aspirations toward an interdisciplinary social psychology. When broadly defined, the attitude concept thus encompasses phenomena such as interpersonal attraction and social values. Attitude theory and research also encompass affect and emotion, cognitions and beliefs, and the prediction of behavior. When social cognition became an important movement in social psychology, I didn't jump on the bandwagon because I had the idea that the study of attitudes included social cognition, along with much else. It was thus the breadth and integrative potential of research and theory on attitudes that seemed so attractive.

My ideas about the centrality of attitude research to social psychology lay behind my goal of writing a book on attitudes that would bring this field of theory and research together and make it more coherent than it then seemed to most social psychologists. I wanted graduate students and psychologists more generally to appreciate the value of what we had collectively created in the study of attitudes. A certain lack of appreciation for the area was apparent in the late 1970s and most of the 1980s. Its decline in popularity probably had several causes—the loss of interest in cognitive consistency theories, the recognition that attitudes often do not predict behaviors, and the rise of social cognition as a distinct specialty area within social psychology. And there was as well in this period the so-called crisis in social psychology that caused some to doubt the value of much of what had gone before, perhaps especially attitude research.

Fortunately, Shelly Chaiken, then a faculty member at the University of Toronto, was willing to collaborate with me on a general book on attitudes (Eagly & Chaiken, 1993). We worked on *The Psychology of Attitudes* for 6 years and ended up with a considerably larger book than either of us had anticipated. Working on this book with Shelly was a highlight of my intellectual journey. Shelly has little tolerance for logical sloppiness or shallow analysis, so every conference with her sharpened my thinking on this book project. We would go back and forth, criticizing one another's chapters and developing them beyond what I had thought possible. In the end, we produced a multithemed saga of real accomplishment in social psychology. To some extent, the book did manage to span the psychological and the social, especially in our efforts to integrate research on attitudes with research on social influence.

Our hopes for this book have largely been fulfilled. It did help people see the integrative potential of attitude theory and the scope of the varied research programs pertaining to attitudes. Quite a few researchers in other areas of psychology also read the book and gained an understanding and appreciation of attitude research and theory. Exceeding my expectations, it has to date garnered 1,483 citations, according to Web of Science.

I have continued to study attitudes. My interest as a graduate student in the construct of psychological involvement lay dormant as not fully developed but eventually led to an integrative meta-analysis with Blair Johnson on the varied approaches to studying involvement and persuasion (Johnson & Eagly, 1989). Yet another major project pertained to memory for attitude-relevant information (Eagly, Chen, Chaiken, & Shaw-Barnes, 1999). In our meta-analysis of this research area, which was one of the first topics systematically investigated in social psychology, some unexpected phenomena emerged. For example, we argued that methodological weaknesses were responsible for some of the seemingly strong early confirmations of the congeniality effect in memory—that is, the principle that people have better memory for information that agrees than disagrees with their attitudes. This project was joined with primary research that clarified the findings of the meta-analysis (Eagly, Kulesa, Brannon, Shaw-Barnes, & Hutson-Comeaux, 2000). These experiments explored the implications of the more thorough processing of uncongenial than congenial information. Consequently, for memorability, there are cross-pressures: The advantages that congenial information has in fitting people's schemas and being generally pleasant are often countered by the more thorough processing of uncongenial information. From this perspective, the apparent absence of effects of attitudes on memory, which are common in research, make more sense. This project untangled one important aspect of the issues involved in understanding attitudinal selectivity in information processing, a topic that I am continuing to pursue with research on selective exposure to information.

INSIGHTS ABOUT METHODS AND MY DISCOVERY OF META-ANALYSIS

For me, as for most social psychologists, initiating a career in the mid-1960s in a psychology department meant becoming an experimental social psychologist. I found this emphasis uncomfortably narrow. Experiments, yes, but why just experiments? There are many ways to do research. Experiments, however thoughtfully designed, generally involve considerable artificiality and raise questions about generalizability to natural settings. It also seemed that many topics in social psychology started with a few experiments that attracted attention for a while. However, enthusiasm would then fade away, as in the case of attitude memory research, because the initial findings failed to be replicated or a host of complicated moderating conditions entered the picture.

Solutions had to be found for what seemed at the time to be a discouraging situation, aspects of which fueled social psychology's crisis of the 1970s. A solution adopted by some was to complement laboratory experiments with a wider range of field and correlational methods. In fact, a portion of my own work has been nonexperimental (e.g., Becker & Eagly, 2004; Eagly & Wood, 1999). The burden of producing nonexperimental analogues of experimental effects helps prevent overemphasis on effects that may mainly reflect specialized laboratory conditions. Another approach is to join experiments together to discover larger patterns in what might seem, at least to many observers, a confusing mix of findings. When findings are systematically analyzed across studies, research literatures can become more cumulative and interpretable. That's why meta-analysis immediately attracted me when I became aware of it in the late 1970s.

I was somewhat pushed into being an early adopter of meta-analysis because of an article by Harris Cooper (1979) on sex differences in conformity, the same topic that I had addressed in a *Psychological Bulletin* article that had appeared one year earlier (Eagly, 1978). I took issue with aspects of Cooper's article, which he had written primarily to illustrate the value of meta-analysis. However, I recognized the superiority of the quantitative integrative methods that he had used for his review, compared with the narrative and vote-counting methods that I had used in my 1978 article. I realized that I should develop my understanding of this topic by undertaking a quantitative review myself. I struggled through this first meta-analysis and published it in the *Psychological Bulletin* (Eagly & Carli, 1981). Having thus learned quite a lot about this new method, I found myself with a powerful tool that I could use in addition to experimentation. I became very enthusiastic about the potential of addressing broader questions by integrating entire research literatures. Meta-analysis offered (and continues to offer) outstanding opportunities to bring together many studies and figure out what they collectively mean. In this way, it is possible to capture some of the larger scope that seemed to be missing from the experimental studies that others and I had conducted on attitudes and other topics.

Adopting this new method brought many challenges—intellectual, methodological, and statistical. Intellectually, I had to learn to think about entire research literatures, some of which were outside of my earlier areas of expertise. Methodologically, I had to come to appreciate the details of other researchers' methods and the relations between methods and study outcomes. And statistically, I had to become much more knowledgeable so that I could understand the wide range of statistical procedures appearing in research articles as well as the new meta-analytic statistics. All in all, delving into meta-analysis was an important step in my intellectual journey—it was not a move that I had anticipated in my early career.

CONCENTRATION ON THE SOCIAL PSYCHOLOGY OF GENDER

Another theme had developed in my research, beginning tentatively with an article on sex differences in susceptibility to social influence (Eagly, 1969). This is the gender theme, which gathered some speed when I published the two reviews of sex differences in conformity, the first in narrative style and the second with meta-analytic methods (Eagly, 1978; Eagly & Carli, 1981).

Why the interest in gender? The late 1960s and the early 1970s was the period of the greatest growth and cultural salience of the women's movement. Feminism posed many unanswered questions about men and women, difference and similarity, and nature and nurture. There was little scientific work to draw on, at least not in social psychology, so this area seemed open to discovery and innovation. In contrast to the attitudes field, which was well stocked with theory and research, the psychology of gender was largely neglected. In fact, the mainstream of social psychology placed little value on this field, and its low status discouraged many from pursuing research on gender. But having gained tenure, I believed that I didn't need to worry all that much about following the crowd. Moreover, I did receive considerable applause for my first major article on gender—the first of the two articles in the *Psychological Bulletin* on gender and influenceability (Eagly, 1978). This paper won two prizes, one from the decidedly feminist Association for Women in Psychology (Distinguished Publication Award) and the other from the progressive Society for the Psychological Study of Social Issues (Gordon Allport Intergroup Relations Prize).

One of the most appealing aspects of gender research was that it put me in contact with other social scientists—initially with developmentalists, personality psychologists, and sociological social psychologists and later with industrial/organizational psychologists. Interest in gender issues was growing rapidly in most of the areas of psychology. Also, through women's studies interdisciplinary groups, especially at Purdue University, where I took a position in 1980, there was welcome contact with scholars in a wide range of other disciplines.

In studying gender, more meta-analyses on sex differences and similarities in social behavior were an obvious direction for me in addition to various types of experiments. Given that few meta-analyses had been conducted, there was considerable interest in the outcomes. The meta-analytic problem, being a two-group comparison, was relatively straightforward. So I tackled altruism and aggression, the good and the bad of social behavior (Eagly & Crowley, 1986; Eagly & Steffen, 1986).

After these projects, I went on to study leadership: Here was an excellent opportunity to be integrative, because gender and leadership questions abounded and were politically and socially important. Also, the relevant studies were spread across several disciplines. Leadership research encompasses not only social and organizational psychology but also political science, sociology, management, education, and other applied areas. Many scholars of leadership value research across the disciplines and are tolerant of a wide range of methods.

My gender and leadership meta-analyses have been strung out over quite a few years. The first one, on leadership style, was published in 1990 (Eagly & Johnson, 1990), and what may be my last, on stereotypes of leaders, is still in progress. In between, I conducted integrative reviews on the emergence of male and female leaders (Eagly & Karau, 1991), evaluations of equivalent male and female leaders (Eagly, Makhijani, & Klonsky, 1992), and the effectiveness of male and female leaders (Eagly, Karau, & Makhijani, 1995). Research on leadership style developed sufficiently over these years that I also published a second meta-analysis on this topic, which focused on studies of the transformational and transactional leadership styles of women and men (Eagly, Johannesen-Schmidt, & van Engen, 2003).

When I began my work on the psychology of gender, social psychologists in particular had produced relatively little theory for understanding gender. And there was very limited research on what seemed to be a fundamental human concern. The lack of attention to gender was a real blind spot in social psychology. For example, Gordon Allport (1954), in his influential book on prejudice, did not consider gender prejudice. Because of the silence of social psychologists, most of the theory that had appeared in textbooks on the psychology of women and gender came from developmental psychology, and psychoanalytic theory lived on in feminist-modified form. In contrast, the traditional message of social psychology—the power of the situation—was missing from theory about gender. Against this background in the 1980s, while I was conducting my first meta-analyses on sex differences, I developed social role theory, which I initially published in a book based on lectures that I gave at the University of Alberta (Eagly, 1987).

Why the emphasis on roles? Like attitude, role is one of the central integrative concepts of the social sciences. Role expectations exist in the minds of individuals and are also shared with other people, producing social structure and culture. The role concept was the key to my development of a theory of gender that emphasizes contextual variation in sex differences and similarities and that gives a major emphasis to the social structural context of behavior. This theory and its extensions have been the focus of most of my work on gender topics (see Eagly, Wood, & Diekman, 2000).

According to social role theory, to the extent that the men and women of a society are differently positioned in the social structure, a variety of mediating processes conspire to make the sexes psychologically different in ways that facilitate performance of their typical roles. Psychological sex differences emerge from general expectations that apply to men and women and from the particular occupational and family roles that are differentially occupied by men and women. Culturally shared expectations, or gender roles, reflect these specific social roles that are typically occupied substantially more by one sex than the other because the characteristics that are required to carry out sex-typical roles become stereotypical of women and men. Women are thus expected to be nurturing and kind (i.e., communal) because they predominate in caretaking roles, and men are expected to be dominant and assertive (i.e., agentic) because they predominate in paid employment roles, especially those yielding higher wages and authority. Sex differences in behaviors and attitudes thus reflect influences arising from membership in the general social categories of men or women, as mediated by socially constructed social roles, socialization processes, and individual psychological processes that include expectancy confirmation sequences, self-regulatory processes, and psychophysiological processes.

After my move to Northwestern University in 1995, I worked on extending social role theory in three quite different directions. The first direction continued the work that I had initiated on leadership, the second addressed the ultimate origins of sex differences, and the third considered the effects of gender on sociopolitical attitudes. The leadership extension followed from the findings of my meta-analyses. The article that I published in the *Psychological Review* organized these projects and other research to support a *role congruity theory* of prejudice against female leaders (Eagly & Karau, 2002). Role congruity theory analyzes the situation of leaders as inevitably occupying both a gender role and a leader role. When these two roles are occupied by women, people's expectations are often in conflict. This conflict, or *role incongruity*, fosters a prejudicial lowering of the evaluation of women as potential leaders and actual leaders, compared with their male counterparts. The presence and extent of this prejudice are hypothesized to vary with many moderator variables (e.g., male domination of leadership role, year data were collected, sex of raters). In analyzing prejudice as an attitudinal phenomenon, I was able to invoke roles and attitudes, my two favorite social psychological constructs.

With gender research becoming a growth area, new contenders entered the picture and vied for attention—most notably, evolutionary psychologists, who analyzed sex differences mainly in terms of sexual selection theory. Their work became increasingly popular in the 1990s, although, I believed, it oversimplified a complex set of questions. I found their theory of mate preferences to be especially incomplete, because it missed obvious alternative explanations to those derived from sexual selection theory. For example, from my perspective, women's preferences for resources and older age in a mate could easily follow from their social position in contemporary society, which was generally not that of primary wage earner. At least this idea seemed as plausible as the evolutionary psychology argument that such a disposition was built into a female mind that was adapted to primeval conditions. Social role theory thus argues that the psychology of women and men stems not primarily from the evolved dispositions postulated by evolutionary psychologists but from the social psychological processes that follow from the social roles occupied disproportionately by women and men. That idea led me to reanalyze David Buss's (1989) influential 37-cultures study of mate preferences. This project established that most of these sex differences in mate preferences were smaller in more gender-equal societies (Eagly & Wood, 1999).

Confrontation with evolutionary psychology required that I study the ultimate origins of psychological sex differences. Over the years when I was giving talks on gender issues and presenting social role theory, every once in a while someone would ask me, "But where do the roles come from?" I would say, that's not really a psychologist's question; we have sociologists and anthropologists to answer it. But as someone who aspired to be an interdisciplinary social scientist, I found that my answer sidestepped a question that I should try to address. I had to do better.

Wendy Wood and I collaborated on a general article on the origins question that appeared in the *Psychological Bulletin* in 2002 (Wood & Eagly, 2002). Here we presented a theory of the origins of the differential placement of men and women into social roles. We identified physical differences between the sexes— primarily female reproductive activity and secondarily male size and strength—as the main determinants of the placement of men and women into social roles. With a review of cross-cultural research in anthropology, we showed that the effects of these physical characteristics of the sexes depend on societies' socioeconomic and ecological environment. These effects are much different in a postindustrial society than in most other societies because of low birthrates and the presence of very few high-status occupations that are highly physically demanding. We labeled our analysis a *biosocial theory* of the origins of sex differences. This article drew on the scholarly literature from anthropology to address psychologists' questions about the origins of sex differences. So once more my intellectual journey bridged psychology and another social science. We also developed links between the biology and the psychology of gender by recognizing the importance of the sex-typed body to role assignments and of the psychophysiological mediating processes that enable and energize role-bound behaviors.

Finally, my gender research has considered the attitudes of men and women on sociopolitical issues. This analysis invoked the social positioning of women and men as the source of the somewhat different political stances of women and men. From this perspective, gender gaps in attitudes and voting behavior are shaped by the divergence of women's interests from those of men; in turn, these divergent interests derive from the gender division of labor. These insights led to a series of studies on sociopolitical attitudes and voting behavior (e.g., Eagly, Diekman, Johannesen-Schmidt, & Koenig, 2004).

THE PRESENT AND FUTURE OF THE JOURNEY

Where is the intellectual journal now? I am happy with what I have accomplished so far in the career journey and hope to accomplish more, mainly the consolidation and further development of the two major themes of my intellectual life, the study of attitudes and of gender. I am currently completing a book on gender and leadership, which is written for general readers and titled *Through the Labyrinth: The Truth About How Women Become Leaders*. In this book, Linda Carli and I deal with the twin issues of women's considerable gains in authority and leadership in most postindustrial societies and the continuing predominance of men in the more powerful leadership roles. The story that we tell is grounded in social role theory and its extensions. Yet, to address this broad topic, we also rely on research by economists, sociologists, and political scientists. So again my intellectual journal carries me into other disciplines. I hope that this book will reach a general audience of educated readers, not merely other social scientists.

Also under construction is a much tighter empirical case for arguing that group stereotypes follow from their groups' typical role occupancies, an essential assumption of social role theory. In the relatively near future I plan in addition to write a general scholarly book on gender, social roles, and the origins of sex differences. Another project, if all goes well, is a second edition of *The Psychology of Attitudes*. Attitude research continues to be central in social psychology, and there is much new work, including the important development of research on implicit attitudes. A new edition would require greater attention to the grounding of attitudes in associational processes that can be automatically elicited by cues related to an attitude object. In the meantime, I serve as department chair at Northwestern University. I sometimes wonder if my knowledge of the scholarly literature on leadership will in any way help me as a department chair.

THE FAMILY CONTEXT

My career journey has been embedded in my life journey, and family is its other main component. As a child, I had parents who were very supportive of education and made sure that my brother and I had good opportunities to develop our intellectual and cultural interests. Because my family was of modest middle-class means, we didn't travel very extensively but took advantage of many educational and cultural opportunities that were available in the cities in which we lived.

From an early age, I was a dedicated student with intellectual interests that my parents encouraged. They supported me in my preference to go away to Harvard/Radcliffe as an undergraduate. Although my subsequent decision to go forward to graduate school and become a professor came as a surprise to my parents, for them it was a pleasant surprise. Having been a very good student at Radcliffe, graduating summa cum laude, it seemed that I could do well in a graduate program. Perhaps the fact that my father was a professor, although of engineering, helped because I had seen this type of career close at hand. Of course, there were very few women professors at that time, and exceedingly few at Harvard, but I did not explicitly recognize that fact as portending career barriers in my own future. Somehow the Radcliffe experience did give quite a few of us women some confidence in our ability, even in those years that preceded the modern feminist movement. I told myself that if I could do well at Harvard, I could do well in a graduate program.

By contemporary standards, people married at an early age in the 1960s. I married at age 23, while a graduate student, to Robert Eagly, an economist and fellow student in the year that I spent in Norway as a Fulbright fellow between my undergraduate and graduate work. My ideas about family were entirely conventional in the sense that I believed that marriage should be followed by children. In relation to having children, my mother maintained, "That's what life is all about." So I didn't want to miss out on such an important part of life. My husband and I have two daughters: Ingrid was born when I was 30 years old, and Ursula when I was 38.

It didn't seem that the career journey should be interrupted by marriage or children, but surely life became far more demanding and complicated after having children. I am most fortunate to have a husband who shared the child rearing and other domestic work and children who were (and remain) physically healthy and psychologically robust. Family has been at least as important and rewarding as career, so the blending has given me a satisfying life. Although on a day-to-day basis there were of course trade-offs between the demands of family and career, in the longer run the two sets of obligations are complementary. I am happier in my career because it did not require giving up motherhood, and I am happier in my family life because it did not require giving up my career. And I am grateful that my life situation offered the opportunity for both a good family life and a good career. I also acknowledge that maintaining my career and family life required dedication to both activities, with little time left over for leisure.

CAREER ADVICE, TENTATIVELY OFFERED

There are so many paths to rewarding careers that I hesitate to offer strongly worded advice. So here are my insights. For me, it has proved valuable to follow my own interests rather than to follow the crowd. Had I followed the crowd, I would have taken up current topics in social cognition in my critical period of early career growth and not written *The Psychology of Attitudes* or learned to meta-analyze or investigated gender and sex differences. By taking these less-traveled paths, which I was convinced should be inherently central to social psychology, I was able to exert leadership and win more visibility than would have been the case on the more traveled paths. I think that, especially in the early and middle phases of a career, researchers should consider taking up topics that are not the focus of lots of other researchers' current studies. Admittedly, such decisions should take into account the likely success of a new departure. Embarking in new directions is not free of risk.

I also encourage young social psychologists to increase their breadth, both methodologically and theoretically, beyond the traditional confines of social psychology. I developed breadth when I was quite young. However, because social psychology moved into a phase of developing its core during my early career, this breadth had little pay-off until somewhat later. In the longer run, breadth proved to be important to my career. The early intellectual background from my undergraduate and graduate programs enhanced my ability to branch out later on.

Understanding human behavior is a long-run endeavor, so good researchers never stop learning. It is abundantly clear that exciting collaborations exist in the direction of biology and neuroscience. Similarly important developments can occur when branching toward the other social sciences, although the advantages may be less obvious at this time. And to be collaborative in these directions, social psychologists need to be appreciative of a wider range of methods than traditionally pursued. And no matter what one's methods, it is important to look beyond one's own studies. To enable researchers to look at entire research literatures, meta-analysis will continue to be important.

It is obvious that anyone's career benefits from outstanding collaborators. My career journey wouldn't have gone at all well without extraordinarily talented graduate students, with whom I developed ideas and studies. From my period at the University of Massachusetts, Shelly Chaiken, Wendy Wood, and Linda Carli, initially graduate students working with me, quickly became colleagues and collaborators. They have become lifelong collaborators who are important to my intellectual life. From my years at Purdue University, Blair Johnson and Steve Karau, once graduate students working with me, have also become long-term outstanding collaborators. More recently my years at Northwestern have also been blessed with superb graduate students: Amanda Diekman, Patrick Kulesa, Anne Koenig, and Paul Eastwick, who are talented collaborators. Faculty colleagues have been essential too, as an audience for ideas and as friendly critics. My new ideas always came out first at brown-bag talks and received comments and critique from the local group. The brown-bag lunch is social psychologists' academic salon, and for me, it has proved to be helpful and motivating.

Finally, perhaps my most important piece of advice for young social psychologists is to work hard and steadily. Keep on researching and writing. Don't be overly discouraged if journals turn down your papers: Appreciate the feedback and move on. It may have been easier to publish in my very early career; journals sometimes accepted papers outright, without requiring the arduous phases of "revise and resubmit" that are now routine. Yet scholarly productivity has always required tenacity and the courage to face criticism. Younger social psychologists must acquire those qualities at the outset of their careers if they are to become successful researchers. The road to an outstanding research career in social psychology, as in other scientific fields, is demanding, perhaps increasingly so, but we now collectively produce much more sophisticated research than we did in the past. The high requirements of a research career in social psychology pay off in building knowledge and contributing to what is one of the most vigorous and exciting of scientific fields.

REFERENCES

Allport, G. W. (1954). *The nature of prejudice*. Cambridge, MA: Perseus Books.

Becker, S., & Eagly, A. H. (2004). The heroism of women and men. *American Psychologist*, 59, 163–178.

Buss, D. M. (1989). Sex differences in human mate preferences: Evolutionary hypotheses tested in 37 cultures. *Behavioral and Brain Sciences*, 12, 1–49.

Chaiken, S. (1980). Heuristic versus systematic information processing and the use of source versus message cues in persuasion. *Journal of Personality and Social Psychology*, 39, 752–766.

Chaiken, S., Liberman, A., & Eagly, A. H. (1989). Heuristic and systematic processing within and beyond the persuasion context. In J. S. Uleman & J. A. Bargh (Eds.), *Unintended thought* (pp. 212–252). New York: Guilford.

Cooper, H. M. (1979). Statistically combining independent studies: Meta-analysis of sex differences in conformity research. *Journal of Personality and Social Psychology*, 37, 131–146.

Eagly, A. H. (1969). Sex differences in the relationship between self-esteem and susceptibility to social influence. *Journal of Personality*, 37, 581–591.

Eagly, A. H. (1974). Comprehensibility of persuasive arguments as a determinant of opinion change. *Journal of Personality and Social Psychology*, 29, 758–773.

Eagly, A. H. (1978). Sex differences in influenceability. *Psychological Bulletin*, 85, 86–116.

Eagly, A. H. (1987). *Sex differences in social behavior: A social-role interpretation*. Hillsdale, NJ: Lawrence Erlbaum.

Eagly, A. H., & Carli, L. L. (1981). Sex of researchers and sex-typed communications as determinants of sex differences in influenceability: A meta-analysis of social influence studies. *Psychological Bulletin*, 90, 1–20.

Eagly, A. H., & Carli, L. L. (2007) *Through the labyrinth: The truth about how women become leaders*. Boston: Harvard Business School Press.

Eagly, A. H., & Chaiken, S. (1993). *The psychology of attitudes*. Fort Worth, TX: Harcourt, Brace, Jovanovich.

Eagly, A. H., Chen, S., Chaiken, S., & Shaw-Barnes, K. (1999). The impact of attitudes on memory: An affair to remember. *Psychological Bulletin, 125*, 64–89.

Eagly, A. H., & Crowley, M. (1986). Gender and helping behavior: A meta-analytic review of the social psychological literature. *Psychological Bulletin, 100*, 283–308.

Eagly, A. H., Diekman, A. B., Johannesen-Schmidt, M. C., & Koenig, A. M. (2004). Gender gaps in sociopolitical attitudes: A social psychological analysis. *Journal of Personality and Social Psychology, 87*, 796–816.

Eagly, A. H., Johannesen-Schmidt, M. C., & van Engen, M. (2003). Transformational, transactional, and laissez-faire leadership styles: A meta-analysis comparing women and men. *Psychological Bulletin, 129*, 569–591.

Eagly, A. H., & Johnson, B. T. (1990). Gender and leadership style: A meta-analysis. *Psychological Bulletin, 108*, 233–256.

Eagly, A. H., & Karau, S. (1991). Gender and the emergence of leaders: A meta-analysis. *Journal of Personality and Social Psychology, 60*, 685–710.

Eagly, A. H., & Karau, S. J. (2002). Role congruity theory of prejudice toward female leaders. *Psychological Review, 109*, 573–598.

Eagly, A. H., Karau, S. J., & Makhijani, M. G. (1995). Gender and the effectiveness of leaders: A meta-analysis. *Psychological Bulletin, 117*, 125–145.

Eagly, A. H., Kulesa, P., Brannon, L. A., Shaw-Barnes, K., & Hutson-Comeaux, S. (2000). Why counterattitudinal messages are as memorable as proattitudinal messages: The importance of active defense against attack. *Personality and Social Psychology Bulletin, 26*, 1392–1408.

Eagly, A. H., Makhijani, M. G., & Klonsky, B. G. (1992). Gender and the evaluation of leaders: A meta-analysis. *Psychological Bulletin, 111*, 3–22.

Eagly, A. H., & Steffen, V. J. (1986). Gender and aggressive behavior: A meta-analytic review of the social psychological literature. *Psychological Bulletin, 100*, 309–330.

Eagly, A. H., & Wood, W. (1999). The origins of sex differences in human behavior: Evolved dispositions versus social roles. *American Psychologist, 54*, 408–423.

Eagly, A. H., Wood, W., & Chaiken, S. (1978). Causal inferences about communicators and their effect on opinion change. *Journal of Personality and Social Psychology, 36*, 424–435.

Eagly, A. H., Wood, W., & Diekman, A. B. (2000). Social role theory of sex differences and similarities: A current appraisal. In T. Eckes & H. M. Trautner (Eds.), *The developmental social psychology of gender* (pp. 123–174). Mahwah, NJ: Lawrence Erlbaum.

Festinger, L. (1957). *A theory of cognitive dissonance.* Evanston, IL: Row, Peterson.

Heider, F. (1958). *The psychology of interpersonal relations.* New York: Wiley.

Johnson, B. T., & Eagly, A. H. (1989). The effects of involvement on persuasion: A meta-analysis. *Psychological Bulletin, 106*, 290–314.

McClelland, D. C. (1961). *The achieving society.* Princeton, NJ: Van Nostrand.

Rosenberg, M. J., Hovland, C. I., McGuire, W. J., Abelson, R. P., & Brehm, J. W. (1960). *Attitude organization and change: An analysis of consistency among attitude components* (pp. 198–232). New Haven, CT: Yale University Press.

Wood, W., & Eagly, A. H. (2002). A cross-cultural analysis of the behavior of women and men: Implications for the origins of sex differences. *Psychological Bulletin, 128*, 699–727.

Life Experiences and Their Legacies

BERNARD WEINER

Department of Psychology, University of California, Los Angeles

*I*n this self-reflection I share with the readers some experiences and the lessons they have taught. I call my bequest "legacies," but they are biases that any reader could reasonably reject. These defining moments or periods occurred early in my career, during graduate school or soon thereafter. Hence, this autobiographical musing ends around 1970, leaving the next 36 years of my life unexamined. The episodes I discuss can be considered boxcars on the train of life, each standing independently yet also linked.

LESSON 1: SELECTING A GRADUATE SCHOOL

In 1956, some 50 years ago, I found myself in the master's degree program of industrial relations at the University of Chicago, where I had obtained my bachelor's degree. I knew nothing about industry and had never been good at relations, so a future in industrial relations did not appear promising. Redirection came unexpectedly. I enrolled in an industrial psychology class taught by Harold Leavitt, a student of Kurt Lewin. This was my first psychology course inasmuch as the undergraduate curriculum at the University of Chicago was based on a Great Books Program. I thought the field of psychology was captured in Freud's *Civilization and Its Discontents*. Following my course enrollment I became Leavitt's research assistant. I was surprised and proud when later seeing my name in a footnote on an article examining communication networks.

Three years later, armed with a master's degree and an honorable discharge from the Army, I made my way to Ann Arbor, Michigan, to be a graduate student at the University of Michigan. This was the only graduate program to which I had applied from my Army post in Huntsville, Alabama, and I am sure that my acceptance was in good part, if not entirely, due to my Leavitt connection. I sought admission to Michigan because I envisioned working with Dan Katz, one of the leading figures in industrial psychology. I shudder when I look back at my naïveté.

As I arrived, Katz was leaving on sabbatical. I was assigned John (or Jack) Atkinson as my temporary advisor. He strongly suggested (i.e., insisted) that I take his motivation course; I then became his teaching assistant. The next year I joined his research group, where I remained and became identified as an Atkinsonian.

During my 4th year of the Ph.D. program in personality, which was the umbrella embracing human motivation, I was studying in the library and noticed an attractive girl at my table. She was reading something with "Supply and Demand" written on the cover.

"Are you an econ major?" I asked, using my most clever opening line (while not really caring about her school major).

"Econ and history," she answered (not really caring to speak with me).

It was arranged that I pick her up at 7:00 for supper. She lived in an upscale academic area of Ann Arbor with her family. My apprehensive knock was answered by a distinguished gentleman, previously unseen by me, with a warm smile. "Hello and welcome," he said, thrusting out his hand. "I'm Dan Katz."

I gulped, or gasped, and replied with a slight stutter: "H-h-hi, I'm B-Bernie Weiner. I came here 3 years ago to be your student."

My fantasy of having Dan Katz as father-in-law rather than mentor came to an abrupt halt after the first disastrous date, reconfirming that I should not major in anything having "relations" in the title. But this life event left me with the first lesson, or rule, or bias that I wish to communicate:

> When selecting a graduate school, do not pursue a person but rather join a pro-gram. Have alternatives. Your sought-after mentor may be unwilling, unable, unavailable, unpleasant, and/or unworthy.

Katz (the elder, not the younger) and I developed a friendly bond, and as editor of the very prestigious *Journal of Abnormal and Social Psychology,* he rejected the first article I ever submitted for publication. In the Gestalt–Lewinian tradition, it concerned serial effects in the recall of incomplete tasks. Katz wrote one of the nicest letters I ever received from an editor, praising the value and promise of this work. I still have his encouraging review.

LESSON 2: CONDUCTING EXPERIMENTAL RESEARCH

Atkinson's theory was the focus on my graduate school life. It contained a straight-forward prediction: Persons highly motivated to achieve desire to undertake inter-mediate difficulty tasks, whereas those low in achievement needs equally prefer easy or difficult alternatives (see Atkinson, 1957). Thus, this was a theory of choice and decision making.

At that time, the University of Michigan had an outstanding program in math-ematical psychology and decision theory. I was friends with many students in that program but particularly with a fellow displaced Chicagoan, Paul Slovic. Paul and I translated Atkinson's concepts into decision-theory language. We concluded that the theory involved variance preferences—persons low in achievement needs were expected to display more variance in their choices, indifferent between easy and difficult tasks, than those high in achievement needs.

We thought about testing the belief that there are stable variance preferences between individuals. Operationalizing this idea was difficult because we could not find meaningful or affordable incentives for our research participants. We did not want to settle for "pretend" scenarios that were to later loom large in my life.

After exploring many possibilities, I suggested to Paul that we use rats as subjects. Motivation psychologists in those days primarily conducted their research on rat populations, and I wanted to do animal research. When rats are hungry, choices involving food are quite meaningful, and we could afford to give away the reward, so this research direction provided a perfect starting point for my animal investigations.

Our reasoning went something like this. We would offer rats 5 pellets of food, for example, when turning left at a choice point and randomly 1 or 9 when turning right. Holding the overall pay-off constant, we could then determine if our animals exhibit stable risk preferences.

Crafting an experimental procedure was not easy. Should there be just one type of food or different incentives? Should we always have the same value alternatives or might we offer, for example, 5 versus 1 or 9 pellets as well as 2 versus 1 or 3 pellets? Should there be spaced or massed trials, because consuming 9 pellets could satisfy hunger? Must left- and right-side alternatives be varied because rats have turning preferences? And how should the choice point be presented? Animal research, we quickly discovered, was not necessarily the royal road to data collection.

We answered the choice-point question by using what was known as a "gap" procedure. When making their selection, the rats had to jump over a substantial gap in the apparatus, hence making an irreversible decision that required cost and commitment. This was a popular methodology at the time.

There were so many unknowns that we decided to first do a pilot study using only one animal. Paul was deathly afraid of rats, and I readily agreed to run the experiment and collect the data, while he would use his mathematical expertise to perform sophisticated statistical analyses.

I selected a curious and friendly rat as our subject. We named him Farfel. For those of you not of Eastern-European Jewish heritage, Webster defines *farfel* as "noodle dough in the form of small pellets or granules." Farfels actually resemble dried dog food, but they are larger and rounder and have less taste. My mother, who came to the United States with my father from a Ukrainian peasant village at the age of 25, used to serve them in chicken soup, where they soaked up the broth and were rather enjoyable. My memory fails to inform me why this name was chosen for our rat.

We began our experiment with Farfel, hoping to find that he would display stable choices. Farfel was very cooperative, eager to get in the runway and make his jump. And why not—he was in rat's paradise. No matter what he did, he received some food. Perhaps not the biggest possible reward on any given trial, but so what? Life was good.

What we failed to notice about Farfel, or perhaps I should say failed to seriously consider, was that he was growing increasingly fat. In fact, it is fair to say he was absolutely obese. One day, as Farfel calculated his decision and jumped, his weight proved his downfall. He did not make it over the gap and fell between the runways. Farfel valiantly held on with his claws, his bulging eyes pleading with me for help, as he tried to prevent falling into research oblivion.

"Paul, get Farfel," I shouted. "He's slipping."

"No way; I am not touching that humongous rat. You get him."

"I can't. I'm holding the data recording sheet."

"Well, put it down."

"Paul, Farfel is running down the hall. Chase him ..."

Yes, during the debate Farfel was already making his way down the corridor. Word has it that his descendants live on in Mason Hall, where the psychology department was housed. Indeed, had we thought about offspring, we could have studied the inheritability of variance preferences. Alas, our experimental quest, and my career as a rat runner, came to an end with the escape and disappearance of Farfel.

This regretful albeit illuminating experience left with me my second set of sage advice to students (although some of the thoughts may roam a bit from this experience):

> Understand and closely observe your research participants. Take part in the experiment. If it does not work on you, don't expect it to work on your subjects. Of course, if your participant population is composed of infants or people from other cultures or if you are studying unconscious determinants of behavior, this may not be reasonable advice. But for many research studies, active participation as a subject is not only possible but necessary.

There seems to be an assumption that our research participants differ from us. When asked about the meaning of his cigar smoking, Freud responded, "A cigar is sometimes just a cigar." I doubt he would have said that about the behavior of his patients. I believe the scientific theory must account for the behavior of the scientist; the research hypothesis should be demonstrable with the research proposer as with the subject, and had Paul and I undergone the experience of Farfel, receiving 100% food reward on endless trials, we would have anticipated his bodily transformation.

LESSON 3: SELECTING A MENTOR

When Odysseus went on his long journey, he needed someone to watch over his son Telemacous, someone who would teach Telemacous moral values and to accept responsibilities in the city-state. He searched for a teacher, sponsor, and exemplar, a person who would facilitate the goals of Telemacous. For this position, Odysseus chose his friend Mentor.

The importance of having someone play the role of mentor in academics cannot be overemphasized. Students with mentors are happier, more productive, promoted more quickly during their academic careers, and overrepresented as award winners.

Initially I did not pursue Atkinson as my mentor, and he did not search for me. Rather, we were thrust upon each other, at least in the first phase of our relationship, by circumstances. In many respects (but not all, as will be seen later),

Atkinson was an ideal mentor. He had personal integrity, he was dedicated to psychology, and he considered science a building process in which each person tries to lay down one brick. He also was a tribal leader. There was a research hierarchy, with him as director. He distinguished members of the in-group (those holding the "correct" theory; i.e., his) from members of the out-group (persons in other tribes, such as drive theorists). He once titled an article "The Final Nail in the Coffin of Drive Theory." He held weekly research meetings at his house, incorporating students at all levels, from postdoctoral visitors to undergraduates. There was one clear criterion to be his advisee—you had to be working on something directly related to the confirmation of his theory; outliers were not accepted. Particularly at the start of my career, I modeled many of these behaviors (I hope not the dogmatic aspects).

As a tribal leader, Jack did not hesitate to make use of his tribal members. I owned an old car that I purchased for $25. Because I used the car sparingly in Ann Arbor, it was shared with friends who were willing to buy gas. Jack would periodically call on me for some errand, such as pushing his car in the winter or driving others to test subjects.

One morning I received a call from Atkinson asking me to help carry some dirt from the local garden store. Of course, I said I would be right over. But first I had to pick up the car from a fellow psychology major who used it for amorous adventures. Jerry H. remains a friend and was famous or infamous for having the most involving and most volatile love relationships. *Love* is perhaps too generous a term; *sexual liaison* is a more accurate description.

I phoned Jerry to tell him I was taking the car back and went to get Atkinson. We proceeded to the garden store and opened the trunk to put in the dirt, and once again I gasped, or gulped. In it were a number of empty liquor bottles, blankets, and assorted condoms. Now although Atkinson was a political liberal, he was a churchgoing conservative. The sexual revolution had not fully hit Ann Arbor and certainly was not going to reach the Atkinson house.

Our eyes locked. These were not the rejecting blue-green pools of Katz the younger, nor were they the fearful eyes of Farfel the fat. Rather, they were the large brown eyes of God, sending forth a verdict of guilty. I looked at Atkinson, stuttered, and said, "J-J-Jack, it is too long a story to tell, and you would not believe it. These are not mine."

I was on my way to becoming an attribution theorist.

Trust was restored as I evenly spread the dirt in the garden, and in exchange Jack put an encouraging inscription regarding my scientific future in one of his books, which remains on my shelf. This leads to my third set of suggestions:

> Find a mentor—someone you respect, admire, and want to be like. Make sure he or she has a research group so you have others from whom to learn and with whom to share ideas. The mentor should be active in research so you can have your name on a publication and come to understand the intricacies and strategies of publication. The mentor should be dedicated to a point of view because, even if you are incorrect, you have a clear direction or guiding light. Finally, maintain your mentor's respect.

LESSON 4: SHEDDING A MENTOR (AND REVISITING EXPERIMENTAL RESEARCH)

The goddess Athena was attracted to Telemacous. She was the daughter of Zeus and had many special gifts, including the power to take the appearance of others. Athena pretended to be Mentor and led Telemacous astray. That is the origin of the phrase "Beware of mentors."

There are many reasons I had to beware of Atkinson. I had been vaguely alerted to them as a student, but they became painfully apparent after I took my first job in 1963 as an assistant professor at the University of Minnesota. I was very fortunate to be offered this position, because I did not publish as a graduate student and the University of Minnesota had a very strong department. It included a cast of colorful characters. Among them was my neighbor, Paul Meehl, the only genius I have ever met. Their program in social psychology was renowned, and Harold Kelley, who was to play a central role later in my life, had left the department for UCLA just two years prior to my arrival. However, I had nothing to do with social psychology and in fact knew little about the area beyond the one brief course I had taken. My appointment was in the personality program, and I was affiliated with the Center for Personality Research, which was directed by Norman Garmezy, respected for his investigations of schizophrenia. Norm became my second mentor, but concerning professional rather than theoretical issues. He did a great deal to further my career, as will soon be elaborated.

My initial interview at the university gave rise to a major job obstacle. I was met at the airport by Gardner Lindzey, a very well-known social psychologist. On the way to the university, Lindzey stopped at a bar. I was somewhat of a teetotaler and very susceptible to the effects of alcohol, which seemed ominous at 11 in the morning, before my job talk. Lindzey ordered his drink, looked me in the eye, and asked what I would have. Again these were not the bewitching eyes of Katz the younger, the frenzied pupils of Farfel the falling, nor the brown eyes of Mentor. Rather, they were the macho eyes of Gardner the great. I was in a lose–lose situation. I can't remember what I replied but suspect it was something like "Got milk?" It must have not been held against me, for about 2 weeks later I received a job offer.

Minnesota's psychology department had a reputation for being the "dustbowl of empiricism." Skinner had been on their faculty, and it was the home of the Minnesota Multiphasic Personality Inventory. It was for this reason that my training presented problems. In the Atkinson tradition, the experimental procedure our tribe followed was first to classify individuals according to their level of achievement needs. Then some experimental manipulation was administered that typically involved choice or persistence of behavior as a function of the difficulty of the alternatives.

This two-phase sequence was fraught with perils. First, achievement needs were assessed with a projective instrument, the Thematic Apperception Test (TAT). A very large population of only males was tested in a group setting. The TAT administration required participants to write stories to four to six outdated-looking pictures. Then these protocols were scored, guided by an established scoring procedure. The experimenter (me) had to therefore read about 1,000 hurriedly and sloppily written story responses to TAT pictures and make decisions concerning the inclusion of a variety of achievement themes. This was intensive and time-consuming work.

Following the TAT administration, those designated as high or low in achievement needs were called back for the experimental manipulation. By the time I completed my scoring, some subjects had fulfilled their experimental requirements. Others would not participate in the second phase of the study. In addition, the experimental manipulation invariably involved deception, particularly failure, with one hour required to run and debrief the subjects, who were tested individually. More than a few participants talked to their friends about the deception, so some other potential participants were unusable.

One consequence of this time-involving procedure and the loss of subjects was that it was possible for me to complete at most two experiments yearly, hardly a fountain of empirical research. To add to these woes, the hit rate for a successful study was low. I previously mentioned that I did not have publications as a graduate student. That was not because Atkinson and I did not conduct research—for three years we repeated an experiment that never worked. In sum, I had reasons to fear the outcome of any later tenure decision.

I therefore began to supplement this research with a different program of study, examining motivational influences on short-term retention. I already revealed that my first submitted (and rejected) article also made use of recall, reflecting my interest in memory. These studies could be conducted in about one-half hour, so an experiment might be completed in one day.

There was great pay-off in this research direction—it resulted in numerous articles, and replication and extension were simple to accomplish. I published a *Psychological Monographs* (Weiner, 1966) with 16 interrelated studies. It followed a monograph written by Julian Rotter (1966) concerning locus of control that became one of the most cited papers in the next two decades and also had an influence on me, although I did not read it at that time. The only claim to fame of my monograph was as the last published by this journal; *Psychological Monographs* came to an end as subscriptions dwindled because the topics were so varied while psychology was becoming increasingly specialized. But I contributed the final nail in the coffin.

I ruminated about why my research on achievement motivation had a hit-or-miss quality and why my experimental work with Atkinson never proved successful. I thought Atkinson's theory was correct (I no longer believe this) and that the experimental manipulations were well conceived. I therefore began to reconsider the TAT as a measure of achievement needs and to address broader issues regarding traits, trait measurement, and the best way to make scientific progress.

Without elaborating my reasoning here, I concluded that situational manipulations take precedence over individual difference research, that there is no generalized trait deserving the label of "need for achievement," and that, if there was, projective measurement was not a solution to the assessment problem. Many psychologists doing achievement-related research were attempting to predict grade point average, or who will drop out of school, or how long one will attempt an impossible anagram, on the basis of a content analysis of stories written about, for example, obscure people performing on a trapeze and/or two persons gazing at one another (oft-used TAT pictures). This approach was doomed to failure. These musings are part of my fourth legacy:

> There should be a time in professional development when a mentor is left behind. This may mean rejecting a mentor or standing on the shoulders to see a little further, or both. All too often I find students following too closely in the footsteps of their advisors, not sufficiently branching out and/or being able to discern the shortcomings of their initial guide.

Many mentors will take pride in this independence. But Atkinson, the tribal leader, did not forgive me for going astray. Perhaps the contents of the car trunk left some lasting doubts.

LESSON 5: ON TEACHING

My parents lived in the vicinity of the University of Chicago, so as an undergraduate student I was able to walk to classes from our apartment. The stroll down Ellis and Greenwood avenues was especially meaningful to me. From the houses and apartments I could hear classical music, and I knew or imagined that my professor and his family were harmoniously playing string quartets, probably Beethoven. My eyes misted with admiration and envy. I thought about a later academic life at a small, liberal arts college; pursuing truth as I lit my pipe, students seated around the fireplace, engaged in serious discussion, petting my golden retriever, and awed by my collection of (read) books.

This image faded as I sought training in industrial relations at the University of Chicago. However, when I undertook the doctoral program at the University of Michigan, this aspiration reappeared. Again, however, it was soon squelched, this time by the pull of a research career at a large university. When I accepted my first position at the University of Minnesota, and later during my career at UCLA, my strategy was to reduce teaching, if possible, because it interfered with my research goals.

My teaching at these institutions was not around the fireplace, but rather I often stood in front of 200 or 300 students, trying to hold their attention. I nevertheless took my teaching role quite seriously, and it was an important part of my life, my self-esteem, and my self-concept.

An early experience at the University of Minnesota was especially traumatic. I was assigned to teach introductory psychology, and the class met at 8 a.m. About 250 of the 350 enrolled students showed up, often late. Some were eating breakfast, others reading the newspaper, and a surprising number were reliving the experience of the prior evening with their significant other. My confidence began to wane; my self-concept as an effective and beloved teacher was crumbling. I did not even own a pipe!

Then I noticed a blue-eyed, blond-haired student whose gaze was fixated on me. His pen constantly moved, writing down each of my precious words. As he wrote, his head vigorously moved up and down and he smiled knowingly, assimilating the new information was his prior knowledge. I thought, this was my fireplace link. If I could reach and change even one person, then it signified I was a good teacher.

This situation continued for the entire semester: empty seats, late arrivals, early hamburgers, rattling newspapers, intertwined hands, and in the midst of this chaos, my prized pupil. At last the semester ended, and a number of students in the lecture hall came down after my final lecture to speak with me. They wanted to take the final early, or late, or not at all. They asked what pages to read, what pages to skip, and what facts to retain. But there, in the background, waited my knight, my student, blue eyes shining. I thought he would say something like this: "Dr. Weiner, this was the best course I have ever taken. It has changed my life. I am a bio-physics honors student but want to switch to psychology. Would you allow me to study with you?" All the while we would be exchanging understanding looks.

Instead, however, in the most primitive and broken English he weakly offered, "Dr. Weiner, I am an exchange student from Finland. I speak very little English and did not understand a word you spoke all semester. Would it be possible to borrow your lecture notes?" This leads to the following advice to the next generation, albeit it may stray just a bit from the story:

> Seek feedback on all aspects of your academic life. Institutions have programs to evaluate and improve teaching. Peers gladly read over manuscripts and have important suggestions. Openly face and address real and perceived shortcomings. One's evaluation and perception of reality, whether good or bad, is likely to differ greatly from the truth.

LESSON 6: REPLICATION AND MULTIPLE-STUDY PUBLICATION

Early in 1965, just 2 years after coming to the University of Minnesota, Garmezy created a shock wave by advising me to go elsewhere. He said the department was in a power struggle and many individuals were going to quit, and I should do the same. As a new assistant professor, I was unaware of this turmoil. He was correct, and a number of the faculty members soon left for other institutions.

Garmezy conveyed that UCLA was building their psychology department. As I indicated, the university had recently hired Hal Kelley. In addition, the clinical program added Elliot Rodnick, who was Garmezy's research collaborator, as its area chair. I assume Garmezy phoned Rodnick, Rodnick spoke to the UCLA psychology department chair, and about 2 weeks later I received a phone call with a job offer from UCLA. This is what is meant by the "old boy's network," and I certainly profited from it. I had never been to California and asked if it would be possible to visit prior to resolving this major life crisis. I landed on a gorgeous March day, leaving behind a number of feet of Minnesota snow, and a decision was reached quickly, before setting foot on campus.

I arrived at UCLA in 1965, along with eight other new assistant professors in the psychology department. The trip across the country was somewhat difficult with our cat, but matters became worse as my wife and I arrived in Los Angeles on the day of the Watts riots. Let me contrast this with my first experiences in Minneapolis. That city gives an award to the "best neighbor," and the 1963 winner lived across the street from our awaiting rental house. When we arrived, the Minneapolis Symphony was playing on our closed-off block. I knew that Minnesota citizens had high regard for university professors, but this welcoming party (for me) was more than I anticipated.

I continued with research on achievement motivation but now eschewed individual difference measurement and searched for studies that could be easily conducted, with multiple persons tested at one time. I wanted to maintain the advantages of memory research while examining more molar and complex motivation phenomena.

Two established psychologists and one graduate student provided the impetus for my research. The psychologists were Rotter, whose monograph I already introduced, and Richard de Charms. Rotter (1966) had introduced the concept of locus of control—the idea that factors affecting task outcome may be distinguished as residing within the individual, such as skill, or in the external environment, such as chance. I initially wondered if individuals high in achievement needs might view their world as determined by skill, while those low in achievement needs consider life more akin to a gambling game. I had not yet moved from a focus on individual differences.

When musing about the association between achievement strivings and locus of control, I read a book by de Charms (1968) titled *Personal Causation*. There he discussed a moral dilemma in which hypothetical persons were described as not repaying a debt either because they could not or did not want to. The obvious dawned on me—internal factors differ from one another in systematic ways, and failure because of low ability will elicit different appraisal than failure caused by lack of effort. Had I any knowledge of social psychology I would have realized that Fritz Heider (1958), who would later be considered my intellectual forefather, already pointed out the ability/effort distinction that provided the foundation for my later work. Heider was not cited by Rotter and had been dismissed by Atkinson as not embracing science, a conclusion with which I concurred when too quickly glancing over Heider's work as a student in Atkinson's seminar.

The graduate student who influenced my thinking was Linda Beckman, my first Ph.D. advisee. Linda approached me after beginning with Hal Kelley (who was going on sabbatical leave). Her doctoral thesis involved asking students the causes of their success and failure. I dismissed this idea as "part of that Heider nonsense" and not worthy of further consideration. She prevailed and was awarded her Ph.D. in 1969.

I also initiated a very simple study with another student, Andy Kukla. In this research we described school children as succeeding or failing and factorially varied whether they had or did not have ability and exerted or did not exert effort. The participants were instructed to evaluate these students. Achievement striving thus was approached from a moral standpoint. That experiment marked a watershed for my research on causal attributions. The studies were easy to conduct, the variables easy to manipulate, the results easy to evaluate and the pattern of findings systematic and easy to replicate. I felt at peace, at least empirically.

A strange thing happened on my way to the publication forum. I submitted a manuscript of about 20 pages, containing three experiments, to the *Journal of Personality and Social Psychology*. The editor at that time was William McGuire. McGuire was extremely critical, insightful, and wordy. He wrote a 10-page, single-spaced editorial response to my article, the length of the manuscript itself, with an invitation to resubmit. By the time I read, processed, and understood his comments, I had conducted a fourth experiment. I included this experiment in the resubmission. McGuire responded with a nearly 7-page, single-spaced editorial response, again asking for a resubmission. I re-sent a manuscript with five experiments. He responded in his usual manner, this time with an abbreviated 3-page comment. Finally, a six-experiment study of approximately 25 pages was accepted and published (Weiner & Kukla, 1970). It subsequently was designated a "citation classic," and I owe much of this to the verbosity of McGuire.

> If possible, publish a series of studies that have within them replication and extension. Be confident about the empirical findings—be willing to bet on full replication. Be open to performing the study in your classroom, without fearing embarrassment.

LESSON 7: CAPITALIZING ON CHANCE

The year was 1967, and my academic career was reasonably underway. The doctoral thesis of Linda Beckman (published in 1970) on the perceived causes of success and failure was progressing, Andy Kukla and I were planning our studies of the evaluative consequences of ability versus effort as causes of success and failure, I was continuing research on memory, and I had established a research group. The direction of my life at UCLA for the next few years seemed clear. Then, quite by chance, an event whose importance I could not have imagined occurred that dramatically influenced my immediate and long-term future.

I was glancing through the *American Psychologist* and noticed a small announcement of a conference on learning, motivation, and education to be held in Sweden in the summer of 1968. Applications to participate in this conference, which was sponsored by NATO, were available. Even though I was older than 30, I had never been to Europe (I was in Asia for a short time during my army service). In addition, many well-known motivation psychologists both from America and Europe were invited to give talks or short seminars. Thus, I was excited about this opportunity. I applied and was accepted to participate, along with about 100 other psychologists and educators from around the world.

To this day, I frequently eat a breakfast of granola, fresh fruit, and yogurt, a practice to which I was introduced in Sweden. And to this day, a number of the people I met there remain friends. Among the individuals I became close with was Heinz Heckhausen, a motivation psychologist at the University of Bochum, Germany, who also studied achievement strivings.

Heckhausen invited me to stop at Bochum on my return trip and deliver some lectures. I met the students in his research group and again developed a new set of friends. Subsequently, two of them became postdoctoral students at UCLA, and this initiated a still-ongoing string of five generations of visitor scholars originating from this research group. My association with German psychologists proved to be central to my productivity and social life, and it continues today.

When I returned from the conference and Germany, a curious letter awaited me. It was an invitation from the Guggenheim Foundation to apply for one of their prestigious fellowships. A very liberal paraphrasing of the letter reads as follows: "A submission does not guarantee a fellowship. Nonetheless, an acceptable application is quite likely to result in a funding." This was a very unusual step for the Guggenheim Foundation to take, rendered even stranger because I had published little and certainly nothing to merit this invitation.

I pondered and pondered how this could be, and eventually I reached a solution. This was sent to the wrong B. Weiner. At that time, a statistics book had just been written by Ben Winer that was the bible for graduate students who wanted to perform an analysis of variance. Ben Winer and I had prior contacts involving the exchanges of letters that reached the wrong B. W(e)iner. Aha, I had it! Guggenheim meant this letter for the deserving Ben Winer.

My ethical being forced contact with Guggenheim to point out their mistake and right the scales of justice. I placed a call to their office and told the tale to their secretary. She somewhat surprised me by saying that I would be connected to Mr. Gordon Ray, the president of the foundation. I repeated the story to the patient Mr. Ray, and he answered as follows: "Son, we are Guggenheim. We do not make mistakes. I am reconnecting you to the secretary."

I later learned that a lecturer at the NATO conference was on the Guggenheim awards committee. I did not have a great deal of interchange with this individual and was taken aback when I saw his name listed among the decision makers. His role will always be an inference, but I am certain the attribution is correct.

I still, however, had to complete an application. I needed to devise a yearlong plan that took me away from my home institution and would appear to be a worthy contribution. Because I just had attended a conference on motivation and education, I proposed writing a book with that title. I am not sure I really intended to do this, but at least I had enough material from the conference to submit a reasonable proposal. I indicated the book would be written in Bochum, Germany, because they had an extensive library and appropriate colleagues.

I therefore left my comfortable UCLA plans behind and embarked on 2 years of travel. The first year was spent considering a job offer at the Graduate Center of the City University of New York, a long and interesting story that I will not tell. The second year was spent in Bochum, Germany. As I became immersed in the proposed book, I found myself drawn to more basic motivation issues and left behind the educational component. The textbook product was titled *Theories of Motivation: From Mechanism to Cognition* (Weiner, 1972) and was published by Markham Press (named after the street where the editor had the idea of founding a press). The cover was avocado green. This book was revised with different publishers and titles in 1980 and 1992. Writing the initial book altered my publication goals and priorities. The deep-pockets cause of this shift was an accidental reading of the *American Psychologist*, which brings me to Rule 7:

Keep abreast of the profession of psychology. Take advantage of conferences and other opportunities, for both professional and social reasons. I relatively neglected to do this in my career and at times (although not always) regret not attending more gatherings, benefiting from the many opportunities they offer, or taking part to any reasonable degree in the profession of psychology. When I engaged in these endeavors, it was very rewarding.

LESSON 8: ON RESPONDING TO CRITICS

The year 1968 was important to me for another reason as well, and indeed this additional experience may have had a greater impact on my career than the conference in Sweden. I mentioned that I inherited my first Ph.D. student, Linda Beckman, from Hal Kelley, in part because Kelley was leaving on sabbatical. He returned in 1968, and one day, while we were both in the mail room, he suggested that *we* should organize a conference on attribution theory.

Although I was conducting research that manipulated beliefs about ability and effort, the causes of achievement outcomes, I certainly did not regard myself as an attribution theorist. That body of work grew from studies in social perception and was imbedded within social psychology, an area I already revealed I knew little about. In fact, I had read nothing written by Kelley at that time and had skipped through Heider. My studies of perceived causality were from the framework of a motivation theorist trying to explain achievement-related behavior, an entirely different tradition.

Thus, my first reaction when Kelley suggested the conference was to ask, "What is attribution theory?" I may have heard this phrase, but I could not articulate to what it referred. Of course, I withheld that knowledge and replied to Kelley, "What a great idea. How do we go about it?" Kelley had already mapped out the details. The plan was to invite four additional participants to join us for three weeks at UCLA, with NSF funding. Edward (Ned) Jones was first choice. I again did not reveal that I had not read any of Jones's publications. Along with the participation of Kelley and Jones, certainly two of the best-known social psychologists in the world, were four assistant professors (including me).

And so it came to pass that six of us met daily for three weeks in the summer of 1969 at UCLA. The mornings were intense discussions, or I should rather say arguments or controversies between Jones and Kelley. I had no idea what all the fuss was about, and the four assistant professors, to the best of my memory, contributed very little. The afternoons were devoted to reading or other activities we planned. At the conclusion of this period of time, we were to write papers, individually or with coauthors, and send these to others in our group for comments. Then we agreed to meet again the following year, at Yale University, for another three weeks to discuss these papers and other issues.

The group decided who would be the best reviewers for the papers. To my horror, Jones and Kelley agreed to serve as my critics. A bulge came in my throat. I regarded them with fear; they were in the McGuire camp: extremely bright, verbal, and highly critical. I wrote my paper while on leave at the Graduate Center of the City University of New York, considering a job shift. At that time I also was being reviewed for tenure at UCLA. Although my record seemingly warranted this promotion, the chair of the department at that time saw little merit in personality or social psychology. It was still the era of the hard–soft split in psychology. Hence, I had reason to be apprehensive about this outcome.

I tried to integrate my thoughts about causal beliefs within the framework of motivation theory. The final manuscript included the names of five of my students (Weiner et al., 1972) and, unlike the other group contributions focusing on social perception, we discussed achievement striving, reinforcement schedules, probability of success, the properties of causes, the meaning of luck, and other topics of main interest to motivation psychologists.

I sent the paper to my students at UCLA and to my readers, Jones and Kelley. Within 5 days I received a reply from Jones. I still remember the dreaded first sentence, and will paraphrase the rest: "Bernie, this paper needs a lot of work. It is far too theoretical and too long. You must add further experiments, get additional data, include some other key conditions and controls, and so on."

It concluded as follows: "Don't send this to Kelley until you make changes. He will kill you. All the best."—Ned.

My worst fears had been realized. I was in a panic. I marshaled my resources as best I could and began to make changes. I knew there was time because Kelley was slow in responding. I did not want to tell him not to read the paper, so took my chances that I would beat him to the punch with an updated version.

I worked extremely hard, phoning my students at UCLA daily, overseeing new research studies, and at the same time shortening the paper, being more constrained theoretically, and incorporating many other suggestions from Jones, the smart and famous.

Alas, just as I was nearing completion of this revision, a large envelope was waiting in my mailbox. Kelley had responded. I read the opening line, and my eyes began to water: "Bernie," the first line said, "this paper needs a lot of work."

I know I had seen that somewhere before. I continued to read: "It has far too much data and not enough theory. Give yourself more space. Don't be in such a rush and shortchange the conceptual part. I suggest you condense the empirical section, get out some of the experimental conditions and controls and expand the theory. By the way, if it is not too late, don't send this to Ned. He will kill you. All the best."—Hal.

I thought this over, made some minimal changes including the presentation of new data and theoretical expansions, and re-sent it to Jones and Kelley. They answered quickly, concluding that the new version was much improved. I assume they did not read the new paper and/or could not remember the old.

We decided to publish a book with our papers (this actually came as a last moment decision at the Yale meetings). The authors were alphabetical, and the book, *Attribution: Perceiving the Causes of Behavior* (Jones et al., 1972), was published after I received tenure and resolved to remain at UCLA. It had a major impact on social psychology and was rereviewed a few years ago in *Contemporary Psychology* under the rubric of "classics revisited." It has been cited thousands of times, and the high tide created by the book raised all of the ships, thrusting me into some visibility in social psychology and motivation.

> Pay attention to your critics, but sometimes not too much attention. If multiple people make the same negative comment, take it quite seriously. If a lot of people do not like the work for different reasons, there is something wrong with the piece. But if someone likes a part that is disliked by others, then have the wisdom to discriminate what needs to be changed and what should stay as is. I have more than half a dozen papers in my file, never published, that are as good as my published works. And I have a larger number of published papers that do not deserve this status. God often evens this scale of justice, especially if the N is large.

SOME FINAL COMMENTS

As I look over this autobiography and consider the course of my early academic career, attribution theory provides some useful language for understanding. Four causes of success and failure reappear in my life:

1. *Luck (both good and bad).* At times, what appeared to be bad luck or of trivial importance proved to be quite fortunate and changed my life. My taking a course in industrial psychology while at the University of Chicago, Dan Katz going on sabbatical as I arrived in Michigan, Farfel falling to the floor, the infighting at the University of Minnesota, McGuire forcing numerous resubmissions, and Kelley going on sabbatical are just a few examples of what appeared to be minor or unfortunate circumstances ultimately acting in my favor and providing new directions in life. That being said, I also recognize that luck comes to the prepared; that is, good luck often requires hard work.
2. *Effort.* By effort I do not mean only scoring endless TATs, resubmitting manuscripts, and conducting series of studies. Even this autobiography required dozens of revisions. But effort has to be channeled; there must be persistence in the pursuit of a topic, multiple studies of the same problem or issue. This brings empirical closure and more theoretical security.
3. *Help from others.* I have surrounded myself with students willing to work with me and visiting scholars interested in attribution theory. They have made countless contributions to my work.
4. *Ability.* If ability had anything to do with my accomplishments, it has been the ability to select the right problem—one that is amenable to research, is to some degree solvable, and brings with it theoretical advancement.

Attribution theory also specifies that causal beliefs give rise to affects: Luck is linked with surprise, ability and effort to pride, and help from others to gratitude. Surprise, pride, and gratitude indeed are dominant in my affective life. I find it quite satisfying that a theory I helped develop can indeed provide some insights into my own life.

REFERENCES

Atkinson, J. W. (1957). Motivational determinants of risk-taking behavior. *Psychological Review, 64*, 359–372.

Beckman, L. (1970). Effects of students' performance on teachers' and observers' attributions of causality. *Journal of Educational Psychology, 61*, 76–82.

De Charms, R. (1968). *Personal causation.* New York: Academic Press.

Heider, F. (1958). *The psychology of interpersonal relations.* New York: Wiley.

Jones, E. E., Kanause, D. E., Kelley, H. H., Nisbett, R. E., Valins, S., & Weiner, B. (1972). *Attribution: Perceiving the causes of behavior.* Morristown, NJ: General Learning Press.

Rotter, J. B. (1966). Generalized expectancies for internal versus external control of reinforcement. *Psychological Monographs, 80*(609).

Weiner, B. (1966). Motivation and memory. *Psychological Monographs, 80*(626).

Weiner, B. (1972). *Theories of motivation: From mechanism to cognition.* Chicago: Markham Press.

Weiner, B., Frieze, I. H., Kukla, A., Reed, L. Rest, S., & Rosenbaum, R. M. (1972). *Perceiving the causes of success and failure.* Morristown, NJ: General Learning Press.

Weiner, B., & Kukla, A. (1970). An attributional analysis of achievement motivation. *Journal of Personality and Social Psychology, 13*, 1–20.

The Journey from the Bronx to Stanford to Abu Ghraib

PHILIP G. ZIMBARDO

Department of Psychology, Stanford University

IN THE BEGINNING WAS THE BRONX

*P*overty is a relative thing; it is easier if you have relatives around to count on and if there are others who are poorer than you. Downward social comparison was a fact of life for us generations before it became a published process. I was fortunate to have both conditions in effect while I was growing up. While affluence buys rich folks the luxury of creating physical distances from neighbors as well as selective exposure to others, for poor folks others are always in your face. That's great if you're a kid living in a crowded urban area. For me it meant that there were always other kids available for play, day and night, right outside my house on the streets and stoops. It also meant that there were always new social learning opportunities lurking out there in the real world when those others were not my friends but my enemies.

The other thing about growing up poor that helped me to become a social psychologist is that it encouraged situational breeding, because I wanted to blame the situations and not the persons for all the failures I saw around me. The economically advantaged prefer to rely on dispositional attributions to account for their favored status in life, since they want to believe that their radiance comes from inherent natural differences favoring them and their kind.

I learned firsthand many of the lessons of social psychology, on a personal experience basis. Prejudice? I was chased and beaten daily for weeks by the neighborhood toughs until one day my mother asked the janitor's son to take me to church on Sunday, and he admitted that he and his buddies were making my life miserable because they thought I was a "dirty Jew boy," big nose, slim, blue eyes, fragile. I was six years old and sickly. Group initiation rituals? To join the East 151 St. Gang, first I had to fight the last kid who was admitted to the gang. I did that reluctantly, because I was so scrawny and did not like to be hurt, and I did not want to hurt anybody. The bloodthirsty kids formed a circular boxing ring, screaming constantly and urging us to hit harder. The fight officially ended when the older kid gave up or the new kid got a bloody nose, which I did as soon as possible. Next, I had to climb to the top branches of a tall corner tree and bring down my sneaker that had been thrown up there by the gang leader, "Popeye, the Armenian." Scary, but not as much as having to crawl through the transom of the fruit store late at night and steal a bag full of fruit to be eaten by the gang. Finally came the strangest ritual of all to a six-year-old. Around the corner was the Stocking Man's Store, a small shop selling women's stockings and undergarments. In front of the store were his goods laid out on a platform resting on orange crates and saw horses—and also a street grill of iron letting air and light into the basement below the store. The final initiation task was to break into the basement and then look up the women's dresses as they shopped above, thereafter to tell the tales of what you had seen to the assembled gang. You were notified in advance that you could not come back up until you saw someone who had no panties; we called them "bloomers" and could regale the masses with the forbidden sexual sights that we had witnessed.

These childish urban initiation rituals seem to tap into some of the same basic aspects of masculine identity, as do adult cultural rituals reported in anthropological accounts of so-called primitive tribes in exotic places. Ingratiation tactics? If you were frail, your survival depended on learning and effectively using finely honed ingratiation tactics to ward off attacks and exploitation by the big, bad kids, to get some of them to take you under their mentoring wings.

The general level of poverty in the many neighborhoods I lived in (we had moved 19 times before I commuted to college at age 18) also meant that play always revolved around group-centered, "people-initiated games" and not commercial toys or TV or solitary activities. And there was no overlap between the world of children and that of adults. They never intruded on our world in the streets except to curtail it for dinner calls and daily taps. There was no Little League or organized soccer; nothing was organized by or watched by adults. We owned the streets; they owned their small tenement apartments. That meant we learned and refined bargaining, negotiating, and conflict resolution strategies on the job without interference by our parents. To that extent then, my earliest informal training as a naive social psychologist came bottom up, directly from the streets in this neighborhood overflowing with diversity.

In those days of the late 1930s and early 1940s, New York could be characterized as having many side-by-side minighettos, where most people living on one street were Irish, around the corner they were all Jewish, across the street were Italians, and down the corner were mostly Blacks. Often a corner candy store or grocery store or bar was the central meeting place where these ethnic divisions would blend in the quest for that particular service. My friends were an amalgam of the whole American melting pot. World War II changed everything. Poor people had jobs and made money, because the demand for workers was high and there was not much available on which to spend money.

Shortly after the war, four simultaneous events changed the nature of the South Bronx from a poor but family-oriented, low-serious-crime neighborhood where I loved living into a chaotic, burned-down place to avoid. Those who had saved money during the war were able to move up the ladder and out of the old neighborhood—mostly these were the Jews who moved north to new housing developments. Into their space vacuum came Puerto Ricans migrating to the land of plenty, many from rural areas and farms into the heart of an urban inner city. They were in conflict with Blacks for the bottom rung of the economic ladder, and new tensions ran high and often exploded into violence. Returning soldiers and mafia contributed drugs to the South Bronx, and drugs created a new lifestyle for local gangs, so turf meant a business domain that was guarded by guns, threats, and action. Finally, as violence escalated and gangs took over, many of the other old timers also moved to safer places, leaving some vacant apartments and tenements behind. Gangs torched the buildings to get rid of the remaining tenants so they could take them over as clubhouses. Landlords, who were not making any money on their rent-controlled, dilapidated buildings also arranged to have them torched to collect the insurance. The South Bronx became a symbol of urban blight, resembling bombed-out European cities.

These dramatic ecological and sociological changes were exciting for me to observe firsthand. I was eager to go beyond mere personal concern to collecting data as these events were unfolding.

As a high school senior at James Monroe High School, I discussed some of these situational upheavals and their consequences with one of my classmates, a very smart, skinny kid, Stanley Milgram. He came from a more affluent neighborhood in that school district; I attended "his" high school by falsely representing my address as being other than the South Bronx. But it was clear to me that I wanted to be either a journalist or a psychologist. I was cured of both desires in my freshman year at Brooklyn College by struggling to do well in English composition and by getting a C grade in introductory psychology (from Evelyn Raskin). That C was an unexpected, alien thorn in my academic career—I ultimately graduated summa, with that one C blemish. The superstar psychologist on our campus, Abraham Maslow, who floated around with an ever-present entourage, was on his way to Brandeis University (to inspire Elliot Aronson) so would not be around to make up for the boring psychology texts, useless lectures, and silly little psychology experiments. I switched to sociology and dual majored in sociology and anthropology, where the professors were asking big questions about the ethics of the atomic bomb, the nature of mass movements, and the differences between bottom-up and top-down revolutions. I glommed on to a wonderful Polish sociologist, Felix Gross, a former colleague of Bronislav Malinowski, who took me under his wing after I had taken more than 15 units of credits with him. He took me camping and always had a story about life in academia in Europe and the need to understand the deeper structure of social phenomena and not settle for the surface appearances. After I helped to review his book on European mass movements, Felix gave me a citation of recognition in the preface. It was so exciting to be in print.

I also was attracted to Charles Lawrence, a sociologist of enormous talent who specialized in race relations and the Negro family. Charlie's infectious smile and wit were a lovely counterpoint to Felix's serious demeanor. He also encouraged me to join the NAACP and to become more socially conscious, which I made efforts to do, but I was more interested in varsity track and fraternity socializing.

The sociological frame enabled me to focus my neighborhood observations into several interesting studies. The first examined the dynamics of prejudice between Puerto Ricans and Negroes in the South Bronx, using interviews and surveys. It was published in a sociological journal during my junior year. The second was an observational and archive data collection of the appeal of the political parties to the minority vote in the South Bronx during the 1952 national election. My third undergraduate foray into field research emerged from observing that despite the norm of tolerance and integration at Brooklyn College, a decidedly socialist stronghold in the 1950s (called by some "The Little Red School House"), self-segregation was apparent in the student cafeteria. I set out to make systematic observations of the seating patterns of Whites and Blacks at each table across the term and over all hours, to reveal that indeed there were some race-exclusive tables. No White ever sat at certain tables even when they were empty, and the same was true of Blacks not sitting at White tables, although, of course, they were not marked as such. I replicated that study at the City College of New York ten years later, because *Brown vs. the Supreme Court* had intervened between my undergraduate experiences and later experiences as an NYU professor. The pattern of self-segregation by race was as evident in 1963 as it had been in 1952.

In my senior year, my buddy Gerry Platt, a psychology major and fraternity brother, talked me into pairing with him in experimental psychology. Although reluctant to get involved with psychology at first, I was soon smitten by the precision of answering specific hypotheses with hard data. Sociologists asked the big questions but never quite had good enough answers, while it became evident that psychologists were asking low-level questions but were good at methodology and analysis. I liked that and realized it was up to me to pose more interesting questions and maybe to do so by wedding my broad interests in the sociology of institutions with the psychology of individuals. After that course, I switched my major to psychology. Although I was a psychology major for only a short while, the major influence on me came from Harold Proshansky, recently out of Ann Arbor, Michigan, and teaching personality theory. His intellectual enemies were people he called "Rat Behaviorists" at Yale. Later in the year, when I was accepted for graduate study at Yale, Hal was distressed, because he wanted me to go to either Michigan or Minnesota. But he gave me valuable fatherly advice to help my transition, first about not letting those narrow S-R ideas get into my head and then to consider changing the way I dressed, because those Yalies would not appreciate the essence of my New York ghetto sartorial style and might reject me. Of course I said that I would not change, that they would have to adjust to me because the clothes were part of my basic self-expression—the blue suede shoes, Billy Eckstein rolled collar shirts, string ties, peg pants, and of course Phi Beta Kappa key hanging proudly from my knee-length key chain.

ON ALMOST BEING THE FIRST BLACK GRADUATE STUDENT AT YALE

Jump ahead to 1959. I have graduated Yale and am in Bonn, Germany, at the International Congress of Psychology presenting my first big-time paper on differentiating between the Freudian version of the concepts of fear and anxiety using Schachter's affiliation paradigm. While talking to Harold Kelley, who had been one of my teachers during my first year of study at Yale before he moved out west to UCLA, I mentioned how difficult it seemed for our Jewish colleagues to deal with being in Germany and relating to Germans, because the wounds of the Holocaust were still open. Hal floored me with his rejoinder, something like, "Well it's probably similar to how you felt at Yale when the faculty assumed you were Negro." Say what? He then went on to recite the battery of circumstantial evidence that led to that reasonable assumption and a major split in the Yale psychology department faculty over whether I should be accepted given my record or rejected given my record. In fact, they did neither. I never received "the accept," "the reject," or "the wait list" letter from them—I got nothing at all.

On April 14, 1954, I had prepared my letter of acceptance to the University of Minnesota to work in the famous social psychology laboratory under the direction of Stanley Schachter, who called me to say that he liked my interests in race relations and group dynamics and would encourage me to develop them. That night I got a call from a Yale professor asking if I was still interested in Yale graduate school because he was coming down to New York City the next day for the Eastern Psychological Association convention and would like to interview me for a possible position as his paid research assistant. He asked me to hold off mailing my letter to Schachter until we had a chance to talk at the bar in the New Yorker Hotel, 10 a.m. sharp. I was excited because Yale was my first choice, because it was close to my home so I could visit often. And it was after all the Ivy League, and Yale and Harvard were the big "It's" in The Bronx.

After he had two double martinis and I pretended to drink mine, and we made small talk, Professor K. C. Montgomery said that he was doing research on exploratory behavior in rats and needed a good research assistant to help him carry out the many studies for which he had just received a big NSF grant. Did I know anything about "running rats"? "Yes, sir" (we ran them out of our apartment regularly and deftly). Could I build equipment? "Certainly, sir, as long as there is a diagram to follow" (my father could be recruited to build anything with Renaissance eloquence, even rat cages, if need be). "OK, then you've got the job, free tuition, and a $1,700 stipend for 20 hours of research assistance. Read these reprints of mine, and come up to the lab before the term starts so we can begin breeding and building the cages." "Sure thing, you won't be sorry you chose me. I will be a good worker." I don't recall if he said, "See you later, *Boy*." Maybe it was my imagination.

When I got to those hallowed halls of Ivy, I quickly became a rat runner of the first degree. I bred hundreds of rats, nursed them, fed them, watered them, and cleaned their shit and cages, after building literally untold numbers of special cages, by hand, some to deprive them of behavioral freedom, others to encourage them in free environment rearing, and still others to deprive them of both behavioral and sensory stimulation. We graduate student rat runners worked around the clock, during holidays (we traded caretaking and running-subjects duties to go home either Easter or Christmas). At first I felt like I was a slave laborer, working my research-assistant butt off up to 40 hours a week in addition to my studies (where I did not excel because I had a weak undergraduate psychology background). I complained to the chair, Claude Buxton, but to no avail. I called my mother just before Christmas to say I was going to quit and come home for good. Wisely she said I could do so but not until the summer, because my sister was using my old bedroom and it would not be right to disrupt her in the middle of her studies (by summer I was cutting the mustard and had no thoughts of leaving ugly New Haven). Montgomery would give me a long to-do list and then disappear. What they concealed was that he was suffering from clinical depression and was in and out of local mental hospitals. The next year he committed suicide.

I'm not sure if it was guilt over Montgomery's death (caused in part by not getting tenure) or the dissonance of convincing myself that living my life in the animal basement wing of the Institute of Human Relations was what I really wanted and not human relations, which I thought I wanted when I was a know-nothing undergraduate in that Gestalt stronghold at Brooklyn College. But whichever it was, I then got totally committed to studying my rats and their data and publishing our findings. I persuaded someone at the NSF to sign over the remaining two years and $38,000 of Montgomery's grant to me, with Professor Fred Sheffield serving ex officio. I wrote and published four articles on this research enterprise, and on the side I published a few more of my own. One was with Neal Miller, whom I think of as my Behaviorist–Experimentalist Mentor Supreme, and the other was with another graduate student, Herbert Barry. We shocked our faculty by getting an article accepted in *Science*, which related the effects of two drugs (the new hot medicine, chlorpromazine, and caffeine) on inhibiting or enhancing sexual behavior in male rats. And Herb and I did it all without faculty involvement. (Incidentally, I have just published an article honoring the memory and contributions of K. C. Montgomery [with Alan Kaleuff from Finland].) But here I was as a relatively new graduate student with an admittedly deficient background in psychology, barely admitted to the Yale psychology department, arguably the best in the nation at that time, with my own large animal laboratory, in charge of a major NSF grant, and with four publications, including being lead author in *Science*. (No, Mom, I think I will stay around here a bit longer.)

I was in my third year, feeling like hot stuff, doing some reanalyses of our *Science* article data in the calculator room, when a faculty member, Bob Cohen, asked me what I was doing. I went into great detail about the merits of this rigorous experimental protocol. He then stopped me to ask if I would do him a favor and look out the window across to the street in front of the medical school and tell me what I saw. I did so, assuming he wanted to know if his beautiful wife, Barbara, was there waiting for him. I said no one was there. He said really, no one? I then told him there were a bunch of people in one group and a couple in another, to which he asked me to try to figure out what the couple was discussing. I examined their body language and made some inferences, with the caveat that I could not be at all sure of the accuracy of my interpretation. Bob then threw the solar plexus punch. "Don't you think that it would be more interesting to spend your career as a psychologist trying to figure out what people mean by their behavior than what white laboratory rats do?" Needless to say, I was furious over being duped into this rather obvious soft-side psychology trap. But when that emotion subsided, it made me think. I had betrayed my origins by giving up my love for observing people and trying to understand the complexities of human interactions for the ready accessibility of rat psychology.

The next term, Bob Cohen and Jack Brehm cotaught a new course in advanced social psychology, which I took and persuaded my roommate Gordon Bower to join me. I had taken basic social psychology as an independent reading course, under the guidance of Leonard Doob, that focused on the classics but stopped sharply at 1950. The main readings of the Cohen–Brehm course were typed copies of Leon Festinger's manuscript titled *A Theory of Cognitive Dissonance*. Brehm had been

Festinger's student, and his thesis was one of the first experiments on dissonance theory. Cohen, who was a student of Michigan's Alvin Zander, was less a methodologist than Brehm and took more of a holistic approach to social psychology, even admitting personality interactions and promoted ideas such as "needs for cognitive clarity." Together, they were a dynamic duo who were delightful to study under and to work with.

I was entranced by Festinger's chutzpah to draw such wide-ranging derivations from such simple assumptions and premises. But more than that was fascinating to my peers and me. Dissonance theory went directly against the very rational, systematic, bottom-up empirical approach dominant in the Yale attitude change program and even in much of the animal behaviorist research since the heady theoretical days of Clark Hull, a few years before my arrival at Yale. We got caught up in the appeal of those nonobvious predictions that challenged the validity of "Bubba psychology," in which everyone's grandmother can predict the outcome of any psychological study described to her. For example, in Hovland's attitude change course, one of our assignments was to construct a table of all existing results in that area by coding them first according to the categories of input/mediating/output variables; then by whether they were stimulus (communication) factors, audience factors, or media or channel factors; and then according to processes borrowed from Hovland's earlier training as Hull's student: message learning or encoding, motivation to accept or resist, message retention, and action consequences. He believed that a comprehensive theory of communication, persuasion, and attitude change could be developed from such a taxonomic approach. But faced with Festinger's daring style of theory formation, this static approach immediately lost its appeal to many of us. However, I felt like a bit of a traitor, because Hovland was my first social psychology mentor, and I learned much from this genius. I had worked with him on issues of judgmental distortion, did some research that was published on semantic ambiguity, and wrote my major area paper reviewing the literature on traditional psychophysical judgment and social psychological judgment. "Mr. Hovland," as everyone reverently called him, told me that he and Muzafer Sherif, his visiting collaborator, found some of it to be useful in their new formulation of latitudes of acceptance and rejection. My doctoral dissertation, jointly sponsored by Cohen and Brehm, pitted predictions from their rational formulation against dissonance theory's rationalizing formulation—and dissonance carried the day and my Ph.D. degree.

I withheld turning in my dissertation until the next year in 1959 to avoid the military draft, which I could escape by turning 26 years old. It helped also to be working at the West Haven Veteran's Hospital as a social psychology postdoctoral trainee, under the supervision of Aaron Hershkowitz, who was steeped in the social ecological approach of Barker and his teachers at the University of Kansas. It was different from anything I had ever studied, focusing on how aspects of the physical environment influenced individual and group responding. I benefited more, though, from the opportunity to wander the wards, talk with patients, and attend clinical staff meetings. I had developed an interest in psychopathology from taking a fabulous course, taught by Irving Janis, which met for a full day a week at the Middletown State Mental Hospital. Janis's real genius was less in experimental social psychology than in experimental psychopathology. He would interview a patient before the class and generate hypotheses about his or her behavior in response to further stimuli, which were then invariably proved to be correct. We each were assigned our own patient on whom we did a complete psychological workup. Although I was auditing the course, I wrote a 60-page report that I later used as course material in my introductory class and in my textbook *Psychology and Life*.

That interest in psychopathology was encouraged by my contact with Irv Sarnoff, a wonderfully creative clinician, also just off that post–World War II train from Michigan to New Haven. He was a rare breed at Yale, because he actually believed in Freudian theory and set out to show that some of Freud's ideas could be translated into ingeniously testable laboratory experiments. Together we did an elegant study to show that Schachter's association of high anxiety to social affiliation was not accurate because he was confusing anxiety with fear. We reasoned, following Freud, that fear as the reaction to an objectively valid, external threat would increase affiliation with others similarly aroused but that anxiety as an irrational evaluation of an objectively harmless stimulus would lead instead to the desire for social isolation—which we found in an interaction between two levels of fear and anxiety.

After we presented that study at the International Congress of Psychology, using a variety of colorful slides to depict the experimental setting and the research procedure, in addition to using the usual convention of presenting slides or overheads of only results, Ned Jones complimented me graciously and recommended we submit it to the *Journal of Personality*, which we did. It was published in 1961. I was feeling a professional high, when Hal Kelley and I had that exchange about my nearly not being admitted to Yale because I was thought to be Black. Seymour Sarason later validated Kelley's recollection of this strange tale in his memoirs. (I worked with Seymour for several years codirecting his project about anxiety in children as he began to move off into community psychology.) So here is the gist of that story.

Hal said that my graduate school application was tabled because there was a split among the faculty on how to deal with it, with me. He went on to tell me that was the case because some were sure I was a Black ghetto kid, or mulatto, while others were less sure, but depending on that diagnosis it would change the way they interpreted my grades, recommendations, and test scores. Once the circumstantial evidence in my file was framed as coming from a minority city kid, then everything seemed to fall into place naturally.

Let me now briefly summarize that evidence contained in my Yale application: interests—listening to modern jazz, Charlie Parker, Lester Young, Dizzy, Miles, Lady Day; favorite reading—*Downbeat* magazine; activities—captain of the track team; major—sociology and anthropology (and also psychology) with top grades in the Negro family in the United States and race relations; extracurricular activities—secretary of the local NAACP chapter; primary recommender—Charles Bradford Lawrence, well-known Negro sociologist, who happened to send his letter on NAACP stationery because he was out of college stationery at home and his letter was late; research evidence—two studies enclosed, one on a publication on the dynamics of intergroup prejudice between Puerto Ricans and Negroes in The Bronx, the other on patterns of racial self-segregation in a college dining facility; my Italian name—Roy Campanella (the famous Brooklyn Dodger catcher at that time was surely Negro with an Italian name). And so it went. Even the GRE scores fit the stereotype, low math scores relative to good verbal scores.

It was not unreasonable for the faculty to assume I was Black. But wait. In those days there was also a required photograph glued to the application, and that cemented the false identification. To save money on the cost of sending out many photos with all my applications, I had one of my graduation photos duplicated cheaply, 10 for a dollar, and they were dark and grainy cheap copies with more contrast than the other applicants' and showed off a skinny dark young man with a pencil moustache wearing some high-style Bronx clothes that were not sold at the J. Press men's clothing shop or the Yale Coop.

Expert psychological reasoning from a false, if not unreasonable, premise, went like this: Good letters of recommendation need discounting, because they obviously reflected reverse biases. This young man will have difficulties adjusting to life at Yale, because there is no one of his kind in the department or in the university so it would be a disservice to him to admit him. Some faculty may have difficulty adjusting to him and his lifestyle, especially those from the South (such as the professor who interviewed me in New York City). But the liberals in attendance argued that it would be good to take one, even if a token one, because this one was not too bad. But if he failed and had to be kicked out, how would that look for the department? In any case, indecision ruled the day, and my application was literally shelved, with an intention of getting back to me later. On the next to the last day of the student acceptances, Gordon Bower, the top admit, deferred to get a master's degree in philosophy of science at the University of Minnesota, and that southern professor with the grant and the drive to explore was suddenly without a research assistant. Maybe he called those on the wait list who either did not want to run rats or by that late date had made a prior commitment elsewhere. That left only me in the null category. Montgomery called; I said I am eligible and eager to come to Yale. But it was curious that he did not offer me the position over the phone. Instead he came to New York; asked a few simple questions, to which I lied; sized me up; and offered me the job on the spot. After Hal Kelley told me this surprising tale, I thought back to that April 15, 1954, day in the bar at the New Yorker Hotel to wonder why Montgomery had to interview me in the flesh, because I could have answered those same questions during his phone call. In those days, no admitted student went through an interview process, so why did he have to see me before he could offer me a research assistantship on his grant money and thereby admission to Yale?

Upon my arrival at Yale, some of the faculty members were indeed sorry to see that I seemed White when they had hoped I would be their first Black. But I don't think my boss man saw it that way. In fact, I now think that had he seen me as Black, he might have informed me that a "more qualified" applicant had already taken the job just that morning before the interview. Maybe, however, I am going too far beyond the data. But the data that I can add in conclusion are that my mixed-message application and transcript also included the line items that I was summa cum laude, junior year Phi Beta Kappa, fellowship winner, fraternity president, varsity athlete with a presidential award for distinguished scholarship, and some other goodies thrown in for good measure. All of that was not sufficient to get me a seat on the first-run bus to New Haven, maybe because it was negated by all that circumstantial evidence that triggered negative stereotypical thinking even among some of the most brilliant scholars and honored psychological researchers in the land.

Although I was nearly the first Black graduate student in the psychology department at Yale, James Jones was able to make that claim many years later. Jim has gone on to make important contributions to the study of racism and prejudice that mark him as one of Yale's important native sons.

LEARNING WHAT MATTERS

It should be evident from this personal travelogue that I learned early many of the most vital lessons in social psychology. From my ghetto experiences, I learned that *situations matter* and also that *culture matters* in shaping human behavior and interpersonal relationships. I learned further that *content matters*, on the basis of my student days as a sociology student and my field observations of prejudice in action and the persuasive appeals made (only) by the American Labor Party to get the minority vote in the 1952 election. What I learned at Yale were two more things that mattered a great deal to me and influenced the rest of my research career: *methodology matters* and *behavior matters*.

The latter are the two residuals of Yale behaviorism that are not given enough credit when we dismiss the rest of the behaviorist manifesto: Learning via principles of reinforcement follows species-universal principles that transcend content, situation, and, of course, culture. It was that misguided arrogant ideology that sidetracked much of psychology for decades, just as Benton Underwood's mindless study of nonsense syllable learning of memory without content delayed the study of meaningful dynamics of memory for narrative and personally significant events. What I learned as an apprentice to Neal Miller and Carl Hovland is the importance of conducting research that was rigorous, operationally as precise as possible, with sufficient preexperimental observation and considerable pretesting to ensure you understood the phenomenon under investigation and how to demonstrate the causal connections your hypothesis advances.

What I got from my years of studying rats was observing and recording their *behavior* rather than inferring what was going on inside their furry little bodies and small brains. So much of my research since then has focused on dependent variables that were observable gross behavior patterns and not just check marks on scales or elicited predictions about how research respondents imagine they would behave in a given situation. But what I learned from Bob Cohen is the message repeated over the years by my colleagues that *people matter* the most. Awareness of that axiom tempers the austerity of any social behaviorism with a compassion for human fragility, a respect for human dignity, and an appreciation of the complexities of the human mind. It has helped me to try to design research that is characterized by both style and substance and an eye for applying what I have learned to improve some aspect of human functioning. I think that the research I reported in my 1969 book *The Cognitive Control of Motivation* is the best example of my attempt to wed the rigorous methodology of my Yale behaviorist training with the rich texture of social–cognitive constructs.

THE YALE CANDY STORE

The Yale psychology department in those golden days of the late 1950s was an enormously overstocked candy store for a kid from The Bronx, and all the candy was free for the asking. Hovland brought to the social area a horde of social psychologists whom we students could learn from and do research with—Irving Janis, Hal Kelley, Bob Abelson, Jack Brehm, Bob Cohen, Bill McGuire, and Milt Rosenberg—and guest lecturers such as Don Campbell, Herb Kelman, and others, such as Muzafer Sherif. And some of us got to visit with Hovland the new social psych lab he helped to create at Bell Labs in New Jersey, headed by Mort Deutsch and Hal Gerard. I also got to work with Seymour Sarason on his research on test anxiety in school children, eventually taking over as codirector when he moved into the area of community psychology in 1959. I was fascinated by the work of Irving, as I noted, and we did a lovely study comparing Freudian distinctions between fear and anxiety within a paradigm developed by Stanley Schachter for studying affiliation processes. Then also on the faculty were John Dollard, Mark May, Leonard Doob, Irving Child, Frank Logan, Bill Kessen, Ed Zigler, Norman Miller, and more oldies but goodies to learn from and work with.

We had a lot of hotshot graduate students as well: Gordon Bower, my roomie and for whom I was best man at his wedding the next year, Roger Shepard, Dave Sears, Jon Friedman, Dean Pruitt, Arnie Lyman, Tim Brock, Lyman Porter, and Buzz Hunt, to name a few who come readily to mind.

I got my first taste of teaching psychology in 1957, when after taking a course in how to teach by Claude Buxton, the chair, I was the first graduate student to be allowed to teach a full course in introductory psychology to the hallowed blues of Yale men. (A professor became sick just before term time, and I was the default value.) I loved every moment of it, and from then to now, my unabashed love affair with teaching has been tempered by my equal passion for doing research.

I deferred my graduation for a year, because our government was still drafting men to age 26 from the Korean War conscription. I got a postdoc fellowship to work at the West Haven VA for a year while also continuing part-time teaching at Yale and part-time codirecting Sarason's anxiety project and publishing with him. Again, as with Janis's abnormal course, I found clinical work really interesting and spent a lot of time just talking with patients and trying to understand how they had become so mentally disturbed.

I had hoped to stay at Yale as a part-time instructor for a few more years, but Miller recommended me to his buddy Howard Kendler for a job opening at NYU in The Bronx. How could I resist going home again? Little did I realize that the short trip from Yale to NYU in The Bronx would be downhill a very long way. That will be our next installment.

NYU (1960–1967)

When I was interviewing for the job at NYU, Chairman Kendler asked me what was more important to me, fame or money. It depends, I answered, on how much of each was at stake, but in general I would prefer fame to money. He replied that he had anticipated that answer given the choices of being an instructor for $6,500 a year versus only $6,000 as an assistant professor—the fame option! He then noted that I liked to teach, and he would see to it that I got as much of that pleasure as possible.

My teaching load was extraordinary—five semester courses each term, most large lecture courses, plus two summer school courses to add some money to my fame. And even that was not sufficient to pay the high cost of living in New York, so one year I taught a 13th course at Yale one afternoon a week, a master's course in the education school on learning. Another year I moonlighted by teaching social psychology at Barnard College. My love of teaching turned into an addiction overload: teaching at least 3 hours a day in class, making new preparations, and grading at night, not to mention keeping office hours, advising majors, being on the medical and dental school advisory committee, and starting and leading a Psi Chi chapter. My teaching was mostly at the uptown Bronx campus, but I also taught graduate classes at the Greenwich Village campus of NYU, went weekly to the evening departmental colloquia, and found time for training and research consulting in experimental and clinical hypnosis at the Morton Prince Clinic for Hypnotherapy. And in my spare time I designed and built a new research laboratory with funds from a new NSF grant, so I could continue with my other passion. If successful I might escape the NYU dungeon.

LOVE AFFAIR WITH TEACHING

Even my horrendous load at NYU did not diminish the joy of teaching psychology that had been nurtured at Yale. Once I was at the lectern, all the daily stresses vanished; I was able to create a sense of personal flow, a total immersion into the 50-minute moment, again and again. Teaching was both my calling and my salvation. I taught large introductory psychology courses fall, winter, and summer and followed them with large social psychology courses, along with a variety of higher level courses. That meant I could gather a bunch of students who "majored in me," taking as many as five sequential courses. Barry Schwartz, Shep Siegel, Ken Fink, Ebbe Ebbesen, and Steve Maier, as well as Ellen Langer and Allen Schatzberg, were part of those golden undergraduate teaching times. All of them are now respected professors in psychology and psychiatry. I won my first distinguished teaching award and realized that to continue teaching and research, I had to use my teaching as a source of research ideas and then recycle into teaching some of my research to create a synergy between these twin passions. I was also blessed with some great graduate teaching assistants, most notably, Scott Fraser.

RESEARCH PROGRAMS

There were five lines of research that I somehow carried out during these hectic years: (a) the psychology of affiliation, following up some ideas based on Stanley Schachter's work; (b) the development of powerful demonstrations of Festinger's theory of cognitive dissonance viewed as the cognitive control of motivation; (c) the conjugate reinforcement as a technique for quantifying subjective states, based on Ogden Lindsey's operant conditioning methodology; (d) the continuation of some of my Yale work on persuasion and attitude change; and (e) the newest, most exciting research based on an idea from William Golding's novel *Lord of the Flies*—deindividuation as facilitating antisocial behavior. It was all within a tradition of experimental social psychology, primarily laboratory research, but with some field studies, such as vandalism of automobiles that I had put on Bronx streets and later those in Palo Alto (which influenced the authors of the broken window theory). I had a great research team for several years and lived in our little lab much of the day and evening when I was not teaching—Ebbe Ebbesen, Scott Fraser, Matty Weisenberg, and others were dedicated research assistants. My NSF research grant helped make it all possible. I also relied on many talented undergraduate research assistants, as I continued to do in my later research at Stanford.

ACTIVISM

I was jarred by the Cuban missile crisis in 1962 and later the horrors of the Vietnam War. My secretary Anne Zeidberg shamed me into activism, because I am a nonpolitical person whose overextended professional life left no time for personal indulgences let alone political involvement. But she made me aware of my role in academia and the need to voice opposition to our mistake of entering and continuing in the war in Vietnam. I organized one of the nation's first all-night teach-ins in 1965 and led a walkout of students and parents at an NYU graduation against giving Robert McNamara, secretary of defense, an honorary degree. I took active parts in other protest movements in New York City and Washington, D.C., against this mindless war and for the new civil rights movement for African Americans. I carried that sense of activism with me to Stanford, where I continued to be energized against the war through a variety of activities. And I am now more fervent than ever in opposing war by our nation, especially the Bush doctrine of preemptive war based on the intuition of some brain trust that another country might pose a danger to U.S. security.

Having been energized as a social-change agent, I helped organize the Harlem Summer Project in 1965 that enlisted student volunteers from NYU and City

College to work in a Harlem church school yard all summer in one of several programs I designed: a kind of Head Start program that taught young children the basics of reading, writing, and arithmetic in small personalized settings using the newest technologies; a program that introduced high school students to the joys of college by having them attend special lectures by top professors at both colleges, visit dorms and varsity team practices, and meet with admissions counselors; and a Black Pride program for teenagers that took them around the city to events that featured Black performers, such as Ella Fitzgerald in practice for a concert, photography exhibits, and more. We financed the project with gifts from fund-raising parties and a small grant of $2,000 from the city that was mostly for free lunches.

TRANSFORMATIVE EXPERIENCES

Several experiences that had a profound impact on my career and thinking about psychology began with my summer school teaching at Stanford in 1963, where I got to be around top-level students and colleagues of the caliber that I had grown accustomed to at Yale and that made me aware of the standards necessary to function at that high level. Sitting in on Festinger's weekly research seminars at his home on the campus was an intellectual treat.

Summer school teaching in Leuven, Belgium, in 1966 similarly changed my lowly self-image, by making it as "the young kid on the Continent" along with a remarkable team of social psychologists from the United States as part of the first summer school of the European Association of Experimental Social Psychology. The U.S. team included Hal Kelley, Bob Zajonc, and Hal Gerard, along with European faculty of Josef Nuttin, Joseph Jaspers, Ragnor Rommetviet, and Jaap Rabbie. We each had a small group of advanced European graduate students to lead in designing, executing, analyzing, and writing a publishable research project in six weeks. The intensive collaboration, with none of my usual endless distractions, was intoxicating, and I flourished. Our group did a study on deindividuation using Belgian military soldiers as our participants, and we were the first team to meet the goals of the summer school. On the way to Leuven, I stopped off in Paris at the invitation of French social psychologists Serge Moscovici and Claude Faucheux to lecture to their graduate students at the Sorbonne for a week. There were wonderfully lively exchanges with the students and my new French colleagues that broadened my perspectives on my work and the significance of psychology. Claude also introduced me to the joys of the fine wine and French cuisine we enjoyed that week in Paris, the most memorable of which for a poor Bronx boy was wild boar in a Madeira-chestnut sauce.

A QUANTUM LEAP IN NATIONAL VISIBILITY

I needed to get an early promotion to increase my lowly assistant professor salary so my family could survive. When I asked Ray Katzell, the head of the NYU psychology department, if he would put me forward for this accelerated step-up a year early, he made clear two things. First, some older faculty thought I was too brash and needed time to mellow (reactions against my antiwar activities), and also that although my career was moving along, I needed to demonstrate a "quantum leap in national visibility" for him to endorse early promotion to associate professor. That meant significantly increasing my publications and invited lectures. I took the bait and then worked even harder to accomplish that ambiguous, open-ended goal. I relinquished any ties to present hedonism and became an over-the-top, future-oriented workaholic.

VISITING AT COLUMBIA UNIVERSITY (1967–1968)

I would hang out at the Columbia social psychology program after my biweekly moonlight teaching at Barnard College (which is across the street), because so many fine social psychologists were there. When Bill McGuire took a leave to check out a job at the University of California, San Diego, I was invited to replace him for the year, which I jumped at. But before I could start, my friend Stan Schachter also took leave to get married, and Bibb Latane left to work with John Darley on bystander intervention research. Before I could feel sorry for being abandoned, I met two remarkable graduate students, Lee Ross and Judy Rodin, who made my year. They were so smart, so professional beyond their years, and so creative that I loved working with them in class, in the lab, and in our regular coffee shop lunches. We published one of the first studies on attributional theory, and later I helped Lee get a job at Stanford and Judy take my job at NYU. Lee and I are still buddies at Stanford, and Judy went on to have an amazing career at Yale, then was the president of the University of Pennsylvania, and now is the head of the Rockefeller Foundation.

I am not sure whether my colleagues viewed my being at Columbia as a sign of my increased national visibility, but it must have helped in some ways to get me a new job at Stanford. One day in December, out of the blue, Al Hastorf, the chair of Stanford's psychology department, called to inform me that I had been selected by the senior faculty to join them as a full professor with tenure! To replace my idol, Leon Festinger! To be part of the best psychology department in the world! And not to have even applied for the position! I must say immodestly that I was able to tell the NYU psychology department head that perhaps this transition from untenured assistant professor at NYU in The Bronx to tenured full professor at Stanford in paradise might define a quantum leap in national visibility. And no thanks; I would not consider staying on, even if someone else did the windows instead of me.

However, it was hard to leave my Bronx family, knowing that I might never return home again. My father had been working for me at NYU as my lab technician, a position he expanded after I left. But I most missed my wonderful mother and my kid brother, Don. My wife, Rose Abdelnour-Zimbardo, and I decided we would separate and eventually divorce after she and our son, Adam, spent the 1968 year at Stanford. Although I called Adam every week and visited with him in New York or at Stanford during holidays and the summer, it was heartbreaking not to be there for him on a daily basis, to be part of his youth. I was fortunate that he came to Stanford for his undergraduate studies and has stayed on living in San Francisco. We are tight buddies, sharing coffee regularly near his home at Jumping Java.

He is now a fine therapist with an MFT degree and a master's specialization in human sexuality.

THE STANFORD DECADES (1968–FOREVER, ALMOST)

I was there, and I was scared. I had been a biggish fish in a little pond, now I was the minnow in the tank of sharks. Hilgard, Atkinson, Bandura, Bower, Maccoby, Mischel, Shepard, Flavell, Pribram, Thompson, Sears, and many more brilliant, creative, productive colleagues abounded there. But freed from the daily grind of survival at NYU and the stressful living in New York City, I felt liberated just to have so much time to think, to plan, to develop ideas, and to get feedback from faculty and students whose input was stimulating. With my new normal teaching load, I could focus on perfecting my teaching and have time to develop teacher-training workshops and seminars and teaching manuals. I was liberated from my excessive teaching load and had only a few courses each quarter, which meant I could put more gusto in each of them and still have more time left over for a little fun on the side. No more hours-long commutes; I could bike to work from the faculty residence in the student dormitory (Cedro) where I lived for free.

The productive juices flowed, and in short order, I wrote an entirely new 8th edition of the textbook *Psychology and Life* (with Floyd Ruch), as well as the instructor's manual, student study guide, reader, and brief edition of that text. In my first three years on the new job, I knocked out *Influencing Attitudes and Changing Behavior* (with Ebbe Ebbesen), *Canvassing for Peace* (with Bob Abelson), a chapter in the *Nebraska Symposium on Motivation*, with some of my best writing, and on the side many professional articles.

Psychology and Life was a big hit, selling more than 100,000 copies, and it made a lot of money. So for the very first time in my life, I no longer felt poor. I traded my borrowed bike for a 1955 Mercedes Benz 350-SL silver bullet convertible, the most beautiful car in the world. And I bought some new suits and joined a spa to exercise and get in shape. I played center field with the psychology department's grad student–faculty softball team that won the Stanford intramural league that summer. I went to my first rock concert at the Fillmore in San Francisco, to shows at Stanford's Frost theater, and to free concerts in Golden Gate Park. I also discovered fine wine in the Napa–Sonoma Valley that changed my drinking habits permanently. I clearly was beginning to blend some hedonism with my excessive future orientation to experience more pleasure in life than my solo work act. But in Stanford's paradise, work comes first, and my eternal struggle between work and play continues to this day.

APPLYING SOCIAL PSYCHOLOGY WISELY AND WELL ALSO MATTERS

In my own research I have tried to move back and forth between studying real-world phenomena in field and laboratory settings and illustrating the applicability of my own research findings and those of my colleagues in a variety of ways. It is my strong belief that short of doing research to test the conceptual adequacy of some theoretical formulation, social psychologists have an obligation to contribute to the enhancement of the human condition through research that applies what we know in sensitive and effective ways—as Elliot Aronson has shown us with the use of his jig-saw classroom technique for promoting cooperation among school children, an intervention that integrates minority children into the mainstream of class activity better than any other available educational tactic. I have used my various research programs as vehicles to promote prison reform and judicial legislation, to reduce urban vandalism, and to help people overcome shyness (in my popular writing, in media appearances, and by establishing a shyness clinic in the community to treat shyness in adults and adolescents). For me, a new mantra emerged: *Application matters.*

THE STANFORD PRISON EXPERIMENT (SPE)

My classes usually involve students in experiential projects, either solo, in pairs, or in teams. In spring 1971, I invited students in my new course, Social Psychology in Action, to select from among a set of 10 projects that combined sociological and psychological features (back to my undergraduate training at Brooklyn College). Teams of 10 to 15 students could choose a topic, then work with a graduate teaching assistant to study it in depth, and either present their project in class or give me the materials to present for them. Many of the projects involved people in an institutional setting, such as older people going to homes for the aged or people becoming prisoners or guards.

The Prison Project Team decided to do a mock prison in their dormitory over a weekend, with half being prisoners and the rest role-playing guards. On Monday during class, their presentation became explosive as they described the intense emotions that experience elicited in them. Some said they could no longer be friends with others who were guards because they felt that showed their true selves. Some were in tears. After class we had an intensive debriefing, but I realized something powerful had happened in that mock prison. However, we could not separate the personal reasons these particular students chose this topic (dispositional factors) from the situational forces acting on them. Only a controlled experiment could do that. Voilà: The idea for the SPE was born after I had discussions with my graduate research team of Craig Haney and Curt Banks and the undergraduate who headed up that class project, David Jaffe.

By now, I can say the rest is history and a history lesson told on our Web site, www.PrisonExp.org, developed by former graduate student Scott Plous and his student Mike Lestik. A Google search of "experiment" reveals it to be the most cited experiment in the world, with about 300 million hits. The SPE and Milgram's obedience research are the bookends of social psychological research that demonstrates the power of situational forces over the individual will to resist. Again it is curious that little Stanley and I were classmates senior year at James Monroe High School in The Bronx and ended up doing comparable research on situational power.

The SPE has had a profound effect on much of my thinking about power and evil and even about better ways to teach in a more truly democratic fashion. It also changed the lives of some of the participants: graduate student Craig Haney; former graduate student, heroine of the SPE who forced its early termination, Christina Maslach (now Mrs. Zimbardo); and our consultant Carlo Prescott, formerly incarcerated for 17 years.

After nearly 35 years, I have finally gotten around to doing a serious write-up of the SPE in a detailed daily chronology, with a whole chapter devoted to each of the 6 days in that basement dungeon and other chapters focused on the first day of the police arrests and the parole board meetings. I wrote it all in a cinematic style: present tense, first-person narrative, with minimal psychological intrusions. Several subsequent chapters deal with its meaning, ethics, and the many extensions and variations it spawned.

THE ABU GHRAIB LITTLE SHOP OF HORRORS

The reason for finally writing such a book about the SPE is the confluence of its messages and visual images with those of the abuses and tortures by American military police prison guards at Iraq's Abu Ghraib prison. The scandal broke in the national and worldwide media in April 2004, when the heroic whistle-blowing of Army Reserve Specialist Joe Darby facilitated the release of the set of horror images of "digitally documented depravity" and the military police doing those dirty deeds. The images of naked men, of prisoners with bags on their heads, and of sexually humiliating poses all brought back a rush of ugly SPE memories long stored away in the crevices of my cortex.

Military leaders and Bush administration leaders all madly rushed to the usual dispositional tactic of blaming the grunts, the perpetrators of evil as the "few bad apples." Such an attribution immediately centers the focus on the characteristics of those "rogue soldiers" and takes the system off the attributional hook for contributing to such violations against humanity. I immediately countered with the banner of social psychology, proclaiming that it was probably a "bad barrel"—the situation—that had corrupted these formerly good American men and women soldiers.

Thus emerged the idea of a new book that sought to understand how such abuses could happen based on the analytical tools of social psychology and particularly what I had learned from ye olde SPE. I became more like an investigative reporter than a social psychologist researcher by first becoming an expert witness for one of those military police guards, Sergeant Chip Frederick, who was in charge of the night shift on the prison tier where these abuses were conducted. As such, I had access to all the digital images, to all the investigative reports, and to this soldier, and then I got to know him, his family, and others who had been at that prison. I now know a great deal more than most other experts about that situation and the military and civilian command personnel responsible for a system that created an impossibly chaotic situation for the soldiers serving as reserve army guards there. I ended my book by putting each of them on trial for their systemic complicity in these abuses—thus assuming a new persona as Zimbardo the Prosecutor.

My book is titled *The Lucifer Effect: Understanding How Good People Turn Evil* (Zimbardo, 2007). It represents my personal journey through the hells of these two prisons, the mock one in the basement of the Stanford Psychology Department and the all-too-real one on Tier 1-A, Abu Ghraib. I really poured my heart, soul, and brain into writing this book. I am too close to it to be objective, so forgive my immodesty in believing it will become an enduring best-seller and the capstone of my career.

LESSONS FOR STUDENTS FROM MY JOURNEYS

So my meandering path through social psychology finds me now studying both situational and dispositional variables and their interaction in research on the psychology of time perspective, the cognitive and social bases of the origins of psychopathology, and the effects of technology on shyness, along with investigating the development of prosocial and antisocial behavior among school children, the role of personality factors in political behavior, the psychological foundations of terrorism, and more. It has been my lifelong passion that those cuddly white rats could never quite fulfill, although it was easier to predict their behavior and publish their data than it is dealing with capricious people and the editors of the *Journal of Personality and Social Psychology*.

My message to the next generation of psychology students, those blessed to be social psychologists, and the others who ought to be is very sexy. Do It With Love, Passion, Arousal, Devotion, and Pride—or go on a different journey.

Love being a psychologist, because figuring out the mysteries of human nature is the most wonderful way to spend your life. And once you have solved a few of its puzzles, you are in a position to determine ways in which you can make life better through your teaching, research, clinical practice, or application of psychological knowledge across many domains.

Don't do psychology in just a nice, gentle way; do it with all-out, unbridled passion, going over the top and being charismatic, not just a good psychologist. Having passion means that you get into the magical moment of flow the moment you engage psychology of any kind, with no past or future, just the totally engaging here and now. Become psychology.

Get excited about what you do as a psychologist. Be aroused by learning new things, by communicating new ideas, and by helping enhance the quality of mental life of individuals and even nations.

Become devoted to a lifelong journey of discovery, of curiosity about the workings of the brain, the mind, and behavior. Remember what matters: content, context, culture, good methodology, and the application of our knowledge to improve the human condition. Have respect for people, animals, and nature.

Be prideful about your major, your career, and your profession—as a psychologist. It is the most complex, compelling, demanding, changing, expanding, deepening field there is. Own it; make it yours. Do it, be it, all the time.

Finally, the difference between my two grandfathers, one a shoemaker and the other, my namesake, a barber, and me, now a celebrated psychologist, is only one thing: education. I was blessed, given the gift of being allowed to be educated, and they were not. They had to work with their hands and not with their minds. In their noble professions they shined maybe hundreds or thousands of shoes and shaved as many faces. But they were not able to touch the minds of their customers as I have been privileged to do as a teacher for 50 years to many thousands of students. So please never take your education for granted; take it as a special gift from your parents, your society, and your teachers that you treasure every day. Find new ways to repay them with your joy in learning and your accomplishments by using what you have learned to enhance the human condition. Dear students of psychology, it is time now for Your Journey. Go in peace and joy.

SUGGESTED READINGS (BOOKS)

Gerrig, R., & Zimbardo, P. G. (2002). *Psychology and life* (16th ed.). Boston: Allyn and Bacon.

Huggins, M., Haritos-Fatouros, M., & Zimbardo, P. G. (2002). *Violence workers: Police torturers and murderers reconstruct Brazilian atrocities*. Berkeley: University of California Press.

Zimbardo, P. G. (1969). *The cognitive control of motivation*. Glenview, IL: Scott, Foresman.

Zimbardo, P. G. (2007). *The Lucifer effect: Understanding how good people turn evil*. New York: Random House.

Zimbardo, P. G., Ebbesen, E. B., & Maslach, C. (1977). *Influencing attitudes and changing behavior* (2nd ed.). Reading, MA: Addison-Wesley.

Zimbardo, P. G., Johnson, R., & Weber, A. (2002). *Psychology: Core concepts* (4th ed.). Boston: Allyn and Bacon.

Zimbardo, P. G., & Leippe, M. (1991). *The psychology of attitude change and social influence*. New York: McGraw-Hill. (Also published in hardcover by Temple University Press)

The Full Cycle of an Interamerican Journey in Social Psychology

AROLDO RODRIGUES

Department of Psychology, California State University, Fresno

*I*n the last pages of his autobiography *The Life of a Psychologist*, Fritz Heider observed that pieces of plain luck were of decisive importance in many of the turning points in his life (Heider, 1983). He then went on to list some of these lucky events and concluded his autobiographical book in this way: "As a matter of fact, if I were inclined to be superstitious, I could believe that a friendly spirit arranged the whole sequence of events in which the powers of fortune were so kind to me" (p. 190).

In 1991, when Harold Kelley retired, I was spending a semester at UCLA and had the privilege of attending the ceremony the Department of Psychology held in recognition of Hal's outstanding career. A book was placed in the department for everybody who wished to write something to Hal, not only in recognition of his accomplishments and his significant contributions to social psychology but also in gratitude for the remarkable human qualities he possessed. I don't recall exactly what I wrote, but I remember distinctly that I ended a two-page message calling his attention to Heider's final sentence in his autobiography and added that perhaps his life and his career were also looked over by a "friendly spirit" who arranged the whole sequence of events in which the powers of fortune were so kind to him.

I don't know if I called Hal's attention to Heider's reference to a friendly spirit or, perhaps more likely, he was already familiar with it. Regardless, in his public appearances after his retirement, he often invoked the friendly spirit when he reminisced on his life. He used it sometimes, however, in a slightly different way. For him, friendly spirits could also be people who happened to be at the right time and at the right place and who had a tremendous beneficial influence in his life. For example, John Thibaut, his research coworker and coauthor in so many endeavors, and Dorothy, his wife, were two constantly mentioned friendly spirits who were so important in his life.

When I pause to reflect on my own career, I am compelled to resort to the friendly spirit idea as first used by Heider.

STARTING A CAREER IN A NONEXISTENT PROFESSION

Fifty-four years ago, when I began a four-year course in psychology in Brazil, psychology as a discipline and as a profession was almost nonexistent there. There was no degree in psychology, the profession was not recognized by law, vocational guidance and counseling were provided by educators, and psychotherapy was exclusively practiced by psychiatrists. Courses in child and adolescent psychology were offered to students graduating in education and social work, general psychology and history of psychology were available to students of philosophy, and an encompassing course titled "psychology" was required of students in medicine who intended to become psychiatrists. The course I entered was not an official one; it was initiated on an experimental basis at the Catholic University of Rio de Janeiro, under the initiative of Hanns Ludwig Lippmann, a German scholar trained in philosophy. Most of the instructors in that course were philosophers, psychiatrists, or educators. At that time, the three most popular professions, and the ones that would give more status and offer more job opportunities to their graduates, were engineering, medicine, and law. After finishing high school, students were screened by a rather severe entrance examination to one of these schools or to the "School of Philosophy," a term used to encompass most everything else in the arts and sciences. In the last three years of high school, students who intended to go into engineering or medicine would follow a curriculum with emphasis on mathematics, physics, chemistry, and biology, and those who were more inclined to become lawyers or to study the disciplines encompassed under the general umbrella of the School of Philosophy (except, of course, physics, chemistry, and mathematics) would follow a set of courses geared toward languages, including Latin, philosophy, and Portuguese grammar and literature.

Because I had not yet made up my mind as to which profession to embrace, I chose the science curriculum, because this would give me more career options. I ended up deciding to become a lawyer, instead of pursuing a career in medicine or engineering, and in March 1952, at the age of 18, I entered law school. Was I enthusiastic about becoming a lawyer? Not really. There were too many engineers and medical doctors in my family, and I wanted to be different, I guess. In any event, there I was, studying to become a lawyer.

In my second year of law school, I came across a newspaper ad announcing the beginning of the first systematic course in psychology. It was being offered in the evenings, and the degree conferred by it could not be legally recognized, for the profession was still nonexistent. Because most of my courses in law school were in the morning, I decided to enroll in this new and, at that time, somewhat exotic course. In hindsight, I know what led me to enroll in that course was my repressed desire to become a medical doctor. Indeed, in the last two years of my psychology course, I spent most weekends in psychiatric hospitals, observing my professors of clinical psychology (all of them, of course, psychiatrists) dealing with mental patients and, often, training myself in the application and interpretation of psychological techniques, such as the Rorschach. I was really in love with clinical psychology; the notion of becoming a social psychologist was a nonexistent region in my life space.

I graduated in law and in psychology by the end of 1956. I was 23 years old. The law degree enabled me to work as a lawyer; the degree in psychology was somewhat useless, as far as jobs were concerned, for the profession had not yet been recognized by law. I was fortunate that, because of the scarcity of trained psychologists, I was called by the founder of the first systematic course in psychology, the aforementioned Hanns Ludwig Lippmann, to teach psychology in his incipient course. I know how horrified the reader must be by this. A recent graduate, after an improvised course—the first course ever offered—was teaching psychology to others! Well, I was horrified too. I did the best I could. I read every book available on the subject of my courses, most of them in French or in Spanish and Spanish translations of books in English, for my command of English was very poor at that time. I consulted frequently with my former instructors, but I knew I was not equipped to be a good teacher. Mornings and afternoons I was working in a law firm to make a living, but not enjoying what I was doing. I loved the evenings, when, one way or the other, I taught my courses in psychology, notwithstanding my shortcomings and my insecurities.

I was, however, more and more determined to follow the profession of a psychology professor, and I started looking for opportunities to go abroad and attain a decent training in the profession I really wanted to embrace. In 1959, the friendly spirit helped me, and I was granted a Fulbright scholarship and instructed to go to the University of Kansas (KU), in Lawrence, to work toward my master's degree. I was thrilled. My English was very poor, but somehow they granted me the scholarship, although with the prerequisite that I spend the summer of 1959 at the American University in Washington, D.C., to go through an intensive course in English. All this happened rather swiftly. So, despite having my wedding scheduled for July 11, 1959, I accepted the scholarship and committed myself to be in Washington 2 days later, spending my honeymoon on a 22-hour plane trip from Rio to D.C. in a four-engine propeller plane, with a short stop in Trinidad.

KU, AND THE IMPACT OF FRITZ HEIDER

At KU I followed a program of studies in clinical psychology. Abnormal psychology, personality, projective techniques, and juvenile delinquency were some of the courses I remember choosing. When I was in Washington trying to improve my English, I came across Fritz Heider's recently published book *The Psychology of Interpersonal Relations*. I was browsing the stacks of a bookstore in Georgetown when I saw this book and noticed that the author was affiliated with KU. I had never heard of Heider, but the fact that he was on the faculty of the university I was about to enter drew my attention to the book, and I bought it. I still have it, with Heider's signature in it. As a coincidence, during the dinner party offered by the Department of Psychology to the entering graduate students, I sat next to an old professor who introduced himself to me as Fritz Heider. At that time Heider was only 63, but he always looked older than he was. We kept a conversation going during the entire dinner, something that was possible because of the help of my wife, Anna Maria, who spoke perfect English and helped me throughout the evening. I was deeply impressed by Heider. His kindness, his sweetness, and his willingness to make me feel comfortable, despite my difficulties in communicating with him, affected me profoundly. I liked him so much that I regretted not being in social psychology and taking the psychology of interpersonal relations course he said he would offer in the spring. There was no room in my schedule of courses in clinical psychology to include Heider's course. I am fortunate that I became his student nevertheless. Advanced general psychology I and II were required of every graduate student, and Heider was the instructor for both. I was very happy with this fortunate coincidence, and my liking and admiration for him grew enormously during that year. As a teacher, he revealed himself as a man of immense knowledge, of extraordinary kindness, and of tolerance for divergent opinions; an exemplar of a true scholar. In addition to having a profound knowledge of psychology, he was capable of navigating with ease through literature, metaphysics, and the philosophy of science. I remember when he was lecturing on the various systems of psychology, and students who favored behaviorism would emphatically proclaim the virtues of this system, just to be followed by others who would hail the contributions of Gestaltism or psychoanalysis with no less vigor. To all Heider would say, "Yes, yes, there is a lot of truth in what you just said."

During my third semester at KU, I was mainly involved with my master's thesis, working under the supervision of Herbert F. Wright, the coauthor with Roger Barker of the book *Midwest and Its Children*. Both Wright and Barker based their research on Lewin's field theory. This was the beginning of my transition from clinical to social psychology. My master's thesis was titled *Affective Reactions of Children and Their Peers in Communities Differing in Size*, and Herbert Wright made available to me data his assistants had collected for his research on social behavior in different communities. In addition, he took great pains correcting my numerous drafts. Without his dedication and willingness to help me beyond the call of duty, I would not have obtained my degree. My knowledge of statistics was extremely limited, and the entire thesis, in its quantitative aspect, did not go beyond means, standard deviations, and correlation coefficients. I regretted once more not having taken Heider's course in interpersonal relations, but now I was graduating at the end of the fall semester and returning to Brazil, and I could not take the course that was offered only in the spring semester.

RETURNING TO BRAZIL, TRANSITIONING FROM CLINICAL TO SOCIAL PSYCHOLOGY, AND COMING BACK TO THE UNITED STATES

With an M.A. degree in psychology from KU, I felt somewhat more confident in my ability to teach, so I quit my law career for good and started teaching full-time at the Catholic University of Rio de Janeiro. The course created in 1953 by Hanns L. Lippmann had picked up momentum and was drawing more and more students. Other universities followed the lead of the Catholic University and began offering four-year courses in psychology. Congress was being pressed to enact a law creating the profession of psychologist. In August 1962, the law was passed, and psychology became a legalized profession with three areas of specialization: industrial, educational, and clinical. A graduate course in counseling was offered to graduates of education and other areas of the social sciences. Therefore, the market for a professor of psychology expanded rapidly. With my M.A. from an American university, I had a head start and was offered several part-time teaching positions. In 1961–1962

I taught several courses in psychology not only at the Catholic University as an assistant professor but also at other institutions on evenings and even Saturdays. Although somewhat more confident, I still felt that I needed further training. Fr. Antonius Benko, a Ph.D. in psychology from the University of Louvain, Belgium, had taken over the coordination of the course created by Hanns Lippmann and encouraged me to go back to the United States to attain my Ph.D. He promised to hold my position at the Catholic University until my return and that a promotion would be automatic should I come back with the degree. With these incentives I applied to UCLA for the 1962–1963 academic year.

Why UCLA? Again several fortuitous occurrences directed me to take this path. In the summer of 1960, my wife and I went on a camping trip from Kansas to California. Los Angeles was one of the few cities in which we stayed at a motel. We spent five days in Los Angeles during which we visited UCLA. I was amazed by its size and modern installations. Moreover, unlike USC, it was located in a beautiful area, surrounded by Beverly Hills, Bel-Air, and Brentwood. Besides, by then I was definitely leaning toward social psychology, and UCLA had distinguished faculty in this area.

I soon realized that a clinical psychologist at that time in Brazil would always be considered a second-class citizen in relation to a psychiatrist. My work with Herbert Wright on psychological ecology acquainted me with Lewin's ideas and with social psychology in general. In the course I took in social psychology at KU, the textbook was the recently published *Social Psychology of Groups* by Thibaut and Kelley. Although I did not like the book at that time, I learned that Kelley was one of the most famous social psychologists in the world and was a member of UCLA's faculty.

In summary, all these forces—the realization that a Ph.D. was needed to adequately pursue a career in academic psychology, the incentive received by Fr. Benko, the desire to change from clinical to social psychology, the acquaintance with Lewin during the work on my M.A. thesis, the glamour of UCLA, and the fact that one of the leading social psychologists was there—constituted strong incentives for me to apply for scholarships and admission to the graduate program at UCLA. The friendly spirit seems to have looked over me again. I was granted a tuition scholarship by the Brazilian government and received a letter from Hal Kelley himself informing me that I had been accepted to the graduate program in psychology at UCLA. I was so thrilled that I could not believe all this was happening. And if all this were not enough, Kelley asked me in his letter if I didn't need financial assistance, for he could offer me either a teaching or a research assistantship. That seemed too good to be true, but it was true, and in August 1962 my wife and I moved back to the United States, I enrolled in the graduate program in psychology at UCLA, and I became Hal Kelley's teaching assistant.

THE UCLA YEARS

By that time my English had improved. Whereas at KU, I would miss about half of what the instructor said in class, at UCLA I missed only 10 or 15%. The first year was a tough one. By the end of it, a medical examination concluded that I probably had a stomach ulcer, a hypothesis that was not confirmed by further testing but that nevertheless illustrates the stress I was experiencing. My class had 53 students. Those who did not attain a B+ average at the end of the first year in six required core courses could not continue toward the Ph.D. degree; they were simply given the option of staying one more semester to write a thesis and obtain a master's degree if their average was at least B−. Only 22 students met the B+ requirement, and I was not one of them. Again the friendly spirit looked over me (or, perhaps, in this particular instance, not a friendly spirit but an actual human being named Harold Kelley), and I was given one semester's probation, during which I had to earn at least one A to make up for previous grades. Thank God I made it, for it would have been extremely disappointing to settle for a second master's degree and, at 30 years of age, it is unlikely that I would have been disposed to apply for admission to some other university. And without the training I received at UCLA, I have no doubt that my career would have turned out completely differently. After four years at UCLA, I obtained my degree. I felt energized and more confident in myself, and I had a strong desire to follow an academic career. I also now felt very adequately trained in methodology, statistics, and, of course, social psychology.

The recognition for what UCLA gave me, and my devotion to what I consider my true alma mater are such that every single car I have owned since 1966 has had a UCLA sticker on the rear windshield. I made several visits to UCLA after my graduation, despite living in Brazil. I kept in close contact with my former professors, particularly with Hal Kelley, Richard Centers, Bert Raven, and David Sears, and also with Bernie Weiner and Hal Gerard, who joined the faculty either when I was about to graduate or later. All of them became very close friends and had an enormous influence on my career.

One of the required courses during the first year of the UCLA graduate program was Psych 206. It consisted of designing and carrying out an experiment and writing the final product in American Psychological Association (APA) format. I had never, ever, run an experiment or witnessed someone running one. I was in a panic. I was supervised by David Sears, who was extremely patient, helpful, and understanding. What was my experiment? Of course, on Heider's balance theory. I attempted to determine which is the best way of changing an imbalanced triad into a balanced one. I finished the course with a B+ and with some nice words of encouragement from Dave. From then on, until the mid-1980s, balance theory was the dominant topic of my research. In 1965 as a student I published the paper "On the Differential Effects of Some Parameters of Balance" (Rodrigues, 1965), and next year I finished my dissertation titled *On the Psycho-logic of Interpersonal Relations*, which dealt with the measurement of tension in triadic interpersonal relations of the type studied by Heider, as well as on biases, other than balance, that influence the tension experienced by people involved in such relationships.

The friendly spirit continued to make it his (or her?) business to help me in my career. Before returning to Brazil in late January 1966 to resume my position at the Catholic University of Rio de Janeiro, I decided to make a stop in Lawrence,

Kansas, to see Heider and one in Ann Arbor, Michigan, to see Ted Newcomb and Bob Zajonc. I wanted to give a copy of my dissertation to Heider and also to two other investigators who were doing influential research on balance, such as Newcomb and Zajonc. Heider had recently retired. I briefed him on my dissertation. He seemed interested but not thrilled, although he said, cordially as always, that it was an interesting and important work. When I asked what he would do now that he had retired, he showed me the numerous notes—the famous notes compiled by Maryann Weiner in *Fritz Heider: The Notebook*—and said something like, "During my entire life I always kept a pad in each room of the house; every time I had an idea that I considered important, I would grab the pad and write it on it. Now I have these piles of notes to go over. This will keep me very busy." That was the first time I learned about the famous notes later brought to light by the monumental work of Maryann. From Lawrence I flew to Detroit and then drove to Ann Arbor. I had enlightening conversations with Newcomb and Zajonc. Both showed more interest in my findings than Heider did. Perhaps my dissertation was empirically sound, but Heider was always more interested in general abstract ideas than in concrete empirical data. Newcomb and Zajonc seemed to me more interested in the empirical part of my work. Two years after my encounter with these two famous social psychologists, Newcomb (1998) published a chapter in Abelson et al.'s *Theories of Cognitive Consistency: A Source-Book* called "Interpersonal Balance," and Zajonc published a chapter in Lindzey and Aronson's second edition of the *Handbook of Social Psychology* on "Cognitive Theories in Social Psychology." Both chapters quoted the data from my dissertation, the chapter by Newcomb doing so on many occasions and reproducing my findings in seven of the chapter's nine tables. After this, no wonder the findings of my dissertation, published in 1967 and 1968 in the *Journal of Personality and Social Psychology* (Rodrigues, 1967) and in the *Journal of Personality* (Rodrigues, 1968), were cited by most textbooks in social psychology published in the 1970s and early 1980s. It was a big boost to my incipient career.

RETURNING TO BRAZIL ONCE AGAIN AND EXPERIENCING FIRSTHAND THE EFFECTS OF THE CRISIS IN SOCIAL PSYCHOLOGY

I returned to Brazil in 1966 with a Ph.D. in psychology, feeling I had a wealth of knowledge to share. After all, I had completed a tough course of studies. I had a solid training in statistics and research methodology. In statistics I had to digest Mosteller's *Probabilities With Statistical Applications*, Walker and Lev's *Statistical Inference,* and Wallis and Roberts's *Statistics: A New Approach*; in experimental design I had to deal with Cox's *Planning of Experiments* and Winer's *Statistical Principles in Experimental Design*. Moreover, I had taken courses with prominent social psychologists such as Hal Kelley, Bert Raven, Dick Centers, and Dave Sears; I had had courses in industrial psychology and educational measurement, which were my two minors; I had passed tough comprehensive exams in my major and minor areas, as well as in history and systems of psychology, and had met the requirement of proficiency in two foreign languages; and I had familiarized myself with Fortran IV, the most recent computer language at the time. I felt, of course, much more confident in my ability to carry out the mission of a university professor than I had ever felt.

In this euphoric state I returned to my position at the Catholic University of Rio de Janeiro. Making me feel even better, I had had my first two daughters in the United States, and my wife was pregnant with our third child. Never before had I been so enthusiastic, so hopeful, and so energized to carry forward my mission as a university professor and to contribute to the development of scientific psychology in my country as I was upon my return from UCLA.

Things went well at first but soon started to change. The huge difference between the facilities I was used to at UCLA and the limitations of the incipient Department of Psychology of the Catholic University immediately convinced me that I had to considerably lower my level of aspiration for research activity. Worse, however—to my deep disappointment—students and colleagues showed very little, if any, interest in my research on balance theory. I remember one evening, as an invited speaker at a meeting of the Brazilian Association of Applied Psychology, I presented a talk on my dissertation. When I finished I was politely applauded, and I waited for questions. There was total silence. Then a member of the board of directors of the association stood up and said, "Professor Rodrigues, your work is very elegant and sophisticated. But tell me, what is the practical application of all that? What use can we make of your findings in the Brazilian reality?" I immediately realized that I was in the wrong place at the wrong time. Brazilian psychologists were interested not in theory and methodology but rather in applications of psychology to improve the condition of the people and to solve social problems. In other words, the crisis of social psychology was already manifesting itself at full strength in Brazil. Skepticism regarding experiments in social psychology, lots of ethical concerns, and almost exclusive interest in applying social psychology to the solution of social problems were the dominant positions. The political atmosphere of the country was favorable to such an approach, for Marxism was making strides, and the emphasis on action research aimed at changing conservative social structures was predominant among students and faculty. I always tried to separate science from politics, and I was having a tough time adjusting to such an environment. My dissatisfaction and frustration reached a point that I decided I had had enough. Although I had come back to Brazil full of good intentions and with hopes of making a difference in the field of psychology, I realized I would not succeed and that I should return to the United States.

AN ATTEMPT TO RETURN TO THE UNITED STATES, AND THE UNEXPECTED EVENTS THAT FOLLOWED

When I learned from a former classmate of mine at UCLA that Claremont Graduate School had an opening for a position of assistant professor, I immediately applied. By the end of 1968 I received a letter from Claremont offering me the position. On one hand I was thrilled, but on the other, I was having a difficult time accepting the offer because I felt I was taking the easier way out and betraying the country that partially sponsored my studies abroad as well as the people who encouraged me and accepted me warmly when I returned to the Catholic University. My conflict did not last long, however. Anna Maria, my wife, told me as soon as she learned about the offer that she would not accompany me back to the United States. At that time, we had four children, ranging from 1 to 5 years of age, and she said it would be too difficult for her to deal with the problems of moving from one country to another with four small children to take care of. I had already asked too much of her in my past two stays in the United States. On both occasions, she graciously accompanied me and even worked to help us financially when I was in graduate school. I could not ask her for more sacrifices. So, with great sorrow, I turned down the offer.

I went through a period of great disappointment and feelings of hopelessness, but, as I realized later, during all that time the friendly spirit had not forgotten me. In the 1960s Leon Festinger was chair of the Transnational Committee on Social Psychology of the Social Sciences Research Council. One of the objectives he pursued during his tenure was to bring together foreign social psychologists who were in contact with fellow social psychologists in the United States but who hardly knew each other. He first brought a group of European social psychologists together through workshops in Belgium, Italy, and Germany. The result of this was the creation of the European Association for Social Psychology in the mid-1960s, which exists to this day. After this success, Festinger turned his attention to Latin America. He began networking with Latin American social psychologists who had attained Ph.D.s in the United States and Europe who, in turn, were asked to establish contact with well-trained social psychologists in their respective countries. In 1969 Festinger went to a congress of the Interamerican Society of Psychology in Montevideo, Uruguay, with the goal of meeting with the social psychologists he had contacted by mail and planting the seed for a future Latin American Association for Social Psychology. On his way to Montevideo, Festinger stopped for a few days in Rio, and I had the opportunity to get well acquainted with him and to establish a friendship that lasted until his death. Following the successful model used in Europe, the Transnational Committee on Social Psychology cosponsored a three-week workshop in Vina del Mar, Chile, in 1971. I went to the meeting, together with several Latin American social psychologists, and we all met for these 3 weeks with three well-known American social psychologists, Morton Deutsch, Leonard Berkowitz, and Harold Gerard, who had been invited to offer workshops.

Festinger's initiative gave rise to several other meetings of Latin American, American, and even European social psychologists. I came to know Serge Moscivici and Henry Tajfel and others through the workshops stimulated by the Transnational Committee on Social Psychology of the SSRC. In 1973 the Latin American Association for Social Psychology was founded, and I was elected its first president. The visibility that my constant interactions with psychologists across the three Americas gave to me was crucial to my election as president of the Interamerican Society of Psychology in 1976. The reason I said the friendly spirit had not forgotten me when I refused the Claremont offer is simple: Had I accepted the position at Claremont, none of this would have happened. It is unlikely that I would have become so closely associated with outstanding American and European social psychologists, in addition to my UCLA friends. Had I accepted the Claremont offer, it is almost certain that I would not have been able to secure letters from Leon Festinger, Ted Newcomb, and Hal Kelley when I applied to become fellow of APA's Division 8, which, I am sure, weighed heavily on the division's favorable decision. And for sure I would not have presided over two important international psychological associations, for I would probably have been more oriented toward American psychology and would have concentrated on meeting the requirements to attain tenure and promotion at Claremont.

Among the distinguished Latin American social psychologists I came to know through Leon's efforts was Jacobo A. Varela, who played a crucial role in helping me deal with the crisis in social psychology, which in Brazil, as I mentioned before, was in full force. Varela coined the term *social technology*, which he defined as "the activity that leads to the design of solutions to social problems by means of combinations of findings derived from different areas of the social sciences" (in Deutsch & Hornstein, 1975, p. 160). Social scientists should follow the lead of colleagues in the natural sciences: When scientists such as Faraday, Henry, and Maxwell made theoretical breakthroughs in the study of sound waves, technologists such as Bell, Morse, and Marconi applied this knowledge to come up with the telephone, the telegraph, and the radio, respectively. Therefore, it is not futile or irrelevant to spend effort designing experiments to test hypotheses derived from theories; this, however, as Lewin always said, must be followed by applications of these findings to concrete social problems. One complements the other, and knowledge should always precede applications.

From then on I always invoked Varela's position when I was accused of doing irrelevant research. Varela deeply impressed Festinger and others when he presented a concrete demonstration of social psychology in action to a selected audience during the 1969 congress of the Interamerican Society of Psychology in Montevideo. Although Varela was an engineer by training, his prodigious intelligence allowed him to accumulate a vast knowledge of psychology, mainly social psychology, and he spent the rest of his life using social technology to solve social problems. His book *Psychological Solutions to Social Problems,* published by Academic Press in 1971, as well as papers in the *American Psychologist* and *Human Nature* and chapters in books edited by Deutsch and Hornstein and by Sachs and Kidd, brought to light examples of social psychology in action. Through the work of Leon, he spent several semesters teaching social technology in universities such as Columbia, Wayne State, and British Columbia at Vancouver. Without his ideas, it would have been much more difficult for me to deal with the repercussion of the crisis in social psychology among my Brazilian and Latin American students and peers.

IN DEFENSE OF ACADEMIC FREEDOM

By the end of the 1970s, my career was going very well. On the Brazilian psychology scene, I was respected by all, although liked by only a few. My perception was that I was equally respected but much better liked in other Latin American countries than in my own. I had many distinguished friends in the United States, in Europe, and in Latin America. My textbook in social psychology, whose first edition came to light in 1972, and which was translated into Spanish in 1976, was being adopted widely in Brazil and in other Latin American countries, primarily in Mexico. This book, by the way, is still the best-selling textbook in social psychology in Brazil and Mexico, and it is now in its 23rd printing. I authored two other books, one in 1975 on research methods and statistics, and another in 1979, a compilation of several of my papers in social psychology. I was full professor and had been chair of the Department of Psychology of the Catholic University of Rio de Janeiro, which at that time was considered one of the best in the country, and I was frequently participating in meetings of the APA. I was securing repeated grants from the Brazilian National Research Council. My collaboration with my American colleagues continued. I wrote a chapter for the book *Interracial Marriage* edited by Stuart and Abt and another on attitude change for the book *La Psicologia Social en el Mundo Hoy*, edited by Whittaker. I carried out work in Brazil with Bert Raven on social power in the schools, and I was working with Ted Newcomb (Rodrigues & Newcomb, 1980) on the preparation of a joint article on balance that we published in 1980. My research on balance theory continued, and after following Newcomb's three-way distinction between balanced, nonbalanced, and positively imbalanced triads in several studies in the laboratory and in the field during the 1970s, I created my own models to predict the amount of tension experienced in balanced and imbalanced triads, in which different weights were assigned to the three main sources of biases—balance, agreement, and attraction. I worked on them with my students and with Saburo Iwawaki, of Japan, who read a paper I published in the *Journal of Social Psychology* (Rodrigues & Dela Coleta, 1983) and became interested in testing my models in Japan (Rodrigues & Iwawaki, 1986). As a result of the creation of the Latin American Association of Social Psychology, I was having frequent contacts with distinguished Latin American social psychologists, such as Jacobo Varela, Rogelio Diaz-Guerrero, Jose Miguel Salazar, Rubén Ardila, Julio Villegas, Euclydes Sanchez, Gerardo Marín, Maritza Montero, Hector Cappello, Luis Ramallo, Oswaldo Romero-García, Jorge García-Bouza, and many others. My adaptation to the Brazilian reality was now completed, and I had ceased longing to return to the United States. I was experiencing a sense of fulfillment, even thinking that I had accomplished much more than I ever dreamed I would when I ventured out into a profession that was literally nonexistent in Brazil in 1953. This pleasant state of affairs, however, was soon to be disrupted.

At the beginning of the 1979 academic year, my wife was a part-timer in the Department of Philosophy of the Catholic University of Rio de Janeiro. That year the department chair censored a couple of books my wife had included in the list of suggested readings for her course. The reading list was very eclectic, including books by Marx, Engels, and other socialist thinkers, as well as books from a Brazilian philosopher, Miguel Reale, who was persona non grata among members of the radical left. My wife was asked to drop Reale's books from the list of readings.

At the same time, I was getting upset with the insistence of the higher administration of the university that all research efforts in the social sciences be geared toward improving the conditions of the populations in the slums of Rio. I considered this a restriction of my academic freedom and was fighting against it. When the censorship of my wife's course occurred, I felt that it was time to speak up against this state of affairs. I wrote a rather long article for one of the most influential and widely read Brazilian newspapers titled "The Curtailment of Academic Freedom From Within," hinting that censorship in universities was being exercised not only from the strong political regime in power at that time but also, and primarily, from within the university. The example of what was happening at the Catholic University was clearly exposed in the article, and a crisis erupted. A debate in the press followed the publication of the article, with those in favor and against my position voicing their opinions. The rector of the Catholic University wrote an article in defense of the university. The "crisis of the Catholic University," as it came to be known, occupied space in Brazilian newspapers all over the country, and even influential governmental institutions expressed their opinion. Antonio Paim (1979) compiled the entire debate in the book *Academic Freedom and Totalitarian Option*. My wife resigned her position. I had tenure and had been associated with the university for 27 years, as a student and a faculty member. It was a very difficult situation. After working in a hostile environment during the months that followed the crisis, I decided to submit my resignation and left the university.

The universities in Brazil at that time were dominated by a leftist ideology. Although I had always refrained from involving myself in public political debates, the position I took in several newspaper articles and letter to the editor against the censorship of my wife's reading list and against the restrictive atmosphere prevailing at the Catholic University led to my inclusion on the radical left's list of personae non gratae. My training in the United States, as well as my adherence to the American model of social psychology, also contributed to my rejection by this group. Because this ideology was overwhelmingly predominant in most Brazilian universities, it is easy to imagine that I had great difficulty finding a new position. I distinctly remember three occasions in which my name was vetoed for the position I was seeking exclusively because of ideological fanaticism. The most eloquent manifestation of such fanaticism and ideological persecution against me happened when I tried to participate in a public contest for full professor of Fluminense Federal University, located just 45 minutes from Rio de Janeiro. When there is an opening at the full professor level of a Federal University in Brazil, a public contest has to be called to fill the vacancy. The candidates must present an original thesis and go through an oral examination and a written examination on their field of specialty and have their vitae evaluated. To be a candidate, one must either be an associate professor Level 4 at a Brazilian Federal University or be recognized by the examination committee as having "notorious knowledge" in one's field. Because by that time I was an APA fellow (Division 8), had published three books and many articles in social psychology in national and international refereed journals, and had been president of three scientific associations of psychology, one of them being the Latin American Association of Social Psychology, I thought I had the necessary credentials to request recognition of notorious knowledge in social psychology. The heavily politicized committee in charge of the contest rejected me. But the funniest part of this episode was that this same committee prepared a reading list to help the candidates to prepare for the contest, and my textbook in social psychology was among the recommended books.

As soon as I left the Catholic University, I was hired by a branch of the Ministry of Education that concerned itself with decreasing illiteracy in Brazil. They had contracted a firm to do research for them, and my role was to oversee this research project and report to them any inadequacies I might find. I was not, of course, pleased with leaving a university career that until very recently had been going so well. Although I kept a part-time appointment at the Getúlio Vargas Foundation, which had a graduate program in psychology, this was far from being a full professor associated with one of the large universities in Rio. The friendly spirit once more decided to help me. I received an offer from the Federal University of Rio Grande do Sul, located in the southernmost state of Brazil, at the frontier with Uruguay and Argentina. The Department of Education wanted to enhance its doctoral program, whose faculty consisted mainly of assistant professors who had recently attained a Ph.D. degree. They needed a senior member on the faculty, and they were interested primarily in academic productivity. They knew that I did not want to leave the city of Rio de Janeiro, so they made me an offer I could not refuse. Full salary, equivalent to full professor, in exchange for one week of work per month! I could not be given tenure, and my contract had to be renewed every year, for a maximum of 4 years. I accepted the offer. During the 4 years I stayed at that university, I published one book, published 16 papers in refereed journals, and gave nine papers at scientific meetings. My temporary job with the Ministry of Education ended after one year, and I had lots of time during my 3 weeks off per month to be productive. At the end of 4 years, in 1983, the Federal University of Rio Grande do Sul informed me that I had to become a full-time professor, because the year-to-year contract could not be extended any longer. I did not want to leave Rio de Janeiro, where my family, which now included my wife and six children, lived in a comfortable house. I was offered a job at a private university called Gama Filho University, which was not among the prominent universities. I had to settle for it, for the elite universities were still censoring my name because of the episode that led to my departure from the Catholic University. I was asked to rebuild a graduate program in psychology at the Gama Filho University. The program was about to be eliminated, and my hiring was the last effort to make it survive. With great effort on my part and decisive cooperation from the administration, the graduate program was back in good standing after a few years. In 1986 a public contest for full professor at the Federal University of Rio de Janeiro was announced. This time, the committee in charge of the contest recognized that I had "notorious knowledge" in social psychology, and I was able to take part in the public contest for the position of full professor. I won it, and after winning a public contest, the law guarantees the position to the winner. I did not have any problems at the Federal University. I was well received by my peers, but after all this turmoil, my enthusiasm for my work in Brazil was again waning.

WHAT ABOUT MY RESEARCH DURING
THESE TROUBLED YEARS?

One constant criticism I used to receive from students and peers was that my book, as well as my classes, relied too much on data obtained in a different culture. Some common questions were these: Are the findings obtained abroad, mainly with American college students, valid for Brazilians? Can social psychological knowledge be generalized to places culturally different? They were not convinced by the argument that the purpose of experiments is to test hypotheses derived from theories and that mundane realism is not of primary concern. They wanted evidence that hypotheses confirmed abroad had applicability to the Brazilian reality.

In an attempt to respond to these criticisms, I initiated a broad program of replications. The results of this program were reported in my presidential address to the Interamerican Society of Psychology in 1981 and expanded in my thesis for the public contest for the position of full professor at the Federal University of Rio de Janeiro in 1986. In 1982 a slightly modified version of my presidential address was published in the *Interamerican Journal of Psychology* under the title "Replication: A Neglected Type of Research in Social Psychology" (Rodrigues, 1982). Among the studies replicated in this program of research were Weiner and Kukla's (1970) work on causal attribution and evaluation of achievement and Weiner, Russel, and Lerman's (1979) research on attribution and affective intensity. Why did I pick these studies to replicate? Again Heider's influence on my work revealed itself. My interest for balance theory was waning after the proposal of my theoretical models and the conditions under which each of them should have the highest predictive value. I read the interview conducted with Fritz Heider by the editors of *New Directions in Attribution Research*, edited by Harvey, Ickes, and Kidd (1976), in which he was asked by the editors, "This is in the area of intersection between your balance and attribution conceptions—is that right?" Heider responded, "Yes, the two are very close together; I can hardly separate them. Because attribution, after all, is making a connection or a relation between some event and a source—a positive relation. And balance is concerned with the fitting or nonfitting of relations" (p. 16).

Therefore, according to Heider, balance and attribution were very much related. Attribution was becoming more and more influential in social psychology, and a friend of mine from UCLA, Bernard Weiner, was becoming one of the leading scholars in this field, from both a theoretical standpoint and an empirical standpoint. I decided then to replicate some of his studies. The results were by and large the same, with a few minor differences that I attributed to cultural idiosyncrasies. I enjoyed carrying out this program of research. I was surprised to verify the transhistorical and transcultural validity of several important social psychological findings, such as the relationship of causal ascription, achievement judgments, and intensity of experienced emotions referred to previously, and also the effects of a unanimous majority on conformity showed by Asch (1952), the preference for balanced over imbalanced triads, the spreading apart between the attraction of chosen and rejected alternatives after a decision as predicted by dissonance theory, Deutsch's hypothesis that equity is the preferable value basis of distributive justice when economic productivity was the goal of the interpersonal relation, Jones and Nisbett's actor–observer hypothesis, the validity of Rotter's locus of control construct, and so on. In several of these replications, a few nuances could be detected that indicated some idiosyncratic tendencies, which could be reasonably explained by cultural characteristics of the samples studied. But by and large the findings were replicated, and I was encouraged to believe that it is not futile to look for universals of social behavior that are transhistorical and transcultural.

After I entered the Federal University of Rio de Janeiro in 1987, most of my time was spent teaching at this university and doing administrative work at Gama Filho University, trying to revive its graduate program. My rate of publication decreased drastically. From 1989 to 1993 I had only four papers, limiting most of my productivity to conferences delivered primarily in meetings sponsored by Brazilian organizations. It seemed to me that the effects of the difficult times since I left the Catholic University were manifesting themselves rather clearly, in the sense that my motivation to continue to carry out the mission of a university professor was decreasing to a degree that began to worry me greatly. In 1991 I would complete 35 years of academic work, the number of working years established by law for a man to retire in Brazil, and I started giving serious consideration to asking for my retirement that year.

Again the friendly spirit came to my rescue. In an attempt to renew and recharge my interest for research, I arranged with the universities where I was working and with two of my UCLA friends, Bert Raven and Bernie Weiner, to spend a semester at UCLA, from January 1991 to June 1991. This event was to have an unexpected influence on my future.

THE WORK WITH BERT RAVEN AND BERNIE WEINER, AND A FORTUITOUS REENCOUNTER WITH BOB LEVINE

In the past I had done some research with Bert Raven, for whom I worked as research assistant during my years at UCLA. We published a couple of papers on power in families and power in schools, and I later did some psychometric analysis on his Interpersonal Power Inventory. Therefore, I welcomed spending some time with him again. My association with Bernie Weiner was more recent, for Bernie joined UCLA a semester before I left. My replications of his studies brought us together, and interacting closely with him was another incentive to spend some time at UCLA. I was elated when all the arrangements for my six-month visit were completed, for my enthusiasm was at an all-time low in Brazil.

As anticipated, I had a great time at UCLA. I attended Bernie's weekly seminars with graduate students and visiting scholars, I sat in Bert's graduate seminar, and I had numerous opportunities to talk about research ideas, which motivated me to get back to the laboratory. One day Bert asked me, "Why don't you try bringing together Bernie's work on attribution and my own work on social power?" That question sparked a strong desire to achieve just that. The result was 12 years of research on attribution and compliant behavior. The essence of my research was to verify how compliant behavior involving a transgression and caused by each one of the six power bases in Raven's taxonomy (reward, coercion, legitimacy, expertise, reference, and information) was perceived in terms of two causal dimensions (internality and controllability); I also hoped to predict—on the basis of Bernie's attributional theory of motivation and emotion and on his theory of social conduct—the affective and behavioral consequences derived from the causal attribution ascribed to the induced compliant behavior. I discussed my idea while at UCLA with both Bert and Bernie, and when I returned to Brazil I continued to be excited about the research project I had in mind. I did some preliminary testing in Brazil, but the project really began when, once more, I came to the United States, now as a professor at California State University, Fresno! How did that happen? Well, the friendly spirit did it again.

While at UCLA, I received a letter that had been sent to Brazil. My secretary at the Gama Filho University forwarded it to me in Los Angeles. The letter was from Bob Levine, then chair of the Department of Psychology of Fresno State, in which he reintroduced himself to me (we had briefly met in Rio, back in 1976, while Bob was spending a sabbatical year at Fluminense Federal University just outside of Rio [the same one that denied me recognition of notorious knowledge]) and said that he would like to interview me about social psychology in Brazil. He proposed different ways of accomplishing that, such as sending me the interview by mail, or doing it by phone, or asking me to record my answers and send back the tape. I immediately grabbed the phone and called him in Fresno. We agreed to meet personally, in Fresno, right after the Western Psychological Association meeting in San Francisco, which I planned to attend. It was a great pleasure to reestablish direct contact with Bob. It was simply delightful to see him again and be introduced to his lovely wife, Trudi. They graciously took me to the Daily Planet, in the Tower District, for dinner. At dinner we set a time for the interview that he and Alex Gonzalez, a social psychologist who was then the provost at Fresno State, would conduct with me the next day at the university. I was looking forward to it. The interview went fine, and when it was over, I asked both Bob and Alex if they saw any possibility for me to apply for a position at Fresno State. Recall that I was very frustrated and bored with my current academic life in Brazil and was thinking seriously about retiring in 1992, when I completed 36 years of service. I asked the question, expecting that they would politely say that the chances were minimum or even nonexistent. To my surprise, both said that this was definitely a possibility and that I should think about my situation seriously. If I came to the conclusion that the best thing to do would be to retire in Brazil and move to Fresno, I should apply for a position at Fresno State.

It is hard for me to describe the emotions I experienced after that encounter. I kept in contact with Bob from then on, finished my time at UCLA, and went back to Brazil with high hopes of finally attaining the goal I had set for myself back in 1968 when I applied to Claremont Graduate School: to become a university professor in the United States. My six children were grown up now, and I could travel to Brazil twice a year to be with them, and they could come here to visit me (and this was exactly what has been happening since I came to Fresno in 1993). I did everything Bob advised me to do, and my résumé was sent to the Department of Psychology of Fresno State. Late in 1992 I received from Stan Ziegler, associate dean of the then School of Natural Sciences, an offer for a tenure-track position of full professor in the Department of Psychology. I was surprised and thrilled at the same time. The friendly spirit had rescued me once again from disaster. This whole new perspective presented to me was overwhelming at that moment. I was then 59 years old and would begin my new career in the fall of 1993, when I was about to become 60. I was in good health and decided to take on the challenge, although I could not hide a fair amount of apprehension about embarking on this adventure, which involved a rather drastic change and posed many challenges so late in my life.

After months fighting the Immigration and Naturalization Service's bureaucracy to obtain legal status to work in the United States, I received a document from one of my daughters, born in the United States and carrying dual citizenship, that finally cleared the way for me to secure a green card and settle the legal situation. All systems were go for the beginning of a new phase of my career, just when I thought that I was inevitably reaching its sunset.

LIFE AT FRESNO STATE

At Fresno State I found the most hospitable environment possible. My colleagues were very friendly and so were the staff and those in high administrative positions with whom I had to interact from time to time. I felt immediately at home. Bob Levine was the department chair, and he helped me in every way he could. A concrete indication of the support I received from my department and from the higher administration was that at the end of my third year, I was given tenure and unanimously elected department chair, a position I held from 1996 to 2003, after being reelected, again unanimously, in 2000.

This friendly and stimulating environment allowed me to carry out the research project conceived at UCLA during my contact with Bert Raven and Bernie Weiner on attribution and power. For more than ten years I conducted a series of experiments, and the findings were published in five journal articles and in eight professional meetings in the United States and abroad. The execution of this research project brought me much joy, and I had the good fortune of attracting several very good students who helped me in this effort. At the end of it, I wrote an unpublished (and perhaps unpublishable) 70-page paper summarizing the entire research. My experiments involved almost 2,000 participants from three countries. The findings were very stable, and clearly showed, among other things, the asymmetrical consequences of compliant behavior caused by reward and coercion from an attributional perspective.

In addition to finding the proper environment to carry out research, the support of Provost Alex Gonzalez, Dean K. P. Wong, and my colleagues and staff in the department allowed me to idealize and carry out a significant event in

1997. When I began my term as department chair, I felt the need to suggest something that would go beyond the routine administrative duties that the job requires. Experimental social psychology was around 100 years old (if we accept Triplett's experiment on social facilitation as its birth), so I proposed, and the faculty approved, the organization of a meeting in which leading figures in the field would present their reflections on these 100 years of experimental social psychology. My acquaintance during the 1960s and the 1970s with famous social psychologists now paid very high dividends. I met several friends at the 7th International Conference on Kurt Lewin, which was held in Los Angeles, in the first week of September 1996. There I approached Hal Kelley, Bert Raven, Al Pepitone, Hal Gerard, and a few others and mentioned my idea to them. Some were very favorable to it, some a little less enthusiastic, and a few not interested at all. I came back to Fresno very encouraged, though. Enough top social psychologists had shown genuine interest in participating in the project and were very supportive of my idea. I then started searching for funding. Once funds were obtained with pledges from the department, the dean, the provost, and the president, I started making official invitations. In a very short time I had secured the endorsement of Len Berkowitz, Mort Deutsch, Hal Gerard, Hal Kelley, Al Pepitone, Bert Raven, and Bob Zajonc. With the help of my colleague Bob Levine, Elliott Aronson and Phil Zimbardo were added to the list. Later we invited Stanley Schachter, who accepted the invitation but could not attend the conference for health reasons. We had formed a dream team of social psychologists. The conference took place at Tenaya Lodge, at the south entrance of Yosemite National Park, on March 15–17, 1997. It turned out to be a memorable event, and a book with the contributions of the participants was later edited by Bob Levine and me and published in 1999 by Basic Books, under the title *Reflections on 100 Years of Experimental Social Psychology*.

After the Yosemite conference project, I kept the chair for several more years, during which I completed my research on attribution and compliant behavior. I left my administrative position in 2003 and once more started thinking about retirement. This time, however, I considered retirement not out of frustration and disappointment, as in the early 1990s, but rather out of the conviction that it was time for me to be replaced by someone with fewer wrinkles, darker hair, and healthier joints. If it were not for the mixed connotation that the expression "mission accomplished" acquired after the Iraq War, I would use it to describe how I felt at the moment. It seems, however, that the friendly spirit had another surprise in store for me. With the support of Provost Jeri Echeverria and Dean K. P. Wong, the possibility of a second Yosemite Conference in Social Psychology emerged, and there I was embarking on one final enterprise before leaving the field. The topic of this new project, career journeys in social psychology, was too tempting to let go by. As the end of my journey was clearly approaching, nothing seemed more fitting than to reflect on it and, I hoped, by making it public, to inspire students by acquainting them with the ups and downs of my professional life. This temptation was irresistible, and that is why I am writing this chapter, associated with people whose contributions to the field and accomplishments in their careers far surpass my own.

What a difference from the early 1990s! I enjoy now a wonderful feeling of accomplishment and great pride and joy at being part of a psychology department in full growth. It has been very gratifying to witness the development of our department. Many excellent new faculty have joined us during the years; they are well trained, full of enthusiasm, and already making significant contributions in their teaching and in their research. The department is well balanced, with new and experienced faculty, and we have recently moved into a new building, with excellent laboratory facilities. There is an atmosphere of excitement and a firm belief in continuous and steady growth.

These years at Fresno State will never be forgotten. They will be securely kept in my inner museum of fond memories. During these years I have been rejuvenated and energized by the atmosphere that I found at this university, and a career that was about to end in the early 1990s after a series of disappointments in Brazil was injected with new blood, which allowed me to accomplish all that I have described and has brought me so much pride and joy.

ASSESSING THE PAST TO ENLIGHTEN THE FUTURE

When I look back over 50 years of a professional career, I find accomplishments that bring me great joy, as well as failures that sadden me. Among the first, I single out the impact of my book *Psicologia Social* [*Social Psychology*], published in 1972 and, more than 30 years later, still widely read, primarily in Brazil and Mexico but also elsewhere in Latin America, Portugal, and Spain. Many printings and several editions have been made, and I am currently working, with my former students and now colleagues Eveline Maria L. Assmar and Bernardo Jablonski, on a new edition. To know that hundreds of thousands of students and professionals have read it is indeed a source of much satisfaction, as is the realization that a great number of instructors have endorsed the book. Because the book is heavily experimental in its approach, I was not expecting it to have such an impact in Latin America, where the predominant position in social psychology has clear sociological and political overtones. The success of my book in such an environment, particularly in Brazil, remains, to date, an unsolved mystery for me. Another fact that comforts me a great deal is that I have been able to merit the trust of my peers. I was elected department chair in Brazil and in the United States; I was elected president of the Brazilian Association of Applied Psychology, of the Latin American Association for Social Psychology, and of the Interamerican Society of Psychology. Also gratifying to me is to have been recognized by the APA, through my election as fellow of its Division 8. A source of utmost satisfaction is to have been instrumental in bringing together a group of remarkable social psychologists to the Yosemite Conferences on Social Psychology of 1997 and 2006. And last, but not least, is that I was welcomed to the Department of Psychology of California State University, Fresno.

But, of course, not everything in my career was gratifying. I regret to have failed in my attempt to change the approach of social psychology in Brazil. My efforts to form a significant group of social psychologists who adhered to contemporary scientific social psychology have been in vain. As I see the panorama of Brazilian social psychology today, I wonder how my book is still being used. A dominant theme in Brazil is social representations; the preferred method of inquiry is content analysis of interview material; the emphasis is on solutions to social problems without the necessary scientific findings to guide specific interventions; and political philosophy, not science, is the driving force that propels the discipline. I fought against this state of affairs and did not succeed. In addition, I was unable to attract students to my view of social psychology or to my research interests. There were, of course, exceptions, but by and large my students did not get excited by my choice of research topics. Only a handful accompanied me in my interest in balance theory. As far as accepting, adhering to, and promoting my approach to social psychology, Eveline Maria L. Assmar and Bernardo Jablonski, who coauthored with me the past two editions of *Social Psychology,* and three other students, José Augusto Dela Coleta, Marilia Ferreira Dela Coleta, Cilio R. Ziviani, and a few others with whom I have, it is unfortunate to say, lost contact, are the only ones to whom I was able to transmit my view of social psychology. It is true that many others who have not chosen social psychology have shown appreciation for my efforts to guide them in the study of scientific psychology, but my attempt to touch a significant number of students capable of changing the picture of social psychology in Brazil clearly failed. Although I thought at the time I was doing the right thing by trying to make students accept the vision of social psychology I had adopted during my training at UCLA, in hindsight I recognize that the tactics I used were inappropriate. I should have been more mindful of cultural differences and proceeded with more cultural sensitivity. But it is comforting to realize that I have more reasons to rejoice than to be sorry about these eventful 50 years.

As I approach the end of my career, what can I tell current and future generations of students to help them in their own paths? My experiences have led me to suggest the following:

1. *Embrace a profession for which you have passion.* As I said at the outset, I was studying law but not enjoying it. Notwithstanding the odds against pursuing a profession in psychology at that time in my country, I overcame numerous obstacles and ended up embracing the profession I had a passion for. Had I renounced my vocation and continued to practice law, it is likely that I would be better off financially today, but it is certain that I would not be as fulfilled as I feel at the end of my career. I would not trade the latter for the former.

2. *Dare to do things that may seem impossible.* I soon realized that graduate training in the United States was fundamental to attaining my professional goals. The big problem was that my English was extremely limited. I can't forget the first day I went to the cafeteria at the American University and asked for a *coke* and was given *coffee* instead. After three weeks of class in one of my courses at KU, I called a classmate who seemed to me to be tolerant and understanding and asked her if there were any assignments. To my surprise and disappointment, there were several already and I was totally unaware of them. But I did not give in. Who would have predicted

that at the end of my career, I would find myself teaching in English in an American university and, more surprising still, being fairly well understood by the students? As Theodore Roosevelt once said, "Far better it is to dare mighty things, to win glorious triumphs, even though checkered by failure, than to live in that great twilight which knows neither victory nor defeat."

3. *Don't be discouraged by setbacks.* When I faced the cold response to my dissertation and to my vision of social psychology upon returning to Brazil after obtaining my Ph.D., I was profoundly disappointed, frustrated, and let down. I experienced similar feelings after resigning my position at the Catholic University, an institution I had been closely associated with for 27 years. On both occasions I bounced back despite all odds because of my determination to overcome adversity.

4. *Stand firmly for what you believe.* I've always deeply cherished academic freedom. When confronted with the curtailment of my wife's intellectual freedom by her department chair and of my own freedom of investigation at the Catholic University of Rio de Janeiro in the late 1970s, I took a firm standing against it, without regard for the costs this attitude could bring to my position at the university. In the long run, the rewards of having stood by my values offset any temporary costs associated with the position I took.

5. *Keep your contacts with mentors and top-notch people in your field.* I always kept alive my acquaintance with Heider, with my UCLA friends, and with the numerous prominent figures I met during my career. I wrote them, I visited them, and I invited them to spend time at the universities where I worked and to attend psychological meetings in Brazil and in Latin America. I looked them up at professional meetings. Do not distance yourselves from your mentors and the significant personalities you meet in graduate school and in your professional life. They will be of help throughout your career.

6. *Seize the opportunities and be optimistic.* Be ready to seize the opportunities that life offers. I was rather depressed and pessimistic regarding the future of my career in the late 1980s. Then the opportunity to spend a semester at UCLA unexpectedly presented itself. I had the good sense and enough optimism left in me to seize this opportunity, which, as I've described, turned my career around. Two years after my 6-month stay at UCLA, I left Brazil, moved to the United States, joined Fresno State, started a new research program, and went from a predominantly pessimistic state to an optimistic one.

7. *Enjoy life as much as you can, because life is very short.* When I wrote this chapter, it struck me how short our lives are, even when we get to be 70 or 80 years old. Some of the events I recaptured here, although they took place 5 or more decades ago, are so vivid in my memory that it is hard to believe that so many years have gone by since they happened. Yes, life goes very fast, and we should enjoy to the fullest the joyful moments it gives us.

Now I have come full cycle. My interamerican journey in social psychology is about to reach the finish line. Soon after this project is over, I will retire and return to Brazil, not to work in any university but to enjoy my children and grandchildren and, very likely, come back every now and then to the United States, a country that is like a second country to me; a country in which I spent one third of my academic life; a country where my oldest daughter, her husband, and their three children live; a country where I made precious friendships that will last forever.

As I conclude these reflections, I recall again the great Fritz Heider. Paraphrasing him, I thank the friendly spirit who has accompanied me in my professional journey and has arranged the whole sequence of events in which the powers of fortune were so unbelievably kind to me.

AUTHOR'S NOTE

I want to express my deep gratitude and indebtedness to Anna Maria and to our children Maria Guadalupe, Maria da Gloria, Anna Cristina, Joao Carlos, Aroldo Luis, and Anna Luiza for their help, support, and motivation in several phases of my career.

REFERENCES

Asch, S. (1952). *Social psychology*. New York: Prentice-Hall.

Deutsch, M., & Hornstein, H. (1975). *Applying social psychology*. New York: Erlbaum.

Harvey, J. H., Ickes, W., & Kidd, R. (1976). *New directions in attribution research* (Vol. 1). New York: Lawrence Erlbaum.

Heider, F. (1983). *The life of a psychologist*. Lawrence: University Press of Kansas.

Newcomb, T. M. (1968). Interpersonal balance. In R. P. Abelson, E. Aronson, W. McGuire, T. M. Newcomb, M. Rosenberg, & P. Tannenbaum (Eds.), *Theories of cognitive consistency: A sourcebook*. Chicago: Rand McNally.

Paim, A. (1979). *Liberdade acadêmica e opção totalitária* [Academic freedom and totalitarian option]. Rio de Janeiro: Ed. Artenova.

Reyes, H., & Varela, J. A. (1980). Conditions required for a technology of the social sciences. In R. Kidd & M. Sachs (Eds.), *Advances in applied social psychology*. Hillsdale, NJ: Lawrence Erlbaum.

Rodrigues, A. (1965). On the differential effects of some parameters of balance. *Journal of Psychology, 61*, 241–250.

Rodrigues, A. (1967). The effects of balance, positivity and agreement in triadic interpersonal relations. *Journal of Personality and Social Psychology, 5*, 472–476.

Rodrigues, A. (1968). The biasing effect of agreement in balanced and imbalanced triads. *Journal of Personality, 36*, 139–153.

Rodrigues, A. (1982). Replication: A neglected type of research in social psychology. *Interamerican Journal of Psychology, 16*, 91–110.

Rodrigues, A., & Dela Coleta, J. A. (1983). On the prediction of preference for triadic interpersonal relations. *Journal of Social Psychology, 121*, 73–80.

Rodrigues, A., & Iwawaki, S. (1986). Testing the validity of different models of interpersonal balance. *Psychologia, XXIX*(3), 123–131.

Rodrigues, A., & Levine, R. V. (1999). *Reflections on 100 years of experimental social psychology*. New York: Basic Books.

Rodrigues, A., & Newcomb, T. M. (1980). The balance principle: Its current status and its integrative function in social psychology. *Interamerican Journal of Psychology, 14*, 85–136.

Varela, J. A. (1971). *Psychological solutions to social problems*. New York: Academic Press.

Weiner, B., & Kukla, A. (1970). An attributional analysis of achievement motivation. *Journal of Personality and Social Psychology, 15*, 1–20.

Weiner, B., Russell, D., & Lerman, D. (1979). The cognition-emotion process in achievement-related contexts. *Journal of Personality and Social Psychology, 37*, 1211–1220.

Introduction, Methods, Results, Discussion
The Story of a Career

ROBERT ROSENTHAL

Department of Psychology, University of California, Riverside

T o give an overview of what lies ahead, I'll begin with a chronology of events, pointing out pieces of good news and bad news, and even worse news, along the way. There will be dates, vignettes, and anecdotes that I am now allowed to tell since entering my anecdotage.

In addition to my chronology, I'll give a sampling of a few of my many teachers, coaches, and mentors, and then I'll report on how a career is like a journal article and that our own personal journal article depends on our career's coauthors, reviewers, and editors. There will also be some details revealing just how much careers can depend on really good luck.

Some of you will be familiar with the well-known World War I flying ace and novelist named Snoopy, close friend of Charlie Brown. From Snoopy I learned that one could rarely do better than to start a story with "It Was a Dark and Stormy Night."

GETTING STARTED (MARCH 2, 1933)

First, the good news, at least for me: I was born that day. The bad news was that it was a terrible time for a German Jewish mother to be having a baby in Nazi Germany. More good news was that my uncle, my mom's brother-in-law, had the insight to know that this was a bad time; the bad news was that he had this insight while driving my mother to the hospital where I was about to be born.

Our family lived in the small cathedral town of Limburg, Germany, but the best place to have a baby delivered was the obstetrics department of the nearby University of Giessen.

Forty-seven years later I returned to the University of Giessen (not in obstetrics) as a short-term visiting professor at the university of my birth, at the invitation of one of its professors, Klaus Scherer, a marvelous former student of mine. Twenty-four years after that, I returned again, to be in grateful receipt of an honorary doctorate from the university of my birth.

LEAVING GERMANY (1939)

We lived in Limburg until 1938, when we left for Cologne and the greater anonymity of a large city. It had become too dangerous for Jews to live where everyone knew who the Jews were and where they lived. And, oh, everyone *did* know, as I learned in a chilling experience. Some 50 years after Hitler came to power, my wife, MaryLu, and I visited the village where my mother had grown up around the turn of the 20th century and during World War I. We asked a railroad worker at the outskirts of the village for directions to my mother's old house. We showed him a photo of the house, and he said, "Ach! Das Judenhaus!"

Oh! The Jew house! No Jews had lived in that village for half a century. Yes, everyone knew where the Jews lived, and some never forgot.

In 1939 we left Germany. We had wanted to come to the United States, but there was a quota and our quota number was too high. Our parents knew we had to get out now or we wouldn't get out at all. We were allowed to go to Southern Africa, and we left Germany by way of Hamburg on the German ship *Watussi*, bound eventually for Salisbury, Southern Rhodesia (now Harari, Zimbabwe). The good news was that it was the last ship out, and we were on it. The ambivalent news was that the *Watussi* was turned into a German troop ship, and, I understand, it was torpedoed and sunk by the Allies on its next voyage.

SOUTHERN RHODESIA (1939–1940)

I started school in Southern Rhodesia. The good news was that I learned to speak English with a British accent (rather a fortunate turn of events, actually).

The bad news was that the British kids beat me up because I was German. But I had a creative first-grade teacher, more good news, who let me out of school 5 minutes early so I'd get a head start on the kids who were going to chase me—an early version of an individualized Head Start program.

WELCOME TO AMERICA (AUTUMN 1940)

In 1940 we were allowed to enter the United States. We left Africa on an Egyptian ship *El Nil*. That ship also became a troop ship shortly thereafter, but for the good guys. One of the troops sailing on the *El Nil* in the very early 1940s was my old friend and colleague, Pat Patullo, an outstanding Harvard administrator and teacher. It took Pat and me 50 years to discover our common travels on the *El Nil*.

I remember our first sight of the New World. No, it was not the Statue of Liberty. It was the Jersey coast of the Hudson River, and the welcoming blinking neon lights said,

Chiclets here, Chiclets there;
Chiclets, Chiclets everywhere.

It was a comfort to know we'd made it to safety and to a land not only of milk and honey but of chewing gum everywhere as well!

New York: PS 89, Queens (1940–1947)

It was at PS 89, Queens, that I first learned about interpersonal expectations—my mom's. I'd get a report card with eight As and an A–. The next day my mom was in the principal's office wondering where she'd failed and what she could do to help me bring up my grades. The wonder of it was that the principal, Selma Week (an educator with whom I corresponded until her death many years later), agreed with my mother. So, of course, I had to get those grades up.

Newtown High School (1947–1949)

More on parental expectations. This time they were my dad's. I was playing a lot of sandlot football then, and my dad, assuming I would be great at it, cautioned me about the drawbacks to a career as a professional football player.

First forays into scientific research. I had read J. B. Rhine's book *New Frontiers of the Mind,* which described Rhine's rigorous experiments in parapsychology. In May 1949, when I was 16, I informed Professor Rhine of Duke University of the following:

> I am conducting experiments similar to yours.

I asked him for a set of Zener cards. Professor Rhine rewarded this presumptuous young whippersnapper by sending a charming, cordial, informative, and inspiring letter that I still have, nearly 60 years later. Happily, about 10 years after his letter, I was able to thank Professor Rhine in person.

Although I have never done serious research on parapsychology, I was asked to review conflicting meta-analyses conducted by pro- and antiparapsychology investigators. I was somewhat surprised to learn that the proparapsychological protagonists did better, less biased, meta-analytic work than did the antis.

I learned a lot about the good news–bad news aspects of scientific attitudes of open-mindedness while serving as a methodological consultant to various groups investigating parapsychological phenomena and methodologies. The good news came in seeing the open-mindedness of Professor William Cochran, the brilliant Harvard statistician, when he and I were both consulting on a large parapsychology research project (he on statistics, and I on experimenter effects). The bad news came in seeing the closed-mindedness of a nationally organized group that didn't like my conclusion that the average quality of serious parapsychological research was well above the average quality of behavioral research in general. Indeed, that group asked me to suppress that conclusion and keep it out of print. That effort to suppress did not work, of course.

Dorsey High School, Los Angeles (1949–1950)

Still more on interpersonal expectations. The family had moved from New York to Los Angeles for my last year of high school. During that year I applied to UCLA's Naval Reserve Officers Training Corps. On graduation I would serve 2 or 3 years

as a beginning naval officer. When I discussed the possibility with my dad, he nodded approvingly and observed that being an *admiral* was an important contribution to the country and I should consider it seriously.

UCLA (AB, 1953; Ph.D., 1956)

Because MaryLu and I had a growing family, I hurried through my undergraduate
and graduate programs, both of which I enjoyed a great deal. As a graduate student
I loved the clinical work despite the ill omen offered me on my first day on the job
as a clinical intern at the Brentwood VA Neuropsychiatric Hospital near UCLA.
Nattily attired in a new blue suit, I crossed the parking lot and heard a voice yelling
from an upstairs ward:

GET THE GUY IN THE BLUE SUIT!

My clinical career improved a good bit after that inauspicious beginning. As a
footnote here, let me add that MaryLu and I met in the 1940s while we were both
"in the theater on Broadway." The theater was the Rialto Theater on Broadway in
downtown Los Angeles. MaryLu was the cashier, and I was the doorman.

University of North Dakota (1957–1962)

My first real academic job offer was from the University of North Dakota. MaryLu
and I went to Grand Forks, North Dakota, to be interviewed. We had a wonderful
3-day visit at the university. MaryLu and I were having a final talk with the Chair,
Hermann Buegel. Years later I learned that when the conversation turned to contract and salary, MaryLu went into a mild form of shock—it appeared we might
actually leave Los Angeles and move to Grand Forks, North Dakota! We did, and
she loved it there! But she never forgot she was an adoptive Californian and always
had it in mind that we might well return to California—which we finally did, only
42 years later, in 1999!

High Adventure on North Dakota Highways

One of my jobs at the University of North Dakota was to organize and direct the
new clinical Ph.D. program. We managed to get a training grant that brought in
five all-star lecturers. They were Harold Kelley from UCLA, Sol Garfield from
Nebraska, William Schofield from Minnesota, Harold Pepinsky from Ohio State,
and O. Hobart Mowrer from Illinois. Their visits gave us a great morale boost
and gave me a chance to save O. Hobart Mowrer's life along with the lives of our
department chair, Hermann Buegel, and my own. We were driving O. Hobart
some 80 miles down to Fargo to catch a train. Hermann was going to drive; Betty,
Hermann's wife, asked me to keep an eye on Hermann and keep him awake—he
tended to nod off at the wheel. "But do it discreetly," she said. I did—I sat in the
back of the car, but I was poised to pounce like a vulture. Hermann drove, and O.
Hobart chatted with us. Sure enough, Hermann fell asleep at the wheel, and I had

to pounce, grabbing the wheel to keep us on the road. Hermann did let me drive the rest of the way to North Dakota's big city: Fargo.

The Shneidman Letter (p = .000011)

Early in my North Dakota career I got what turned out to be a very spooky letter from my very first VA clinical supervisor, Ed Shneidman, the brilliant cofounder of the field of clinical suicidology. He invited me to accept a clinical research position with his new Suicide Prevention Center. In that letter he recognized it would be a tough choice for me—a clinician/research career back in good old Los Angeles versus an academic career that might take us anywhere. His letter referred to the choice—the clinical track versus a hypothesized career from North Dakota to Ohio State to Harvard. That letter still sends chills up my spine. Two years later I was at Ohio State as a visiting associate professor, and a year after that I was invited to accept a nonladder appointment at Harvard. I figured the odds of Ed's predicting the correct sequence of my next two jobs was about 1 in 2.25 million. Considering only the top 20% of all colleges and universities, the odds go to about 1 in 90,000. Ah, well, maybe J. B. Rhine, the parapsychologist, was right!

The Good News–Bad News Lunch

Thinking about the year we spent at Ohio State reminded me of one of the most instructive days of my career. It was in the fall of 1960, and Julian Rotter, Al Scodel, Shep Liverant, and I were going to the Faculty Club for lunch, as we often did. On the way to the elevator, we stopped to pick up our mail, and we began opening it as we waited for the elevator. What I learned that day is that no matter how bleak fortunes appear to be, they can get worse, and no matter how bleak, they can also get better. I also learned about the unreliability of judgments of the quality of scientific work. I had two letters that day, one from the leading social psychological journal of the time, the other from the American Association for the Advancement of Science. The first of these letters rejected for publication a paper written with Kermit Fode, a graduate student working with me. The second letter notified me that this same rejected paper, "Three Experiments in Experimenter Bias," had been awarded the 1960 AAAS sociopsychology prize for the best social science research of the year. Go figure!

(As a footnote to the experience of getting those letters: I've since discovered that you can tell the age of psychologists by how they feel about getting mail. Young psychologists [as I was back then] love it—it brings them into contact with the rest of the scientific world. Old-timers [as I am right now] dread it—they know that the primary purpose of mail is to create work for the recipient.)

No Class, No Breeding

We had a final year (1961–1962) at North Dakota after our year at Ohio State. That year marked my coming-of-age as a completely uncouth North Dakota backwoodsman, totally lacking in class and good breeding. I'd heard of a high-level (by invitation only, I learned later) conference on communication, including nonverbal communication, to be held at the University of Indiana in May 1962. I wrote to the organizer, the famous semiotician Tom Sebeok, and asked whether I could attend the conference. He kindly overlooked my lack of couth and let me come. That's where I met Margaret Mead, Ray Birdwhistell, Erving Goffman, Edward Hall, Weston LaBarre, George Mahl, and other stars of that ilk! It showed that lacking couth can be quite rewarding.

Harvard (1962–1999)

There were 36 great years spent at Harvard, and nothing about it drove us away—but it wasn't in California. Actually, there was also this major power struggle with my good friend and squash partner, Jerry Kagan. It was over the chairmanship. It was fortunate for me that Jerry lost that struggle, and so he had to be chairman of the department—first. They got me later.

University of California, Riverside (1999–Into the New Millennium)

Since January 1999 we've been back in California, and I've been greatly enjoying my excellent new colleagues and students.

TEACHERS, COACHES, AND MENTORS: A SAMPLE

That concludes my chronology and brings us to a very quick look at just a sampling of my teachers, coaches, and mentors. Most of them started out as teachers or colleagues, but some of them started out as my students and became my teachers, coaches, and mentors. In fact, two of them, Robin DiMatteo and Howard Friedman, had been such students and have now become my teachers; both of them are distinguished professors of psychology here at UC Riverside.

My oldest friend, colleague, collaborator, teacher, coach, and mentor is Ralph Rosnow. He is also responsible for ruining my character by having spoiled me for more than 40 years, beginning back when we both started the Boston phases of our careers. He spoiled me when he invited me to collaborate with him in his ongoing research program. He educated me in matters historical, philosophical, and theoretical. And then whenever I needed cheering up, he wrote a book and put my name on it. That does wonders for your morale! I must have needed a lot of cheering up, because Ralph did that a lot of times, and he's still doing it.

Among the other teachers, coaches, and mentors who made me look good were several who taught me to be a good clinician, including, especially, George Hohmann and Ed Shneidman, two of my clinical supervisors; Joseph Gengerelli, who taught me how to analyze my dissertation data (using a mechanical calculator—a Friden); and Bruno Klopfer, the chair of my doctoral committee and, incidentally, the person who brought the Rorschach to America.

The pre–Ralph Rosnow teachers who introduced me to fundamental ideas about the nature of science included three UCLA professors: the psychologist Irving Maltzman, the philosopher Abraham Kaplan, and the sociologist Donald Cressey. Donald Cressey's course in criminology was huge, and on the first day of class he asked everyone to list all the things they had ever stolen. He read aloud these anonymous lists, and when he got to mine he said he wanted whoever wrote it to see him after class, and so I met him personally. What I'd written was "I haven't stolen anything, but I'm young and eager to learn."

My understanding of statistical issues and procedures greatly benefited from my contacts with Bill Cochran, Fred Mosteller, and Paul Holland, whose courses I sat in on when, as a newly minted professor, I realized how much there was I didn't know. Jack Cohen's writings about power and effect sizes influenced me profoundly over the years, though it was only quite recently and all too briefly that I got to know Jack in person. That happened when Jack, Bob Abelson, and I began to think collectively about how psychologists use and think about statistical inference and how we might go about doing better. We were able to enlist nine of the best quantitative scholars in the country to help us think about these matters as members of the American Psychological Association's (APA's) Board of Scientific Affairs' Task Force on Statistical Inference. Let me brag also about our task force's senior advisors: Lee Cronbach, Paul Meehl, Fred Mosteller, and John Tukey.

For the past 35 years or so I have been coached in statistical matters by my friend and colleague Don Rubin. For all those years we have been collaborating on papers in the area of data analysis. This collaboration proceeds as follows: I ask him questions, he answers them, and he then insists we publish alphabetically. What a country! Between Don's articles and Ralph's books, I have long had it made!

When you're working in controversial areas and you're young and you're at the University of North Dakota in the 1950s, it pays to have some very senior mentors and advisors. I was lucky enough to have such mentors when I sorely needed them. They included Don Campbell, Harold Pepinsky, and Hank Riecken.

Don Campbell—Mentor at a Distance

Since December 1, 1958, Don Campbell has been my mentor at a distance. In a letter he wrote that day, he agreed to participate in a symposium I was organizing for the APA to be held the following summer in Cincinnati. (Other members of that symposium were Martin Orne, Walter Reitman, and Hank Riecken.)

Don took me under his wing in the organization of that symposium and later saw me through some tough times when, first, most psychologists thought I was crazy for believing that psychological experimenters could unintentionally influence their research subjects to respond in accordance with the experimenters' expectations, and, second, when some highly placed critics tried to stop the publication of the book describing the research with Lenore Jacobson on teachers' expectation effects in classrooms. Don intervened on my behalf, and *Pygmalion in the Classroom* was published after all!

Because this occasion of a career retrospective forced me to think so hard about my career, it struck me that we need a model of a research career. Then I realized that such a model already exists: it is the structure of a journal article!

THE JOURNAL ARTICLE AS A MODEL
OF A RESEARCH CAREER

The journal article, it turns out, serves as an excellent model of a research career. Careers, like journal articles, have an introduction, a methods section, a results section, a discussion section, sometimes a summary, often an abstract, and always, gulp, a conclusion.

The introduction section of a research career is made up of the areas of our field that interest us, that engage us, that motivate us—they are the questions we want to address in our research career.

The methods section of a research career is made up of the ways we go about addressing the questions that engage us. We make up our methods section out of the following:

experiments,
or surveys,
or psychoanalysis,
or secondary analysis,
or content analysis,
or path analysis,
or factor analysis,
or meta-analysis,
or computer simulation,
or participant observation,
or canonical correlation,
or back translation,
or factor rotation,
or a combination

of these and other methods.

But, for the most part, we develop characteristic ways of addressing our basic questions; that, then, is our personal methods section.

The results section of a research career is made up of the things we find out about the issues of interest to us by having applied our methods of finding them out. Often our careers are identified with our results.

In the discussion section of our research career, we are permitted to go beyond our data:

sometimes to *soar* beyond our data,
sometimes to *adore* our data,
sometimes to *abhor* our data,

sometimes to *roar* about our data,
sometimes to *bore* about our data,
sometimes to *war* about our data,
sometimes to *ignore* our data—
(or other people's data)!

If we have been active researchers in the results section of our careers, we earn the right to a discussion section on the basis of a Judeo-Christian–Buddhist ethic, that is, of having paid our dues. It really *is* quite analogous to the discussion section of a research journal article. Your results have been your ticket of admission to the more speculative discussion section. No results section—no discussion section! That is sometimes called the *principle of earned speculation* and sometimes the *law of warranted chitchat.*

In the discussion section of our research career, we are, therefore, authorized to wax philosophic, perhaps even theological. If and when we do, our rascally younger colleagues are likely to say to one another, amidst a great shaking of heads, that we have begun "cramming for our finals." I actually had not quite yet thought of myself as having arrived in the discussion section of my research career. However, occasions such as this do make me wonder.

You will notice that I have said nothing about the article's conclusion. That part of the model I don't even want to *think* about!

AN ACCIDENTAL JOURNAL ARTICLE (CAREER)

My research interests include some that are more methodological (e.g., data analysis, contrast analysis, and meta-analysis) and some that are more substantive (e.g., dyadic interaction, nonverbal communication, and interpersonal self-fulfilling prophecies).

All of these interests grew directly or indirectly from a single, simple unexpected event in the introduction section of my journal article. Some 50 years ago, I ruined the results of my doctoral dissertation at UCLA. Here's what happened.

"An Attempt at the Experimental Induction of the Defense Mechanism of Projection"

With the foregoing as its almost unbearable title, my dissertation employed a total of 108 subjects: 36 college men, 36 college women, and 36 hospitalized patients with paranoid symptomatology. Each of these three groups was further divided into three subgroups receiving success, failure, or neutral experience on a task structured as, and simulating, a standardized test of intelligence. Before the subjects' experimental conditions were imposed, they were asked to rate the degree of success or failure of persons pictured in photographs. Immediately after the experimental manipulation, the subjects were asked to rate an equivalent set of photos on their degree of success or failure. The dependent variable was the magnitude of the difference scores between pre- and postratings of the photographs. It was hypothesized that the success condition would lead to the subsequent perception of other people as more successful, whereas the failure condition would lead to the subsequent perception of other people as having failed more, as measured by the pre- and postrating difference scores.

In an attack of studently compulsivity, an attack that greatly influenced my scholarly future, I did a statistical analysis that was extraneous to the main purpose of the dissertation. In this analysis I compared the mean *pre*treatment ratings of the three experimental conditions. The pretreatment rating mean of the success condition was substantially and significantly lower than the mean of either of the other two conditions. It must be emphasized that these three treatment groups had not yet undergone their treatment; they were only destined to become the subjects of the three conditions. If the success group started out lower than the other groups, then, even if there were no differences among the three conditions in their posttreatment photo ratings, the success group would show the greatest gain, a result favoring one of my hypotheses, namely, that projection of the good could occur just as well as projection of the bad. Without my awareness, the cards had perhaps been stacked in favor of obtaining results supporting one of my hypotheses. It should be noted that the success and failure groups' instructions had been identical during the pretreatment rating phase of the experiment.

The problem, apparently, was that I knew for each subject which experimental treatment he or she would subsequently be administered. As I noted in 1956 with some dismay, "The implication is that in some subtle manner, perhaps by tone, or manner, or gestures, or general atmosphere, the experimenter, although formally testing the success and failure groups in an identical way, influenced the success subjects to make lower initial ratings and thus increase the experimenter's probability of verifying his hypothesis" (Rosenthal, 1956, p. 44).

THE SEARCH FOR COMPANY

When I discussed these strange goings-on with some faculty members, they seemed not overly surprised. A not very reassuring response was "Oh, yes, we lose a few Ph.D. dissertations now and then because of problems like that." There followed a frantic search of the literature for references to this phenomenon, which I then called *unconscious experimenter bias.* As far back as Ebbinghaus (1885), psychologists had been referring to something like this phenomenon, including such notables as Oskar Pfungst (1911), of Clever Hans fame, Ivan Pavlov (Gruenberg, 1929), and Saul Rosenzweig (1933). It was unfortunate that none of these investigators (or even later ones) had explicitly designed and conducted an experiment to test the hypothesis of unconscious experimenter bias; that remained to be done.

There is something I want to add about the paper by Rosenzweig, which appeared the same year as Harry Murray's paper on a process similar to Freud's defense mechanism of projection (cited earlier) and, incidentally, the same year that I appeared. In my own several reviews of the literature (e.g., in 1956 and 1966), I had completely missed the Rosenzweig paper. I believe it was Ralph Rosnow who called my attention to Rosenzweig's extraordinarily insightful and prophetic paper. Not only did Rosenzweig anticipate the problem of unconscious experimenter bias but he also anticipated virtually the entire area now referred to as the *social psychology of the psychological experiment*. The Rosenzweig paper makes good reading even today, some 75 years later. There is a superb appreciation of the Rosenzweig paper in Ralph Rosnow's brilliant 1981 book about the methodology of social inquiry, *Paradigms in Transition*.

THE PRODUCTION OF COMPANY

If it was my unconscious experimenter bias that had led to the puzzling and disconcerting results of my dissertation, then presumably we could produce the phenomenon in our own laboratory, with several experimenters rather than just one. Producing the phenomenon in this way would yield not only the scientific benefit of demonstrating an interesting and important concept but also the considerable personal benefit of showing that I was not alone in having unintentionally affected the results of my research by virtue of my bias or expectancy.

There followed a series of studies employing human subjects in which we found that when experimenters were led to expect certain research findings, they were more likely to obtain those findings. These studies were met with incredulity by many investigators who worked with human subjects. However, investigators who worked with animal subjects often nodded knowingly and told me that was the kind of phenomenon that encouraged them to work with animal subjects. In due course, then, we began to work with animal subjects and found that when experimenters were led to believe that they were working with maze-bright rats, the rats learned faster than did the rats randomly assigned to experimenters who had been led to believe that their rats were dull. That result surprised many psychologists who worked with animal subjects, but it would not have surprised Pavlov or Pfungst, or Bertrand Russell, who in 1927 said, "Animals studied by Americans rush about frantically, with an incredible display of hustle and pep, and at last achieve the desired result by chance. Animals observed by Germans sit still and think, and at last evolve the solution out of their inner consciousness" (pp. 29–30).

Our experiments on the effects of investigators' expectancies on the behavior of their research subjects should be distinguished from the much-older tradition of examining the effects of investigators' expectations, theories, or predilections on their observations or interpretations of nature. Examples of such effects have been summarized elsewhere, and there is continuing lively interest in these topics (Rosnow & Rosenthal, 1997).

TEACHER EXPECTATION EFFECTS
AND AN ESSENTIAL PRINCIPAL

If rats became brighter when expected to, then it should not be far-fetched to think that children could become brighter when expected to by their teachers. Indeed,

Kenneth Clark (1963) had for years been saying that teachers' expectations could be very important determinants of children's intellectual performance. Clark's ideas and our research should have sent us right into the schools to study teacher expectations, but that's not what happened.

What did happen was that after we had completed about a dozen studies of experimenter expectancy effects (we no longer used the term *unconscious experimenter bias*), I summarized our results in a 1963 paper for the *American Scientist*. (As an aside, I should note that although this research had begun in 1958, and although there had been more than a dozen papers, none of them had been able to find their way into an APA publication. During these years of nonpublication, there were three "psychological sponsors" who provided enormous intellectual stimulation and personal encouragement: Don Campbell, Harold Pepinsky, and Hank Riecken; I owe them all a great deal, as I mentioned earlier.)

I concluded this 1963 paper by wondering whether the same interpersonal expectancy effects found in psychological experimenters might not also be found in physicians, psychotherapists, employers, and teachers (subsequent research showed that indeed it could be found in all these practitioners). "When master teachers tell their apprentices that a pupil appears to be a slow learner, is this prophecy then self-fulfilled?" was the paraphrased closing line of this paper (Rosenthal, 1963, p. 280).

Among the reprint requests for this paper was one from Lenore F. Jacobson, the principal of an elementary school in South San Francisco, California. I sent her a stack of unpublished papers and thought no more about it. On November 18, 1963, Lenore wrote me a letter telling of her interest in the problem of teacher expectations. She ended her letter with the following line: "If you ever 'graduate' to classroom children, please let me know whether I can be of assistance" (Jacobson, personal communication, November 18, 1963).

On November 27, 1963, I accepted Lenore's offer of assistance and asked whether she would consider collaborating on a project to investigate teacher expectancy effects. A tentative experimental design was suggested in this letter as well.

On December 3, 1963, Lenore replied, mainly to discuss concerns over the ethical and organizational implications of creating false expectations for superior performance in teachers. If this problem could be solved, her school would be ideal, she felt, with children from primarily lower class backgrounds. Lenore also suggested gently that I was "a bit naive" to think one could just *tell* teachers to expect some of their pupils to be "diamonds in the rough." We would have to administer some new test to the children, a test the teachers would not know.

Phone calls and letters followed, and in January 1964, I made a trip to South San Francisco to settle on a final design and to meet with the school district's administrators to obtain their approval. This approval was forthcoming because of the leadership of the school superintendent, Dr. Paul Nielsen. Approval for this research had already been obtained from Robert L. Hall, program director for Sociology and Social Psychology for the National Science Foundation, which had been supporting much of the early work on experimenter expectancy effects.

The Pygmalion experiment showed results consistent with the earlier work on human and animal subjects. But we still didn't know exactly *how* one person's expectations for another's behavior came to serve as self-fulfilling prophecy. In an effort to find mediating variables, we began to study nonverbal behavior, especially in dyadic interaction. That was more than 40 years ago.

At about the same time, criticisms of our human and animal studies and our classroom studies became more and more common, and most of the criticisms were of a statistical nature.

Trying to understand and evaluate these criticisms led me to study quantitative matters more systematically. That was when I sat in on courses taught by Bill Cochran, Fred Mosteller, and Paul Holland, and when I first met Don Rubin, who was finishing his Ph.D. with Bill Cochran.

It was also about then that I began to become especially interested in issues of replication, statistical significance, contrast analysis, and meta-analysis. Much of it probably was simple self-defense.

A Position Statement

Although these quantitative–methodological matters have engaged my interest now for many years, this chapter is not the place to go into any detail about them. But there is a brief position statement I can make here that addresses an issue that the APA's Task Force on Statistical Inference and I felt to be quite important, namely, that we should increase our data analytic emphasis on effect size estimation while decreasing our emphasis on significance testing. The position statement comes in two very short parts:

Part I. The Problem
Oh, F is large and p is small
That's why we are walking tall.
What it means we need not mull
Just so we reject the null.
Or chi-square large and p near nil
Results like that, they fill the bill.
What if meaning requires a poll?
Never mind, we're on a roll!
The message we have learned too well?
Significance! That rings the bell!
Part II. The Implications
The moral of our little tale?
That we mortals may be frail
When we feel a p near zero
Makes us out to be a hero.
But tell us then, is it too late?
Can we perhaps avoid our fate?
Replace that wish to null-reject
Report the size of the effect.

That may not ensure our glory
But at least it tells a story
That is just the kind of yield
Needed to advance our field.

CONCLUSION

It's been a long time since that 1956 doctoral dissertation showed a significant treatment effect before the treatment had been administered. Along the way there have been a lot of studies in laboratories and in classrooms, clinics, and courtrooms to show that expectancy effects occur, and there have been a lot of studies to investigate how they occur. We've learned something about that and about some related things as well, for example, about a number of data analytic issues including the quantitative summary of research domains and various processes of nonverbal communication. Of course, much of what we really wanted to know is still not known. But perhaps that's not too bad. It's true that finding the answer is the outcome we want, but the looking itself, when it's done with as good colleagues and as good students as I've had, is not so bad either.*

AUTHOR'S NOTE

This chapter is based in part on the Annual Career Retrospective presented on April 16, 2000, at the meeting of the Western Psychological Association held in Portland, Oregon.

REFERENCES

Clark, K. B. (1963). Educational stimulation of racially disadvantaged children. In A. H. Passow (Ed.), *Education in depressed areas* (pp. 142–162). New York: Bureau of Publications, Teachers College, Columbia University.

Ebbinghaus, H. (1885). *Memory: A contribution to experimental psychology* (H. A. Ruger & C. E. Bussenius, Trans.). New York: Teachers College, Columbia University. (Original work published 1913)

Gruenberg, B. C. (1929). *The story of evolution.* Princeton, NJ: Van Nostrand.

Pfungst, O. (1911). *Clever Hans (The horse of Mr. von Osten): A contribution to experimental, animal, and human psychology* (C. L. Rahn, Trans.). New York: Holt. (Reissued by Holt, Rinehart & Winston, 1965)

---

* If I were asked to state what I thought I might have contributed to our field, if anything, the answer would be brief and simple; it's the students, of course! It's the 52 Ph.D.s and all the other graduate and undergraduate students with whom I have been privileged to work for some 50 years. It's seeing the work they have done, are doing, and will be doing. And what makes it go on and on is seeing the work *their* students have done, are doing, and will be doing. Yes, it's the students; they make me very, very proud!

Rosenthal, R. (1956). *An attempt at the experimental induction of the defense mechanism of projection*. Unpublished doctoral dissertation, University of California at Los Angeles.

Rosenthal, R. (1963). On the social psychology of the psychological experiment: The experimenter's hypothesis as unintended determinant of experimental results. *American Scientist, 51*, 268–283.

Rosenthal, R. (1966). *Experimenter effects in behavioral research*. New York: Appleton-Century-Crofts.

Rosenzweig, S. (1933). The experimental situation as a psychological problem. *Psychological Review, 40*, 337–354.

Rosnow, R. L. (1981). *Paradigms in transition: The methodology of social inquiry*. New York: Oxford University Press.

Rosnow, R. L., & Rosenthal, R. (1997). *People studying people: Artifacts and ethics in behavioral research*. New York: Freeman.

Russell, B. (1927). *Philosophy*. New York: Norton.

An Autobiography
Why Did Culture Shape My Career?

HARRY C. TRIANDIS

Department of Psychology, University of Illinois

I have had a long and satisfying life. Now at age 80 I can search for the factors that made it so. I will start by giving some advice to those who are starting their careers:

1. *Choose to do what you feel passionate about.* Success requires many hours per week, almost without interruption. You cannot sustain such effort unless you love what you do. Some psychologists have defined "genius" as loving to work 70 hours a week on something!

2. *Be modest and do not expect too much.* Mozart went to an early grave (at age 35) because, in my opinion, he wanted in his 20s and 30s to have the fame he had as a child. In his mid-30s he was still very productive (he had just composed the *Magic Flute*), yet he was depressed and stressed. Stress reduces the immune system, and thus he was not able to respond to infections. Do not think about fame and immortality. Rather use the attitude that you are a student all your life. Deal with your students as junior colleagues and friends.

3. *Early in your career, if there is a good opportunity, get involved in some controversy.* When I was an assistant professor, Rokeach, a very important social psychologist, argued that prejudice was due to differences in belief. I wrote a short critical paper that argued that there is more to prejudice than that. Especially in the case of intimate behaviors, people discriminate those of a different race because of their race. This paper for a few years was my most quoted paper. The race versus belief controversy generated a lot of research, and my name was placed on the map of social psychology at a point in my career when most people would not have known anything about me.

Because I have written other partial autobiographies (Triandis, 1997, 1999, in press), I will avoid in this autobiography materials that I covered elsewhere. Nevertheless, some points must be restated, so that the present account can stand on its own.

THE FIRST 20 YEARS

I was raised in Greece, mainly in Athens. Like most children, I enjoyed seeing pictures of exotic animals, such as elephants and zebras, but I was truly fascinated by another set of exotic animals: tourists! They wore strange clothes, jewelry, and hats, such as turbans or ones with feathers, and spoke strange languages. When I was between 10 and 12 years old, I used to visit the archaeological museum, which was near our apartment, because I was interested both in the exhibits and in the tourists. I knew enough French and German to be able to talk with some of them and find out more about them. Most of them seemed to be able to speak some of those languages (French in the 1930s was *the* international language, the way English is now), and at times I was able to help them, and in a few cases they gave me some candy. Only about 6 million people spoke Greek at that time (it is now 11 million). Clearly, one had to learn other languages. In fact, in my family everybody spoke several languages. My relatives were fluent in French and German, and some could speak English. During the Italian occupation of Corfu, I also learned some Italian, so that I could read books that interested me in that language, because they were the only recently published books available to me.

Learning languages is important for a future cross-cultural psychologist. One gets into another culture by learning its language, and when I started cross-cultural research, I often asked myself whether a construct I was working with had a counterpart in the other languages that I spoke.

The tourists stopped coming when the Second World War started. I went to a French high school, but it closed. Athens was occupied by the Nazis, who made no provisions for the food supplies of the population, and an estimated 125,000 people died of hunger. I was *very* hungry, and that had a silver lining: I now eat everything and like all food. I was fortunate that my maternal grandfather was a rural physician on the island of Corfu, and by moving there we had fruit, vegetables, and olive oil, and in exchange for oil we had some meat from the black market.

Corfu was occupied by the Italians, who unlike the Germans made an effort to treat the population decently. Thus life in occupied Corfu was not bad. The Italians made an effort to be nice to the population in hopes of annexing the Ionian Islands after the war. They gave advice to the farmers, built some roads, and constructed a very nice swimming area. They used loudspeakers on the main square of the city to broadcast classical music.

The contact with tourists and later the contrast between the Germans and Italians suggested that culture shapes behavior. But why do cultures differ? How do the differences develop? I was curious to find out, and I would have started studying this problem, but in high school I did not have the tools to do it.

As part of their effort to impose Italian on Corfu, the Italians sent the Greek teachers back to the mainland. The students went on strike, and for one year I did not go to school. I spent my time reading a 24-volume encyclopedia, so that this was the time in my life when I learned more than in any other period. I was curious to find out what the world was like, and a good encyclopedia in the hands of an interested 15-year-old can do wonders.

In 1943 the Italians got out of the war, but the Germans wanted them to continue fighting. The Italians were in Corfu, so the Nazis bombed the city to make them surrender. In one night, September 14, half the city was set on fire by Nazi incendiary bombs. It was a terrible shock. My mother and I walked to the country house of her first cousins, 9 kilometers from the city. Some 25 other friends and relatives were also there as refugees, and they spent the next 3 months or so in that large villa. My aunts were immensely cheerful and welcoming, and they organized all kinds of dances and other events to keep us happy. It was a fun experience, because there were a number of boys and girls my age, and we had a good time in spite of the occasional bombings. We expected the Allies to invade Corfu and fight the Germans.

It was natural that with such an expectation I had to learn English, so at the age of 17 I started studying with my mother's old teacher. She was a terrific teacher, and in 6 months I was almost fluent. All I needed was some practice. My mother discovered a patient at the local mental hospital who had an English mother and a Greek father. When he became mentally ill, in Switzerland, he was sent to Corfu, but by the time we met he was more than 70 years old and his mental illness was in full remission. The hospital kept him for life and allowed him to go out to give some lessons so he could have some pocket money. He spoke excellent English, and this allowed me to practice.

My first job, at age 19, was as an interpreter for an American colonel who was a UN observer of the referendum that brought back the king. The colonel had a cockney-speaking driver, whom I could not understand, so the colonel had to translate for me. One night a couple of homosexuals approached the driver and wanted him to come to their room. The communication was from Greek to English, to cockney English, to English, to Greek! The driver was not interested in them. He said they were "peculiar."

When the war ended, we moved back to Athens, and then the big issue was what to study. I was interested in everything, which means I had no idea where to go. Because I liked math and physics and my father was an engineer, it made some sense to study engineering. Thus I went to the Technical University, but just after the war things were disorganized. The lectures were terribly overcrowded, with 600 kids sitting on top of tables and the like. It made sense to transfer to a university that had not suffered from the war. Thus, with a Canadian scholarship, I went to McGill University in Montreal. I graduated 3 years later with honors. In 1951 there were many jobs for engineers. Procter & Gamble (P&G) offered me a job, with $250 per month. That was terrific, because my image of a great salary was $400. I accepted in writing. But then an engineering research job offer for $225 arrived. I liked the idea of research more, and so I went to my professor and asked if I could accept that job, though I had accepted the P&G job. He said with great emotion that having accepted a job in writing is like "swearing on a stack of bibles." Thus, I never became a research engineer!

The P&G job was easy, and I had time to do an executive MBA-type course (Thursday night and all day Saturday, for 2 years) at the University of Toronto. There I met psychology and was so taken by it that I quit my job and went back to McGill for one year to get all the undergraduate psychology I needed for graduate school.

The course that changed my life was called "Human Relations in Industry." It was given by psychologist Bob Joyner. He had studied with Carl Rogers in Chicago, and Rogers's view of education was that students should generate their own curriculum. There were six of us in the course, and when we arrived in class Joyner told us, "The university thinks that I am the instructor, but *you* are going to decide what to study and how to study it." After some negotiation, we asked for a reading list. He came up with 200 books—anthropology, human relations in industry, psychology, sociology. We read books and presented summaries in class. Joyner made comments, but he was definitely nondirective in the classroom. For me, this was an excellent course, because I had the time to read, and I sampled widely. But the others, who had more demanding jobs, did not learn very much. I tried this course format in Illinois, and again there were two students who learned a great deal and the rest did very little. Given my experience reading the encyclopedia and taking this course, I think that Rogers is right, except that it works *only* for those who are highly motivated and do not have competing courses or jobs. But in any case, that was the course that changed my life. I suddenly realized that one can make a living in the social sciences.

The only requirement was a Ph.D. But to do graduate work I needed to learn some undergraduate psychology. So I quit my job at P&G and went back to McGill for a year of intensive study of undergraduate psychology. It was an excellent experience, with faculty such as Don Hebb (president of the American Psychological Association [APA]), Jim Olds (physiological psychologist who discovered the locus of rewards in the brain), and Wally Lambert (later a famous psycholinguist). Lambert was just out of graduate school, so he arranged for me to study with his brother Bill (1919–2005) at Cornell. Bill was one of the great polymaths of our field. He had studied at the social relations department at Harvard and saw social psychology as closely linked to anthropology and sociology. In fact, he is the only person I know who was at different points in his career the chair of the anthropology, psychology, and sociology departments. He ended up as dean of the graduate school at Cornell. One of his strong interests was cross-cultural psychology, and he was on the team of Whiting and Child, who organized the famous six-cultures project. After I graduated he published *Mothers of Six-Cultures*, with my first wife, Leigh Minturn.

One can trace intellectual traditions by examining who got his doctorate with whom. Lambert got it with Richard Solomon (1918–1995), who got his doctorate at Brown with Harold Schlosberg (1904–1964), who got his doctorate at Princeton with Herbert Langfield (1879–1958), who got his doctorate in Berlin with Carl Stumpf (1848–1936). Stumpf had an interest in music, as well as psychology, and collected primitive musical sounds from many cultures, which shows that my intellectual great, great, great grandfather was a kind of cross-cultural psychologist!

Cornell was an excellent choice for me. At Cornell, three professors, who supervise course selection and all work including the dissertation, guide the student's graduate study. The chair of my committee was Bill Lambert, and the other two were William Foot Whyte of *Street Corner Society* fame, a book I had read in Bob Joyner's course, and Art Ryan, who taught statistics and industrial psychology. They suggested that I study anthropology as well as psychology and take an experimental course in the methods of the social sciences that was offered because Cornell had received a grant from the Social Science Research Council. It was a wonderful full-year course that trained students in all the methods of the social sciences—ethnography, systematic observations, content analysis, experiments, survey methods, test construction, and the use of the Human Relations Area Files. The student had the opportunity to use each of the methods under the supervision of a graduate student who had some experience using that method. Thus the idea of doing multimethod research, and looking for convergence across methods, was established in that course.

In my first year in graduate school, I was exposed to Osgood's *Experimental Psychology*. I also read his *The Measurement of Meaning* and got in touch with Osgood and suggested that it would be a good idea to replicate his study of the structure of affective meaning (evaluation, potency, and activity) in another culture, with monolingual participants. He was enthusiastic, and we applied to the National Institute of Public Health and obtained a $5,000 grant for me to go to Greece to collect the data. Osgood analyzed it, and we published it (Triandis & Osgood, 1958). While I was in Greece for the summer, I also collected data for a replication of Schlosberg's theory of emotion, with a peasant sample that had not seen any movies. The structure of emotions that emerged (Triandis & Lambert, 1958) was the same as the one in the United States, and that started Ekman and others in their study of the universality of some emotions. Thus the data collection after my first year in graduate school resulted in two publications in the best social psychology journal.

My first paper at a scientific meeting, during my second year of graduate work, was in New York, at the meetings of the Eastern Psychological Association. I gave a paper on the replication of Schlosberg's theory of emotion in Greece. Schlosberg was in the audience, and he stood up and complimented me. It is difficult to describe how important that was. Schlosberg at the time was Mr. Psychology, because he was the author of the experimental psychology text that all graduate students had to master. To get a positive comment from him was instant imprinting to go to conferences! When I retired at age 71, Walter Lonner, who came to Illinois for the event, commented, "Harry has never seen a conference that he did not like." One piece of advice to academics is to go to conferences. It is stimulating, and one establishes important links to the profession.

When I was about to graduate, Osgood went to Lanier, then head of the Department of Psychology at Illinois, and told him that I was "a catch." Lanier offered me the job sight unseen. It was a fantastic offer of $6,800 per year, which the Cornell professors told me to accept without hesitation. Thus in 1958 I started at Illinois, in a department that already had several former presidents of the APA (e.g., Lee Cronbach, Joe Hunt, Hobard Mowrer). Over the years I had offers from other places, but the university always matched the offer, and thus it was impossible for me to leave.

The social psychology program at Illinois that first year consisted of Fred Fiedler, Bill McGuire, Ivan Steiner, and me. The first year, while Fiedler was on sabbatical in the Netherlands, I rented his house. When he returned from his sabbatical, we became close friends. Bill McGuire had his office next to mine, and we usually had lunch together.

Fiedler was a master in getting grants. In fact, he was so well connected in Washington, D.C., that the Office of Naval Research came to him with the message that the chief of naval operations wanted each sailor to become an ambassador, and they wanted him to organize the project. Could he accept a grant to do that? Fiedler put together a team: Osgood, Stolurow, and me. I was given the job of finding out how to study culture. Osgood was to study how to communicate the information to the sailors, Fiedler was to study how to lead the sailors, and Stolurow was to study how to put all the information into computer training programs. With almost a million dollars, we started working on our tasks.

In the 1950s "culture" was a peripheral concept in psychology. To get tenure I had to work on mainstream topics. So I worked on attitudes in general and prejudice in particular. I started working on the measurement of social distance, and I developed a method that could measure social distance toward stimuli that differed in race, social class, religion, nationality, and other attributes. I focused on studies of social distance across cultures. In Triandis (1961) I objected to Milt Rokeach's argument that intergroup attitudes were the result of perceived differences in beliefs (see above).

In Triandis and Davis (1965), I provided what is perhaps a definite formulation of the race versus belief issue, but it reverberated in the literature for a few additional years. I emphasized that there are norms for behavior toward African Americans, and belief by itself is an incomplete explanation of discrimination. As usual in such controversies, both positions are viable under some circumstances, and Bill McGuire is correct in arguing that every theoretical position is defensible some of the time under some circumstances.

My emphasis on norms did of course overlap with the views of Muzafer Sherif, and after I met him at the APA meetings in Los Angeles, we became good friends. I published in one of his edited books, and years later I contributed one of the essays for the volume that was published in his honor (Triandis, 1992).

The social distance studies gave me something to talk about when in 1960 I went to my first international congress of psychology in Bonn, Germany. I gave my paper on social distance and suggested that it might be good to replicate this work in other countries. At the end of my lecture, Earl Davis, an American who had received his doctorate at the University of Munich in Germany, offered to replicate the study. We became friends, and he later came to Illinois as my research associate for a few years. Finally, he became professor in Dublin, Ireland. When Takezawa, a Japanese professor, visited Illinois, I suggested that he collect similar data in Japan. That became the Triandis, Davis, and Takezawa (1965) paper. In 1961 I went to Copenhagen for the International Association of Applied Psychology meeting. Little did I know at that time that I would become president of that association 29 years later.

During my 1964–1965 sabbatical, I went around the world talking to colleagues about the Navy project (see above). I spent some time in Hawaii, where Osgood had taken his sabbatical, and then went on to Japan. At that time the visit of a "visiting fireman" from the United States was exotic enough that there was a special meeting of the Japanese Psychological Association to hear me talk. Some students asked for my autograph! I worked with Yasumasa Tanaka and discussed the project with Jiujitzu Misumi. Tanaka taught at Gakushin University, where the relatives of the Emperor of Japan go. In that university a professor is not allowed to make any mistakes. Thus Tanaka did not own a car, because if one has a car one might make a mistake (e.g., drive too fast!). He took taxis everywhere. I loved Japan, especially the gardens, and I consider the visit to the Katzura villa's garden in Kyoto as one of the great aesthetic experiences of my life.

Next was a stop in Hong Kong, where I spent some time at the University of Hong Kong, and after that was Malaysia and Thailand and discussions with colleagues at Chulalankorn University.

India, which was my next stop, was a unique experience for a cross-cultural psychologist. It is so rich in cultural diversity, with scores of languages and cultures. The first stop was in Calcutta, where I had my first culture shock. Arriving at 4 in the morning, the sight of thousands of seemingly dead bodies illuminated by the airport bus lights left an indelible impression. I later found out that these people sleep outside to save money to send to their villages. I talked with Rhea Das at the Indian Statistical Institute and gave a colloquium at the university. After my colloquium the students were asked to leave the room so the professors could ask questions! Hierarchy is powerful in the culture. After the students left, the professors did not have any questions!

Then came Benares (Veranassi), where the full scale of Indian mysticism could be observed on the banks of the river Ganges. Next came New Delhi and again a special meeting of the Indian Psychological Association and discussions with Professor Kupaswami. Later I contributed a chapter in a book published in honor of Kupaswami. After a trip to Agra and the Taj Mahal, I traveled to Jaipur, where I stayed at a hotel that used to be a palace. On the train between Agra and Jaipur, I met the minister of that state, who invited me to tea. He had an elegant house, and I was introduced to his son, who took me around to see his university. I asked him if he had any trouble getting books out of the library, and he said, "No, I just send my servants." Again hierarchy is an important aspect of Indian culture!

The next stop was Bangalore, where I was met by Shanmugam, who collected the India data for Triandis, Vassiliou, Vassiliou, Tanaka, and Shanmugam (1972). He drove me to Mysore, where he lived. I had communicated with the only Western hotel in Mysore, which sent me a card that had two options: "we have" and "we do not have" a room for you. The second option had a cross. I assumed that there was no room, so I asked Shanmugam to find another room. The room that I was shown had too many lizards, and so I asked if another room could be found. He arranged for me to stay at the palace of the Maharaja, but the room could not be ready for 24 hours. Rather than spend a night with the lizards, I went back to the Western hotel and asked if by chance they had a cancellation for that night. The clerk was astonished, because they expected me. I asked how come they sent a card that had a cross on "we do not have a room." He answered, "We cross out the categories that do not apply."

After Mysore was Bombay, where the standard tour takes one to the temples of the Parsis, who do not bury their dead but expose them to vultures. The Parsis are an endogamous religion, and their numbers are getting smaller every year. The next country was Iran. The University of Illinois had a research station in Teheran, and I visited the personnel and then went to Isfahan. The local poets were justified to claim that "half the world is Isfahan." I found it delightful, with one of the largest squares in the world surrounded by mosques, palaces, and other buildings, as well as a bazaar. The blue and white tiles on all the buildings created a sense of unity like one experiences at the Piazza San Marco in Venice.

Israel was the next stop. I had corresponded with Uriel Foa, who booked me at the King David hotel in Jerusalem, an unnecessary luxury, and at an equally fancy place in Haifa. We became good friends and remained so until his untimely death. I arranged for him to come to Illinois, where he taught for a few years; later I wrote his obituary for the *American Psychologist*.

The major stop on that trip around the world was in Athens, where I worked at the Athenian Institute of Anthropos. Vasso Vassiliou was my collaborator, and her husband, George, was a wise consultant. Vasso did survey research, so she included my questions in her surveys, and the data were from representative samples of the two largest cities in Greece. Of course, social psychologists usually obtain student samples, so getting samples representative of the urban population of a country was special. We later coauthored the major chapter of Triandis et al. (1972).

While in Greece I went back and forth to other parts of Europe, giving colloquia at such places as Leuven (Belgium), Strasbourg (France), Cologne (Germany), Neuchâtel (Switzerland), and Milan (Italy). One of my cross-cultural mistakes was to give my talk at Leuven in French. I had not realized that in the Flemish part of Belgium, it would have been better to give it in English. The language divisions in that country are important, so that some years later Leuven split into a Flemish Leuven and a French Louvin (south of Brussels). They split the library so that one campus has the odd-numbered volumes of the journals whereas the other has the even-numbered volumes! On the other hand, the same lecture in France was greatly appreciated.

The trip around the world resulted in the selection of collaborators for the Navy project. A number of research projects were completed, and the work was published in *The Analysis of Subjective Culture* (Triandis et al., 1972). In the process of developing different ways of studying culture, I developed the behavioral differential, the role differential (Triandis, Vassiliou, & Nassiakou, 1968), the antecedent-consequent method of measuring values, and methods for the equivalent measurement of constructs across cultures (Triandis, 1992; Triandis et al., 1965), and I emphasized methods that avoided translation, because concepts do not map accurately across cultures. Studies of stereotypes were also made possible because of this Office of Naval Research project.

In 1960 Osgood started his major cross-cultural study of affective meaning and had a group of consultants come to Illinois to help with the design. They included Clyde Kluckhom, an anthropologist from Harvard, who wrote what is, in my opinion, the best chapter ever on culture and behavior, in the *Handbook of Social Psychology* (1954). I was delighted to meet him. In connection with the cross-cultural measurement of affective meaning project, Osgood held conferences in Dubrovnik, Yugoslavia, in 1963 and Teheran, Iran, in 1967. I went to both of these conferences and established close relationships with some of the people who worked on that project as well as on the Navy project.

Up to 1960 the major effort in cross-cultural psychology was to check on the generality of findings obtained in the West (Triandis, 1978). Replications were the name of the game. But after that, we started worrying that cultures might have their own unique ways of constructing reality. We distinguished emic (culture-specific) and etic (culture-general) constructs. The issue then became how can one use both emics and etics and make the measurements comparable across cultures, so that one may be able to both say something about the worldview of each culture and compare cultures. Numerous publications were generated around this topic. I developed a method that used a common metric but standardized the measurements separately in each culture (Triandis, 1992; Triandis et al., 1965).

The emic elements of culture extracted in such studies were converted into episodes, in which a person from one culture is interacting with a person from another culture. The "culture assimilator" (Fiedler, Mitchell, & Triandis, 1971) is a programmed learning experience, in which the learner studies 100 such episodes and makes attributions about why persons from the other culture behave in a specific way. After making each attribution, the learner goes to another page, where feedback about the attribution (correct or incorrect) is provided. Much cultural information is provided in the feedback, and eventually the learner begins to make "isomorphic attributions" to the attributions typically made by people from the other culture. In short, the learner gets into the shoes of people from the other culture.

Random assignment of participants to both training and no-training groups allowed for the evaluation of the effectiveness of this training. It was shown that people experienced less culture shock when they were assimilator trained than when they had received other kinds of training. Culture assimilators are now a standard method of cross-cultural training and were widely used by the Navy, but I do not think they succeeded in making many sailors good ambassadors. That was a well-intentioned but unrealistic goal. There are now special kinds of assimilators, based on individualism–collectivism theory and other theoretical perspectives.

About that time, Len Berkowitz asked me to do a chapter on culture for his series, so I read a lot and put together a review of the field (Triandis, 1964). People perceive others quite differently across cultures. Unless we take this into account, we are bound to have cross-cultural misunderstandings.

In 1967 I went to a conference organized by Henri Tajfel and Herb Kelman in Ibadan, Nigeria. Situated on the campus of the University of Ibadan, the conference brought together about a dozen Western and a dozen African psychologists. The meeting was designed to stimulate research and collaboration. It made a deep impression on me, because the Tunisians introduced me to the concept of "intellectual colonialism." It included the accusation that Western psychologists collect data in exotic cultures and do not involve the local social scientists in their publications. I became very sensitive to this problem, and ever since then I have included local scientists in my studies. This turned out to be extremely valuable. Subsequently, very often when I analyzed some data and developed an interpretation of what they indicated, my collaborators had a different interpretation than what I showed them. I often ended up adopting their views. This is especially important when naming factors in factor analyses. This view became central to my discussions of cross-cultural methodology in Triandis et al. (1972) and the discussion of cross-cultural ethics (Tapp, Kelman, Triandis, Wrightsman, & Coelho, 1974).

Three years after I arrived in Illinois, Marty Fishbein joined our group. I felt that his theory of behavior as a function of norms and attitudes was not sufficiently broad. Behavior is often a function of habits and of the self-concept (Am I the kind of person who does that? Am I capable of doing this?). Finally, it is important to consider whether facilitating conditions, such as the setting, make it easy or difficult to behave. Thus I developed a more complicated model for the prediction of behavior (Triandis, 1977). I argued that each of the independent variables of the model has a weight that depends on culture. This model turned out to be useful, although it is more widely used by medical personnel (Reach, 2005) than in social psychology.

Cornell invited me back in 1968, at their International Studies Center. It was a wonderful opportunity to have a free year, which I spent writing two books (Triandis, 1971; Triandis et al., 1972).

By the nearly 1970s I had attained some reputation in the culture and psychology area. Thus the *Annual Review of Anthropology* and the *Annual Review of Psychology* asked me to do chapters on cross-cultural psychology. In 1972 I was asked by Allyn and Bacon to edit a *Handbook of Cross-Cultural Psychology*. This became a major undertaking, because the six volumes required 8 years to put together. It was a lot of work, but Lee Cronbach stated that it established cross-cultural psychology as a separate field. In the late 1980s Phil Zimbardo asked me to do a book on culture for his social psychology series. That resulted in Triandis (1994). I also edited the international volume of the *Handbook of Industrial and Organizational Psychology* (Triandis, Dunnette, & Hough, 1994).

In 1973 I was invited by the Venezuelan National Science Foundation to give some lectures in Caracas. I was impressed by the inequality that one could see in that country: people lived in newspaper-covered huts in the middle of that city, but on the other hand I was invited for a swim at a private club where the swimming pool was so large that it accommodated a small island. After Venezuela I visited Mexico City, where I met Rogelio Diaz-Guerrero, with whom I developed a research project on factors that Mexican women, of different social classes, consider important when they make the decision to have one more child. This visit later developed a special relationship with Mexico. I was subsequently invited to give several keynote addresses to meetings of social psychologists in that country. On several occasions my friends translated an English paper into Spanish, and I read it in Spanish, because many young social psychologists there do not understand English. This way some of my research became familiar to the young social psychologists in that country.

In 1974 I took my second trip around the world, with stops in New Zealand, Australia, Iran, and the Netherlands. I visited the Institute of Aboriginal Affairs in Canberra, Australia, a magnificent capital city built with an eye to the future. I was most impressed by the difference between Australian aborigines, who have very mild manners, and the much more outspoken African Americans. They may look somewhat similar, but their culture is very different. Also in 1974, at the meetings of the Interamerican Society of Psychology (SIP), in Bogotá, Colombia, I was elected vice president of the SIP. To my horror I was introduced to the audience as a member of the *junta directiva*. I did not cherish the idea of being a member of any *junta*, a term that is used in Greece to refer to a dictatorship.

At a conference on cross-cultural psychology at the New York Academy of Sciences, I had a sharp disagreement with Margaret Mead, who rejected any information obtained with psychological methods, such as rating scales. This is, of course, a fundamental debate, and I hold the position that we need all methods and convergence across them.

The exploration of what can be obtained if the methods of subjective culture are used with different participants resulted in studies of blacks and whites (Triandis, 1976), and Hispanics (e.g., Marin & Triandis, 1985). For example, "ecosystem distrust" was identified among blacks who had never held a job. They were suspicious of every aspect of their social environment, and that is quite understandable in a sample where reinforcements are chaotic. Also, the *simpatia* script was found among Hispanics (Triandis, Marin, Lisansky, & Betancourt, 1984). They tend to expect social interaction to be more positive and less negative than do non-Hispanics, and that has implications for many misunderstandings in interactions involving these two groups.

In 1978 I gave a week of lectures in Hawaii, and that started a long association with that island. I returned many times, including two sabbaticals at the East–West Center, where I wrote one of my most important papers (Triandis, 1989) and a book (Triandis, 1995).

In 1973 I met Geert Hofstede at the International Congress of Applied Psychology in Liege, Belgium. He had a large data set on the values of IBM employees from different parts of the world, which he offered to show me. So we went to Brussels, and I had a look at it. I told him that it was a terrific data set. He eventually put it together, and when I was asked by Sage Publications to evaluate the book for publication (Hofstede, 1980), I provided an enthusiastic review and found that the individualism–collectivism dimension was especially interesting. It connected well with my findings in Greece (Triandis et al., 1968), which was, when I studied it in the middle 1960s, quite collectivist. It also fit the Hispanic data very well (Marin & Triandis, 1985). Thus my interest in these constructs became the focus of considerable research. Exactly how should the constructs be defined (Hui & Triandis, 1986; Triandis, Bontempo, Villareal, Asai, & Lucca, 1988)? How can the constructs be distinguished from related constructs? What cognitive processes are involved? How should the constructs be measured (Triandis et al., 1988; Triandis, McCusker, & Hui, 1990; and many others)? What are their antecedents (Triandis & Trafimow, 2001)? What are their consequences (Triandis et al., 2001)?

As the relationship between culture and psychology was further explored, cross-cultural, cultural, and indigenous psychologies were advocated. I argued that we need all of these ways of studying the culture–psychology link and must use multimethod perspectives. When we obtain convergence of findings across these approaches, we have a solid basis for describing the culture–psychology relationship. Culture and personality can be examined from all three of these perspectives (Triandis & Suh, 2002).

Returning to a previous interest in intergroup relations, I developed a model (Triandis, Kurowski, & Gelfand, 1994) that includes variables such as Cultural Distance, the History of Previous Conflict, and the Knowledge of the Other Culture as determinants of the Perceived Similarity between a respondent and the person from the other culture. Perceived Similarity was hypothesized to predict Satisfaction With the Relationship, which was also determined by the Availability of Opportunities for Contact. Satisfaction was then hypothesized to predict Intergroup Attitudes and the Intention for Further Interaction. An empirical test by Goto and Chan obtained support for this model for both Whites and African Americans. However, structural equation modeling showed that the White sample required an additional path between Cultural Distance and Intergroup Attitudes, and the African American sample required an additional path between the History of Conflict and Intergroup Attitudes.

The rest is history. The field has picked up the constructs I worked with, and they have been connected to many aspects of social behavior. I linked collectivism and lying to out-groups and vertical individualism and cheating (Triandis et al., 2001). This may explain deception in American academia (making up fictitious data, especially in biological research) and business (e.g., Enron). A highly competitive culture may increase the use of deception (Triandis et al., 2001).

SOME MISCELLANEOUS MEMORIES

In 1979 I gave an invited address to the Interamerican Congress of Psychology in Lima, Peru. I spoke about attitude change, and one member of the audience criticized me for not giving them any clues on how Peru could win its next war with Chile (in 1898 these two countries had a war, which Peru lost, so they are dreaming of revenge)! In less-developed countries, psychologists are expected to provide *useful* applied conclusions.

In 1983 I went to India for a second time, this time as a distinguished Fulbright professor. In each city I visited, I was to give three lectures, at three different universities or institutes, and each venue could choose one of the nine proposed topics for me to discuss. It was a bit like being a concert pianist, giving a recital in different cities. The Fulbright people were most generous. A member of the Fulbright program and an interpreter accompanied me throughout the trip. I lectured in Delhi, Hyderabad, Patna, Bhubaneshwar, Puna, Bombay, and Ahmedabad, ending in Anand, a dairy cooperative that had its own university. I traveled by train and by air. At the end of the trip, I took 3 days on my own in Srinagar, Kashmir. The Fulbright people were overprotective, worrying about my safety in Kashmir. Sadly, this beautiful place is no longer safe, but when I was there I did not experience any trouble. The location of Srinagar near the Himalayas is enchanting. Lake Dahl was covered with flowers. The Shalimar gardens were memorable. It seems that the Muslim rulers put a lot of money in their gardens, because they could not put it in representational art.

At the meetings of the SIP in Quito, Ecuador, the members of the *junta directiva* were given the keys of the city. As I mentioned earlier, *junta* has bad connotations in Greek. I was elected president of the SIP, and my executive committee voted to have the next meeting in Cuba. As conference organizer I had to go to Cuba, which was not easy for an American, given the embargo. Americans were not allowed to spend any money in Cuba, so all my expenses were covered by the Cubans. The Cuban government provided a car and driver. During the inauguration of the congress, the vice president of Cuba, a fellow who looked like an American senator, pressed me to do something about the embargo. I explained that the Reagan administration had very little respect for social psychologists, whom they confused with socialists. I doubted that anyone would listen.

That year the United Nations Educational, Scientific, and Cultural Organization (UNESCO) asked me to participate in a panel, held in Buenos Aires, Argentina, that would organize a major cross-cultural study of values. In the typical UNESCO manner, the panel had a mixture of specialists and nationalities. I was the American psychologist. There was a Polish sociologist, a Ghanaian geographer, a Filipino anthropologist, a Japanese statistician, a Brazilian jurist, a Chilian philosopher, and an Uruguaian city planner. UNESCO was represented by a French consultant. Because I was the only one who knew English, French, and Spanish, the three languages of the committee, I was asked to chair the meeting. The meeting was translated into these three languages, and the professional interpreters depended on me to get them out of a bind when there was a technical term they did not understand. At one point the French consultant was talking about *ce virus qui est Dallas,* and the interpreter panicked. "What is this virus?" she asked me. I explained that it was just a television program!

Unfortunately, while the idea of different disciplines and nationalities is commendable, the reality is that we spent the whole week trying to understand each other. At the end, nothing was accomplished. I was given the task of drafting a research proposal that would be circulated among the delegates. I did so, but just at that moment the United States pulled out of UNESCO, and they could not circulate a proposal drafted by an American!

In 1986 I spent a week at Churchill College of the University of Cambridge, in England. I ate at the high table, while the students ate at a lower level. Dinner started with the head of the college using a Latin invocation. Wines and spirits were widely available before, during, and after dinner. In fact, while the faculty pay is low by American standards, the faculty, which is at the very top of the profession, was compensated, in part, by free food and drink. I had the impression that for some of them the drinking was an important aspect of their life at the college.

In 1987 I was invited to the celebrations of the 150th anniversary of the inauguration of the University of Athens, and I received an honorary degree from that university. The celebrations included a buffet dinner at the palace where I discussed Greece's foreign policy with the foreign minister and had delightful chats with delegates from the major European universities, such as my friend (and fellow psychologist) Peter Drendt, who was rector magnificus of the University of Amsterdam. Melina Mercuri (star of *Never on Sunday*), who by then was minister of culture, gave a wonderful cocktail party at the Yacht Club, and we were taken on a trip to Delphi with a superb tourist guide.

That year also I had my first trip to China, where I gave colloquia in Beijing, Shanghai, and Hanzhu and visited Shu Tzo. The major event of 1988 was a 6-week course on the methods of social psychology, organized by the National Academy of Sciences and the Chinese Institute of Psychology at Beijing, China. Prior to that visit I had a conference in Bielefeld, Germany, on how to teach German professors about American culture and a stop in Athens to talk at the meeting of the Greek Psychological Society. To reach China I went around the world for a third time.

Traveling through China without a guide was a challenge, but we managed. I had acquired enough Chinese to be able to buy a ticket or understand that there was no room at a hotel. Guilin, with its romantic mountain formations, and the trip on the river Li were unforgettable. Xian, with the terracotta statues and many other sites, was a great experience, but the agent at the airport would not reconfirm my previously confirmed reservations to Beijing. My wife and I showed up early for the flight, having explained, to a Chinese fellow passenger in a taxi, about the lack of reconfirmation. He took over and told the airport people that if I did not show up in Beijing on time, a major hydroelectric dam would not get constructed! They put us on the plane, and we arrived in Beijing on time, where we were received by a delegation from the Institute of Psychology. For the first night's banquet, they had Kentucky Fried chicken. I told them right away that we preferred Chinese food.

We were treated royally. We had a car and driver to take us to the interesting sites around the city, including the Great Wall, which we visited in two different places. At one point in time a traffic jam developed on the Great Wall, and taking advantage of my height I became a traffic policeman and disentangled it. The Chinese were amazed by my 6-foot-4-inch height and brought their children to see me and be photographed with me. In 6 weeks, of course, I was able to see Beijing in much detail, and we were treated to a side trip to Shan Du, where the emperors used to spend their summer. The trip by train was a bit trying, because the railway station was so crowded. We had just read a novel titled *I Lost My Wife in the Beijing Railway Station*, and my wife had the feeling that she would lose me in that mass of humanity.

We were housed in a Mongolian *yurt*, but with TV and a nice bathroom. The garden where the emperor spent his time was delightful. One emperor went around and picked the best view of some part of the garden and wrote a poem about it, which is shown at each site. The wealth of the Chinese emperor is indicated by the fact that he wanted the Dalai Lama to visit him, and the Dalai Lama expressed his concern that he might not be comfortable in Shan Du. So the emperor had a copy of the Patala Palace, in Tibet, built in Shan Du!

As president-elect of the International Association of Applied Psychology (IAAP), I was responsible for organizing its 1994 Congress of the IAAP in Madrid, Spain. I had to go to Madrid several times in the 1990–1994 period, and my wife and I did extensive sightseeing throughout Spain and Portugal. The local organizer Jose Maria Prieto was systematic and terribly well organized, so the congress was a great success. My job as president started in Kyoto, Japan, in 1990, at the previous meeting of the IAAP. At the inauguration of the Madrid congress, I spoke in Spanish (of course, the text was prepared by my Spanish friends), French (the second official language of the IAAP), and English. As is normal in such meetings, the organizers of subsequent meetings arrange to have their embassies host the executive committee and some of the important psychologists. The Greek embassy hosted such a meeting, and of course I chatted with the staff in Greek.

All this travel resulted in many interpersonal connections and a lot of cooperative research. My list of publications shows the names of many colleagues from around the world.

THE LAST YEARS IN ILLINOIS

In 1990 I did some consulting for NASA on the question of how cultural differences between Russians and Americans could be accommodated on the space module. The following year as president-elect of the Society for Comparative Research, a society that consists of anthropologists and psychologists as well as others who do comparative work, I had to organize its annual meeting. I did it in Puerto Rico, where Nydia Lucca and her husband, Angel Paccheco, who had been visitors in Illinois, resided, so I had very competent local persons to do it. I spent 2 months on the abstracts of the papers, making sure that each paper was given at the optimal time and place. I invited Shalom Schwartz of the Hebrew University in Jerusalem to give the keynote address, and he did a marvelous job. Dick Nisbett, who was just starting his cross-cultural work, came to learn more about what we were doing. The meeting included some very lively local dancers and was pronounced a great success.

The 1991 European Congress of Psychology was held in Budapest, a beautiful city on the Danube. My social psychologist friend Ibolya Vary-Szilagii found an apartment for us and also arranged for us to spend some time at the villa of the Hungarian Academy of Sciences on Lake Balaton. The food at the villa was very rich with eggs, at breakfast, lunch, and dinner. I inquired about life expectancy there and was told that it was 55. No wonder! In connection with that meeting, the International Association of Cross-Cultural Psychology met in Debgrecen, Hungary, a charming provincial town. After these meetings in the company of five other members of that association, we went to Poland, where Pavl Boski arranged for a joint meeting with Polish psychologists to introduce them to cross-cultural issues.

As universities in the less-developed countries develop, they must acquire some useful norms from the countries that have had more experience with academic life. This has resulted in my selecting the faculty of new universities on Crete and on Cyprus. My travels continued, but to avoid a travelogue I will not mention any more of them, except for an especially enjoyable conference in Padova, Italy, in 1997. This was one of the major universities of the world in the 16th and 17th centuries. One can see the chair that was used by Galileo Galilei for his teaching. Among the students of that university were Copernicus (the founder of modern astronomy) and Harvey (the founder of modern medicine; he found how the heart works and how the blood circulates). The first anatomy laboratory was established there, and it became one of the leading medical schools in the world. My wife and I always enjoy Italy, and Padova is such a good location for a trip to Venice.

I retired in 1997, at age 71, and my wife, John Adamopoulos, and the department at Illinois organized a splendid meeting, with many of the leading cross-cultural psychologists and some of my former students. Half the meeting was thought provoking, with serious papers that resulted in a publication (Adamopoulos & Kashima, 1999), and the other half was funny, with different people pulling my leg one way or another. John Berry presented to me the second edition of the *Handbook of Cross-Cultural Psychology*. It was moving to see that my work was being continued.

AFTER RETIREMENT

I taught for a few years in different places, wanting to stay in touch with students and to talk about my ideas for the future of the field. These places included the University of California, Irvine; the University of Hawaii; the Nanyang Institute of Technology in Singapore (twice); and Victoria University in New Zealand. With more time during this period I did even more sightseeing, at places such as Bali, Indonesia; Bora-Bora in Tahiti; and a number of places on the coast of Malaysia.

I was given all kinds of fancy titles, such as "Chancellor's Visiting Professor" (at the University of California), "Distinguished Visiting Scholar" (at Hawaii), "Shaw Chair Professor," and "Goh Tjoel Kok Professor" (in Singapore). I gave colloquia in Tartu, Estonia, and Geneva, Switzerland, and participated in conferences in Cyprus, Indonesia, Poland, Sweden, and Taiwan. In 2001 I was at conferences in the Netherlands, Germany, and Singapore. In 2004 I went around the world for a fourth time, to give lectures in Taiwan and a course in Athens, Greece, for the bankers of the European Union.

But the events of 9/11/01 shook me up. I had to find out about terrorism and its causes. I read widely, and I am currently writing a book, tentatively titled *A Clash of Fantasies: Cognitively Simple Self-Deceptions in Everyday Life.*

THE SATISFACTIONS FROM STUDENTS

Nothing is more satisfying for an academic than good students. They become like his children, and they carry on the work that he cherishes. I was very lucky in that respect, primarily because Illinois has always been rated as having one of the best psychology departments in the world. Of course there have also been some disappointments, in the sense that the person did not become prominent, and I lost track of what he or she is doing. In any case, consider the following list of names, in the order in which I had them as students:

- Josie Naidoo, from South Africa, who became a professor of psychology at Laurier University in Canada (she has now retired);
- Al Bass, who became the head of the Department of Psychology at Wayne State, in Detroit;
- Yang Ku-Shu, from Taiwan, who became the most distinguished Chinese psychologist alive, vice president of the Academia Sinica, and developer of a Chinese indigenous psychology;
- Robert Ewen, who has written a book on personality that is in its fifth edition;
- Earl Davis, who became a professor in Dublin, Ireland;
- Wally Loh, who took degrees in both psychology and law and was, when I last saw him, dean of the law school at the University of Washington, Seattle;

- Andy Davidson, who is the associate dean of the School of Public Health at Columbia University in New York;
- Terry Mitchell, who is a professor at the University of Washington, Seattle;
- Jack Feldman, who is a professor at Georgia Institute of Technology;
- Rabi Baghat, from India, who is a professor at the University of Memphis, Tennessee;
- Rosita Albert, from Brazil, who was my research associate and is now a professor at the University of Minnesota;
- Don Carlston, who is a professor at Purdue University;
- John Adamopoulos, from Greece, who is a professor of psychology at Governor's State University in Allentown, Michigan;
- Harry Hui, from Hong Kong, who is now a senior lecturer at the University of Hong Kong;
- Kwok Leung, from Hong Kong, who is a chair professor at City University in Hong Kong;
- Bernadette Setiadi, from Indonesia, who is the head of psychology at the University of Indonesia;
- Yoshi Kashima, from Japan, who is now at the University of Melbourne in Australia and the editor of the *Asian Journal of Social Psychology*; his wife, Emiko, was also my student and teaches in Australia;
- Darius Chan, who is at the Chinese University of Hong Kong;
- Marcelo Villareal, from Mexico, who is a consultant in Monterey, Mexico;
- Robert Bontempo, who is an adjunct professor at Columbia University and also a very successful consultant in New York City;
- Sharon Goto, who is at Pomona College, in California;
- Chris McCusker, who taught at Yale for years;
- Michele Gelfand, who is an associate professor at the University of Maryland and has developed a very important, NSF-supported program of research on cultural tightness;
- Darm Bhawuk, who heads the program on international management at the University of Hawaii; and
- Arzu Wasti, from Turkey, my last Ph.D., who is an associate professor at Sabanci University in Istanbul, Turkey; she received an award for her work at a ceremony attended by the president of the Turkish Republic.

At the International Congress of Applied Psychology in July 2006, there was a symposium on the occasion of my 80th birthday. Adamopoulos (Greece), Baghat (India), Bhawuk (Nepal), Gelfand (the United States), and Leung (Hong Kong) gave papers linking their current research to what I had done in the past. Peter Smith (professor emeritus at the University of Sheffield, England) did a masterful job identifying the major themes of my career and linking them to the papers of the former students. It was like a memorial, where people say nice things about the dearly departed. But I was there! It was one of the most satisfying events in my life.

CONCLUSIONS

Humans are social animals, and much research shows that the good life requires that people be connected to one another. Yet strife and competition disconnect people and make them miserable. Universally humans praise peace and harmony but act so as to make them unlikely. My purpose in life has been to try to increase the subjective well-being of as many humans as possible. That means I have wanted to increase the physical and mental health of at least some and to see them living long, satisfying lives. To help people increase their well-being, it is necessary, among other things, to understand where cultural differences come from and how we can decrease the way such differences create social distance, conflict, and other divisions. Much of my career has been focused on these goals.

It has been most satisfying that I was able to achieve some of these goals. I think I helped colleagues and students understand the factors that create cultural differences and how to take them into account in planning international organizations and activities. Some of this work developed methods that provide cross-cultural training. Some of my books were translated into German, Spanish, Japanese, Russian, and Farsi (Iran). My research received several awards, from several psychological associations. I established friendships around the world. I lectured in some 60 countries and certainly covered the most populous ones, with perhaps more than half of the world's population.

Perhaps most satisfying are the good students and the links with colleagues all over the world. As I said when I started this paper, connections among humans lead to the good life. Every day as I respond to my e-mail, I receive one or two requests for advice on plans for a new research project, from some corner of the world. I feel connected, and that is the most important aspect of the good life. Of course connections can be achieved in different ways. A person staying in a small village where he knows everyone can be as connected as I have been. It is just that my connections have been international.

Looking back, I note that there were many points when my career could have gone in a different direction. I could have been a research engineer, an editor of journals, or an administrator. I conclude with my earlier advice: Do what you feel most passionate about. To succeed you must work very hard, but it is well worth the effort.

REFERENCES

Adamopoulos, J., & Kashima, Y. (1999). *Social psychology and cultural context*. Thousand Oaks, CA: Sage Publications.

Fiedler, F. E., Mitchell, T., & Triandis, H. C. (1971). The culture assimilator: An approach to cross-cultural training. *Journal of Applied Psychology, 55*, 95–102.

Hofstede, G. (1980). *Culture's consequences*. Thousand Oaks, CA: Sage Publications.

Hui, H. C., & Triandis, H. C. (1986). Individualism-collectivism: A study of cross-cultural researchers. *Journal of Cross-Cultural Psychology, 17*, 225–248.

Marin, G., & Triandis, H. C. (1985). Allocentrism as an important characteristic of the behavior of Latin Americans and Hispanics. In R. Diaz-Guerrero (Ed.), *Cross-cultural and national studies in social psychology* (pp. 85–104). Amsterdam: North Holland.

Reach, G. (2005). Role of habit in adherence to medical treatment. *Diabetic Medicine, 22*, 415–420.

Tapp, J. L., Kelman, H. C., Triandis, H. C., Wrightsman, L., & Coelho, G. (1974). Continuing concerns in cross-cultural ethics: A report. *International Journal of Psychology, 9*, 231–249.

Triandis, H. C. (1961). A note on Rokeach's theory of prejudice. *Journal of Abnormal and Social Psychology, 62*, 184–186.

Triandis, H. C. (1964). Cultural influences upon cognitive processes. In L. Berkowitz (Ed.), *Advances in experimental social psychology* (pp. 1–48). New York: Academic Press.

Triandis, H. C. (1971). *Attitude and attitude change.* New York: Wiley.

Triandis, H. C. (1976). *Variations in Black and White perceptions of the social environment.* Urbana-Champaign: University of Illinois Press.

Triandis, H. C. (1977). *Interpersonal behavior.* Monterey, CA: Brooks/Cole.

Triandis, H. C. (1978). Some universals of social behavior. *Personality and Social Psychology Bulletin, 4*, 1–16.

Triandis, H. C. (1989). Self and social behavior in differing cultural contexts. *Psychological Review, 96*, 506–520.

Triandis, H. C. (1992). Cross-cultural research in social psychology. In D. Granberg & G. Sarup (Eds.), *Social judgment and intergroup relations: Essays in honor of Muzafer Sherif* (pp. 229–244). New York: Springer-Verlag.

Triandis, H. C. (1994). *Culture and social behavior.* New York: McGraw-Hill.

Triandis, H. C. (1995). *Individualism and collectivism.* Boulder, CO: Westview.

Triandis, H. C. (1997). Raised in a collectivist culture, one may become an individualist. In M. H. Bond (Ed.), *Working at the interface of cultures: Eighteen lives in social science* (pp. 38–46). London: Routledge.

Triandis, H. C. (1999). Odysseus wandered for 10, I wondered for 50 years. In W. J. Lonner, D. L. Dinnel, D. K. Forgays, & S. A. Hayes (Eds.), *Merging past, present, and future in cross-cultural psychology* (pp. 46–50). Lisse, the Netherlands: Swets & Zeitlinger.

Triandis, H. C. (in press). The satisfactions of a career in cultural psychology. In D. G. Oster (Ed.), *Life as a psychologist: Career, choices, and insights from veterans.* Westport, CT: Greenwood Press.

Triandis, H. C., Bontempo, R., Villareal, M. J., Asai, M., & Lucca, N. (1988). Individualism and collectivism: Cross-cultural perspectives on self-ingroup relationships. *Journal of Personality and Social Psychology, 54*, 323–338.

Triandis, H. C., Carnevale, P., Gelfand, M., Robert, C., Wasti, A., Probst, T., Kashima, E., Dragonas, T., Chan, D., Chen, X. P., Kim, U., deDreu, C., van de Vliert, E., Iwao, S., Ohbuchi, K.-L., & Schmidt, P. (2001). Culture, personality and deception: A multilevel approach. *International Journal of Cross-Cultural Management, 1*, 73–90.

Triandis, H. C., & Davis, E. E. (1965). Race and belief as determinants of behavioral intentions. *Journal of Personality and Social Psychology, 2*, 715–725.

Triandis, H. C., Davis, E. E., & Takezawa, S. I. (1965). Some determinants of social distance among American, German and Japanese students. *Journal of Personality and Social Psychology, 2*, 540–551.

Triandis, H. C., Dunnette, M., & Hough, L. (Eds.). (1994). *Handbook of industrial and organizational psychology* (2nd ed., Vol. 4). Palo Alto: Consulting Psychologists Press.

Triandis, H. C., Kurowski, L. L., & Gelfand, M. J. (1994). Workplace diversity. In H. C. Triandis, M. Dunnette, & L. Hough (Eds.), *Handbook of industrial and organizational psychology* (2nd ed., Vol. 4, pp. 769–827). Palo Alto: Consulting Psychologists Press.

Triandis, H. C., & Lambert, W. W. (1958). A restatement and test of Schlosberg's theory of emotion with two kinds of subjects from Greece. *Journal of Abnormal and Social Psychology, 56,* 321–328.

Triandis, H. C., Marin, G., Lisansky, J., & Betancourt, H. (1984). Simpatia as a cultural script of Hispanics. *Journal of Personality and Social Psychology, 47,* 1363–1375.

Triandis, H. C., McCusker, C., & Hui, C. H. (1990). Multimethod probes of individualism and collectivism. *Journal of Personality and Social Psychology, 59,* 1006–1020.

Triandis, H. C., & Osgood, C. E. (1958). A comparative factorial analysis of semantic structures of monolingual Greek and American students. *Journal of Abnormal and Social Psychology, 57,* 187–196.

Triandis, H. C., & Suh, E. M. (2002). Cultural influences on personality. *Annual Review of Psychology, 53,* 133–160.

Triandis, H. C., & Trafimow, D. (2001). Cross-national prevalence of collectivism. In C. Sedikides & M. B. Brewer (Eds.), *Individual self, relational self, collective self* (pp. 259–276). Philadelphia. Psychology Press.

Triandis, H. C., Vassiliou, V., & Nassiakou, M. (1968). Three cross-cultural studies of subjective culture. *Journal of Personality and Social Psychology Monograph Supplement, 8*(4), 1–42.

Triandis, H. C., Vassiliou, V., Vassiliou, G., Tanaka, Y., & Shanmugam, A. V. (1972). *The analysis of subjective culture.* New York: Wiley.

Toward Understanding Social Power
A Personal Odyssey

BERTRAM H. RAVEN

Department of Psychology, University of California, Los Angeles

*T*hough most of us date the beginnings of the field of social psychology to the turn of the century, with the publication of two textbooks with that title, by E. A. Ross and William McDougall, it is generally conceded that the major growth of the field can be seen in the period after World War II, when a number of young people, fresh out of military service, entered universities. Many of these were children of parents who had immigrated from Germany, Poland, Russia, and other parts of Eastern Europe, and a substantial number were Jewish. They had spent their early childhood in the Great Depression and seen or experienced first-hand its hardships and inequities. They matured during the presidency of Franklin Roosevelt and were excited by the hopes of the New Deal, which they saw as offering greater security and economic and social justice. Some were excited by what had been characterized as the great social experiment in the Soviet Union, only to have their hopes dashed as they learned more about it. They witnessed the horrors of Hitler and Nazism and later learned of the horrors of the Holocaust. Thrilled by the victories of World War II, they looked hopefully toward an era of world peace, with justice and racial and ethnic harmony for all. They hoped to understand and contribute to such changes in some way. I was one of these.

FAMILY ROOTS

My own family roots go back to a small town in Belarus, in Tsarist Russia, where my parents had a small *kreml,* or general store. My three oldest sisters, Clara, Anne, and Min, were born and spent their early childhood there. My family got along well with its Russian neighbors but did have the experience of pogroms led by Cossacks. This life was too restrictive for my father. Hearing of a program, sponsored by a wealthy Bavarian Jewish baron Moritz von Hirsch, to resettle Russian Jews on the pampas of Argentina, he left my mother to look after the girls and the store and went off to Argentina. He was excited by his new life but was homesick, and he didn't have the means to bring his family to Argentina—so he went back to Belarus, only to be told by the count who controlled that district that he couldn't stay. It seems that the count thought he might be dangerous because all the peasants came to hear from him what life was like in the new world. The legal reason given was that while my father was gone, they had taken a census of Jews in that district, and because my father had been absent, he had not been counted—so they did not have a place for him. My father left his family again, this time to homestead in Alberta, Canada. My mother and the girls joined him later. They stayed there for a year, long enough for my brother, Jay, to be born, then decided that the soil was too rocky to farm and the weather was too cold, so they went off again, to join some cousins in Youngstown, Ohio. My sister, Frances, was born there, and 5 years later I came along. Eventually, my father started an auto wrecking business, which supported our family through the Depression. While not living in luxury, we had enough for our basic needs, but not much beyond that.

To support his large family through the Depression, my father worked long hours, from daybreak to late at night, 7 days a week. We did not see very much of him. By the time he got home, exhausted, from his business, it was past our bedtime. From him the major thing we got was sustenance, as well as a role model of dedication, reliability, acceptance of responsibility, and a readiness to try new and different things.

MY MOTHER

My mother's influence was much greater. She was a most remarkable woman. It is difficult to imagine that she had had no formal education whatsoever. After all, she was trained to cook, sew, care for her children, and keep a kosher, Jewish home. Beyond that no other education was considered necessary. Yet she managed to learn a lot on her own. The boys in the Jewish shtetl community, including my father, attended *cheder,* classes where they learned to read and write in Yiddish and to read the Torah and pray in Hebrew. My mother, as a little girl, was excluded, but she sat by the door and listened, so that she eventually learned to read in Yiddish. In another life, I think she might have become a great naturalist. She told me how as a child she watched, with amazement, little fishes in the nearby pond in the forest, watched as their tails fell off and they developed legs and became frogs. This she discovered on her own. I listened intently, but a fish becoming a frog? It stretched my credibility. She studied the frogs as they swam and imitated them, so that she became quite an effective swimmer herself. We all spoke Yiddish at home, and I talked in Yiddish to her and to my father as long as they lived.

My mother told me many folktales and stories of rabbinical ages and devils. A number of these tales, I later learned, actually came from Aesop. How she learned them I would never know. Somehow she also learned a lot about history, about the Tsar Alexander II, who freed the slaves (actually serfs) and made life easier for Jews—for which, of course, he was assassinated. She told me of the Russo-Japanese war and how the overly confident Russians were soundly defeated at a place called "Par-Tar-Tour," which I learned, much later, was more generally known as "Port Arthur." She told me of the conspiratorial conviction of the French captain Dreyfus for treachery, framed by his anti-Semitic superiors and imprisoned in that horrible place called "Chortra Utra" (Russian for "Devil's Island"), and of his eventual vindication. She related the blood libel conviction of a man named Beilis who was accused of murdering a young Russian boy, so that his blood could be used for a Passover ritual. From her I developed a particularly strong sense of Jewish identity and an awareness of anti-Semitism and a deep dedication to the Zionist dream of a state where Jews could be independent and free of abuse. At home we always spoke in Yiddish, and I insisted on doing this even outside the home. My sister was often embarrassed when I would speak to her loudly in Yiddish while we were riding on the streetcar.

Our mother also introduced me to music. She sang songs in Russian, Hebrew, and, mostly, Yiddish. She would crank up our Victrola and play records. We heard Russian operatic music sung by the great basso Feodor Chaliapin. One of her favorites was Saint-Saens's *Danse Macabre,* during which she would relate the imagery of the dead arising to dance at midnight until the cock crowed in the morning. (All of this in Yiddish, of course.) She encouraged Jay and me to play the clarinet. (Jay later played in the Youngstown Symphony Orchestra and taught music in schools and universities.) It was not just for the love of learning: For Russian Jewish mothers of her generation, a major fear was that their sons would be forced into the Russian army, never to be seen again. If a war came, which she always considered likely, it was better to serve in a military band and play music for people rather than to shoot at them and be shot at in return. (Jay, indeed, served during World War II in the National Air Forces Band in Washington.) Music became a major interest for me, and until I entered the army, I was most interested in a career in music.

EDUCATIONAL ASPIRATIONS

From our mother, who had had no formal education whatsoever, we all learned so much, but especially an admiration for learning and education: Our older sister Clara set high academic standards for all of us. She worked her way through college and was a student at Michigan when she got a call telling her that she had a baby brother. (Clara insisted that it came as a complete surprise.) She later continued with a master's degree in bacteriology, an MD degree from Northwestern with a specialty in pathology, and a postdoctoral fellowship at the University of Liverpool in Britain. After considerable persistence, she became one of the first women commissioned in the U.S. Army Medical Corps, eventually reaching the rank of colonel. Her later years were distinguished by her pioneer research on sudden infant death syndrome while she was the medical examiner for Wayne County, Michigan.

None of my other siblings could really match that, but each excelled in at least one field, but usually in several fields. Given this, it came as something of a shock for our family when I failed the very first semester of the first grade. My sisters tell me that this was because I could not understand English. Perhaps. But I also had a bad case of whooping cough, which kept me out of school for quite a while. I never had that experience again. However, that failure had a particularly important impact on my later life, as we shall see later. In any event, I was under continual pressure at school, because we all went through the same school system, and my teachers' expectations were based on the performance of one of my successful siblings: My Latin teacher made me stay after school, even though my work was satisfactory, because, after all, I was a brother of Min, who was an outstanding Latin scholar. Clara was tops in math and the sciences. Jay was a talented musician. Frances would take it on herself to mediate with my teachers—something my mother could not do. But at home, I was simply expected to do well. If I brought an all-A report card home to my father, he would simply glance at it and sign it. If I had a B, he would hesitate just a bit, show mild surprise ("Bs too?"), sign it, hand it back to me, and go back to reading his newspaper.

Schooling took up most of my waking hours, because, like most Jewish boys, and many Jewish girls, we followed each day of school with an additional session at Hebrew school, to which we had to transport ourselves with two city buses. Once I got to high school, I would often get to school by 7:00 a.m. to practice my clarinet, saxophone, and cello. Somehow, going on to college was something I just expected to do. I didn't know exactly how, because I knew that my father could not afford to support me. So I worked and saved. On Saturdays and holidays, I worked in a shoe store. By the time I was 15, I was working summers in a foundry, where we were making parts for World War II navy vessels. Later I began playing clarinet and tenor saxophone in dance bands on weekends and sometimes during the week. But that work was irregular, so I took a job playing Friday, Saturday, and occasionally Sunday nights with a small combo at the Blue Crystal nightclub. This began to worry my mother some, because I would leave home at 8:30 p.m. and return at 2:00 a.m. She would never tell me that I could not do something. Instead, she would ask if I really needed to do all those things. I told her I could use the money, but, even more, the musical experience might be good for me, because that might eventually be my profession. When I got home from my nightclub gig at 2:30 in the morning, I would find her waiting for me.

A SUMMER WITH THE CIRCUS

In the summer of 1944, I accepted a position in the Cole Brothers circus band, along with my very oldest friend, Jack Hollander, whom I met in first grade. At $38.50 per week, with room and board, it paid even more than working in the foundry, and, of course, it would offer a different musical experience, which I thought would be useful. We traveled by train from one town to the next, sleeping on the circus train. To fill a gap in the band, I was asked to play the part of a baritone horn with my tenor saxophone. The first days were quite an ordeal, particularly because I had to transpose and sight read, skipping from one musical number to the next to coordinate with the clowns, trapeze artists, the woman on the waltzing horse, animal trainers, and others. I wrote home often and described the interesting things I was observing—observations that became all the more meaningful to me later on, from the perspectives of social psychology and anthropology. There was the very firm caste system between those in the "Big Top" (the major circus performance) and the "Side Show" with the freaks, fire-eaters, bearded ladies, and exotic dancers. We had many southerners in the circus, and there were signs of prejudice against African Americans, but the Big Top–Side Show caste system overrode that. In addition, there was a status hierarchy within the castes, from the circus owners, the Big Top headliners, the trapeze artists, bandsmen, the cowboys and dancers, the clowns, and the roustabouts. That status was clearly represented in terms of their location on the circus train, with those of superior status at the rear of the train and lesser status toward the front. I was particularly well situated to make social observations when the train was moving, because my bunk was next to the Pie Car, a section where circus personnel could gather for drinks, card games with some experienced poker players, slot machines, and general social activities. I described this social system later on in an introduction to a chapter on social structure in the social psychology text that Jeff Rubin and I wrote (Raven & Rubin, 1983). I also wrote up my observations for an anthropology course at Michigan years later, and my professor, Horace Miner, encouraged me to take some time off, go back. He could get funding for me to do an anthropological participant observation study of caste and class in a circus community.

MILITARY SERVICE

I left the circus in August 1944, having learned a lot more than music, and went home in time for my last semester in high school. I turned 18 in September and had to register for selective service, but I was deferred so that I could graduate in January. Here my life was most clearly affected by my having to repeat the first grade: By joining the army in January rather than September, I missed out on some of the worst parts of World War II, including the Battle of the Bulge in Europe and some of the bloodier battles in the Pacific.

On high school graduation day, I received the expected letter, with the now familiar salutation: "Greetings from the President of the United States." Ten days later I was quickly shipped off to Fort Knox to be trained as a medium tank crewman. The wars in Europe and the Pacific were still at their height, and there was a rush to train replacements for the heavy casualties, particularly in the infantry and armored units. Musicians were not a priority.

Military service was certainly not what I enjoyed doing, but I accepted my duty as a loyal citizen, ready to do what was required, particularly in combat against an unquestionably evil enemy. I could understand having to learn how to fire various weapons, to drive the tank, to bayonet dummies made to look like the enemy, to go on long marches to build up our endurance, and so on. What I could not understand was what we called "chicken shit": being ordered, without any explanation, to do silly things, such as wearing boots with differing lacing on odd and even days, walking around in puddles of water, having our footlockers arranged in meticulous patterns, saluting officers, and so on. How could those silly things serve the war effort? Only many years later did I feel I understood why. It was, of course, a matter of power. We were being trained in automatic, unquestioning obedience to authority—legitimate position power, rather than following a more normal expectation of clear explanations (informational power). In battle conditions there was no time for explanations, questions, or even the slightest deviation from a direct order. As Alfred Lord Tennyson put it, "Ours is not to reason why," because once we got into battle situations, it could be fatal to require that we obey only orders for which we felt that there was a clear logical explanation. And later still, I also understood the dangers of unquestioned obedience to legitimate power as demonstrated so dramatically in research by Stanley Milgram (1974).

The lieutenant in charge of our unit in basic training even offered some advice to the men about how to deal with an uncomfortable power–dominance situation. He said that when we are walking in Louisville with our girlfriends, we might feel uncomfortable having to salute a commissioned officer coming our way, because it might make us look less powerful, maybe less masculine. But, understand, he said, that military protocol requires that the commissioned officer salute back in return. So he advised us to say to the young woman, "Hey! See that captain coming toward us? Watch me make him salute me." He was, of course, anticipating what we today call reframing, important for a soldier who wanted his female friend to see him in the most powerful light.

It was while we were in a quarter-ton truck, coming off of bivouac, that one of the other soldiers told us that he had just heard that our president, Franklin Roosevelt, had died. I asked him to say it again, because I didn't think that I heard him. It was so hard to believe. We had never really known another president. We felt a very deep personal loss, the immensity of which became even more over the years, as we gained additional knowledge about the importance of his role in getting us past the Great Depression and in introducing social legislation that would forever change our country and the world. It was only later that we could get a better understanding of this truly charismatic leader and his sensitivity to the bases of power (Gold & Raven, 1992).

Before we completed our basic training, we were relieved to hear the news of our victory in Europe. A great relief, but it guaranteed that we would all be going to the Far East. Given our armored training, and with Allied forces driving the Japanese from the South Pacific, we fully expected to be in the forefront of an invasion of Japan. We were given a short leave before being transferred to Fort Ord, California, to continue combat training while we waited our place on the next ships. It was while we were there that we heard about the explosion of bombs of tremendous magnitude in Hiroshima and Nagasaki. Knowing what we know now about the immensity of the damage and suffering, it is uncomfortable to remember that I, and everyone around me at the time, felt a sense of triumph and relief at the news.

We were at sea when we heard about the Japanese surrender. We eventually landed in the Philippines. The war was over, and there was no need for tank crews. I spent a year there: First I helped to process long-term veterans for their return home, and then I was assigned to the 86th Infantry Division. Meanwhile, I had a chance to experience another completely different social culture, to see ethnocentrism among our American armed forces, and to witness firsthand the devastation of war. But with the war over, I felt that I was wasting so much time. I was bored. I was fascinated but repelled by military regulations—chicken shit all over again. Why should there now be even greater concern about unquestioned obedience to senseless commands? Then I began to have my own experiences as I began to move up the ranks to corporal, sergeant, and eventually first sergeant in the Headquarters Company. It was a position with which I never felt comfortable, but it allowed me to experience and gain more insights about power in military situations and especially the effects of power on the power holder.

Meanwhile, I had some time to read all sorts of books—my first contact with paperback books, distributed by the U.S. Armed Forces Institute. And I had my first exposure to psychology. I signed up for a course called Psychology and Life, using Floyd Ruch's text (which Phil Zimbardo later successfully transformed into one of the most popular texts). I was fascinated: This is what I wanted to study! I wrote a letter to the Department of Psychology at Ohio State, saying that I wanted information on their psychology courses, because I wanted to go there and work toward a Ph.D. They sent me materials with a condescending note saying that they appreciated my inquiry, but I should know that I would have to receive a bachelor's degree and a master's degree first.

OHIO STATE UNIVERSITY

After 14 months in the Philippines, I finally returned home and enrolled at Ohio State University as soon as I possibly could. My family did not have the funds to support me in college. But what about all of the money I had stashed away in war bonds—from the shoe store, the foundry, the circus, the bands, the bond a month I purchased patriotically from my army pay? It amounted to very little—inflation had eaten most of it! In 1944, however, Congress passed the GI Bill, one of the most social revolutionary measures in American history. Higher education, which had previously been available mainly to children of well-to-do parents, plus a few who were able to win scholarships, suddenly became available to any veteran whom the colleges would accept. It provided college support for 12 months plus an additional month for each month in the service, including tuition, books, and some subsistence money. It is difficult to fathom how greatly the GI Bill affected academia and, indeed, most aspects of life in the United States, as these millions of young veterans eagerly took advantage of the new educational opportunities available to them.

After I declared my major in psychology, my father asked me to explain to him exactly what it was that I was studying, because people were asking him. One of my cousins asked, "So you're going to college?" "Yes." "And what is it you are studying at college?" "Psychology." "Psychology? Well, I guess, it is better than not going to college altogether." It is gratifying to realize that in the years since then psychology as a field of study is more widely understood and appreciated.

I was very excited to be at the university. I leafed through course descriptions in the college catalog like a kid in a candy store. But I couldn't take all of them. I had 34 months of support from the GI Bill, which would not take me through the Ph.D., and I had a lot of time to make up. So I took as many courses each term as I could—as many as 23 units per quarter. I kept quite busy with classes but still could not keep out of campus political activities. This was a politically turbulent period, with many veterans returning and looking toward a better world. I joined student groups to work toward racial equality and social legislation—Progressive Citizens Committee, Student Non-Violent Coordinating Committee, Students for Democratic Action. We demonstrated, organized petitions, and tested the effectiveness of new state accommodations laws that forbade racial discrimination in restaurants. Within the groups, I was able to get some experience and insight into political strategies, particularly in confrontations between progressive Democrats and Communists.

A BRIEF ENCOUNTER WITH BEHAVIORISM AND ANIMAL RESEARCH

The Department of Psychology was heavily oriented toward behaviorism and learning theory, and we got a heavy dose of that in introductory psychology classes. I was particularly intrigued by the carefully developed and systematic learning theory of Clark Hull. I even had a turn at animal research, with Delos Wickens, studying learning and delayed reaction. I was given a cage with three rats and developed a complicated apparatus. Wickens was impressed with the learning patterns but encouraged me to increase their rate of the learning by increasing motivation, that is, by reducing their food supply. One morning I found that two rats had killed and eaten the third and thus ended my experience with animal research. A course in sociology opened up new perspectives.

INTRODUCTION TO SOCIAL PSYCHOLOGY

When I discovered there was a field called "social psychology," a field that dealt with social issues and problems that were important and exciting to me, I thought it was almost too good to be true. My first course in social psychology was with Donald Campbell, then fresh out of his graduate work at the University of California, Berkeley. From him I received inspiration and direction that serves me even to the present day. For my courses with Campbell, I wrote two overly ambitious term papers. The first was a historical analysis of social psychological issues in Jewish identity. The second was a paper on "revivalist religions." That was stimulated by a book by Hadley Cantril that explored religious groups such as the Kingdom of Father Divine, Bishop Cherry and the Black Jews, and the so-called Oxford Movement. Essentially, I was looking at the ways in which an ambitious religious leader might manipulate the minds and behaviors of his followers. It was a topic that excited me, and I wanted to explore it further, but I soon realized that it was not the sort of thing that one could investigate with the stringent scientific approach of laboratory experimentation. So I put that topic aside—put it aside for more than 50 years.

Discovering Kurt Lewin. I started doing some reading on my own. From sociology, I was fascinated by a book by Everett Stonequist called *The Marginal Man.* That one really seemed to hit home, because he was exploring people with roots and identities in two cultures. Such marginality, he wrote, can be a source of serious identity conflict, but it may also have positive effects, particularly in social sensitivity. When I discussed this with Donald Campbell, he suggested that I read Kurt Lewin. In Lewin's *Resolving Social Conflicts* (Lewin, 1948; edited by Dorwin Cartwright), there were articles that presented in more psychological terms some of the issues raised by Stonequist—especially chapters titled "Psychosocial Problems of Minority Groups," "Self-Hatred among Jews," and "Bringing Up the Jewish Child." I was excited to learn that it was possible to explore complex social phenomena with controlled laboratory experiments: Lewin, Lippitt, and White's experiments on democratic, autocratic, and laissez-faire leadership (so very relevant when we had just seen the effects of autocratic leadership in Hitler's Germany); experiments on group decision and social change; and Festinger's experiment on the role of group belongingness in a voting situation. That these studies provided answers that were also consistent with my values and ideology made them all the more satisfying. I began to read further in the Ohio State Arps Hall reading room. I found the journal *Human Relations,* then the first issues of a new social psychological journal, the *Journal of Social Issues.* The very first issues of JSI included an article by Ronald Lippitt, "To Be or Not to Be—a Jew," and a series of articles on racial and religious prejudice in everyday life by Kurt Lewin, Daniel Katz, Gardner Murphy, and Gordon Allport. Later issues focused on problems of reeducation, bureaucracy, conflict and cooperation in industry, and military occupation in Germany and Japan as tests of democracy.

Social psychology! Clearly that was the way to go. After talking to Donald Campbell, I knew there was only one place to go—the interdisciplinary program in social psychology at the University of Michigan, and I couldn't wait to get there. By taking as many units as possible and going to summer session, I completed my bachelor of arts in eight successive quarters—in 2 fiscal years. And in three more quarters, I completed my master's requirements. I then applied to only one graduate program—the doctoral program in social psychology at the University of Michigan. To my good fortune, I was accepted.

THE UNIVERSITY OF MICHIGAN AND THE RESEARCH CENTER FOR GROUP DYNAMICS

Sadly, Kurt Lewin had died in 1948. I always regretted that I had never had an opportunity to meet him. He founded the Research Center for Group Dynamics at MIT and was later invited to move it to Ann Arbor. Several of those people whom I identified with Kurt Lewin were there: Dorwin Cartwright was the director, and Ronald Lippitt was also there (whom I associated with the experiment on democratic, autocratic, and laissez-faire leadership). And then there was John R. P. French, who had been involved in studies of group decision and participatory decision making in organizational settings. And Leon Festinger, whose name I knew from his experiment on the role of group belongingness in a voting situation.

Shortly after I received my invitation to enter the Michigan social psychology doctoral program, I was excited to receive a call from Leon Festinger. He was in Columbus for a Midwestern Psychological Association convention and wanted to meet with me. We met over drinks. My good friend and roommate, Joe Masling, joined us.

Festinger described his research program on pressures toward uniformity in groups and communications with deviant members. He then asked me about my interest in that area (of course, I was extremely interested) and then asked some questions about me and my master's thesis. Finally, he said, there was one more question: Could I mix drinks? I would have had to confess that my experience in that sphere was limited to mixing Manischewitz Concord with Manischewitz Malaga. Fortunately, Joe told Festinger not to worry, he would teach me. That assurance was apparently sufficient, because Festinger offered me a research assistantship. I was ecstatic, especially because I now felt assured that I would continue to have funding even after support from the GI Bill ran out.

My first assignment was to help a new study director to code data on his research on communications in hierarchies. His name was Harold Kelley. Kelley became one of my closest friends, mentor, and colleagues, for more than half a century. Another close colleague was a fellow student, Harold Gerard, who was also my office mate. One of the studies that we carried out together examined the "influence process in the presence of extreme deviates" (Festinger, Gerard, Hymovitch, Kelley, & Raven, 1952). Out of Festinger's program developed an amazingly productive series of experiments and studies by members of that group and their subsequent collaborators, not only at Michigan but elsewhere. Most of us continued to look to Festinger for direction even after he left Michigan and we had completed our doctorates—from communication and group pressures toward uniformity, to social comparison processes, to dissonance theory.

New graduate students in the social psychology program and Research Center for Group Dynamics (RCGD) had come from universities where students were expected to behave in a very respectful manner toward professors, always addressing them as Professor or Doctor. It therefore required some adjustment to a university setting where professors were addressed by their first names—Leon, Al (Zander), Jack (French), Hal (Kelley), Al (Pepitone), Ted (Newcomb), Dan (Katz). This seemed quite consistent with an ideology that emphasized democratization and collegiality. We found only one indication of status recognition: Dorwin Cartwright, the director of RCGD, was called "Doc." But even this exception proved illusory—Cartwright was always called "Doc" even when he was in high school.

Many of the other students who were then research assistants became important contributors to social psychology: Arthur Robert Cohen, Sidney Rosen, Ezra Stotland, George Levinger, and, later, Robert Zajonc.

THE DOCTORAL PROGRAM IN SOCIAL PSYCHOLOGY

Entering the doctoral program in social psychology at the University of Michigan was like a dream come true. The program was headed by Theodore Newcomb, with whose work I was very familiar, and by Daniel Katz, who had studied with Floyd Allport and who was a source of wisdom and a role model for all of us. The program included faculty from sociology and psychology, and a major aim was to create hybrids who cut across the two disciplines such that they could later become faculty in sociology or psychology. Those of us with master's degrees in psychology took more course work in sociology, and vise versa. It also seemed to have a strong sense of social purpose, attempts to apply our theory and research to the solution of social problems. The students in the program were dedicated to the program and its purpose of relating social psychology to social issues and problems, and included many who would become important figures in the field.

The reading list for our preliminary examinations was huge, full of references from sociology, psychology, political science, philosophy, and related fields. Students soon realized that it would be physically impossible to cover all of these materials, so we organized into study groups with members assigned to read and summarize specific articles and books. The summaries were reproduced on "ditto," the state of the art in reproduction of that day, discussed at the study group meetings and then circulated to other groups.

Obman and Podelka's theory of amorphous structure. At one of the lighter moments of our group sessions, we collectively agreed that I should take on a particularly challenging assignment: Soon all of the study groups received a summary titled "Important Information You Should Know About the Influential Obman and Podelka Amorphous Structure Theory." The document went on to say that this influential but rarely cited theory specifically dealt with the second question on our preliminary exam, whatever that might be—"the amorphous structure theory of personality … or leadership … or attitude change … ." Each student was asked to refer to this theory in writing on the second question in the preliminary examination. Not everyone followed through, for various understandable reasons, but several of us did. Ezra Stotland said he forgot to do so but begged to have his blue book back so that he could add an important additional reference. We had images of the faculty readers being intrigued by this reference with which so many students were apparently familiar and would ask us for details after the exam. We were disappointed that none did so, though we heard that one professor cited it in a lecture. But Obman and Podelka became part of the folklore of the Research Center for Group Dynamics. The names of the two authors, incidentally, were taken from my Russian dictionary, meaning "fraud" and "falsification."

MY DOCTORAL DISSERTATION

My doctoral thesis grew out of my research with Leon Festinger. It was a study of the ways in which group pressure can contribute first to change in behavior, followed by change in belief. This was consistent with Festinger's theory of cognitive dissonance, which appeared several years later. The subject would read a case study of a juvenile delinquent accused of murder, including various relevant bits of information, often inconsistent, from witnesses and family. After taking a position, rating the delinquent on a guilt–innocence scale, the subject would learn that all others in the group were in sharp disagreement with him/her. Pressure toward conformity was great, because the deviant subject could be expelled from the group. We found that, indeed, most subjects changed toward the group norm, but if they were first asked to write a report summarizing all of the information, content analysis revealed that that report would be affected before the opinion change took place. And if that written report were to be shown to the group, then the group effects on the report, as well as on the opinion, would be even greater. Thus it seemed that group pressures may first change our behavior, and the change in behavior affects our perceptions, our recollections, and eventually our opinions (Raven, 1959b). I have continued to cite that study today on occasion when testifying on the validity of eyewitness testimony in criminal trials.

Before I could complete my doctoral dissertation, Leon Festinger left for a position at the University of Minnesota. I completed my doctoral studies and dissertation under the sponsorship of John R. P. French Jr. I stayed on at the Research Center for Group Dynamics as a research associate with a lectureship in psychology. French and I offered some courses together and continued with research on the bases of social power. It was for our theory of the bases of social power that we are both best known. More about this later.

TEACHING AND RESEARCH IN THE NETHERLANDS

The amazingly creative GI Bill, which greatly influenced higher education following World War II, had its parallel at the international level in the Fulbright program. When the war ended, American armed forces left behind huge stocks of surplus property in various countries. Rather than asking the host nations to pay the United States for such property, Senator J. William Fulbright offered a plan whereby such funds would instead be used to promote international communication and understanding—to provide for American academics to go to foreign universities to study, carry out research, and offer instruction and for foreign scholars to come to the United States. That program continues to this day, with funds provided by congressional appropriation. The Research Center for Group Dynamics was particularly eager to promote its approach to research, especially the use of controlled laboratory experimentation on important social psychological issues. For some reason, the Netherlands was particularly receptive to such cooperative ventures. With support from various sources—including Fulbright—Leon Festinger, Stanley Schachter, Ben Willerman, Albert Pepitone, Harold Gerard, Henry Riecken, and I soon participated in this effort.

Following my 1-year postdoctoral lectureship and research position at Michigan, I accepted an invitation from Professor Tony Oldendorff of the Catholic University of Nijmegen in the Netherlands to come there as a visiting professor and a research scholar at the Sociological Research Center under the Fulbright program. I offered instruction in Nijmegen and Utrecht. In keeping with the interest at the center, I also developed an experiment on the interdependence in group problem solving, on the effects of clear goals and clear paths to goals in development of influence and cohesiveness in groups (Raven & Rietsema, 1957). Several Dutch students worked with me as part of their research practicum experience. I have continued my friendship with several of these students even to this day.

Experimental social psychology was virtually unknown in the Netherlands in the 1950s. The acceptance of this approach took several years, but thanks in part to the collective effort of American social psychologists, especially those associated with RCGD, social psychology in the Netherlands has gained a well-deserved international reputation. In 2003, I was honored to be invited by the social psychology graduate students of Amsterdam as the opening speaker in a special international symposium titled "The Struggle for Power," at which I presented our most recent research and theoretical developments in that area.

In addition to the interesting and useful experience of teaching and doing research in a different academic setting, I also learned a lot about the terrible effects of World War II, and especially the diabolical influence strategies whereby the German occupiers were successful in implementing the Holocaust, which destroyed most of Dutch Jewry. I stayed in a pension run by a Dutch Jewish woman and her daughter, who had managed to survive but still suffered severe effects from their experiences.

A side trip to Israel. On a quite different note, during the winter break I traveled through Italy and Greece and eventually to Israel. It was a vacation, but I also hoped to find traces of my maternal grandfather. He disappeared from Odessa in 1918, and my mother, knowing his Zionist commitment, believed that he might have emigrated to Israel. Though the search for my grandfather was unsuccessful, my visit resulted in a very important event: I met an English girl, Celia Cutler, who was doing a year of service to Israel working on a kibbutz—a collective farm. It was a very casual meeting, but we met again later in London, and in Holland, and we continued with a 6-year intercontinental courtship by mail. In 1961, after I was firmly established at UCLA, Celia traveled from London to Los Angeles with her wedding dress on her arm. We had a beautiful wedding with colleagues, students, friends, and family in attendance. It has been a wonderful partnership, with our son, Jonathan, and daughter, Michelle, and three grandchildren.

STUDYING GROUP EFFECTIVENESS IN AIR DEFENSE CREWS

At the end of 1956, I accepted a position with what was then the Systems Development Division of the RAND Corporation. In response to the so-called cold war, the U.S. Air Defense Command had established a network of radar surveillance sites covering the entire country to detect unknown aircraft and protect against a sneak bombing attack. All air flights were filed and recorded, and when an unknown "blip" appeared on the radarscope, a signal was sent to the nearest fighter base to scramble, identify, and control, or even eliminate, possible enemy flights. Making use of newly developing computers, RAND developed means to simulate air defense crises as a crew-training device. The Systems Development Division was established to implement this program, and a large number of sociologists, psychologists, and education specialists were hired to implement it. I was hired as part of a small group to study the effectiveness of the program. It seemed like a wonderful opportunity to continue my research on interdependence in group problem solving. The task of the air defense crew required a high level of cooperation and task distribution, between the men observing their radar screens, communications from adjacent stations, plotting the movements of aircraft on the radar screen on a plotting board, checking with flight reports from airfields, and directing fighter jets to scramble and intercept questionable aircraft. It seemed like an ideal situation to test group theories about leadership, stresses in different parts of a social system, communication, and coordination. We carried out several carefully controlled experiments, with actual air defense crews whom we instructed to behave naturally, which were published in classified reports. One day a general in the Air Defense Command came to examine our program while we were conducting one of our experiments. He was appalled. "There seems to be a complete loss of discipline and military decors! What is that corporal doing behind the plotting board with his tie loose?" Again, chicken shit? To my good fortune, I was offered a position as a social psychologist at UCLA. And I have been there ever since.

SOCIAL PSYCHOLOGY AT UCLA

The Department of Psychology at UCLA in 1956 was quite respectable, but social psychology was not its forte. Then, as now, the department was in the Division of Life Sciences, rather than Social Sciences, and in the tradition of Shepherd Ivory Franz and Knight Dunlap, its major reputation was in physiological and comparative psychology and learning theory. But at that time, the University of California system and UCLA in particular were going through a period of rapid growth, and we were fortunate to have department chairs who encouraged social psychology. Within a few years, we were joined by Harold Kelley, my friend and colleague from my Michigan days, then David Sears, Barry Collins, Hal Gerard, Bernie Weiner, and Anne Peplau. Out of social psychology, we later developed a concentration in health psychology and added Shelley Taylor and Christine Dunkel Schetter. Before long we were recognized as one of the major centers in social psychology. One of my esteemed Michigan mentors, Theodore Newcomb, told me that when he came across promising students in social psychology, he told them that UCLA was the place to go. What greater compliment for our social psychology program?

RESEARCH ON INTERDEPENDENCE
IN GROUP PROBLEM SOLVING

One of my long-term interests in social psychology has focused on interdependence in group problem solving. This included our research in the Netherlands and at the Systems Development Division. I won't dwell much on this topic but will describe briefly our studies on interdependence in triads (three-person groups).

There had been controversy in social psychology regarding the advantages and disadvantages of cooperation versus competition in team effectiveness. Some reported that competition activates the competitors to work harder and faster, thus increasing their productivity. Others reported that cooperation leads to sharing and coordination, so as to lead to greater productivity. The answer seemed to be that it depends on various factors, two of which are the degree of interdependence with regard to group goals versus individual goals and also interdependence in the means necessary to pursue such goals. At a meeting of the Topology Group, composed of former colleagues of Kurt Lewin and their students, Alex Bavelas suggested a triangular board problem, which seemed ideal for investigating these two variables.

The problem presented to the triad was as follows: Each participant sat at a corner of the large triangular board with a knob or set screw that allowed him/her to raise or lower that corner. In front of each set screw was a small carpenter's spirit level perpendicular to that subject's line of sight, with the bubble off center. The task was to center three spirit levels. In an individualistic or competitive condition, the subjects were told, "Try to center your spirit level before either of the others." In a cooperative condition, it was, "Try to get the whole board level (all three bubbles centered) as quickly as possible—faster than the other groups." It should be clear that each subject could not affect the bubble on his or her own spirit level. This could be accomplished only by persuading one subject to lower his or her corner and/or influencing the other subject to raise his or hers. But the subject could alter the centering of the other two spirit levels. The group was then completely interdependent. When the task was presented as "get the entire board level as soon as possible" (center all three spirit levels), then the group moved rapidly to solve the problem. When the task was presented as "try to get your spirit level centered before the other two," the task became much more difficult and often impossible, with each subject trying to get the other two to assist him or her while resisting their attempts to influence him or her. Later we began to examine other patterns of interdependence by changing the direction of the spirit levels. The basic finding was that interdependence with respect to means was a major factor in determining whether cooperation or competition would lead to greater group effectiveness (Raven & Eachus, 1963; Raven & Shaw, 1970).

In 1962–1963, on my first sabbatical leave from UCLA, I was fortunate to receive support from a Guggenheim fellowship to continue my research on interdependence in Israel. Moving from the laboratory, we attempted to study effects of social norms for cooperation versus competition as represented in Israeli kibbutzim and moshavim (collective farms). Unfortunately, we could not get the triangular board to Israel in time, so we resorted to a form of the prisoner's dilemma experiment. To our surprise, the participants in even the most doctrinaire collectivist movements tended to be competitive and even exploitative in this prisoner's dilemma situation. In our postsession interviews, it appears that the young kibbutzniks interpreted the prisoner's dilemma situation as a game, a test of their ability to outsmart their partners. Thus social norms for cooperation did not apply. The most cooperative and altruistic players were young American students who were about to join a kibbutz on a short-term basis (Raven & Leff, 1965). For them, it seemed, the situation was seen not as simply a game but as an opportunity for them to demonstrate their commitment to the collectivity norms of the kibbutz.

THEORY AND RESEARCH ON INTERPERSONAL INFLUENCE AND SOCIAL POWER

I have departed from my chronological sequence to save for last my longest term research commitment: interpersonal influence and social power. Following Festinger's departure, Jack French and I met regularly to develop long-range research plans. In an article titled "An Analysis of Compliant Behavior," Festinger

(1954) noted that, in response to influence attempts from others, we change our behavior but only so long as the influencing agent is able to observe us. In other situations, we not only change our behavior but privately accept the change, so that it continues even when the agent cannot observe us. The former change, in which observability is important, occurs when the agent offers a reward for compliance or threatens punishment for noncompliance. My thesis, in part, followed from that differentiation. But now French and I began to explore other factors affecting change in belief and behavior. Under the leadership of Dorwin Cartwright, most members of the Research Center for Group Dynamics began to study various aspects of social power. French had had longtime experience in industrial and organizational psychology, so in our first meetings, we focused on the relationship between supervisor and subordinate. The Michigan emphasis on a discipline of social psychology, which drew from both sociology and psychology, helped broaden our perspective. We examined the experimental literature and our own experiences, and from this we developed the bases of power topology, which has been referred to as one of the most frequently cited approaches in the social power literature.

THE SIX BASES OF SOCIAL POWER

Our theory originally proposed six bases of power, resources that an influencing agent might use in changing the beliefs, attitudes, or behaviors of a target of influence: Reward, Coercion, Legitimacy, Expertise, Reference, and Informational (French & Raven, 1959; Raven, 1965). Festinger's analysis, it seemed, focused on three of these: Reward and Coercion (threat of punishment) would lead to change where observability was critical ("My supervisor can offer me a promotion, or fire me, so I will do as he says—so long as he can see me doing it."); Information (based on the persuasive content of the influence attempt) did not require observability ("My supervisor convinced me that this was really the best way to do my job, so I do it that way, whether or not he can see me doing it."). What French and I added was the notion of "social dependence," the extent to which the target must relate the changed behavior to the influencing agent—when informational power is operative, and the changed behavior is accepted, the target can completely forget the fact that change was requested by the agent but still continue to comply. For these three bases of power, social dependence and observability go hand in hand.

But are there influence situations in which the change is socially dependent but where observability is *not* an important consideration? We looked for various examples and came up with three such influence situations: Legitimate Power ("He is my supervisor, and therefore I feel obliged to do as he asks, whether or not I understand why."), Expert Power ("He knows much more about this than I do, and even if I don't understand it, this must be the best way to do this."), and Referent Power ("I identify with my supervisor or see him as a model, so I do as he says, even if I don't understand, and I am not concerned about his rewarding or punishing me.").

FURTHER DIFFERENTIATION

Though these six bases of power are widely cited in the organizational literature (in some cases, Informational Power is omitted, because it was not included in the original French and Raven [1959] paper), there has been continual development of the typology, based on additional research (Raven, 1992; Raven, Schwarzwald, & Koslowski, 1998). The original six bases are still included, but with further differentiation: In our original statement, Coercive and Reward Power were presented in terms of tangible rewards and real physical threats—threats of being fired or fined, promises of monetary rewards and bonuses or promotion within an organization, and so on. However, it should be clear that personal approval from someone whom we like can result in quite powerful reward power, and a threat of rejection or disapproval from someone whom we value highly can serve as a source for powerful coercive power. Considering personal, as well as impersonal, forms of reward and coercion helped us to understand certain forms of influence where surveillance was important but which had previously been inappropriately categorized as Referent Power.

Legitimate Power stems from social norms requiring that the target of influence comply with the request or order of the influencing agent. *Legitimate Position Power* (a concept that we adopted from Weber, 1922/1957) is the most obvious form of legitimate power and stems from a social norm that requires that we obey people who are in a superior position in a formal or informal social structure, such as a supervisor or a higher ranking military officer influencing a subordinate. Other examples, reflecting various cultural norms, might be the right of parents to influence children, of older people to influence younger people, of teachers to influence students, and of police officers to influence citizens. There are some more subtle forms of legitimate power, based on other social norms: *Legitimate Power of Reciprocity.* The reciprocity norm (Gouldner, 1960) states that if someone does something beneficial for us then we should feel an obligation to reciprocate by doing as he or she asks ("My supervisor helped me when I needed it, so now I feel obliged to do as he asks."). *Legitimate Power of Equity*: This might also be referred to as a *compensatory norm* ("My supervisor has really worked very long hours on this job" or "I have really messed up on my job and caused him great difficulty" and therefore "I owe it to him to do as he asks.") (Walster, Walster & Berscheid, 1978). *Legitimate Power of Responsibility*: According to this social responsibility norm, we have some obligation to help others who cannot help themselves or to help others who are dependent on us ("My supervisor really cannot get his work done without my assistance; because I am in position to help him, I feel obligated to do so.") (Berkowitz & Daniels, 1963). This form of legitimate power has sometimes been referred to as the *power of the powerless*.

THE POWER–INTERACTION MODEL OF INTERPERSONAL INFLUENCE

The bases of power are included within a larger context through the development of a power–interaction model of interpersonal influence (Raven, 1992). The model begins with a consideration of the motivation for influence and the use of power, then the factors that lead to the choice of power strategy, the preparatory devices for implementing the bases of power, the manner in which a power strategy is utilized, the effective changes or lack of change in the target of influence, the after-effects, and the readjustment of the perceptions and choices of future strategies by the agent.

Typically, the agent's motivation for influence will be very obvious, the purpose being to attain some goal or desirable outcome. He or she will then use the basis of power that will accomplish that end most expeditiously and effectively. Often, the situation will affect what bases of power will be selected. One should, of course, expect differing power strategies to be operative by a supervisor in a supermarket, a warden in a prison, the leader of a Boy Scout troop, a parent with a child, a teacher in a classroom, and so on.

In addition, the selection of power strategies will vary according to how the agent views the target and even more how he or she believes that the target views the agent. In an early analysis, Douglas McGregor (1960) distinguished between "Theory X" supervisors and "Theory Y" supervisors. The former believes that workers cannot be trusted and that they do not really like their work and try to do as little as they can get away with. For Theory X supervisors, one might then expect greater use of Coercive Power and Legitimate Position Power, and the distrusting supervisor would be very concerned about maintaining surveillance. By contrast, Theory Y supervisors, with a more positive view of workers, seeing them motivated to do the best they can, are more likely to rely on Informational and Expert Power, and perhaps Legitimate Power of Dependence, with greater trust and less emphasis on surveillance. The basic point is that an influencing agent, motivated to achieve the most positive outcome, will select bases of power in terms of his or her perceptions of what works in that specific relationship.

Another sort of motivation that might affect the choice of power strategies is the attitude of the influencing agent toward the target of influence. It is, of course, the agent's perception of the target that will help determine what basis of power would be effective or ineffective, but, in addition, a strong negative feeling toward the target might lead to a choice of harsh bases of power, such as impersonal coercion, even when that power strategy might not be the most efficient or effective. Similarly, a strong positive feeling toward the target might preclude the use of a harsh basis of power, even when, objectively, it might seem most appropriate.

The agent might also go through a cost-benefit analysis of the influence strategy. Informational influence or persuasion would ordinarily be highly desirable but may require more time and effort than is available. Coercion, as we had indicated, may result in more rapid compliance but carries with it the costs of having to maintain surveillance, the hostility of an unhappy subordinate, and sometimes the violation of one's personal value system or generally accepted social norms. The legitimacy of dependence ("I need your help.") may lead to a loss of respect and perhaps may imply an obligation to return the favor. Referent power, which emphasizes similarity, may undermine the target's respect for the agent's superiority in expertise and legitimacy of position. In addition, as we have noted, power holders, because of their personalities, experiences, values, or force of habit, may tend to prefer some bases of power over others.

Following the influence attempt, the agent will want to assess the effects. Was it successful? Is there evidence that the target has actually accepted the influence, has actually altered his or her behavior in accordance with the outcome desired by the influencing agent? Does the target really accept the change personally, or is the change socially dependent? Is surveillance important for the change to continue—will the target revert to earlier behavior patterns as soon as the agent cannot continue to check on the degree of compliance? Will the target subsequently internalize the changes in his or her behavior?

How about secondary effects? How has the influence attempt, successful or not, affected the target's perception and evaluation of the agent? Has respect for the agent diminished? Is there greater personal liking or disliking? Have the power bases previously available to the agent increased or decreased in their potency? The agent may then attempt to repair the damage and reassess his or her relationship with the target. If the influence attempt was unsuccessful, then it is likely that the agent will try again. But this time the agent's motivations may change: Whereas previously he or she had wanted merely to achieve the extrinsic goal, he or she now may have developed some hostility toward the target, which in turn will affect the choice of influence strategy the second time around. The agent's success or failure will also lead to a reassessment of the available bases of power and the development of a quite different strategy.

Though originally developed with the supervisor–subordinate relationship in mind, the bases of power analysis have since been applied to many other settings, including husbands and wives influencing one another (Raven, Centers, & Rodrigues, 1975), political figures influencing one another (Gold & Raven, 1992; Raven, 1990), school counselors influencing teachers (Erchul & Raven, 1997), police captains influencing police officers (Schwarzwald, Koslowski, & Agassi, 2001), infection control personnel in hospitals influencing physicians and nurses (Raven, Freeman, & Haley, 1982), and religious figures using power as a mechanism of social control (Raven, 1999). The initial controlled laboratory experiments have led to studies in the field and to the development of an Interpersonal Power Inventory, which was developed and tested in various cultures by Aroldo Rodrigues in Brazil (Rodrigues & Raven, 1974), Haruki Sakai in Japan, Joseph Schwarzwald and Meni Koslowski in Israel, and Antonio Pierro in Italy and Greece (Pierro, de Grada, Raven, & Kruglanski, 2004).

Our bases of power analysis have been cited as a classic and the most frequently utilized model of dyadic power in the social psychological and industrial/organizational literature (e.g., House, 1993; Mintzberg, 1983). In any event, it is gratifying to see theory and research using this model in so many diverse settings.

A LONG JOURNEY

Our journey has touched on three centuries—from the late 19th century to the 21st century. Preparing this chapter has been an interesting and exciting experience in its own right. It is not often that we examine where we are and then try to trace the route by which we got there. I can't help but appreciate the many people, circumstances, and experiences that have determined my direction and accomplishment. In a lecture on Lewinian field theory, I have attempted to dramatize it with the following illustration from a high school physics class: A plate of glass is placed over a bar magnet, and iron filings are scattered about the glass. The filings form a distinctive pattern, which represent the magnetic field. If we take a pencil and move some of the filings, we find not only that they change but also that the entire field is affected, as the pattern of filings that represent that field. One's life journey can be considered in that same light—a small alteration of circumstances: if my father had stayed in Argentina, if I had not had to repeat the first grade and entered the army a few months earlier, if I had not run across Kurt Lewin's books in the library or had not taken my first social psychology with Donald Campbell, if Festinger had not left suddenly for Minnesota. Any of these circumstances might have dramatically affected my dedication to research on social power or the manner in which I approached it. We should also expect that when my own beliefs, attitudes, and behaviors changed, they likely affected many others with whom I came in contact, and thence others with whom they interacted.

We may recall that my mother, in influencing our behavior, never used threats of punishment or promises of reward—power strategies that other children often experienced. Her approach was to gently raise questions about my activities: Did I really want to do that? Had I considered the implications and consequences of my choices? She then accepted my decision, even if it was contrary to her preferences. This information power was supplemented by legitimate power of reciprocity, as she dedicated herself fully to the needs of her family. With the wisdom she acquired without formal education, she had great affect not only on my decisions in specific instances but also on my own influence strategies. These in turn were reflected in our theories and in our behaviors. Our children have, indeed, commented on the social influence experiences that they encountered in our home—and tell us that these in turn have affected the power strategies that they use with others, including our grandchildren.

Thank you for taking this journey with me. I hope that it may give the reader some insights into the factors that have contributed to the directions of your life journey, including a better understanding of the influence strategies that you use and the ways in which you respond to influence strategies used by others.

FOR STUDENTS INTERESTED IN PURSUING A CAREER IN SOCIAL PSYCHOLOGY

I assume that you have already explored various options and have decided that social psychology is indeed a discipline to which you would like to dedicate the next 50 years. As with any such commitment, you should certainly review the reasons and motives for your choice. Why psychology? Why especially social psychology? There might be some person whose work led you in that direction. Or perhaps there was a topic in social psychology that captured your attention. What was it?

1. *Commit yourself to an area of research and study.* If you are fortunate, you will find a topic about which you can feel passionate, and it will serve as a beacon that will give you direction. You cannot possibly become an expert in all the various areas in social psychology. Nobody can. But if you can focus on something that is exciting and important to you, you may be on your way to becoming a known expert in that area. It doesn't mean you can't change or focus on other things. Some other topic may grab your attention later on. Or you may become bored or lose interest in the topic you chose initially. So change, but at least give it a good try. As you study that phenomenon, you will become more sophisticated. You will discover nuances you never considered. You may find that topic is broader than you originally anticipated, and you will begin to narrow your focus. In my case, I was fortunate to find an interest in social influence, developed through my readings and my experiences at the Research Center for Group Dynamics. That general interest became more focused on interpersonal influence and social power. That choice did not restrict me from exploring other areas, especially interdependence.

2. *Find a mentor.* Connecting with someone whose work you find exciting, someone who can provide guidance and direction, can be extremely important. Actually, that mentor may not necessarily be someone with whom you are in close contact. My first mentor was Kurt Lewin, whom I was never able to meet, which is unfortunate. But reading his works excited me and had an impact on my thinking even to the present day. There were several other mentors who also greatly influenced me at various stages of my career: Donald Campbell, Leon Festinger, Daniel Katz, John R. P. French, and Harold Kelley.

3. *Value your colleagues and peers.* It is very helpful to have others to whom you can turn, whom you can count on to exchange ideas, and with whom you can test your ideas. If they can be collaborators as well, that will be even better. With modern developments in communication technology, it is no longer necessary that they be physically present. Some of my most productive professional interactions have been conducted over the Internet and with e-mail.

4. *Don't lose sight of the real world.* Much of what you will study in your formal course work will focus on theory and methodology. We social psychologists are particularly sensitive and sometimes defensive about meeting scientific criteria. We are judged to a great extent on the number of publications that we are able to have published in respected scientific journals. Unfortunately, such emphasis sometimes causes us to lose sight of what our field is all about, on its important value in applications and in the solution to social problems and issues. Some of the research published in scientific journals is difficult to justify in terms of its actual value to our society and is not of much interest to those who are not social psychologists. Don't lose sight of what we are here for. Always look for interesting examples of social psychological phenomena in everyday life, and include these in your writings and in your teaching.

5. *Develop a tolerance for frustration and disappointment.* What I have discussed are ideals we should try to find and hope for. Unfortunately, it does not always work out that way. Studies do not always work out as planned. Your best journal article may be rejected. When that happens, you will often find you have learned a lot in the development of the study and in examining why your original expectations were not fulfilled. Our chosen mentors may have clay feet. Funding for our research may not always be available. Be prepared for disappointments. But, of great importance, it helps to *have a good sense of humor.*

REFERENCES

Berkowitz, L., & Daniels, L. R. (1963). Responsibility and dependence. *Journal of Abnormal Psychology, 66,* 429–436.

Erchul, W. P., & Raven, B. H. (1997). Social power in school consultation: A contemporary view of French and Raven's bases of power model. *Journal of School Psychology, 35,* 137–171.

Erchul, W. P., Raven, B. H., & Ray, A. G. (2000). School psychologists' perceptions of social power bases in teacher consultation. *Journal of Educational and Psychological Consultation, 12,* 1–23.

Festinger, L. (1954). An analysis of compliant behavior. In M. Sherif & M. O. Wilson (Eds.), *Group relations at the cross-roads* (pp. 232–256). New York: Harper.

Festinger, L., Gerard, H. B., Hymovitch, B., Kelley, H. H., & Raven, B. H. (1952). The influence process in the presence of extreme deviates. *Human Relations, 5,* 327–346.

French, J. R. P., Jr., & Raven, B. H. (1959). The bases of social power. In D. Cartwright (Ed.), *Studies in social power* (pp. 150–167). Ann Arbor, MI: Institute for Social Research.

Gold, G. J., & Raven, B. H. (1992). Interpersonal influence strategies in the Churchill-Roosevelt bases-for-destroyers exchange. *Journal of Social Behavior and Personality, 7,* 245–272.

Gouldner, A. W. (1960). The norm of reciprocity: A preliminary statement. *American Sociological Review, 35,* 161–178.

House, J. S. (1993). John R. P. French, Jr.: A Lewinian's Levinian. *Journal of Social Issues, 49*(4), 221–226.

Lewin, K. (1948). *Resolving social conflicts.* New York: Harper.

McGregor, D. (1960). *The human side of enterprise.* New York: McGraw-Hill.

Milgram, S. (1974). *Obedience to authority: An experimental view.* New York: Harper & Row.

Mintzberg, H. (1983). *Power in and around organizations.* Englewood Cliffs, NJ: Prentice Hall.

Pierro, A., de Grada, E., Raven, B. H., & Kruglanski, A. W. (2004). Fonti, antecedenti e consequenti del potere in contesti organizzativi. In A. Pierro (Ed.), *Potere e leadership* (pp. 33–58). Roma: Carrocci.

Raven, B. H. (1959a). Social influence and power. In I. D. Steiner & M. Fishbein (Eds.), *Current studies in social psychology* (pp. 371–382). New York: Holt, Rinehart, & Winston.

Raven, B. H. (1959b). Social influence on opinions and the communication of related content. *Journal of Abnormal and Social Psychology, 58,* 119–128.

Raven, B. H. (1965) Social influence and social power, In I. D. Steiner & M. Fishbein (Eds.), *Current studies in social psychology.* New York: Holt, Rinehart, and Winston.

Raven, B. H. (1990). Political application of the psychology of interpersonal influence and social power. *Political Psychology, 11,* 493–520.

Raven, B. H. (1992). A power/interaction model of interpersonal influence: French and Raven thirty years later. *Journal of Social Behavior and Personality, 7*, 217–244.

Raven, B. H. (1999). Influence, power, religion, and the mechanisms of social control. *Journal of Social Issues, 55*(1), 161–186.

Raven, B. H., Centers, R., & Rodrigues, A. (1975). The bases of conjugal power. In R. E. Cromwell & O. H. Olson (Eds.), *Power in families* (pp. 217–234). New York: Halstead.

Raven, B. H., & Eachus, H. T. (1963). Cooperation and competition in means-interdependent triads. *Journal of Abnormal and Social Psychology, 67*, 307–316.

Raven, B. H., Freeman, H. E., & Haley, R. W. (1982). Social science perspectives in hospital infection control. In A. W. Johnson, O. Grusky, & B. H. Raven (Eds.), *Contemporary health services: Social science perspectives* (pp. 239–276). Boston: Auburn House.

Raven, B. H., & Leff, W. (1965). The effects of partner's behavior and culture upon strategy in a two-person game. *Scripta Hierosaolymitana, 14*, 82–97.

Raven, B. H., & Rietsema, J. (1957). The effects of varied clarity of group goal and group path upon the individual and his relationship to his group. *Human Relations, 10*, 29–45.

Raven, B. H., & Rubin, J. Z .(1983). *Social Psychology*. New York: John Wiley & Sons.

Raven, B. H., Schwarzwald, J., & Koslowski, M. (1998). Conceptualizing and measuring a power/interaction model of interpersonal influence. *Journal of Applied Social Psychology, 28*, 307–332.

Raven, B. H., & Shaw, J. I. (1970). Interdependence and group problem-solving in the triad. *Journal of Personality and Social Psychology, 14*, 157–165.

Rodrigues, A., & Raven, B. H. (1974). *Teacher and peer power in Brazilian schools*. Paper presented at the Western Psychological Association convention, San Francisco, CA.

Schwarzwald, J., Koslowski, M., & Agassi, V. (2001). Captain's leadership type and police officers' compliance to power bases. *European Journal of Work and Organizational Psychology, 10*, 273–290.

Walster, H. E., Walster, G. W., & Berscheid, E. (1978). *Equity theory and research*. Boston: Allyn & Bacon.

Weber, M. (1957). *The theory of social and economic organization*. Glencoe, IL: Free Press. (Original work published 1922)

A Social Psychologist Examines His Past and Looks to the Future

HAROLD B. GERARD

Department of Psychology, University of California, Los Angeles

I entered Brooklyn College in the fall of 1939 at age 16, declaring myself a physics major. Immediately after Pearl Harbor, I dropped out of college to become an aviation cadet. I had the flying bug. Family resistance prevented me from enlisting, so instead I went to work in a defense plant, the Johns-Hartford Tool Company in Hartford, Connecticut, that manufactured punches and dies for stamping out shells for various caliber bullets. I was a setup man for the lathes and milling machines. I did enlist in the Signal Corps in March 1942. I took a crash course (crash courses of all kinds were whipped up in those early days of the war) in electrical engineering at New York University, after which I was sent to the Lexington Signal Depot in Lexington, Kentucky, for another crash course in radar. I remember being totally fascinated with what was designated the SCR547 (SCR for Signal Corps Radio), a large ground radar station. After my tour of duty in Lexington, I was determined to pursue a career in electrical engineering after the war.

I was finally able to apply to become an aviation cadet, but by the time I was accepted I was in Newport News, Virginia, awaiting overseas shipment, which, to my dismay, put me in a high-priority category, out of reach of the Army Air Corps. I tried every which way to transfer from the Signal Corps to the Air Corps, but it was a lost cause. I even pleaded for help to the army chaplain in the Newport News embarkation camp. I was told to reapply once I got overseas, which I tried to do, but further complications intervened. It was just not meant to be. When I was eventually shipped overseas in January 1944 to take part in the invasion of Europe, through no design on my part, I was, because of my engineering background, assigned to teach electronics and radio repair at the American School Center in Shrivenham, England. I finally got into the war after the Battle of the Bulge, but that's another story.

After I was discharged in December 1945, I immediately returned to Brooklyn College. Hiroshima and Nagasaki cured me of wanting to be a physicist or an engineer. I decided instead to become a social scientist to help me make some sense of the war experience, which I found so devastating. I was haunted by the Holocaust, and I still am. I became completely caught up in some of the courses I was taking at Brooklyn College. In a philosophy course, I read *Logic and the Scientific Method* by Morris Cohen and Ernest Nagel (1934). I still own and treasure that original copy, which is now quite tattered. Nothing I read before or have read since has had the impact on me of that book. It literally changed my way of seeing the world. I began to devour everything Morris Cohen had written, including his wonderfully sweet autobiography *A Dreamer's Journey*, which began with his childhood in Russia. Even though I never met Cohen, I consider him, along with

Leon Festinger, one of my mentors. Cohen, incidentally, was one of Festinger's teachers at New York's City College, where Cohen taught for many years. When I eventually went to work with Leon, he suggested that I read Cohen and Nagel. I assured him that I had already internalized it.

I was a veritable sponge in my postwar stint at Brooklyn College, soaking up everything. I took a course in economic analysis and was encouraged by the instructor, Eli Shapiro, to follow him for graduate work to the University of Chicago, where he had just taken a job. Chicago was *the* place to study economic analysis, and it still is, I suspect. Shapiro invited me to his apartment for a steak dinner and to meet his wife. My wife to be, Dorothy (I had just gotten engaged), would not consider living in Chicago. It was windy and full of gangsters and meat-packing houses.

I was nearly sidetracked into art history by a course I took with Leo Balet, an inspired teacher, who also took a shine to me. Sidney Siegel, the instructor in the introductory sociology course I was also taking, encouraged me to become a sociologist. So instead of economics at Chicago, I opted to go to Columbia University in sociology, which turned out to be a mistake. That was the easy way out, because we would remain in New York.

GRADUATE SCHOOL

In my first semester at Columbia, I had courses with Robert MacIver, Robert Lynd, Theodore Abel, Paul Lazarsfeld, and Robert Merton. Quite a lineup! Merton's lectures were the most impressive. He was erudite, well organized, and dynamic; one of the best lecturers I had ever heard. I wanted desperately to work with him. So I approached him after one of his lectures, and—miraculously—he put me to work. He turned me loose with a deck of IBM cards that held data from a housing study of his that was supported by the Lavenberg Foundation. He also gave me a key to the facilities of the Bureau of Social Research, which was located in the scary Hell's Kitchen part of Manhattan. I was an as-green-as-it-gets first-year graduate student, and I was to somehow make sense of those data. I would go to the bureau nearly every evening, when the place was dark and totally deserted, and run my cards through the counter-sorter over and over again, looking for relationships in the data. It was strictly a fishing expedition.

I was given a fixed appointment time every week with Merton, during which I would report my latest findings. He was as cold and severe face-to-face as he was warm and engaging behind the lectern. Gradually I came to dread those weekly meetings and was looking for a way to quit. I was rescued by an unfortunate turn of events; Merton had a heart attack—not the first, I learned—which put him out of commission for some time. I just never went back to him, and I never did find out what happened to the work I had already done.

When I was finally able to get an appointment with Robert Lynd, the coauthor, with his wife, of the famous Middletown study, to discuss a proposal I had for a master's thesis, he threw me for a loop. At the time Dorothy and I were living in a predominantly Black housing project in Queens, and I wanted some guidance for conducting a participant observation study of racial contact. With his experience, Lynd seemed like the perfect mentor. When I described my proposal to him, his response, which I remember verbatim, was, "Son, that's like pissin' through a knot-hole!" Instead he suggested that I do a study of how Keynsian economic principles would meet obstacles if applied to the United States! (He was evidently enamored of the English Fabians.) What a topic for a greenhorn like me! So that was that. Lazarsfeld's course was taught most of the time by his assistant Patricia Kendall, whom I believe he eventually married. Columbia's sociology department had all those stars, but I found it a disconcerting, anomic, and uncongenial place.

In my second semester at Columbia, I took a course with Margaret Mead. On the basis of a term paper I wrote for the course, she offered to sponsor me if I would switch to the anthropology department. She even offered me a Viking Fund fellowship to support my future fieldwork. Again, Dorothy prevailed on me to refuse Mead's offer, because she did not want to spend a year or two some-where like central New Guinea, contracting malaria. Incidentally, Mead suffered periodic bouts of malaria, which she had contracted in New Guinea, so there was something to Dorothy's concern.

Mead and Ruth Benedict were jointly involved in a program of Research on Contemporary Cultures (RCC). A number of their graduate students had con-ducted their dissertation research on various ethnic groups, such as contemporary Japanese, Polish, Italian, German, Syrian, East European, and middle-eastern Jews. Mead had discussed some of that research in class. So when it came time for me to select a topic for a term paper, I decided to study differential ethnic reactions to a single crisis situation, to see if the conclusions reached in the RCC research rang true with regard to how people from different ethnic backgrounds reacted to the same crisis. Mead agreed to give me access to the RCC materials.

I made a historical search for a crisis to which people from a number of ethnic groups that were represented in the RCC materials were exposed. Initially, I con-sidered physical calamities such as earthquakes, hurricanes, or tidal waves, but I was unable to come up with a physical calamity that filled the bill. Someone, I don't remember who, suggested labor strikes as a possibility. A great suggestion. I finally found the Lawrence, Massachusetts, textile strike of 1912. To my delight, workers representing 17 ethnic groups were involved, and the Lawrence Library had an extensive archive of materials on the strike, mostly in the form of newspaper accounts of the day. The Lawrence strike was one of the bitterest, most protracted strikes in American labor history. It was organized by the International Workers of the World, the "Wobblies," the forerunner of the American Communist Party.

To make a long story short, I traipsed up to Lawrence with Dorothy and spent many hours perusing the archival materials. I also interviewed Elizabeth Gurley Flynn, who had been one of the strike's organizers, at the American Communist Party headquarters in New York City. I was unable to interview the other two orga-nizers, Joe Ettor and Arturo Giovanitti. Ettor had moved to California to make wine, and Giovanitti, a brilliant poet who named his firstborn son Lenin (they call him Len), refused to see me. I tried to get Len, who was an organizer for the ILGWU, the garment workers union, to help me, to no avail. His father had refused to speak to him for years. In any event, I was able to discuss the strike with

Elizabeth Gurley Flynn, a beautiful and remarkable woman, in the inner sanctum of Communist Party headquarters. Her memory of the strike and the principals involved was still vivid after 35 years.

The paper I wrote for Mead represented my very first halting research effort. I attempted to tie in events occurring during the strike, that is, the behavior of the strikers, to the RCC materials. The workers did behave true to form. For example, the Italians were the first to strike. The Germans spent most of their time arguing politics in their beer hall. The Polish women made a cordon by locking arms and pushed scabs off the sidewalks. The Jews shipped their firstborn son off to New York City. Unexpectedly, the only suicide was a Pole. Recently, while clearing my files of old papers, I came across my copy of the paper, which is quite long. If I must say so myself, it's not half bad. Mead evidently liked it, because, on the strength of it, she invited me to spend a day with her at the Museum of Natural History where she had her offices. She was one of the museum's curators. I arrived there bright and early and left after dark, exhausted. My memory of that day is still crystal clear. Mead held me in thrall for the entire day as I accompanied her on the whirlwind of her various activities. I got a real sense of what a day in the life of a serious academic is like. Unlike me, she didn't waste a minute.

When I called Mead the following day to refuse her offer to sponsor me, she asked me, "Well then what *do* you want to do?" She seemed to be interested in furthering my career. I had recently read the Lewin, Lippitt, and White article on experimentally created autocratic, democratic, and laissez-faire group atmospheres in groups of young boys, which had so impressed me. Also, while at Brooklyn College, I had attended a lecture given by Kurt Lewin to the Psychology Club. More than 50 years later, I still remember that lecture on what he called quasi-stationary equilibria. I answered Mead's question about what I wanted to do by saying that I would like to study with Kurt Lewin. She informed me that, unfortunately, he had just died, but that Ronald Lippitt, a coauthor of the paper I had read, was at the University of Michigan and that she knew Lippitt quite well because they had worked on a project together during the war. She picked up the phone and called Lippitt, and that's how the ball got rolling. Eventually, I formally applied to the social psychology program at the University of Michigan and was accepted. I'm sure a good word from Margaret Mead helped.

I had applied to two graduate programs, Michigan's and Cornell's School of Industrial and Labor Relations. I had also recently read William Foote Whyte's (1955) stunning book *Street Corner Society*, which was a detailed study of a street corner gang. I remember an intriguing and important finding of a positive relationship between the members' bowling scores and their relative status in the gang. The initial status of the members did not depend on how well they bowled. Status expectations had somehow induced pressures that influenced performance. Because Whyte was in Cornell's labor relations school, I applied to study with him. Cornell also accepted me but could not guarantee financial support, although they said they probably would be able to support me. Because Michigan guaranteed me a paid assistantship in the Research Center for Group Dynamics, I chose Michigan. I would also have $75 a month on the GI Bill. I'm not sure what I would have done had Cornell come through with money at the last minute. To this day I'm still intrigued by Whyte's finding, which may reflect a general tendency for performance in a group to be influenced by status expectations.

My first job as a graduate student was working with Ronald Lippitt on a study of a group of young Germans who had been brought to this country to be "democratized." However, as a born experimentalist, I was soon drawn to the work Leon Festinger and his research group were doing. Bert Raven and Hal Kelley were in that group. Luckily I was able to switch to working with Leon. Thus began a 40-year career thinking about and designing experiments to study social influence processes and attitude change.

When I joined Festinger's research group, they were hard at work testing derivations from his then theory of "informal social communication" (Festinger, 1950), which grew out of the study Festinger and two of his students had conducted in a student housing community (Festinger, Schachter, & Back, 1950). The general idea behind the theory was that in any group, over time, differences of opinion will tend to equilibrate. Furthermore, certain group characteristics will affect how quickly and to what extent opinion equilibration will occur. The mediating conceptual variable, *pressures toward uniformity*, will be moderated by the *cohesiveness* of the group and the degree of *homogeneity* of the group members, that is, how similar in background they are to one another. Other factors external to the group that bring pressure to bear on it, such as the importance of being steadfast in the face of confrontation, will also tend to intensify and hasten movement toward uniformity of opinion.

Festinger had an idée fixe from the time of his doctoral dissertation in 1942, which was his concern with how man copes with discrepancy. In his dissertation he studied, in a laboratory context, the effect on a person's level of aspiration on a task of knowing that the performance of a superior, inferior, or same status group was different from his or her own performance. In a subsequent experiment (Festinger, 1947), he studied the effect on a person's voting behavior of knowing that others in various comparison groups had voted differently. The work he was doing when I joined him was in the same vein but in an experimental context with considerable refinement that enabled us to track the process of opinion equilibration over time.

Where did this equilibration model come from? Festinger's mentor, Kurt Lewin, had developed a model of the person that took into account both the person's momentary needs and the activities available to him or her through which those needs could be satisfied. Lewin conceived of the *inner person* as having what he called a need system that consists of need regions that may be in various degrees of tension in relation to one another. If a particular need is in tension relative to the rest of the system, the person will tend to engage in some activity that will reduce the tension in that need region, that is, satisfy that need, so that need tension across the entire need system would tend to equilibrate. Lewin also argued that the boundaries between adjacent regions are what he called *semipermeable,* borrowing a term from cell biology. To the degree that need-region boundaries are permeable, tension in the system will tend to spread rapidly across boundaries. In Festinger's opinion-equilibration model, the group's degree of cohesiveness played a conceptual role analogous to Lewin's notion of semipermeability between adjacent need regions. Equilibration models in psychology were not new. In his *Project for a Scientific Psychology,* written in 1895, Freud argued that the function of the entire nervous system is, through activity, to reduce excitation, that is, to equilibrate excitation across the system.

As what must have seemed a natural segue, Festinger much later followed his concern with discrepancy to an even more fundamental phenomenal level—perception—in which, for example, he used prismatic distortion to study the effects of discrepant information from two different sensory modalities, tactile and visual perception (Cohen & Festinger, 1967). In carrying out that work, he devised some ingenious "brass instrument" type apparatus, which impressed me when I visited him at the New School for Social Research, his last academic position.

In his last book, which is on archaeology, Festinger (1983) transposed his concern with discrepancy to human history, where he examined how prehistoric and ancient man solved the problem posed by the growing discrepancy between a burgeoning population and a limited food supply. Agriculture was the solution. In his inimitable fashion, he turned the pessimistic Malthusian dilemma on its ear by arguing from historical data that through man's intrepid ingenuity our species will survive.

In the research we carried out at the University of Michigan in the early 1950s, we devised methods for manipulating characteristics of the group such as the degree of cohesiveness and member homogeneity and studied the way in which and how quickly opinion equilibration occurred. I must say those were heady days. We were at the frontier of attitude and opinion research and the effects of the group on its members. We were inventing new research paradigms to test hypotheses derived from a general theory of social influence processes, something no one before had ever done.

The only other previous attempt to test derivations from a general theory of social influence was the work of the towering intellect, French sociologist Emile Durkheim. His classic study of suicide published in 1897 represents such an attempt. It was the first piece of research of a social phenomenon based on systematic data collection. Durkheim argued that "social facts," which he also called "collective representations," arise sui generis as a consequence of group life, and the greater the number of collective representations a group has, such as beliefs and rituals, the less the anomie experienced by its group members and therefore the less likely will a group member be to commit suicide. On the basis of this theory, Durkheim predicted and found that Catholics were least likely and Protestants most likely to commit suicide. Jews fell in the middle.

Festinger's term *group standards* is really synonymous with the concept of collective representations coined by Durkheim. Because Festinger and Durkheim were after the same thing, the effects on the individual of the beliefs and behavior of group members, it is not surprising that there is an underlying similarity in their conceptions. The unique aspect of what we were doing, however, was that we created experimental situations within which to study the process. Durkheim took the process as a given, whereas we studied the process by creating social contexts and manipulating moderating variables. The laboratory research on opinion comparison was begun at the Massachusetts Institute of Technology and carried forward at Michigan, where I did my apprenticeship, participating in three studies (Festinger,

Gerard, Hymovitch, Kelley, & Raven, 1952; Gerard, 1953, 1954). Because my dissertation required two people to run it, Leon allowed me to hire someone to help me. That someone was Bob Zajonc, who was paid something like 65¢ an hour. At the time, Bob was a student in the sociology department. Yes, that's true. The rest is history.

When Festinger left Michigan for the University of Minnesota in 1951, he offered to take me with him, but I was happy in Ann Arbor. However, I did want to finish my dissertation with him. My doctoral committee agreed to let me use a preliminary study as my dissertation. I therefore finished with Leon as my chair in the record time of a year and a half. I may still hold the record.

In Minnesota, Festinger extended the theory of social comparison processes to encompass how we come to assess our abilities. He and his students at Minnesota devised ability comparison experiments that were analogous to the earlier opinion comparison ones. Those experiments revealed clear tendencies for the person to use the performance of others as referents for judging his or her ability. In this research Festinger made a full circle back to his level of aspiration dissertation research. He had once again demonstrated the social determinants of self-ability estimates. One of Festinger's former students, Stanley Schachter, extended the theory even further to the comparison of emotions.

RETURN TO NEW YORK

I reluctantly left Ann Arbor in the fall of 1952 (Michigan was such a nurturing environment) to take my first postgraduate school job working with Morton Deutsch at New York University. Mort had a contract with the air force to study group formation and group functioning, and my salary was paid out of that contract. Along with Jim Farr and Phil Lichtenberg, we conducted a number of laboratory studies on group formation. In addition, Mort and I studied staff work at Mitchell Air Force Base on Long Island, at Maxwell Air Force Base in Alabama, and in the Pentagon. We spent a great deal of time on that study and wrote a lengthy report for the air force. The report was classified "top secret," so I couldn't read it after I had helped write it because my security clearance was up to only "confidential." I never found out why I hadn't received "top secret" clearance, but I suspect it was because a close family member belonged to the Communist Party. I had also signed petitions that were suspect, and when I was much younger, I had marched in a May Day parade. When Eisenhower took office in 1953, he appointed Charles Wilson as secretary of defense. Wilson, in deciding to tighten up the defense budget, zeroed in on psychological research, and, bingo, Mort lost his contract and I, of course, lost my job. When I was hired, Stuart Cook, the director of the Research Center for Human Relations where Mort was a staff member, assured me of at least 5 years of employment. Cook rushed to make good on his promise by offering me another position in the Research Center working with Isadore Chein on a long-term drug study, but I declined the offer. I was determined to remain an experimental social psychologist.

I remember vividly the American Psychological Association meeting that September. So many people were in my boat because of Charlie Wilson and were scurrying around looking for jobs. I had a wife and two young children to feed, so I literally took the first job that came along, an assistant professorship in the psychology department at the University of Buffalo for the munificent salary of $5,500 a year. A mistake, not because the job was bad but because Dorothy found the winter unbearable. I must say I wasn't prepared for all that snow either.

But, to backtrack to NYU, while I was there I got to puzzling over Solomon Asch's (1956) classic conformity experiments. Asch had framed the problem in strictly informational terms. What is the person going to do when confronted by unanimous disagreement about something from a group of peers? He found that fully a third of the subjects yielded at least part of the time to the discrepant group judgments, even though they were clearly wrong. Festinger also couched his "informal social communication" theory in informational terms. I had the strong suspicion that in Asch's experiments and in ours, strong normative pressures were also operating. In both experimental paradigms, subjects were in face-to-face contact with the other subjects (or paid participants in Asch's studies and in some of ours). Both types of face-to-face encounters must have been rife with concern by each of the group members as to how he or she would be regarded by the others. As I saw it, there were probably two motives operating: the desire to make a correct judgment and the desire to be accepted by the others.

In our studies, one of the key variables was group cohesiveness. The experimental manipulation of cohesiveness we used in most of those studies was to try to convince subjects in the high-cohesive condition that, on the basis of premeasures we took, they would like each other and should get on well together. The instructions to the low-cohesive groups were very lukewarm. (Of course, assignment to conditions was made on a random basis.) Clearly, those instructions would tend to induce differential status concerns, with the subjects in the high-cohesive groups being more concerned about how they would be regarded by other group members. Yet Festinger insisted he was studying the effects of the opinions of others about the matter at hand, for example, how to treat "Johnny Rocco," a delinquent boy who had committed a crime. He virtually ignored the effect of normative pressures.

I decided to tease apart the effect of normative versus informational influence, and I asked Mort to collaborate with me. Given that I had acquired some electrical know-how in the army, I built the conformity apparatus that Mort and I used in the first experiment and I used in a number of subsequent ones. It was designed to eliminate normative pressures. Most psychologists are familiar with the setup. Richard Crutchfield and others subsequently built other similar versions of it. It was actually ultrasimple. Four subjects were run at a time, each seated in a cubicle facing the front of the room where the stimulus material was displayed. We used Asch's stimuli, which consisted of a single line at the left and three comparison lines of different lengths presented on the right, one of which was equal in length to the single line on the left. Each subject indicated his or her choice of correct comparison line by depressing one of three switches. The choices of the others were displayed on a three-by-four matrix of red bull's-eye lights on a panel in front of the subject. The subterfuge was that all four subjects were told that they were "subject number 3" and all of them responded simultaneously. I ran the experiment, and Mort was hidden behind a screen feeding in a prearranged sequence of judgments (the same sequence Asch used) for subjects "1," "2," and "4" such that the subject found that he or she disagreed with a unanimous majority on 24 of the 36 trials. Mort also recorded their choices.

To compare the cubicle treatment with Asch's original setup, we ran an approximately equal number of subjects, four at a time, in the face-to-face situation, three of whom were paid participants. As we predicted, the combined effect of informational and normative influence in the face-to-face situation produced much more yielding as compared with the cubicle situation, which we referred to as the "anonymous" treatment. "Anonymous" was really a misnomer, because the subjects saw each other when they arrived for the experiment, and, more important, they assumed that they would see each other again before leaving the laboratory. That expectation must have induced normative pressures. A subject who deviated from the majority might have been concerned about what the others would think of him or her and how they would react to him or her after the experiment was over. So my hunch is that the cubicle situation served to reduce normative pressures considerably but certainly did not eliminate them completely. To reduce them even further, we would have had to create a situation in which subjects did not see each other upon both arriving and leaving. Such a situation, however, might arouse suspicion that the experiment was rigged.

The one really positive event of my one-year sojourn in Buffalo was meeting Edward (Ned) Jones. Ned grew up in Buffalo. His father, Edward, Sr., was a long-time member of the psychology department. By the time I joined the department, Ed had retired. One day he called, insisting that Dorothy and I come to lunch to meet his son and his son's wife, Ginnie. I didn't realize it at the time, but that was a fateful meeting. A year or so later, I received a letter from Ned telling me that he was bogged down trying to write a social psychology textbook and asked if I would collaborate on it with him. I flatly refused, saying that writing textbooks is not part of my self-image, or some such disclaimer. He wouldn't take no for an answer and proceeded to send me drafts of chapters on perception that he had already written. As I read the material, I became more and more intrigued; my resistance melted away. I was very impressed with the level of Ned's scholarship and his grasp of the field of what was then called social perception. That was in the preattribution theory days. More about the book later.

Dorothy and I were rescued from the next Niagara Frontier winter by an offer of a Fulbright fellowship to Holland. Bert Raven had been there during the year we were in Buffalo, and he paved the way for us. We had an absolutely wonderful year in Holland and met some lovely people. Jacob Rabbie was assigned to me as my assistant, and we managed to do some research together. I was so impressed with him that I helped him work out graduate training at Yale. When he finished his Ph.D., he was offered the professorship of social psychology at the University of Utrecht. He recently retired from that position.

While in Holland, we were not relishing a return to Buffalo; one traumatizing winter was enough. I had an offer from my alma mater, Brooklyn College, with a much higher salary than Buffalo's, but the teaching load was onerous, five courses a semester. Olive Lester, the chairwoman of the Buffalo department, had twisted the dean's arm to give me a raise. He did, $150 for the year; $12 and change a month!

One reason for returning to Buffalo was that I was to begin medical school that fall. I had started some research on emotion using physiological measurement within the context of the Asch conformity paradigm and also was following up Schachter's work on the social comparison of emotion. Rightly or wrongly, I concluded that if I wanted to really immerse myself in that work, medical training would give me a leg up. The dean of the medical school had worked out a decelerated program for me that would enable me to take the medical courses and continue my teaching and research. Even so, we both dreaded at least six more snowy and windy winters in Buffalo.

THE BELL LABS

As luck would have it, Mort Deutsch came to our rescue. With the guidance and stewardship of Carl Hovland, AT&T had decided to form a social science communication department to be housed at the Bell Telephone Laboratories in Murray Hill, New Jersey. Carl got the labs to hire Mort, and Mort hired me. When I asked the powers that were at the labs why in the world they wanted to support research in social psychology, I received a simple answer: "Since there are 750,000 people working in the Bell System, whatever you may discover about people, and how they relate to one another, is potentially useful to us." An acceptable answer. Our department was unique in corporate America. There were 3,500 members of technical staff in the labs, only 150 of whom were in the research department, to which we 8 belonged. We were part of an elite group. Those not in the research department were involved in applications to the communication industry.

I spent a very happy and productive 6 years at the labs, mostly exploring more fully the psychology underlying the Asch conformity paradigm. I made a foray into the use of physiological measurement, work I had begun in Buffalo, to study the emotional impact of the situation on the subject. I kept coming back to an experience with one participant in the face-to-face treatment in the experiment I ran with Mort at NYU. When he entered the laboratory room, the subject was extremely friendly toward the three paid participants, who, he believed, were also naïve subjects like he was. When he found himself in disagreement with them on most trials, he became quite upset. At some point he asked to leave the room. When he returned, he looked sick and visibly shaken. I became worried and suggested that we discontinue the session. He absolutely refused to stop and continued through all 36 trials, not yielding to the others on a single trial. After the experiment was over and I explained the subterfuge to him, his entire body relaxed, and he sighed with relief. Color returned to his face. I asked him why he had left the room. "To vomit," he said. He did not yield, but at what a price! He wanted so much to be accepted and liked by the others and was afraid he would not be because he had stood his ground against them. There you have normative pressure operating with a vengeance. It was very important for this subject to both be correct and liked. At the Bell Labs I began to study the emotional consequences of deviation and yielding, inspired by my memory of that subject.

The work situation at the Bell Labs was as perfect as it gets. The people were great and so was my salary. If I needed anything, all I had to do was requisition it. One of the engineers designed an impressive new version of the conformity apparatus that ran and collected data automatically. During my sixth year there, however, a change in the administration at AT&T occurred, and the new vice president in charge was not as supportive of our department as was the previous vice president. Pressure began to build, mostly in subtle ways, for us to do something that would be directly useful to the Bell System. Mort actually did do some consulting for one of the so-called operating companies. While at the labs, I received job offers from time to time, which I turned down because things at the labs were going along so swimmingly.

THE MOVE WEST

When the "do something for Ma Bell" pressure began to build, I happened to be approached by the Riverside campus of the University of California. After a very pleasant visit there, I decided to take the job. So in the fall of 1962, my family and I made the trek to California, and I was back in academia. As part of the negotiation with Riverside, they agreed to my taking a leave of absence for a year after the first year. Ned Jones and I had been working fairly steadily on the textbook and had reached a point where we needed to spend time together to finish it. We managed to wangle an invitation for both of us to the Center for Advanced Studies in the Behavioral Sciences at Stanford for the academic year 1963–1964. So after a year in Riverside, we headed north to Stanford.

Working with Ned every day was a joy. We saw eye to eye on most everything, which was surprising because we had come out of different traditions. Ned was trained more or less as a clinician at Harvard, and I had come out of the Lewinian tradition. I consider that year one of the high points of my career. We did manage to nearly finish the book, and we were both pleased with the fruits of our labor. We were each responsible for writing first drafts of eight chapters. Each time one of us finished a chapter, he would give it to the other to work it over. Both of us were ruthless in revising each other's work. After the revision, the chapter was given a going-over by the original author of the chapter, and back and forth it went. In that way, each chapter went through four or five revisions, until it was acceptable to both of us. It was truly a labor of love. Ned challenged me and I him at every step of the way. My gray matter got a real workout! I haven't been as intellectually stimulated since.

One of the chapters in the book for which I had primary responsibility was titled "Action, Choice, and Dissonance," which necessitated my digging into the mushrooming literature on dissonance theory. What most intrigued me was the controversy between Festinger and his followers on one side and critics such as Irving Janis and Milton Rosenberg on the other, who argued that the counterintuitive finding of the inverse relationship between attitude change and reward was due to various artifacts.

I remember one occasion when I drove Festinger from Stanford (he had moved to Stanford by then) to the San Francisco airport. We had some time to kill before his departure and decided to have a drink while we waited for his plane. I questioned him about the Janis and Rosenberg studies, which he dismissed with some simple but telling criticism. "Aren't you going to take them on?" I asked. He answered by saying something to the effect that he had more fertile fields to plow, or other fish to fry. That was about the time he was getting heavily involved in the perception research, so we went on to discuss how to implement an ocular system for producing prismatic distortion. So that was that. Given Festinger's considerable impact on social psychology—arguably more than anyone else—it is rather amazing that he spent so little time—about 20 years—working among us, from the early 1940s to the early 1960s.

When I arrived back in Riverside, I had the good fortune to work with three talented graduate students, Edward Conolley, Linda Fleischer, and Roland Wilhelmy, and several exceptionally good undergraduates, among them Jon Atzet and Grover Mathewson. The three graduate students did their dissertations on problems related to dissonance theory, as did Mathewson. Conolley and Wilhelmy tested derivations from a general theory we were developing that encompassed both dissonance and incentive effects, and Fleischer, using a pupilary dilation measure, studied what Jones and I called "the basic antinomy"—the radical change, as described by Festinger, of the psychology underlying the pre- versus postdecisional situation. We eventually published an account of the theory and the supporting experimental studies (Gerard, Conolley, & Wilhelmy, 1974).

The Riverside school district was at that time in the post–*Brown v. the Board of Education* turmoil. The school board eventually voted unanimously to desegregate the schools, a decision that put me in a quandary. There I was, on the spot, literally. In my naïveté, I was convinced that desegregation would give a boost to minority students' academic performance. I was in a position to document the change and study the mediating processes that would presumably produce it. But did I want to leave the pristine confines of the laboratory for the messiness and unpredictability of the real world? I knew that a study in the schools would take a great deal of time and money—I didn't realize then how much of each would be involved—but I decided to do it. (When Leon heard about my involvement in the study, he said, "Hal, I thought you were an intelligent man.") A number of us on the campus, including Norman Miller, formed a consortium with personnel in the school district and began to mount the study in 1965, the year before desegregation was to be implemented, to take premeasures. The California State Department of Education came through with money, as did the National Institute of Child Health and Human Development.

We selected a sample of 1,800 children from all the elementary grades that included the three major ethnic groups: Mexican American, Black, and what we dubbed Anglo. We tracked the children yearly from 1965 through 1971, taking measures not only on the children but also on their teachers and parents. In most of the schools, there wasn't any space that we could use for testing the children, so we rented air-conditioned trailers that were set up in the school yards. Our staff grew to 150! I was called on the carpet twice by the dean, once because our computer programmer was caught shoplifting a pair of shoes and again because a member of our testing staff was accused of molesting one of the children. Somehow I was to blame for not having screened prospective employees carefully enough! I was so wiped out by that first year's effort that I ended up in the hospital.

A number of publications came out of the work, including a volume edited by Norman Miller and me (Gerard & Miller, 1979). Most of the measures we used were bootstrapped. (We received very little help from the existing developmental literature.) There are enough data from our study to plum for the next hundred years, literally. We had time only to skim the surface, looking at the most obvious relationships. Generally speaking, the results were pretty depressing. By comparing cross-sectional achievement data for the predesegregation year with the longitudinal postdesegregation data, it was clear that, overall, the performance gap between the Anglos and the two minority groups did not change; there was no apparent salutary effect of desegregation on school performance. As the children moved through the grades, the achievement gap widened as it had for the predesegregation data.

We did find an interesting relationship between the degree of the teacher's prejudice and the academic performance of the minority children in her class and their acceptance by their Anglo classmates. We used an unobtrusive measure of the teacher's prejudice from the way in which she evaluated the academic ability of the children in her class. Each teacher rated all the children in her class on 27 semantic differential type scales, a number of which tapped her evaluation of the child's intelligence and academic performance. By comparing those evaluations with objective measures of performance from the state-mandated achievement tests, we were able to generate a prejudice ratio for each teacher based on how much she underestimated the performance of minority children versus Anglo children in her class. Nearly all teachers, some more than others, underestimated the performance of the minority children. The measure seemed to work like a charm. We found impressive correlations between a teacher's prejudice score and how well a minority child did in her class, as measured by the change in the child's performance from before to after being in her class, and also with how well accepted the child was by his or her Anglo peers, as reflected by sociometric measures. The teacher apparently modeled for the children. It is therefore not surprising that the achievement gap widens as children move through the grades. This is not the place to go into the full panoply of the data, but those nuggets do stand out.

ON TO UCLA

My last major effort working in mainstream social psychology is reported in Gerard and Orive (1987). We developed an overall theory of the dynamics of opinion formation that encompasses both social comparison and dissonance processes. The basic notions behind the model are that an opinion represents a preparatory set for action and that a given action has some required level of opinion preparedness (OP). Requiredness level (RL), which is the cornerstone of the theory, is, in turn, a function of both the immediacy and the importance of the anticipated action. The theory relies heavily on earlier conceptions of the nature of conflict, as formulated by Lewin (e.g., 1938), Hull (1938), and Miller (e.g., 1959), and on Allport's (1924) theory of the reciprocal effects of what he called social projection.

In Jones and Gerard (1967), cognitive dissonance is cast within a framework of action with a pragmatic, functional basis. Dissonance, which Festinger argues is strictly a postdecisional state of mind, is rather viewed by us as induced by cognitions having incompatible behavioral implications. After a person makes a decision, the negative features of the chosen alternative and the positive features of the rejected one(s) induce action tendencies in the person (P)—approach toward the rejected alternative(s) and avoidance of the chosen one—that are incompatible with maintaining an unequivocal behavioral orientation (UBO) toward transaction with the chosen alternative and interfering with effective transaction with it. Viewed in this light, dissonance reduction is an attempt to reduce or eliminate these incompatible tendencies in the service of maintaining UBO. The imperative induced by an impending transaction with X requires that P develop a well-formed opinion toward X, enabling P to transact unconflictedly with X.

As far back as 1931, Kurt Lewin proposed what he called a "force field" analysis of conflict that he subsequently elaborated further. In this analysis, he proposed that as P moves closer to transaction with X, its positive features gradually loom larger, and if there are anticipated negative consequences attendant on transaction, those features loom larger still. In effect, if anticipated transaction portends both positive and negative consequences, two psychological gradients develop: a positive one, which starts early and increases with a shallow slope as P nears transaction, and a negative one, which starts later and increases more sharply with decreasing distance.

Lewin gives the example of a little boy at the beach whose rubber swan is floating near the water's edge. (In Germany they must have rubber swans rather than rubber ducks.) As the boy moves closer to the swan, its attractiveness increases; I assume that is due to the anticipated growing joy of finally having it. The boy, as it happens, is afraid of the water, and as he approaches the swan, his fear of the water mounts rapidly, more rapidly than his joy at getting closer to the swan. Because of the configuration of force fields of the swan and the water, the boy will stop at the point where the force fields are equal and opposite: in gradient terms, where the positive and negative gradients cross. If the boy moves forward of the equilibrium point, his fear of the water will increase relative to his desire for the swan, so he will retreat. If he retreats beyond the equilibrium point, his desire for the swan will be greater than his fear of the water, which will move him forward again. All of this will result in his vacillating near the water's edge.

For the child to resolve his conflict, he must have a restructuring of the gradient configuration. He has to overcome his fear of the water, that is, lower the negative gradient or raise the positive one so that it is everywhere above the negative gradient. This cognitive restructuring will enable the child to enter the water and fetch the rubber swan.

As White and Gerard (1981) demonstrated, dissonance arousal is not inherently a postdecisional mental state, although it is often that, but induced by an awareness that accommodation is necessary for UBO to be maintained in the face of transaction. In the White and Gerard experiment, the subject chose between two closely valued alternatives, anticipating immediate or delayed transaction, either 10 minutes or 30 minutes later, with the chosen one. The typical postdecisional spreading apart in value of the alternatives, the chosen one increasing relative to the rejected one, occurred only when anticipated transaction was to be immediate but not when it was delayed, even though subjects in all three conditions had made a decision. It was analogous to the problem of the little boy and his rubber swan. To enable him to fetch the swan, which he wanted immediately, he had to do the cognitive work necessary to enter the water. Subjects in the "immediate" condition in the experiment were under the gun, so to speak.

Lewin argued that there are two basic kinds of conflict. One occurs when the positive and negative force fields emanate from separate sources, as in the boy and swan example (the positive force field from the swan and the negative one from the water). The other basic conflict situation is one in which one activity embodies both positive and negative features, as in the cases of a boy wanting to climb a tree but being afraid of falling out of it, or someone wanting to eat a gooey hot fudge sundae but being concerned about its calories. The so-called forced compliance paradigm invented by Festinger and Carlsmith (1959) is prototypical of the first kind of conflict; the subject is offered a positive inducement to lie to the next subject, a negative counterattitudinal act. For the subject to engage in the lie, some form of accommodation is necessary; the less the inducement to lie, the greater will be the accommodation to maintain UBO. Rabbie, Brehm, and Cohen (1959) found that the subject's merely agreeing to engage in counterattitudinal behavior, without actually engaging in the behavior itself, was enough to induce accommodation. Because transaction was to be immediate, an opinion-forming imperative was induced.

In an experiment utilizing a double-approach avoidance conflict (each alternative embodied both a positive and a negative feature), Gerard and White (1983) found that postchoice dissonance reduction consists of reducing ambivalent feelings toward the chosen alternative but not toward the rejected one, which is in line with the results of the previously described study. Consistent with our theoretical framework, the subject's efforts were focused primarily on the negative feature of the chosen alternative, attempting to increase its value. Both the positive and negative features of the rejected alternative and the positive feature of the chosen one did not change appreciably in value. Festinger would have predicted that, in addition to the decrease in the negativity of the chosen alternative, the positive feature of the rejected alternative would be denigrated, which did not occur.

In our model of opinion dynamics, cognitive work is necessitated when there is a discrepancy between P's RL for the transaction facing him or her and his or her OP for that transaction. When OP is at or above RL, P is sufficiently prepared for transaction; therefore no increase in net support is necessary. When OP is below RL, however, P will be motivated to reduce the discrepancy. Two basic strategies for doing that are possible: lowering RL or raising OP (or both). Lowering RL may be possible by either postponing transaction with X, if that is possible, or reducing X's importance (or both), the two factors that determine RL. A result of lowering RL is a tendency to reduce opinion extremity. This follows from two related consequences: RL lowering reduces the level of OP needed to reach the RL, and because there is a monotonically increasing relationship between OP and net support, the lower the OP, the less extreme will be the opinion. Early important work by Suchman (1950) on the relationship between opinion intensity and opinion extremity clearly shows that the two variables are related in a U-shaped function, such that more extreme opinions, either pro or con, are held with greater intensity. By this line of reasoning, it therefore follows that a less extreme opinion will result from lowering RL, a consequence that can easily be tested. It would also follow that lowering RL will tend to make P more vulnerable to social influence, another consequence that can easily be tested. In addition, subjects for whom an issue had low importance were vulnerable to weak arguments presented by a highly credible source but not to the same arguments presented by a source of low credibility. This suggests that a so-called expert can have such an effect, in spite of weak arguments, because RL is low. Initial opinion was not firm, making the subject more vulnerable to persuasion.

In addition to RL lowering, opinion uncertainty may induce information generation in the service of lowering the OP–RL discrepancy, which, in turn, will result in a tendency for P to polarize his or her opinion. This is the basis for Petty and Cacioppo's contention that thought is required for durable opinion change, which is supported by Cialdini, who found that enduring opinion polarization emerged only for an important transaction that could not be delayed. In effect, net support had increased because of the action imperative, which polarized the subject's opinion.

Support for an opinion may be provided by direct issue-relevant information or by indirect social support. P may increase direct support by adding supportive cognitions, by subtracting nonsupportive ones, or by changing the weights of cognitions related to the issue. Indirect support may consist of the opinion of an expert, group consensus, or fabricated consensus.

Although F. H. Allport's (1924) description of the process was incomplete, he was, to my knowledge, the first to describe fabricated consensus through a process he called social projection. He developed the theory as a way of understanding crowd behavior, which was one of the central concerns of early social psychologists. Allport identified three steps: projection, reciprocal consensus, and increased opinion extremity. The tendency for P to project his or her opinion onto others is at the heart of informational social comparison. In the early social comparison studies, the manipulation of both cohesiveness and homogeneity was tantamount to providing the subject with differential opportunity to project his or her opinion on the other group members. Social projection occurs irrespective of whether P is below his or her RL. It may provide an avenue of increasing OP by adding fabricated consensus information as supporting cognitions. And if P's OP is below RL, it will tend to polarize P's opinion.

Allport's analysis helps us understand the social dynamics underlying crowd behavior, but he left out two critical features. First, for P to project his or her opinion onto others, P must judge them to be cooriented with him or her, that is, to share the same vantage point (or values) with regard to X, the issue at hand. Second, for P's opinion to polarize, his or her OP must be below his or her RL. The first condition can be seen as the necessary condition for polarization to occur, and the second one can be seen as the sufficient condition for it to occur.

Wolfgang Wagner, an Austrian postdoc who worked with me, ran two experiments that are reported in Gerard and Orive (1987) that studied the effect of coorientation, opinion importance, and measurement delay on opinion polarization. In the first study, subjects were run in same-sex groups of four in which, with false feedback, the subject was led to believe that the others either shared or did not share his or her value perspective. This would presumably influence the degree to which the subject could utilize social projection to fabricate a consensus to increase OP. To vary RL, which would affect the degree to which the subject would be motivated to engage in information generation, Wagner utilized a manipulation I had used in my dissertation (Gerard, 1953). Subjects were told that they were each going to debate someone not in their present group on the opinion issue, the "Johnny Rocco" case, immediately after the present session, next week, or possibly not at all. Following that, the subject indicated his or her opinion on a 7-point scale as to whether Johnny should receive harsh or lenient treatment for his crime. The subjects never actually discussed the case or had the debate. The results were in line with the theory. It was only under high similarity and anticipated immediate confrontation that opinions polarized significantly. RL was high and social projection was possible, confirming the necessary and sufficient conditions Allport had failed to note.

PSYCHOANALYSIS ENTERS THE PICTURE

In 1969, I married for the second time, this time to a psychoanalytically minded clinical psychologist who was determined to get me interested in psychodynamics. We met at the Interamerican Congress of Psychology in Montevideo on April Fool's Day, 1969.

I resisted Desy as long as I could, but eventually I capitulated to acknowledging the importance of personality dynamics in social interaction, especially of emotions, that we social psychologists had all but ignored. By the 1970s, social psychology had become dominated by the cognitive revolution that had swept most of psychology. My own work, which I've already discussed, fit the prevailing cognitive cast. I began to have a strong, sneaking suspicion that an important ingredient of social life was missing from our work. Social psychology had ignored the gut, where we really live. A sad commentary is that the study of personality, which tends to focus on affect, has nearly faded out of existence in American academic psychology. At UCLA we no longer have a personality area.

As part of Desy's campaign to convert me, she got me hooked into the psychoanalytic doings in Los Angeles. I took a course with her, taught by a local analyst, on the work of Melanie Klein and Wilfred Bion, which was an eye-opener. I began to familiarize myself with that literature. Also, Desy was in supervision with the leading Kleinian analyst in town and tape-recorded her supervision sessions with him. He was trained in London within the tradition established by Melanie Klein. She cajoled me into listening to the tapes. Her campaign was compelling. More and more, I developed a sinking feeling that we social psychologists were missing the boat. There is much more to social interaction than is represented in the research in mainstream social psychology.

It took a lot of doing for me to overcome my stereotype of clinicians as soft headed for me to become one. I decided that if I were going to develop some kind of purchase on the emotional underpinnings of social interaction, I ought to go whole hog into the enterprise. So in 1982, at age 59, I entered psychoanalytic training, one of the oldest candidates ever, if not the oldest. I finished my training ten years later, during which I *had* developed a sense of how the mind functions from being both on the couch and behind it.

On one hand, I had become dissatisfied with the bland cast that had overtaken social psychology. But now I was confronted by both the lack of rigor and the systematic research in the psychoanalytic literature. The question as I saw it was how was I going to marry my newfound knowledge of the mind with my background as an experimentalist to bring some harder science into the new field I had entered.

REFLECTIONS AND PROJECTIONS

Writing this chapter has made me aware of how happenstance determined, at various points, the direction of my career. I didn't start out, as some do, with a burning desire to do a particular thing and doggedly stay the course. Rather, I kept getting sidetracked. If Dorothy, my first wife, had shared my enthusiasm about my doing graduate work in economics at the University of Chicago or my taking Margaret Mead up on her offer to be my mentor, my career would have been quite different. Or if Cornell had been able to offer me financial support, I may have worked with William Foote Whyte and become an industrial anthropologist of sorts. If my studies at Columbia and the work I did with Robert Merton had been less fraught with anxiety, I might have stayed with sociology. If Elliot Aronson had not convinced me to attend the Interamerican Congress of Psychology with him in Mexico City in 1967, where we had such a good time, I never would have been at the next congress in Montevideo, where I met Desy, who eventually became a major influence in my becoming a psychoanalyst.

Back even further—to the beginning. When I was born, I was slated to become a doctor like my mother's oldest brother, Jacob. Unfortunately, my mother died when I was very young. I am quite certain that had she lived, I would have ended up in medical school. She was a very determined lady. As a matter of fact, when my mother's three brothers found out that I had decided against medical school, I had a lot of explaining to do. They felt responsible for seeing that their sister's wish be fulfilled. They called a meeting where I was on the carpet, having to justify my decision. They really put the pressure on. I eventually prevailed, but just barely. I suspect that my decision to enroll in the University of Buffalo Medical School was in part motivated by guilt at not having fulfilled my mother's wish.

All this makes me wonder whether my career experience is atypical or if others take this kind of random walk through life. In any event, my career has had its frustrations, but, by and large, it has been quite satisfying. Would I exchange it for one of those missed opportunities? I'm not sure.

I know that many of my friends believe that I dropped out of social psychology to become a psychoanalyst. After all, I stopped publishing in mainstream journals. Nothing could be further from the truth. I had reached a point at which I lost the old excitement about my research. The journals were being filled with more and more methodologically sophisticated research with less and less real meaning for me. I was disturbed by a sense of ennui that I had begun to feel. Fortunately, at that moment I rediscovered psychoanalysis, and this time around, the work of Melanie Klein. I could see the potential in it for illuminating the problems we social psychologists study. I was determined to learn more about the recent developments in psychoanalysis. To immerse myself in psychoanalysis, I had to declare a time-out to be retrained. But, rest assured, I am as committed to social psychology as I ever was, probably more so.

I shared the misconceptions of psychoanalysis held by most psychologists and promulgated in most introductory textbooks that psychoanalysis was a useless and lengthy intellectual exercise focused on reconstructing the patient's past and had little effect on the patient's current behavior. In fact, psychoanalysis can be a form of treatment that focuses on the patient's behavior toward the analyst in the here and now, and it is anything but a purely intellectual exercise. It is also essentially a social psychological enterprise.

Up through the 1950s, psychoanalysis had been the dominant theory of personality and the preferred method of treatment. Since then, psychoanalysis has lost its currency in academic psychology. Graduate training in clinical psychology shifted to the cognitive and behavioral approaches. So I was swimming against the tide when I decided to go into psychoanalytic training in 1982.

Psychoanalysis has been very short on research, one of the reasons it has fallen under a cloud. There is a growing realization that good research is needed. By research the psychoanalytic establishment means clinical outcome studies to assess the efficacy of psychoanalytic treatment. It is therefore surprising to me that both the American Psychoanalytic Association and the International Psychoanalytic Association have partially funded my research, which is completely theoretical.

When interest in psychoanalysis by psychologists was cresting in the 1940s and 1950s, a great deal of cross-fertilization between personality and social psychology took place. In our textbook, Jones and I detailed the fruits of the infusion that took place, which culminated in the so-called New Look studies of Jerome Bruner, Leo Postman, George Klein, and others. That work demonstrated the effects of unconscious motivation on perception. In the late 1930s and early 1940s, a number of the faculty members in the Yale psychology department were psychoanalyzed. That immersion led to the work on the frustration–aggression hypothesis, spearheaded by Neal Miller (1941). Psychoanalysis was part of the zeitgeist in those days. Unfortunately, it never got a firm, permanent foothold in psychology, partly because of the difficulty of translating the theory into hypotheses that were testable in the laboratory. Also, the sense was that studies of psychological development in children were necessary to test psychoanalytic hypotheses. These studies are difficult and costly to do. Because the residues of infancy and childhood are very much alive in us in the present and can be activated experimentally, as I hope I've demonstrated in my research, it is not really necessary to limit oneself to developmental studies. I believe we are now on the threshold of returning to that natural connection between personality and social behavior with a much more sophisticated theory of the unconscious and its effects as well as a more highly developed research armamentarium. This has the potential for creating a new New Look. I hope that young social psychologists will rise to the challenge and usher in a new millennium for a social psychology that is grounded in the emotional substratum of mind Freud discovered.

REFERENCES

Allport, F. H. (1924). *Social psychology*. Cambridge, MA: Riverside Press.

Asch, S. E. (1956). Studies of independence and conformity: A minority of one against a unanimous majority. *Psychological Monographs, 70,* 416.

Cohen, M., & Nagel, E. (1934). *Logic and scientific method*. New York: Harcourt.

Coren, S., & Festinger, L. (1967). An alternative view of the "Gibson normalizing effect." *Perception and Psychophysics, 2,* 621–626.

Festinger, L. (1947). The role of group belongingness in a voting situation. *Human Relations, 1,* 184–200.

Festinger, L. (1950). Informal social communication. *Psychological Review, 57,* 271–282.

Festinger, L. (1983). *The human legacy*. New York: Columbia University Press.

Festinger, L., & Carlsmith, J. M. (1959). Cognitive consequences of forced compliance. *Journal of Abnormal and Social Psychology, 58,* 203–210.

Festinger, L., Gerard, H. B., Hymovitch, B., Kelley, H. H., & Raven, B. H. (1952). The influence process in the presence of extreme deviates. *Human Relations, 5,* 327–346.

Festinger, L., Schachter, S., & Back, K. (1950). *Social pressures in informal groups: A study of human factors in housing*. New York: Harper.

Gerard, H. B. (1953). The effect of different dimensions of disagreement on the communication process in small groups. *Human Relations, 6,* 249–271.

Gerard, H. B. (1954) The anchorage of opinions in face-to-face groups. *Human Relations, 7,* 313–326.

Gerard, H. B., Conolley, E. S., & Wilhelmy, R. A. (1974). Compliance, justification and cognitive change. In L. Berkowitz (Ed.), *Advance in experimental social psychology* (Vol. 7). New York: Academic Press.

Gerard, H. B., & Miller, N. (1979). *School desegregation*. New York: Plenum.

Gerard, H. B., & Orive, R. (1987). The dynamics of opinion formation. In L. Berkowitz (Ed.), *Advance in experimental social psychology* (Vol. 20). New York: Academic Press.

Gerard, H. B., & White, G. L. (1983). Post-decisional reevaluation of choice alternatives. *Personality and Social Psychology Bulletin, 9,* 365–369.

Hull, C. L. (1938). The goal gradient hypothesis applied to some "field force" problems in the behavior of young children. *Psychological Review, 45,* 271–299.

Lewin, K. (1938). The conceptual representation and measurement of psychological forces. *Contributions to Psychological Theory, 1,* 4.

Miller, N. E. (1941). The frustration-aggression hypothesis. *Psychological Review, 48,* 337–342.

Miller, N. E. (1959). Liberalization of basic S-R concepts: Extensions to conflict behavior, motivation, and social learning. In S. Koch (Ed.), *Psychology: A study of a science* (Vol. 3). New York: McGraw-Hill.

Rabbie, J. M., Brehm, J. W., & Cohen, A. R. (1959). Verbalization and reaction to cognitive dissonance. *Journal of Personality, 27,* 407–417.

White, G. L., & Gerard, H. B. (1981). Postdecision evaluation of choice alternatives as a function of valence of alternatives, choice, and expected delay of choice consequences. *Journal of Research in Personality, 15,* 371–382.

Whyte, W. F. (1955). *Street corner society* (2nd ed.). Chicago: University of Chicago Press.

Some Reflections on 50 Years in Social Psychology

HAROLD H. KELLEY

Department of Psychology, University of California, Los Angeles

I came from a rural background. My father was a farmer in the small town of Delano, located some 90 miles south of Fresno. Like most college-bound youngsters there, from Delano High School I went on to Bakersfield Junior College, and then to Cal, that is, Berkeley. I can no longer reconstruct exactly why I became a psychology major, but I did well in my studies. On graduating with a master's degree in 1943, I had the good fortune to go directly into the Aviation Psychology Program of the army air force. There I worked under the direction of Stuart Cook ("Captain Cook," in those days), developing selection tests and analyzing how various aircrew members did their jobs (e.g., landing a plane, interpreting airborne radar signals).

Heider concludes his autobiography (1983) with a reference to "a friendly spirit" that arranged the sequence of events in which fortune was so kind to him. I resonate strongly to Heider's comment, because it applies to my life as well. Surely the relationship with Stuart Cook was the work of such a spirit. I came to trust his judgment fully, and it was on his strong urging that, at the end of the war, I enrolled in the group psychology program at MIT. That decision landed me in what became one of the most influential groups of social psychologists and gave me a head start on a productive career in the field.

We can think of social psychology, located as it is between the social and the psychological, as standing between two counterposed mirrors, the one the mirror of the *individual* and the second the mirror of the *group*. We can look into the one, or we can look into the other. But when we look into either one, we see reflections from the other, including its reflections of the mirror we're viewing directly.

Using that metaphor (and with apologies to Charles Horton Cooley), I will chronicle my career path under four counterposings of the *individual* and the *group*:

1. The individual *or* the group? (What is the proper focus of our field? Which mirror do we look directly into?)
2. The individual *versus* the group? (The "person" versus the "interpersonal situation" as causes of behavior? When we see behavior, in which mirror does its image originate?)
3. The individual *from* the group? (How are individual differences related to or derived from the group? When we look into the individual mirror, what are we seeing from the other side?)
4. The individual *against* the group? (When are individuals independent of the group? When are images in the individual mirror independent of those in the other?)

Those four themes have been important in social psychology over the past century and are, to varying degrees, reflected in my own 50 years of work. These are my recollections about *why* certain things went as they did during those years.

THE INDIVIDUAL OR THE GROUP

This concerns the basic question of what is the proper subject matter of social psychology. At MIT we were taught that a group is more than the sum of its parts. Our version of social psychology was focused on "dynamic wholes," closely interconnected—that is, interdependent—sets of individuals. By virtue of their past or their ongoing interaction, they have complex and dense ties—linkages via communication networks, influence via sociometric and status positions, and so on. That focus was contrasted with that of earlier social psychologists, who argued that only individuals are real and a group is no more than the sum of individuals' actions.

In research, the individual focus was illustrated by Triplett's and similar work that examined such things as the effect of observers on a person's activities. In this tradition, experiments usually used strangers as subjects, and the interaction was highly constrained and, generally, brief.

The group focus is well illustrated by the leadership studies at Iowa, by Festinger, Schachter, and Back's study of a housing project at MIT; by Deutsch's study of contrasting classroom incentive systems; and by Thibaut's laboratory study using gangs from Boston neighborhoods. My own work on first impressions wasn't in that vein, though, like Mort Deutsch, I received a Ph.D. from MIT in *group* psychology. The studies were marked by the use of ongoing groups and by the effort put into documenting the processes within those groups.

From 1950 to 1955, my role at Yale, in Carl Hovland's program, was to bring a group focus to bear on mass communication processes. That was in contrast to Hovland's orientation (with its learning theoretic focus on the individual's comprehension, learning, and retention of information) and Janis's similar individualistic focus on personality and psychodynamics. The group and individual orientations were never brought into confrontation. They existed side by side, which reflected Hovland's open personality and the value he attached to eclecticism.

In the late 1940s and the 1950s, the major focus was the group one, set in place mainly by the group dynamics people. But then, I think it is clear, the group focus began to blur and was gradually pretty much replaced by the individual focus. This shift occasioned Steiner's famous question in 1974: "Whatever happened to the group in social psychology?" In this shift, much of the study of groups has been left to neighboring disciplines (sociology, communication, education, management, etc.).

That shift leads me to think that the group focus in social psychology does not afford a stable intellectual orientation for psychologists. To mix metaphors a bit, it is not a firm place for us to stand. Ned Jones wrote, "In a curious way, social psychology has always been ambivalent about the study of groups per se" (Jones, 1985, p. 77). I offer two possible reasons for this instability of our attention to groups:

1. An institutional reason concerns the relative prestige of various locations in the scientific hierarchy. In the reductionistic aspects of our shift toward the individual, perhaps there is a seeking of hard-science legitimacy and prestige—a disengagement from the softer (perhaps, the more sociological) parts of social psychology and an identification with the hard-science parts.
2. The other reason may be found in the problem that Bob Cohen (or was it Stan Schachter?) identified as "Bubba psychology": This is the natural desire to try to surprise and impress one's Bubba and one's colleagues. I argue (as I did in Kelley, 1992) that avoiding the commonplace or obvious takes us in one or both directions away from the intermediate level of observable behavior in groups—either to more *micro*levels (reductionistic) or to more *macro*levels (collective, cultural). Leon Festinger's scientific career might be examined in these terms, with his moves away from groups, first downward to microlevels of individual motivation, and later to motion of the eyeball, and finally upward to the macrolevels of paleontology and history.

In the Thibaut and Kelley collaboration, which began in 1953, John and I *did* achieve a stable focus on phenomena at the group level. We did so by hitting on a comprehensive and systematic theory, the elements of which others might regard as mundane but the *combinatorial* structure of which brings order to numerous interpersonal and intergroup phenomena.

So, another friendly spirit story concerns the Thibaut and Kelley collaboration and how it came about. In 1952, Gardner Lindzey wrote me at Yale asking me to write a chapter on groups for the new handbook he was editing and suggesting that I ask Irv Janis to be a coauthor. I posed the question to Irv, and he declined. I then asked Thibaut (who had been a fellow graduate student at MIT), and he accepted. John and I found that we greatly enjoyed working together, our minds and temperaments meshed well, and we produced a chapter of which we were rather proud. On the merits of that chapter (at least in part), we were invited to the Ford Center (Center for Advanced Study in the Behavioral Sciences in Stanford) as a team. We intended to write a textbook on groups, perhaps along the line of Homans's *The Human Group*. But we got sidetracked into economic models (I remember drawing numerous indifference curves on the blackboard), and then we got caught up with pay-off matrices. Luce and Raiffa had just written their survey of game theory, and we studied a draft copy then available at the center. Our book turned out to be a theoretical work that, in its use of outcome matrices (in a more relaxed way than the pay-off matrices are used in game theory), provided a strongly analytic and organizing approach to group interdependence—an approach we eventually came to call "interdependence theory."

So our collaboration was importantly determined by some good luck and helpful accidents—Janis's other competing tasks; the formation of the Ford Center at that time, which gave us the year to work together; the Luce and Raiffa manuscript; and so on. The Thibaut and Kelley collaboration surely had the benefit of arrangements by one of Heider's friendly spirits.

That collaboration continued until John's death in 1986. Further developments in our theory are described below. Over the years, we continued our joint theoretical work, but our respective lines of empirical work diverged rather markedly. I became increasingly obsessed with the dyad, which I felt I could eventually master intellectually. Reflecting his longtime interests in moral and political philosophy, John's work increasingly consisted of experimental studies of social organizations, norms, and processes. Prominent among those was his brilliant work, with Laurens Walker (a colleague from the UNC law school), on procedural justice. I have no doubt that John was the single most important intellectual influence on my career and work in social psychology.

THE INDIVIDUAL VERSUS THE GROUP (AS CAUSES OF BEHAVIOR)

This second counterposing of individual and group refers to the "person versus situation" attribution problem. The "situation" almost always involves one or more other persons, so the "person–situation" contrast is a special case of the individual–group contrast. Is an observed behavior due to the "person" or is it due to the "group"; that is, due to pressures from other persons? This, of course, is one of the central questions raised by the attribution perspective in social psychology.

My role in the development of attribution theory was that of bringing together under one tent a number of lines of prior and ongoing work. So—a brief story about why and how the "Kelley Cube" came about: At Minnesota we "social relations" people (Stan Schachter, Ben Willerman, Ken Ring, Jerry Singer, Ladd Wheeler, etc.) had read and discussed Heider's book, and I had written a review for *Contemporary Psychology*. I had long been a fan of Thibaut and Henry Riecken's paper on perception of conformity to requests for help from more and less powerful people, and then at UCLA Ken Ring and Arie Kruglanski had done doctoral theses taking off from some of Thibaut's work. From Minnesota days, I was familiar with Schachter's arousal-affect work, which lent itself to attributional interpretations. I had studied the Jones and Davis paper, "From Acts to Dispositions." And I interacted at UCLA with Melvin Seeman, a sociology colleague steeped in Rotter's locus of control ideas. So my head and notes were full of causal perception and attribution-related stuff. Then came the invitation to write a paper for the Nebraska Symposium, and I did the obvious thing, which was to draw together those various strands of thought.

Now, pardon a homely metaphor: The theoretical fruit were hanging high in the tree, ripe and ready for picking, and I happened to be in the orchard at the top of the ladder. (The imagery comes naturally to a farm boy from Delano.) My point is that possessing the particular combination of information and opportunity I had, almost any respectable social psychologist could have written that attribution paper. (This point is also suggested by Ken Ring's and Daryl Bem's subsequent comments, which implied that a similar synthesis was close to the surface of their thinking.) Again, Heider's friendly spirit smiled on me. I should add that the Kelley Cube was included only at the last minute, as a visual aid for the lecture. If I had relied entirely on words, as I had originally intended, people wouldn't have had the Kelley Cube to play hacky-sack with all these years.

To back up a little, much of the earliest work on person perception after World War II was concerned with *accuracy* of judgments of other people, until it was discouraged by Cronbach's critique of the methodology. Then, following leads in Asch's early work, there came the extensive study of judgments of nouns and adjectives, as illustrated by Norman Anderson's work and Charles Osgood's monumental studies of the meaning of concepts.

The attribution approach was different from the earlier work in that it avoided issues of accuracy and different from the later work in that it dealt with interpretations of behavior rather than adjectives. The new questions concerned the causal explanation for the behavior—whether due to the individual and, therefore, informative about that person, or due to the group or situational context. Equally important about the attribution perspective was that it was clear that such attributions make a difference. This was shown in the work on misattributions (inspired by Schachter's work on labeling of arousal) and soon in Bernie Weiner's studies of affect, moral judgments, and behavior in relation to person–situation attributions.

The major impact of the ANOVA model was not in its direct use but in the broader questions it stimulated. Raised first by Leslie MacArthur's research, these questions concerned biases in the use of the covariance information and in the tendency to make "person versus situation" attributions. Those issues came to the forefront in the Jones et al. attribution book—the *Orange* book.

Schachter was, in some ways, the friendly spirit responsible for that book. When I happened to be in New York, he suggested that I invite Dick Nisbett and Stuart Valins to come out to UCLA to discuss attribution problems. It was natural and easy at that time, with the executive secretary of the appropriate NSF review panel at that time being Kelly Shaver, to get funds for a workshop on attribution. I also invited Ned Jones and two other UCLA participants—Bernie Weiner and Dave Kanouse. We met at UCLA in August 1969 and continued a bit later at Yale. Again, my (i.e., our) good luck held, and the book was quite influential. You may remember that it was printed on beige paper, for which we must credit Hurricane Agnes, which, in the summer of 1972, produced floods in Pennsylvania that reduced the printer's supply of paper to that lovely creamy beige.

Most directly traceable to that workshop and most notable in its influence was the Jones and Nisbett chapter on the actor–observer discrepancy, the hypothesis being that actors tend to attribute their behavior to the situation but observers tend to attribute it to the actors. The latter became the focus of much of Ned's subsequent work on insufficient discounting (or "correspondence bias" as he called it), and the basis of work that led to Lee Ross's famous concept of the "fundamental attribution error." (So we see that questions of accuracy crept back into social perception work after all.)

THE INDIVIDUAL FROM THE GROUP

This third counterposing of "individual" and "group" concerns how individual differences are related to—derived from—the group. Here I want to describe my own shift in attitudes toward individual difference and personality research, and how the Thibaut and Kelley analysis of interdependence patterns became a platform for analyzing how individual differences are defined and shaped by interdependence.

As I remember it, in the early days we experimentalists were rather supercilious in our attitudes toward colleagues who used personality measures and studied individual differences. We were "real" scientists, using the experimental method, drawing firm conclusions about cause and effect, and not fooling around with mushy correlational data. *Except*—except when it served our own purposes, as in using "take measures" (a highly relevant and contemporaneous individual difference assessment) to sort our experimental subjects and "clarify" our experimental results.

I shared that attitude. Yet individual differences played a crucial role in one of my best studies—with Tony Stahelski—on cooperators versus competitors, their interaction in the prisoner's dilemma game, and the behavioral assimilation of the cooperators to the competitors. In their interplay, competitors quickly begin to act like cooperators, but this assimilation goes unnoticed by the competitors and serves only to substantiate their misanthropic beliefs that almost all people are, deep down, competitive like themselves.

That was a nice model. And it was a first step in bringing together my interests in interdependence and attribution—interests I had previously tended to keep separate.

Not long after, I tired of laboratory experiments with gamelike tasks and turned to using questionnaires to study real dyads—young couples in love and in ongoing relationships. My first interest was in whether we could extract from their reports the 2 × 2 outcome matrices latent in the problems they encountered in their lives. The answer is, "Well sort of, but 2 × 2 matrices aren't quite adequate for the job," that is, the job of describing natural interpersonal situations. Far better descriptions are provided by transition lists, which I presented in my 1984 paper.

In the course of that work, it became clear that people's satisfactions and dissatisfactions with each other are greatly influenced by the general interpersonal dispositions they attribute to each other. So "attribution" shifted from a peripheral to a central position in my work on interdependence. It began to make sense to think of people as being outcome interdependent not only in their actions but also in their attitudes and dispositions.

That view of interdependence was reflected in Thibaut's and my 1978 book. With an advance from Wiley, we moved our families to Morelia (Michoacan) for a month and then quickly lost interest in the original plan, which was to write a revision of our 1959 book. Instead, we worked on two new ideas: (a) a thorough analysis of the domain of 2 × 2 outcome patterns to identify all the major problems, opportunities, dilemmas, and so on that such situations present to interdependent people, and (b) a causal model of behavior in such situations. That model distinguishes between the underlying ("given") situation and the transformed ("effective") situation. The latter reflects the new situation created by the attitudes they bring to bear on the concrete problem—such attitudes as cooperativeness, fairness, dominance, and so on. This is a systematic, logical way of identifying and distinguishing the individual differences that are relevant to interdependent life. We were heavily influenced in that elaboration of the theory by Chuck McClintock and his colleagues' work on social orientations—work that continues to be very useful in its explanation and prediction of social interaction.

I might note that in writing the 1978 book, John Thibaut and I became increasingly aware of how greatly our theory depended on various key ideas from Kurt Lewin's writings. Those ideas include, for example, interdependence, contemporaneity, taxonomy of situations, cognitive restructuring of the field, goal conflict, motivational properties of conflict, and (in transition lists) locomotion through a "space" defined by paths and goals. The relation of our theory to Lewin's has been questioned by various commentators over the years, and some writers have even regarded us as disloyal renegades from the Lewin camp. Our experience in belatedly appreciating our theoretical indebtedness to Lewin piques my interest in the recent resurgence of interest in Lewinian "field theory," as evidenced by the very active Society for the Advancement of Field Theory (with much leadership from two fellow MIT students, Kurt Back and Albert Pepitone), Ross and Nisbett's use of Lewinian ideas in their 1991 book *The Person and the Situation,* and the 1996 Society of Personality and Social Psychology (SPSP) symposium on Lewin in San Francisco.

In the 1978 and 1979 books, our "group" focus merged with an "individual" focus. In a sense, we became able to look into both mirrors at once, though for our purposes the group mirror was the primary one and the images in the individual mirror were closely coordinated with those on the group side. In brief, the Thibaut and Kelley theory expanded to include a psychology of individual differences. So I now see a basis for creating tight theoretical linkages between social and personality psychology. The idea, expressed in the 1982 Cartwright symposium paper and developed somewhat further in two recent papers (Kelley, 1997a, 1997b), is to derive logically the relevant personal dispositions from the problems and opportunities presented by situations. Accordingly, the dispositions a person is likely to have are a function of the sample of interdependence situations that person has experienced and of the pattern of tendencies the person has been able to negotiate with the various partners in those situations.

My research on young couples naturally led to contact with other social psychologists working on relationships. Another brief story concerns the increasing involvement of social psychologists in the close or personal relationship field, that is, in work on love, jealousy, commitment, arguments, divorce, and so on. The pioneers in this involvement were Elaine Walster and Ellen Berscheid. Despite encountering considerable prejudice against the scientific study of personal phenomena, in the 1970s they published impressive research on feelings of fairness, interpersonal attraction, and love. At a conference at Vanderbilt, John Harvey suggested to Berscheid and me that a group should be assembled to write a broad-gauge book for the field of close relationships. Again, the NSF supported a workshop at UCLA; we assembled a cadre of nine fine social, clinical, and developmental psychologists; and after some Sturm und Drang, we published *Close Relationships* in 1983. Meantime, there were the beginnings of interdisciplinary organizational activities in that field. A signal event was a 1982 conference at Wisconsin on relationships, arranged by Steve Duck and Elaine Walster. That was the first in a series of meetings that evolved into an ongoing international organization (the International Society for the Study of Personal Relationships). The ISSPR brought experimental social psychologists into contact with researchers from sociology, family studies, and communication. Partly through the ideas in the *Close Relationship* book and through the authors' participation in that organization, the influence of social psychologists—their theories and their methods—have become diffused through what has come to be known as the "personal relationship" field. Again, the friendly spirit smiled on us.

THE INDIVIDUAL AGAINST THE GROUP

The broad question here concerns when a group member can stand up against the group, maintaining independence of behavior or belief while still retaining membership.

The Festinger program on cohesiveness and pressures toward uniformity (with Schachter and Kurt Back) emphasized the effectiveness of groups in bringing their members into line. A similar emphasis on the power of the group setting was present in many of the key studies in the 1950s and 1960s—those by Asch, Milgram, Newcomb, Sherif, Zimbardo, and others.

Several of my studies at Yale raised questions about when an individual might resist those pressures, for example, by being highly valued in the group or by having strong direct evidence from one's own senses. A similar counteremphasis existed (implicitly) in the risky shift studies and (explicitly) in Moscovici's work on minority group influence—the influence of an initially divergent minority.

The same issue was raised later in my ANOVA model, which explicitly counterposed group versus individual information sources, in the form, respectively, of the consensus versus consistency criteria. One of my favorite studies, with John Harvey, provided a neat experimental demonstration of the effect of informational consistency on confidence in one's judgment—something we demonstrated experimentally, where before it had been indicated only by correlational evidence.

The possible behavioral independence of a person was, of course, one of the major questions for interdependence theory. The (logical and perhaps mundane) generalization was that behavioral independence is possible when you are less dependent on others than they are on you. This generalization proves to have implications for a variety of basic events in close relationships, such as who has the most say in its affairs, who is most free to deviate from its norms, who is least likely to worry about being left by the partner, and who, indeed, is most likely to be left.

Interdependence, Lewin's criterion for a real group, comes in several forms. The Thibaut and Kelley 1959 book focused on outcome interdependence, but as our second 1968 handbook chapter emphasized, social psychology also yielded a great deal of evidence about information interdependence, for example, in the Bavelas-inspired communication network studies, the sharing of information in Elliot Aronson's jigsaw classes, and recent studies of jury decisions.

It has now become clear to me that the analysis of the interdependence between an individual member and the group requires even further differentiation. They are interdependent in their concrete outcomes, but they are also interdependent in how they use their outcome control (as in being cooperative or competitive, altruistic or selfish). They are interdependent in their control over movement into, through, and out of situations, but they are also interdependent in how they use those controls (as in being a leader or follower, active or passive). Similarly, they are interdependent in the information they control (i.e., to which they have access) but also in how they use that information (in their attentiveness, carefulness of analysis, etc.). Particularly important is their interdependence in the communication of information (as in being open, honest, and trusting or secretive, deceitful, and suspicious).

These comments are not meant to overwhelm the reader with the obvious but merely meant to highlight the multidimensional nature of the relation between the individual member and the group. At each of these nexuses of interdependence, the member has power over the group and the group has power over him or her.

For the question at hand, of when a member can stand up against a group, these distinctions suggest that the social influence effects from the earlier work (by Festinger, Asch, Milgram, etc.) are not subject to simple interpretations. Over the years, we have been much impressed by those results and have placed various dramatic interpretations on them. However, I believe that we do not yet know what mix of factors separate the conformers from the nonconformers under the various conditions. The utilitarian, coordinative, solidarity, ethical, reality, and self-regard factors in most acts of conformity versus resistance are, in my judgment, quite complex. Given this list of factors, it is not surprising that, for example, the subjects in Asch's line-judging experiment were deeply disturbed by discrepancies between their own and their fellows' judgments. That disturbance surely reflected, in part, their puzzlement about reality considerations. But they must also have been perplexed about possible concrete rewards and costs, group incoordination, the demonstration of "good membership," the ethics of their fellows, and the consequences of their verbalizations for their self-regard. This multidimensional perspective leads me to warn against blithely oversimplified and, too often, cynically misanthropic interpretations of conformity.

CONCLUDING COMMENT

By now the reader will probably have been overdosed on the friendly spirits and my stories. However, in those comments I do not exaggerate my feelings about how and why my career proceeded as it did. It is clear to me that the course of my work and the roster of people I've worked with have been influenced very much by various chance events and timely opportunities. Perhaps the stories suggest that the *process* of my work—the interactions, meetings, working groups—are more salient in my memories than are the *results* of that work. That is not entirely correct. I have decided not to use this occasion to lay out the cumulative results of the theoretical work that John Thibaut and I began and that I continue to this day. In that regard, I'm hoping that the benevolent causal structure of my world will continue to be what it has been in the past and that there will be a few more smiles from the friendly spirits. But that is to challenge fate, and I do better to wish for the spirits to smile on the future of social psychology.

REFERENCES

Heider, F. (1983). *The life of a psychologist: An autobiography*. Lawrence: University of Press of Kansas.

Jones, E. E. (1985). Major developments in social psychology during the past five decades. In G. Lindzey & E. Aronson (Eds.), *Handbook of social psychology* (3rd ed., pp. 47–107). New York: Random House.

Kelley, H. H. (1992). Common-sense psychology and scientific psychology. *Annual Review of Psychology, 43*, 1–23.

Kelley, H. H. (1997a). Expanding the analysis of social orientations by reference to the sequential-temporal structure of situations. *European Journal of Social Psychology, 27*, 373–404.

Kelley, H. H. (1997b). The "stimulus field" for interpersonal phenomena: The source of language and thought about interpersonal events. *Personality and Social Psychology Review, 1*, 140–169.

A Career That Spans the History of Modern Social Psychology

MORTON DEUTSCH

Teachers College, Columbia University

My career almost spans the existence of modern social psychology. I entered the City College of New York (CCNY) in 1935 at the age of fifteen: two-and-a-half years younger than most students, as a premed major with the idea of becoming a psychiatrist, having been intrigued by the writings of Sigmund Freud, some of which I read before college. I was drawn to psychoanalysis undoubtedly because it appeared to be so relevant to the personal issues with which I was struggling, and also because it was so radical and rebellious (it seemed to be so in the early and mid-1930s). During my adolescence, I was also politically radical and somewhat rebellious toward authority, helping to organize a student strike against the terrible food in the high school lunchroom and, later, a strike against the summer resort owners who were exploiting the college student waiters, of whom I was one.

The 1930s were a turbulent period, internationally as well as domestically. The economic depression; labor unrest; the rise of Nazism and other forms of totalitarianism; the Spanish civil war; the ideas of Marx, Freud, and Albert Einstein; and the impending Second World War were shaping the intellectual atmosphere that affected psychology. Several members of the psychology faculty at CCNY were active in creating the Psychologist League, the precursor to the Society for the Psychological Study of Social Issues (SPSSI). Thus when I became disenchanted with the idea of being a premed student after dissecting a pig in a biology lab, I was happy to switch to a psychology major: It was a simpatico faculty. Psychology was a part of the Department of Philosophy at CCNY when I started my major in it. Morris Raphael Cohen, the distinguished philosopher of science, was the leading intellectual figure at CCNY, and his influence permeated the atmosphere.

At CCNY Max Hertzman introduced me to the ideas of Kurt Lewin and other Gestalt theorists. And under Walter Scott Neff's direction, I conducted my first laboratory experiment, a variation on Sherif's study of social norms, employing the autokinetic effect. As I now recall, in it I introduced a stooge who constantly judged the stationary speck of light in a dark room as having moved a substantial distance in one direction. (Most subjects see the light as moving small distances in varying directions.) The stooge had a considerable impact on the judgments made by the naive majority of subjects. The findings of this pilot study anticipated later research by Serge Moscovici on minority influence.

My first exposure to Lewin's writings was in two undergraduate courses, taken simultaneously: social psychology and personality and motivation. In the social psychology course, one of our textbooks was J. F. Brown's *Psychology and the*

Social Order (1936). This was an ambitious, challenging, and curious text that tried to apply to the major social issues of the 1930s Lewinian and Marxian ideas, with a sprinkling of the Riemanian geometry employed by Einstein in his theory of relativity. To a naive 17-year-old undergraduate student like me, it was a very impressive and inspiring book showing how social science could shed light on the urgent problems of our time.

In the personality and motivation course, I read Lewin's *Dynamic Theory of Personality* (1935) and *Principles of Topological Psychology* (1936). I also read his *Conceptual Representation and Measurement of Psychological Forces* (1938) as an undergraduate, but I cannot recall when. I, and others, experienced great intellectual excitement on reading these books more than 60 years ago. A *Dynamic Theory of Personality* consisted of a collection of independent articles, previously published in the early 1930s, whereas the other books made a brilliant but flawed attempt to articulate the foundations of a scientific psychology with the aid of topology. They were mind openers. These books are permeated by a view of the nature of psychological science different from what was then traditional. The new view was characterized by Lewin as the "Galilean mode of thought," which was contrasted with the classical "Aristotelian mode." In my writings on field theory, I have characterized in some detail Lewin's approach to psychological theorizing, his metatheory.

Although I was impressed by Lewin's writings, my career aspirations in psychology were still focused on becoming a psychoanalytic psychologist as I decided to do graduate work in psychology. My undergraduate experiences, in as well as outside the classroom, led me to believe that an integration of psychoanalysis, Marxism, and scientific method, as exemplified by Lewin's work, could be achieved. In the 1930s such influential figures as Wilhelm Reich, Erich Fromm, Max Horkheimer, Theodor Adorno, and Else Frenkel-Brunswik, as well as many others, were trying to develop an integration of psychoanalysis and Marxism. Also at this time, some psychoanalytic theorists such as David Rappaport were intrigued by the idea that research conducted by Lewin and his students on tension systems could be viewed as a form of experimental psychoanalysis.

I am not sure why I was advised to go to the University of Pennsylvania to take my master's degree. Possibly it was because it had a well-established psychological clinic and two faculty members, Frances Irwin and Malcolm Preston, who were sympathetic to Lewin's ideas. I had some interesting clinical experiences there working with children, largely without supervision, but the course work seemed dull and antiquated in comparison with my undergraduate courses at CCNY. I earned the reputation of being a radical by challenging what I considered to be racist statements about Negro intelligence in a course on psychological measurement given by Morris Viteles.

After earning my M.A. degree in 1940, I started a rotating clinical internship at three New York state institutions: one was for the feebleminded (Letchworth Village), another for delinquent boys (Warwick), and a third for psychotic children and adults (Rockland State Hospital). During my internship I became skilled in diagnostic testing and clinical interventions with a considerable variety of inmates, more widely read in psychoanalysis, and more aware of how some capable inmates were unjustly retained in the institution because of the valuable services they performed for it or its staff.

I also had the good fortune to meet Clark Hull (the famous learning theorist) while he was visiting a former doctoral student of his, a staff psychologist at Letchworth Village. He was a remarkably generous and tolerant person. We had several long discussions, one related to his recently published book developing a hypothetico-deductive system for rote learning. I had read the book and was somewhat critical of it from two perspectives: the perspective of Gestalt psychology and of Morris Cohen and Ernst Nagel's book on scientific method, both of which I had been thoroughly indoctrinated in while I was an undergraduate at CCNY. Hull seemed genuinely interested in what I had to say even though I was an overly brash 20-year-old pipsqueak. We had another interesting discussion in which he gave me advice on how to seduce a woman. He told me that, on a date, I should carry a handkerchief permeated with perspiration. He explained that sweat and sexual feelings were associated together because of their joint occurrence during sexual intercourse and that sweat would arouse sexual feelings. In retrospect, I realize that he must have been joking, because his suggestion never worked for me.

When Pearl Harbor was bombed in December 1941, I was still in my psychology internship. Shortly thereafter, I joined the air force. I flew in 30 bombing missions against the Germans. During combat I saw many of our planes as well as German planes shot down, and I also saw the massive damage inflicted by our bombs and those of the Royal Air Force on occupied Europe and Germany. Moreover, being stationed in England, I saw the great destruction wrecked by the German air raids and felt the common apprehensions while sitting in air-raid shelters during German bombings. Although I had no doubt of the justness of the war against the Nazis, I was appalled by its destructiveness.

After my demobilization, I contacted some psychology faculty members I knew at CCNY to ask for advice with regard to resuming graduate work in psychology. I discussed with them my somewhat confused interests in getting clinical training, in studying with Lewin because of his work on democratic and autocratic leadership, and in doing psychological research. As a result of these conversations, I decided to apply for admission to the doctoral programs at the University of Chicago (where Carl Rogers and L. L. Thurstone were the leading lights), at Yale University (where Donald Marquis was chairman and where Clark Hull was the major attraction), and at MIT (where Kurt Lewin had established a new graduate program and the Research Center for Group Dynamics [RCGD]). As one of the first of the returning soldiers, I had no trouble in getting interviews or admission at all three schools. I was most impressed by Kurt Lewin and his vision of his newly established research center and so decided to take my Ph.D. at MIT.

MY AUTOBIOGRAPHY AS A SOCIAL PSYCHOLOGIST

I date the start of my career as a social psychologist to my first meeting with Lewin, in which I was enthralled by him and committed myself to studying at his center. He had arranged for me to meet him for breakfast at a midtown hotel in New York in August 1945. Even though it was very hot, I dressed formally—with jacket and tie—to meet with this distinguished professor. Our meeting time was 8:30 a.m., but he did not appear until about 9:00 a.m. He came bustling in, cheerfully looking around for me, his face bright pink from a recent sunburn. He was not wearing a jacket or a tie, and his manner was quite informal. I recognized him from a picture that I had seen and introduced myself, and we set off for the hotel's dining room. But they would not admit us because he had no jacket or tie (how things have changed). We then went to a nearby coffee shop. I do not remember much about the conversation other than that I described my education, experience, and interests, and he described his plans for the new center. I was being treated as an equal; I felt somewhat courted; I was experiencing a trancelike sensation of intellectual illumination with new insights constantly bubbling forth from this brilliant, enthusiastic, effervescent, youthful, middle-aged man. He spoke a colloquial American, often with malapropisms, and he was both endearing and charming. I left the interview with no doubt that I wanted to study with Lewin. I also left in a dazed sense of enlightenment, but I could not specifically identify what I was enlightened about when I later tried to pin it down for myself.

I had a similar experience a month later when I went to MIT to study and work with Lewin. He discussed with me some work he was then doing with the Commission on Community Interrelations of the American Jewish Congress (a commission he helped to establish) to reduce anti-Semitism and other forms of prejudice. His discussion of the issues was intensely illuminating when I was with him, but I could not define it afterward when I was alone. At the end of our meeting, he asked me to prepare a review of the essence of the literature on prejudice, and he indicated that it should be brief and that he needed it in three days. I felt good. I was being treated as a serious professional and was given a responsible and challenging task. Lewin's treatment of me was, I believe, typical of his relations with his colleagues and students. He would discuss a topic with great enthusiasm and insight, he would ignite one's interest, and he would encourage one to get involved in a task that was intellectually challenging, giving complete freedom for one to work on it as one saw fit.

Shortly after arriving at MIT, I noticed a very attractive young woman, named Lydia Shapiro, who would occasionally pop into the center. She was working under Lewin's direction as an interviewer for a study on self-hatred among Jews. We started to get to know one another over cherry Cokes and jelly donuts. Being supported on the GI Bill, I was a cheapskate, and she did like jelly donuts. I don't recall the specifics, but somehow I assigned to supervise her work. After learning that she spent much of her supposed work time sunning herself on the banks of the Charles River, I fired her. About a year and a half later, on June 1, 1947, we got married. Stan Schachter and Al Pepitone, with whom I was sharing an apartment, were my best men at the wedding. In moments of marital tension, I have accused Lydia of marrying me to get even, but she asserts it was pure masochism on her part. In our 60 years of marriage, I have had splendid opportunities to study conflict as a participant observer.

Immediately after our honeymoon in Quebec, we went to Bethel in Maine for the first National Training Laboratory (NTL). I served on its research staff with other students from the RCGD at MIT and from the Harvard Department of Social Relations. Lydia and another woman were the rumrunners for the workshop; Bethel was a dry town, and they had to drive 20 miles to buy the liquor to keep the workshop staff and participants well lubricated.

The first NTL was a natural follow-up of the Connecticut Workshop on Intergroup Relations held during the summer of 1946. As I now recall it, the training staff consisted of Ron Lippitt, Ken Benne, and Lee Bradford, and the research staff consisted of Murray Horowitz, Mef Seeman, and me. One evening, following a lengthy workshop day, Lewin, the workshop participants, the trainers, and the researchers were all sitting around a conference table when one of the participants turned to the researchers and asked us what we were doing. We said that we were keeping track of the patterns of interaction among the group. He then asked us to describe what we had noted; Lewin suggested that would be an interesting thing to do. We summarized our impressions, and this led to a lively, productive discussion among the participants that all of us felt was a valuable, insightful, learning experience. This was the embryo of the T-group and sensitivity training that was given birth at the first NTL in 1947.

I would now say that the researchers at the first NTL did not fully appreciate the importance of the new procedures and new movement being developed. The evangelical tone of some of the trainers appalled many of us, with the result that there was considerable unhappiness among the researchers that summer of 1947. Today many of us recognize the NTL as the birthplace of much of applied social psychology, especially in the area of organizational psychology.

Lewin assembled a remarkable group of faculty and students to compose the RCGD at MIT. For the faculty, he initially recruited Dorwin Cartwright, Leon Festinger, Ronald Lippitt, and Marian Radke (now Radke-Yarrow). Jack French and Alvin Zander were to join later. The small group of 12 students included Kurt Back, Alex Bavelas, David Emery, Gordon Hearn, Murray Horowitz, David Jenkins, Albert Pepitone, Stanley Schachter, Richard Snyder, John Thibaut, Ben Willerman, and me. These initial faculty and students were extraordinarily productive, and they played a pivotal role in developing modern social psychology in its applied and its basic aspects. As I write these past two sentences, it strikes me that all of the students and the key faculty members were men. This was quite a change for Lewin; in Berlin most of his students were women (e.g., Bluma Zeigarnik, Tamara Dembo, Eugenia Hanfmann, Maria Ovsiankina, and Anitra Karsten). It is interesting to speculate how modern social psychology's development might have differed if the student group included a substantial number of women.

Lewin died suddenly on February 11, 1947, of a heart attack. The RCGD had been functioning for considerably less than two years when he died. Yet in this brief period of time he had established an institution that would strongly influence the development of modern social psychology.

My career in social psychology has been greatly affected by Kurt Lewin and my experiences at the RCGD. First, I probably would not have been a social psychologist were it not for the inspiring interview with him in the summer of 1945. Second, the intellectual atmosphere created by Lewin at the RCGD strongly shaped my dissertation and my value orientation as a social psychologist. Lewin was not only an original, tough-minded theorist and researcher with a profound interest in the philosophy and methodology of science but also a tenderhearted psychologist who was deeply involved with developing psychological knowledge that would be relevant to important human concerns. Lewin was both tough-minded and tenderhearted; he provided a scientific role model that I have tried to emulate. Like Lewin, I have wanted my theory and research to be relevant to important social issues, but I also wanted my work to be scientifically rigorous and tough-minded. As a student, I was drawn to both the tough-mindedness of Festinger's work and to the direct social relevance of Lippitt's approach and did not feel the need to identify with one and derogate the other.

MY DISSERTATION STUDY

My dissertation started off with an interest in issues of war and peace (atomic bombs had been dropped on Hiroshima and Nagasaki shortly before I resumed my graduate studies) and with an image of the possible ways that the nations composing the newly formed United Nations Security Council would interact. The atmosphere at the center, still persisting after Lewin's premature death, led me to turn this social concern about the risk of nuclear war into a theoretically oriented, experimental investigation of the effects of cooperative and competitive processes. The specific problem that I was first interested in took on a more generalized form. It had been transformed into an attempt to understand the fundamental features of cooperative and competitive relations and the consequences of these different types of interdependencies in a way that would be generally applicable to the relations among individuals, groups, or nations. The problem had become a theoretical one, with the broad scientific goal of attempting to interrelate and give insight into a variety of phenomena through several fundamental concepts and basic propositions. The intellectual atmosphere at the center pushed its students to theory building. Lewin's favorite slogan was, "There is nothing so practical as a good theory."

As I reflect back on the intellectual roots of my dissertation, I see it was influenced not only by Lewin's theoretical interest in social interdependence but also by the Marxist concern with two different systems of distributive justice: a cooperative egalitarian one and a competitive meritocratic one. In addition, the writings of George Herbert Mead affected my way of thinking about cooperation and its importance to civilized life.

This study, in addition to being the takeoff point for much of my subsequent work, has helped to stimulate the development of a movement toward cooperative learning in the schools under the leadership of David and Roger Johnson. Although cooperative learning has many ancestors and can be traced back for at least 2,000 years, my dissertation helped to initiate the development of a systematic theoretical and research base for cooperative learning. Hundreds of research studies have since been done on the relative impact of cooperative, competitive, and individualistic learning (see Johnson & Johnson, 1989). These various studies are quite consistent with one another and with my initial theoretical work and research on the effects of cooperation and competition (Deutsch, 1949a, 1949b) in indicating favorable effects on students. Through cooperative learning, students develop a considerably greater commitment, helpfulness, and caring for one another regardless of differences in ability level, ethnic background, gender, social class, and physical ability. They develop more skill in taking the perspective of others, emotionally and cognitively. They develop greater self-esteem and a greater sense of being valued by their classmates. They develop more positive attitudes toward learning, school, and their teachers. They usually learn more in the subjects they are studying by cooperative learning, and they also acquire more of the skills and attitudes that are conducive to effective collaboration with others.

THE RESEARCH CENTER FOR HUMAN RELATIONS

After earning my Ph.D. from MIT in the summer of 1948, I joined the Research Center for Human Relations (then at the New School) headed by Stuart Cook. The war against Nazism had stimulated a considerable interest among psychologists in understanding prejudice and how to overcome it, and financial support for research in this area was available from Jewish organizations such as the American Jewish Congress as well as from federal agencies. Among the many groups receiving funding for work in this area were members of the Berkeley Public Opinion Study and the former Frankfurt Institute of Social Research, who produced *The Authoritarian Personality* (Adorno, Frenkel-Brunswik, Levinson, & Sanford, 1950); Lewin's MIT Center, which developed not only the first workshop for reducing prejudice and improving intergroup relations but also action research "to help social agencies that were developing programs aimed at reducing prejudice and discrimination"; and the Harvard group working with G. W. Allport (1954b) on creating an integrated overview of the nature of prejudice and ways of reducing it.

The Research Center for Human Relations was in 1948 also mainly funded by agencies interested in reducing prejudice. As soon as I joined, I became involved in a study of interracial housing that I conducted with Mary Evan Collins. We started with an "experience survey" of knowledgeable public housing officials to identify the important factors affecting interracial relations in housing projects. On the basis of this survey, we decided that the residential pattern—whether the races were segregated or integrated within the housing project—was a critical determinant. We then set out to identify housing projects that were otherwise similar but differed in terms of whether black and white residents lived in separate buildings or were integrated within each building. We were able to identify biracial segregated public housing developments in Newark, New Jersey, and racially integrated ones in New York City that were roughly similar. We then did an extensive interview and a small observational study in the projects, and by the use of various controls, we created a quasi–ex post facto experiment. Despite the obvious methodological limitations of such a study, it was clear that the two types of projects differed profoundly in terms of the kinds of contacts between the two races and the attitudes that they developed toward each other.

This study (Deutsch & Collins, 1951) had important social consequences. As the executive director of the Newark Public Housing Authority stated in a postscript to our book *Interracial Housing*, "The partial segregation which has characterized public housing in Newark will no longer obtain. In large measure, this change in fundamental policy reflects the impact of the study reported in this book. The study has served as a catalyst to the re-examination of our basic interracial policies in housing and as a stimulus to this change." It also led me to become active on an SPSSI committee concerned with intergroup relations. Over the next several years, this committee gave talks before policy-oriented groups as well as helped lawyers who were challenging racial segregation in various suits brought before federal courts. The committee also contributed material to the legal brief that was cited in the 1954 Supreme Court decision *Brown v. the Board of Education*, which outlawed racial segregation in schools and other publicly supported facilities.

In 1949 the Research Center for Human Relations moved to New York University (NYU), and I became a member of its graduate faculty in psychology. Here I worked collaboratively with Marie Jahoda and Stuart Cook on an SPSSI-sponsored textbook, *Research Methods in Social Relations* (Jahoda, Deutsch, & Cook, 1951), one of the earliest—if not the earliest—of its kind. To help me overcome my Kafkaesque, Germanic style of writing, Mitzi pinned on my wall a slogan that stated, "You don't have to write complex sentences to be profound." It was a good reminder as well as a subtle way of deflating my pompous persona of theorist-basic researcher with which I had emerged from my graduate studies.

At NYU I also worked collaboratively with Harold Gerard on a laboratory study of normative and informational influence on individual judgment and a study of decision making among high-level air force officers. In addition, with support from the Office of Naval Research, I was able to start a program of research on factors affecting the initiation of cooperation. Hal had introduced me to Howard Raiffa, who in turn introduced me to the Prisoner's Dilemma (PD), which I soon turned into a useful research format for investigating trust and suspicion (Deutsch, 1973). I was probably the first psychologist to use the PD game in research. Unfortunately, the PD game (like the Asch situation and the Skinner box) became an easy format for conducting experimental studies, and as a result a torrent of studies followed—most of which had no theoretical significance.

I added to my busy schedule by undertaking training as a psychoanalyst at the Postgraduate Center for Mental Health, which had an eclectic orientation rather than a commitment to one or another school of psychoanalysis. It involved not only my own analysis (three times per week) but also 6 to 9 hours of classes, 20 hours of psychoanalytic psychotherapy work, and 2 to 3 hours of supervision per week. It was hectic, but I was young. It was an extremely valuable supplement to my work as an experimental social psychologist, which gives perspectives only on very narrow cross-sections of people's lives. Psychoanalysis provided a longitudinal, developmental view in addition to glimpses into the internal psychodynamics underlying a person's behavior in conflict situations. My psychoanalytic work stimulated my research interest in such topics as trust and suspicion and conflict. It has been a two-way street. My social psychological work on conflict, negotiation, and mediation has affected my therapeutic approach to the conflicts experienced by patients as well as my approach to marital therapy. I continued a small private practice until about 15 years ago, when I wanted to have more freedom to travel. The practice was personally rewarding. I helped a number of people, it enabled me to stay in touch with my own inner life, and it provided a welcome supplement to my academic salary.

During my tenure at NYU, most of my salary was paid out of soft money, from research grants or other monies from outside sources. As McCarthyism developed increasing strength in the early 1950s, social science and social scientists became targets of attack, being labeled as "radical," "fellow travelers," "communist sympathizers," and the like. If your personal library contained books by Karl Marx, if you had participated in interracial groups challenging segregation, if a friend was or had been a member of the Communist Party, and so on, you were suspect and might be purged from your position. During the height of the McCarthy period, many funding agencies no longer were willing to support research dealing with prejudice or interracial relations, and there was much talk of reducing federal support for social science research. Thus I was happy to accept when Carl Hovland, in 1956, invited me to help establish a new basic research group in psychology at the Bell Telephone Laboratories. Bell Labs had an excellent reputation for its support of basic research, and this is what I wanted to do, without the constant problem of raising money.

Much to my surprise, even during the worst part of McCarthyism I never had any problems, and my funding from the Office of Naval Research or the air force did not stop. Although never a communist, I had many of the characteristics of the usual suspect. It is possible that I was not harassed because I had received a security clearance from the air force in the early 1950s before doing research on its decision making.

THE BELL LABORATORIES

Bell Labs was, by academic standards, a luxurious place to work. I received a good salary and had no trouble getting research assistants, equipment, secretarial help, and travel money as well as much freedom to do what I wanted. I was able to hire Bob Krauss and Norah Rosenau, then graduate students at NYU, to work as my research assistants. I was also able to add Hal Gerard and Sy Rosenberg to our research staff. It was a productive group. At Bell Labs, Bob Krauss and I developed and conducted research with the Acme-Bolt Trucking game; we also started on our book *Theories in Social Psychology* (Deutsch & Krauss, 1965). I did various other studies on the interpretation of praise and criticism, dissonance and defensiveness, and effects of group size and task structure on group processes and performance (e.g., "The Interpretation of Praise and Criticism," Deutsch, 1961, 1962).

In addition, while at the Bell Labs, I was its unofficial peacenik, criticizing the strategic thinking among establishment intellectuals and coediting the book *Preventing World War III* (Wright, Evan, & Deutsch, 1962). During this period I was quite active in the SPSSI, articulating some of the social psychological assumptions underlying our national policy and even becoming its president.

Although Bell Labs was in many respects a fine place to work, it had its problems. Compared to a university, it was a stiff organization: It had a clear hierarchical structure; it had fairly set hours of work and vacation (from which I was a tolerated deviant); the lab had no small, offbeat, informal eating places that served wine or beer; and there were few students and little ethnic or racial diversity.

In addition, there were specific problems related to our psychological research unit. Although it was located in the Bell Labs in Murray Hill, New Jersey, the Personnel Research Group at AT&T had been instrumental in getting the unit established and thought that we should be primarily working closely with them on problems with which they needed help. None of us who had come to Bell Labs at Carl Hovland's urging had this view, and apparently Carl did not either. The administrative head of our unit was a former member of the AT&T Personnel Research Group. An uncomfortable power struggle developed about what we should be doing, which Bell Labs ultimately won. But because of the dispute and also because we were the oddballs of the Bell Labs (which was composed mainly of physical scientists and mathematicians), we were the constant object of high-level attention. We had visits from the president of AT&T, the president of Western Electric, the presidents of various Bell Telephone companies, and so on, and at each visit our group would have to put on a show, lasting one or two days, in which we would demonstrate our research. During one of these visits, when a committee came in order to make a recommendation about the future of our group, we received word that Bob and I had just been awarded the American Association for the Advancement of Science (AAAS) sociopsychology prize for the research we had done at the Bell Labs with the Acme-Bolt Trucking game (Deutsch & Krauss, 1962). This apparently laid to rest the doubts about our group.

In addition to the people I recruited for my research group on interpersonal processes, Alex Bavelas, another key staff member selected by Hovland, recruited Herbert Jenkins, a Skinnerian who did his research on learning using pigeons. Herb must have had several people a day ask him, jokingly, "Going to replace the telephone with pigeons, eh?" After a year or so, Bavelas quit the labs, feeling that it was not a receptive environment for what he wanted to do. Jenkins then recruited Roger Shepard, who started his brilliant work on multidimensional scaling there.

While at the labs, I was consulted by its administration on problems such as how to improve the creativity of their researchers, how to apply social science knowledge to improve the functioning of the various telephone companies, and how to improve race relations. As I recall, I gave many potentially useful suggestions, none of which were implemented. I also suggested that they hire Henry Riecken to establish a social science development group to develop existing social science knowledge for use in the Bell system. Although Bell interviewed Riecken, they did not implement this idea either.

Hovland died in 1961, and about a year later I started to think about leaving the labs. I was getting tired of commuting from New York City to Murray Hill; I missed working with graduate students and working in the looser, less hierarchical atmosphere of a university; and I was bored by the special attention that our group was receiving. My memory of the specifics is unclear, but around this time I was approached by Teachers College to consider an appointment to replace Goodwin

Watson, who was retiring, and to head its doctoral program in social psychology. Teachers College was attractive to me because Lydia and I were determined to continue living in New York, I would have freedom to create a new social psychology program, and I was interested in education. I received other feelers from nearby institutions (the Department of Management at Yale University and the Department of Psychiatry at the Albert Einstein College of Medicine) that would have provided higher salaries and more affluent settings, but they did not have the lure of shaping a social psychology program.

TEACHERS COLLEGE

When I joined Teachers College in September 1963, I had a strong view of what I wanted the new social psychology program to be like. I wanted it to attract students and turn out graduates who would be tough-minded and tenderhearted, who would be as knowledgeable and expert in theory and research as the best of the pure experimental social psychologists, and who would also be concerned with developing and applying social psychological knowledge to the urgent and important social problems of our time. In other words, I wanted to develop a program that would overcome the split that had developed between the laboratory and applied social psychology during the 1950s and the early 1960s. As I have indicated earlier, the differences between the sharp-minded and sharp-tongued Festinger and the evangelical, unsystematic Lippitt were precursors of this split, which widened into a chasm in the decade after Lewin's death.

Although the split was understandable in terms of the insecurities of both sides in a young discipline, it was harmful and stupid from my perspective. It polluted the atmosphere of social psychology. When I left Bell Labs (a tough-minded institution) to join Teachers College (a tenderhearted one), I thought that my experimental colleagues would consider this to be a loss of status for me and that my new colleagues would be concerned that I would be overly critical and scientistic (rather than scientific) as well as out of touch with practical realities. However, by the time I came to Teachers College, I felt sufficiently secure in my own identity as a social psychologist not to be concerned by colleagues who would deprecate either tenderheartedness or tough-mindedness.

I was fortunate when I came to Teachers College in several respects. First, although Teachers College, like most schools of education, has relatively little money for research by its faculty or stipends for its graduate students, I was able to bring in outside funding to get the social psychology program off to a good start: The National Science Foundation (NSF) gave funds to build a well-equipped social psychology laboratory, the Office of Naval Research (ONR) supported my research, and the National Institute of Mental Health (NIMH) provided a training grant that would support most of our graduate students. Second, we were able to attract many excellent students who fit our criteria of being tough-minded and tenderhearted, including Harvey Hornstein, David Johnson, Jeffrey Rubin, Roy Lewicki, Barbara Bunker, Madeleine Heilman, Kenneth Kressel, Charles Judd Jr., Janice Steil, Michelle Fine, Ivan Lansberg, Louis Medvene, Susan Boardman, Sandra

Horowitz, Susan Opotow, Eben Weitzman, Martha Gephart, Adrienne Asch, and Peter Coleman. Third, our program was initially small enough for us to be a very cohesive group that mainly worked cooperatively on interrelated research projects under my direction. We could have frequent informal lunches together during which we discussed politics, diets, Jackie Ferguson (our fascinating secretary who mothered us all), and research and theory. Many good ideas emerged from these lunches. Finally, the change from Bell Labs to Teachers College accelerated a shift in focus and labeling of my research. At the Bell Labs, I and others came to view the Acme-Bolt Trucking game as a bargaining game, so I began to think of studies that employed it as bargaining or negotiation studies and more generally as con-flict studies. This was a shift away from labeling them as studies of the conditions affecting the initiation of cooperation.

With a change in labeling, I began to reframe the question underlying much of my research from "What are the conditions that give rise to cooperation rather than competition?" to "What are the conditions that give rise to constructive rather than destructive processes of resolving conflict?" At a conceptual level, the two questions are very similar. Nevertheless, the latter phrasing is much sexier; it reso-nates directly to many aspects of life and to the other social sciences and psychol-ogy. And it is also directly connected to many of the social issues with which I was concerned: war and peace, intergroup relations, class conflict, and family conflict.

It was a productive reframing that led to much research in our social psychol-ogy laboratory by my students and me. My book *The Resolution of Conflict: Con-structive and Destructive Processes*, published in 1973, summarized much of this research and had considerable impact in the social sciences. It helped to provide a new way of thinking about conflict and broadened the focus of the field to include constructive conflicts as well as destructive ones.

Our research into the question central to *The Resolution of Conflict* started off with the assumption that if the parties involved in a conflict situation had a cooperative rather than competitive orientation toward one another, they would be more likely to engage in a constructive process of conflict resolution. In my earlier research on the effects of cooperation and competition on group process, I had demonstrated that a cooperative process was more productive than a competi-tive process in dealing with a problem that a group faces. I reasoned that the same would be true in a mixed-motive situation of conflict. A conflict could be viewed as a mutual problem facing the conflicting parties. Our initial research on trust and suspicion employing the Prisoner's Dilemma game strongly supported my reason-ing, as did subsequent research employing other experimental formats. I believe that this is a very important result that has considerable theoretical and practical significance.

At a theoretical level, it enabled me to link my prior characterization of coop-eration and competitive social processes to the nature of the processes of conflict resolution that would typically give rise to constructive or destructive outcomes. That is, I had found a way to characterize the central features of constructive and destructive *processes* of conflict resolution; doing so represented a major advance beyond the characterization of *outcomes* as constructive or destructive. This not only was important in itself but also opened up a new possibility that we would be able to develop insight into the conditions that initiated or stimulated the development of cooperative-constructive versus competitive-destructive processes of conflict.

Although the gaming conflicts in the laboratory during this period (1963–1973) were relatively benign, the conflicts in the outside world were not. During this period the cold war escalated; the Berlin crisis occurred; the brothers John and Robert Kennedy and Martin Luther King Jr. were assassinated; the United States was increasingly involved in the Vietnam War; there were teach-ins, campus upheavals, race riots, Woodstock, love-ins, and communes; the new left was emerging; and so on. I was not immune to the effects of these events, personally or professionally.

On a professional level, as a result of *Preventing World War III* (of which I was coeditor), my activities in the SPSSI, my various speeches, and our conflict studies, I became identified as one of the psychologists (along with Ralph White, Charles Osgood, Irving Janis, Jerome Frank, and Herbert Kelman) concerned with war and peace issues. I was invited to participate in meetings on the Berlin crisis, arms control, deterrence, Soviet–U.S. relations, and so on. Some involved high-level diplomats, others involved people in the defense establishment, others were at the United Nations, and still others were with citizen groups or social scientists. During the 1960s I was also trying to get more of my fellow psychologists involved in these issues. I took the opportunity of several addresses to speak to these issues: My 1960 SPSSI presidential address was "Psychological Alternatives to War"; my 1966 New York State Psychological Association talk was "Vietnam and the Start of World War III: Some Psychological Parallels"; my 1968 Eastern Psychological Association presentation was "Socially Relevant Science"; and my Kurt Lewin Memorial Award address was "Conflicts: Productive and Destructive."

About the time I was finishing the manuscript for my conflict book, in May 1972, I received from Melvin J. Lerner, then at the University of Waterloo, an invitation to participate in a conference titled "Contributions to a Just Society." Mel had been an NYU social psychology student who had worked with Isadore Chein but had taken some courses with me. Shortly after the conference, he asked me to contribute to the *Journal of Social Issues* volume on the justice motive that he was editing. The two papers I wrote as a result of his urgings were "Awakening the Sense of Injustice" (Deutsch, 1974) and "Equity, Equality, and Need: What Determines Which Value Will Be Used as the Basis of Distributive Justice?" (Deutsch, 1976). In preparing these papers, I reviewed the existing work on the social psychology of justice and became quite dissatisfied with the dominant approach to this area: equity theory. My dissatisfaction led me to write an extensive critique of equity theory in 1977 (Deutsch, 1978) and, with the support of the National Science Foundation, to embark on a program of research on the social psychology of distributive justice. This program was, without my full recognition, something I had been engaged in for many years. Like Molière's bourgeois gentleman, I had been "speaking justice" all the time without being aware of it. My dissertation study could be thought of as a study of two different systems of distributive justice: cooperative egalitarian and competitive meritocratic. Our research on bargaining and conflict had direct relevance to a central question in the social psychology of justice, namely, What are the conditions that facilitate the establishment of a stable system of justice among interactants that they will consider to be fair?

The year 1982 was particularly satisfying for me. I made two important addresses. In one, my presidential address to the International Society of Political Psychology, I developed the concept of "malignant conflict" and described the processes involved in such conflicts and used this discussion as a basis for analyzing the cold war between the United States and the Soviet Union (e.g., Deutsch, 1983a). The reaction of the audience was very gratifying. In various follow-ups (e.g., interviews, talks, conferences, pamphlets) it received considerable attention.

The second address was my inaugural lecture as the E. L. Thorndike Professor of Psychology and Education at Teachers College. I admired Thorndike both as a psychologist and as a person (after reading an extensive biography of him), but I felt his views about race reflected the ignorance and bigotry prevalent in his time. In my opening remarks, I expressed my admiration for Thorndike but dissociated myself from his statements about racial and ethnic groups. My address was essentially a review of my work in social psychology. However, in a concluding section, I indicated my intention to help to further develop the educational implications and applications of my work on cooperation and conflict resolution. To this end, I proposed establishing a center at Teachers College that would foster cooperative learning and constructive conflict resolution in the schools. At that time I vainly hoped that I might be able to induce a former student of mine to direct, administer, and raise funds for such a center; I never liked doing administrative work or raising funds, even though I had been reasonably successful in doing so during my career. In 1986, with the aid of a small grant from President Michael Timpane ($9,600), I started the center that I later ambitiously named the International Center for Cooperation and Conflict Resolution (ICCCR).

In 1982 I also published the paper "Interdependence and Psychological Orientation," which integrated several strands in my work. Mike Wish and I (while Mike was on the faculty at Teachers College) did some initial work on characterizing the fundamental dimensions of interpersonal relations. This work grew out of some research that my students and I were doing on marital conflict; we felt it would be useful to go beyond personality descriptions of the individual spouses so that we would be able to characterize the couple as a couple in terms of their relations to one another. Using various data collection procedures and multidimensional scaling methods, we (Wish, Deutsch, & Kaplan, 1976) came up with five dimensions: cooperation–competition, power distribution, task-oriented versus social–emotional, formal versus informal, and intensity of the relationship.

Previously, I had done much to characterize the social psychological properties of the first dimension, cooperation–competition. Now I sought to do this for the others. Undoubtedly influenced by the popularity of the cognitive approach, I labeled my first attempt "modes of thought." But this title did not seem to be sufficiently inclusive. It appeared to me evident that cognitive processes differ in types of social relations, and I wanted to sketch the nature of some of these differences. However, I also thought that the psychological differences among the types of social relations were not confined to the cognitive processes: Various motivational and moral dispositions were involved as well. It had been customary to consider these latter predispositions as more enduring characteristics of the individual and to label them "personality traits" or "character orientations." Because my emphasis is on the situationally induced nature and, hence, temporariness of such predispositions, these labels did not seem fitting either. Thus I settled on the term "psychological orientation" to capture the basic theme of this paper, namely, that people orient themselves differently to different types of social relations and that these orientations reflect and are reflected in various cognitive processes, motivational tendencies, and moral dispositions.

At the time, I was not doing research in cognitive social psychology, but I was sympathetic to it for two reasons. First, as someone greatly influenced by the Gestalt psychologists as well as by Lewin and Fritz Heider, I felt perceptual and cognitive processes were very important. Second, I felt it was a healthy reaction to the antimentalist views of B. F. Skinner and his followers, which were quite popular in psychology in the 1960s and 1970s. My sympathies for the cognitive approach possibly unconsciously led me to suppress the significant differences between it and my emphasis on psychological orientations. Psychological orientations involve the cognitive but also the motivational and moral orientations. In the 1980s, cognitive social psychologists neglected both the motivational and moral aspects of people's orientations to social relations.

After publishing *Distributive Justice* (1985), I sought funding from NSF for a program of basic research related to some of the ideas in my paper "Interdependence and Psychological Orientation." It is unfortunate that my proposal was not funded. By this time our NIMH-supported, predoctoral training program was no longer in existence; the NIMH's interest had turned toward postdoctoral training. Teachers College provided no funds for research or for graduate research assistants and little secretarial support or money for travel or equipment. It was also a period in which academic appointments became scarce. The consequence was that our doctoral students increasingly became part-time students who often had full-time jobs. In addition, they became more interested in nonacademic positions and more frequently decided to specialize in the organizational rather than in the social psychology component of our doctoral program in social and organizational psychology.

In this context I discontinued my basic research, which had been primarily conducted in the laboratory. From 1985 on, I continued to write and publish papers mainly for small conferences related to conflict or justice, several as award addresses for honors I was receiving and a number by invitation of editors of books or special journal issues. Among the more than 60 articles I have published since 1985, several titles stand out: "On Negotiating the Non-Negotiable"; "Psychological Consequences of Different Forms of Social Organization"; "The Psychological Roots of Moral Exclusion"; "Sixty Years of Conflict"; "Equality and Economic Efficiency: Is There a Trade-Off?"; "Kurt Lewin: The Tough-Minded and Tenderhearted Scientist"; "Educating for a Peaceful World"; "The Effects of Training in Cooperative Learning and Conflict Resolution in an Alternative High School"; "Constructive Conflict Resolution: Theory, Research, and Practice"; "The Mediation of Interethnic Conflict" (with Peter Coleman); "William James: The First Peace Psychologist"; "Constructive Conflict Management for the World Today"; "Mediation and Difficult Conflicts"; "The Interplay Between International and External Conflict"; and "A Framework for Thinking About Oppression and Its Change." I also contributed to and coedited *The Handbook of Conflict Resolution: Theory and Practice*.

THE INTERNATIONAL CENTER FOR COOPERATION AND CONFLICT RESOLUTION

In 1986 I started the center that I promised in my Thorndike inaugural address. Our first activity was a workshop to which I invited the superintendents of school districts in and around New York City as well as representatives of several foundations who might become interested in financing the activities of our center. In addition to introductory remarks made by the president of Teachers College and me, the workshop consisted of a series of miniseminars chosen to reflect the kinds of activities in which our center would engage: cooperative learning, the constructive use of controversy in teaching, conflict resolution training in schools, the training of student mediators, and research evaluation of programs. A leading expert conducted each seminar (e.g., David and Roger Johnson led the seminars on cooperative learning and the constructive use of controversy).

As the result of this workshop, one of the superintendents invited us to develop a program of cooperative learning in his wealthy, suburban school district and to evaluate the program. We sought without success to broaden the program to include conflict resolution training. However, the superintendent was helpful in arranging for us to meet with the superintendent of a nearby, comparable school district that would serve as a control. We approached several foundations for funds but were rejected, until I noticed in a publication that Hank Riecken was on the board of the W. T. Grant Foundation. I contacted Hank and told him of our plans and hopes, and he arranged for me to meet with the president and him. Both were enthusiastic about our plans, which called for support for 5 years at a level of $200,000 per year, and they asked me to write a detailed proposal for submission to the board. The board approved the project for 3 years and indicated that after the first year we should obtain half our funds from other sources. At the time I did not realize that this was a customary but nasty policy of many foundations—forcing one to remain continuously in a fund-raising mode.

We began the project with a preliminary workshop in which David Johnson got a group of senior, influential teachers involved in cooperative learning. They became enthusiastic supporters. Our next step, which proved to be fatal, was to introduce the questionnaires, observational measures, and other recorded data we wished to obtain. We needed permissions from the school board and from the school personnel and parents of the students. When the school board learned that we were interested not only in studying academic achievement but also in measuring social skills, social relations, and psychological adjustment, they were horrified and canceled permission to do the study in their district. As the superintendent regretfully explained, the political attitudes of the board members were to the right of Attila the Hun, and they thought of mental health as a dangerous, explosive topic.

At this point I was sorry that I had left the social psychology laboratory to do research in field settings. However, Ellen Raider, who had joined our center as training director after we were funded, came up with the center-saving suggestion that we move our project to an inner-city, alternative high school where she knew the principal and associate principal. Luckily, the foundation was happy to approve the move; they preferred that our research be done with inner-city youth.

I shall not describe the many headaches and heartaches we had in carrying out our research, other than to indicate that we were training overworked and fatigued but dedicated teachers, most of whose students lived in poor and difficult circumstances and often did not have the reading or writing skills necessary for successful work as high school students. Also, to put it bluntly, the physical conditions of the school and neighborhood were horrible. Many aspects of the project were not executed as well as we had planned: the training of the teachers; the measurement of the effects on students; the duration of the study; the records kept by the school on student attendance, dropouts, and disruptions; and so on. By the standards of a laboratory experiment, it was very unsatisfactory research. Yet I must say that I came out of this study with a great deal of appreciation of those researchers who are foolhardy enough to leave the laboratory. They must have the kind of administrative and social skills, flexibility, ingenuity, statistical wizardry, and frustration tolerance rarely required in laboratory studies.

Despite our problems, much to our surprise, we were able to demonstrate that our training had important and significant effects on the students. In brief, the data showed that as students improved in managing their conflicts (whether or not because of the training in conflict resolution or cooperative learning), they experienced increased social support and less victimization from others. This improvement in their relations with others led to greater self-esteem as well as fewer feelings of anxiety and depression and more frequent positive feelings of well-being. Their higher self-esteem, in turn, produced a greater sense of personal control over their fates. The increases in their sense of personal control and in their positive feelings of well-being led to higher academic performances. There is also indirect evidence that the work readiness and actual work performance of students were also improved. Our data further indicated that students, teachers, and administrators had generally positive views about the training and its results.

This study was the first longitudinal study of the effects of cooperative learning and conflict resolution training conducted in a very difficult school environment. It was also the first to go beyond the measurement of consumer satisfaction. Its positive results were consistent with our theoretical model and with results obtained in smaller, brief studies in experimental classrooms. In part because the study was conducted in the New York City school system, the city's board of education made a contract with the ICCCR in 1992–1994. The contract specified that the ICCCR would train two key faculty or staff people from every high school in New York City so that one would become sufficiently expert to be able to train students, teachers, and parents in constructive conflict resolution and the other would become sufficiently expert in mediation to be able to establish and administer an effective mediation center at the school, with students functioning as mediators.

The ICCCR continues to do conflict resolution training in various school systems and in other contexts, such as the United Nations. More recently, as a prelude to offering graduate studies in conflict resolution at Teachers College, Ellen Raider conducted workshops on conflict resolution with various members of the faculty. The graduate studies now exist as one of the concentrations in the degree programs in social and organizational psychology as well as a certificate program for nondegree students.

I have been the organizer for a faculty seminar on conflict resolution from which the book *The Handbook of Conflict Resolution: Theory and Practice* was published by Jossey-Bass in 2000. I wrote four chapters for it and served as its editor along with Peter Coleman, who is the new director of the ICCCR. Recently, Eric Marcus joined Peter and me in editing a revised and expanded edition of the *Handbook* (Deutsch, Coleman, & Marcus, 2006). After the ending of the seminar on conflict resolution, I initiated another faculty seminar on oppression. It started with an earlier version of my paper "A Framework for Thinking About Oppression and Its Change." The seminar gave rise to a conference on interrupting oppression and sustaining justice at Teachers College on February 27–28, 2004. In turn, the conference led to the publication of a special issue of the journal *Social Justice Research* in 2006.

CONCLUSION

As I look back on my career, several things stand out for me.

Luck. I was lucky to go to CCNY, which had two young faculty members, Max Hertzman and Walter Scott Neff, who stimulated my interest in Lewin and in social psychological research. I was extremely lucky to be a student at the RCGD at MIT, where I was able to become part of a small, innovative group of faculty and students who had a major impact on the development of modern social psychology. Moreover, my career got off to a quick start largely as a result of the prodding of Stuart Cook, who had me involved in writing two books shortly after I obtained my Ph.D. Also, I was very fortunate to be able to receive financial support for my research throughout most of my career. In addition, I have had the opportunity to work with many excellent, productive students who have stimulated me and contributed much to my research. Not least, I was lucky enough to marry a woman whose esthetic sensibility and practical skills helped to create a congenial and supportive home environment that enabled me to focus my attention on scholarly activities rather than on such household activities as fixing things (which I never could do anyway).

Continuing themes. My work on social psychology has been dominated by two continuing themes with which I have been preoccupied throughout my career. One is my intellectual interest in cooperation and competition, which has been expressed in my theorizing and research on the effects of cooperation and competition, our studies of conflict processes, and our work on distributive justice. I have continued to believe that these foci are central to understanding social life and also that a "social" social psychology rather than an "individual" social psychology would have these as its fundamental concerns. The second continuing interrelated theme has been the development of my work so that it has social relevance to key social problems. Sometimes images, derived from such social problems as war and peace, prejudice, marital conflict, and injustice, would be the starting point for the development of a theoretical analysis or an experimental study. At other times I would use theory and research (other social scientists' as well as my own) in an attempt to shed light on important social issues. The two themes of my career have contributed to important applications, particularly in the field of education, where I am considered to be one of the parents of cooperative learning and conflict resolution training.

Episodic research. Occasionally, I strayed from the two themes just described to do single studies that expressed my reservations about some of the fashionable theorizing and research. I took potshots at Solomon Asch's neglect of group factors in his conformity studies, at Festinger's omission of defensiveness in his dissonance theorizing, at equity theory's assumption of greater productivity when people are rewarded in proportion to their performance, at social perception studies that ignored the social and institutional context in which social acts are imbedded, and at Henri Tajfel's initial assumption that the mere awareness of a difference among a collection of individuals will promote group formation. My straying was usually short-lived, because my primary interests were in the two themes described above and I was not sufficiently energetic to take on additional themes.

The social context. I grew up in a time when, as a Jew, I experienced many instances of prejudice, blatant as well as subtle, and could observe the gross acts of injustice being suffered by blacks. In my youth and adolescence, there was the economic depression, union organizing, the Spanish civil war, and the emergence of fascism, Nazism, and Stalinism. I was politically engaged—contributing lunch money to the Spanish loyalists, organizing strikes in high school and in a summer resort, participating in a sit-in against the fascist ambassador, and so forth. It is no wonder that I was attracted to Lewin, whom I saw as taking psychology in a direction that would enable it to contribute to the development of a democratic, cooperative society that was free of prejudice.

The activist theme in my career as a social psychologist undoubtedly reflects the social context of my youth. The social context also helps to explain why I did not become a political activist or union organizer. In my family, among my fellow (mostly Jewish) students, and in my high school and college, there was a strong emphasis on ideas and intellectual achievement. Our heroes were those who contributed to the world through their ideas—Darwin, Marx, Freud, and Einstein. They had exemplified Lewin's dictum, recalled earlier, that "there is nothing so practical as a good theory." This has been the second theme of my career.

I conclude with the hope that future social psychologists will be more concerned than we have been with characterizing the socially relevant properties of individuals and the psychologically relevant attributes of social structures. To oversimplify it, I hope that they will provide a successful integration of the orientations of three of the intellectual heroes of my youth: Freud, Marx, and Lewin.

REFERENCES

Adorno, T. W., Frenkel-Brunswik, E., Levinson, D. J., & Sanford, R. N. (1950). *The author-itarian personality.* New York: Harper.

Allport, G. W. (1954a). The historical background of modern social psychology. In G. Lindzey (Ed.), *Handbook of social psychology (Vol. 1).* Cambridge, MA: Addison-Wesley.

———. (1954b). *The nature of prejudice.* Reading, MA: Addison-Wesley.

Deutsch, M. (1949a). An experimental study of effects of cooperation and competition upon group processes. *Human Relations, 2,* 199–231.

———. (1949b). A theory of cooperation and competition. *Human Relations, 2,* 129–151.

———. (1961). The interpretation of praise and criticism as a function of their social context. *Journal of Abnormal and Social Psychology, 62,* 391–400.

———. (1973). *The resolution of conflict: Constructive and destructive processes.* New Haven, CT: Yale University Press.

———.(1974). Awakening the sense of injustice. In M. Lerner & M. Ross (Eds.), *The quest for justice.* New York: Holt.

———. (1978). The social psychology of justice. In *Proceedings of the international symposium on social psychology* (pp. 23–46). Kyoto, Japan: Japanese Group Dynamics Association.

———. (1982). Interdependence and psychological orientation. In V. Derlega & J. L. Grzelek (Eds.), *Cooperation and helping behavior: Theories and research* (pp. 15–42). New York: Academic Press.

———. (1983a). Conflict resolution: Theory and practice. *Political Psychology, 4,* 431–453.

———. (1983b). Current perspectives on justice. *European Journal of Social Psychology, 13,*305–319.

———. (1983c). Preventing World War III: A psychological perspective. *Political Psychology, 3,* 3–31.

———. (1985). *Distributive justice: A social psychological perspective.* New Haven, CT: Yale University Press.

Deutsch, M., Coleman, P. T., & Marcus, E. (2006). *The handbook of conflict resolution: Theory and practice,* revised and enlarged 2nd ed. San Francisco: Jossey-Bass.

Deutsch, M., & Collins, M. E. (1951). *Interracial housing: A psychological evaluation of a social experiment.* Minneapolis: University of Minnesota Press.

Deutsch, M., & Krauss, R. (1962). Studies of interpersonal bargaining. *Journal of Conflict Resolution, 6,* 52–76.

———. (1965). *Theories in social psychology.* New York: Basic Books.

Jahoda, M., Deutsch, M., & Cook, S. W. (1951). *Research methods in social relations.* New York: Holt and Dryden.

Johnson, D. W., & Johnson, R. T. (1989). *Cooperation and competition: Theory and research.* Edina, MN: Interaction.

Lewin, K. (1935). *A dynamic theory of personality.* New York: McGraw-Hill.

———.(1936). *Principles of topological psychology.* New York: McGraw-Hill.

———. (1938). *The conceptual representation and measurement of psychological forces.* Durham, NC: Duke University Press.

Wish, M., Deutsch, M., & Kaplan, S. (1976). Perceived dimensions of interpersonal relations. *Journal of Personality and Social Psychology, 33,* 409–420.

Wright, Q., Evan, W. M., & Deutsch, M. (Eds.). (1962). *Preventing World War III: Some proposals.* New York: Simon and Schuster.

Conclusions
Looking Back to Inspire the Future

ROBERT LEVINE AND LYNNETTE ZELEZNY

Department of Psychology, California State University, Fresno

Winston Churchill once observed that the further one can see into the past, the longer that person is able to project into the future. In this book, we have journeyed through the histories of 13 outstanding social psychologists spanning the modern era of social psychology. Looking back at these journeys, what lessons can scholars and future students take away? In this final chapter, we will try to highlight some coherent trends and shared advice that emerged from these career histories.

COMMONALITIES AND DIFFERENCES IN THE STORIES

In the introduction to this book, we questioned whether commonalities would emerge in the career paths of the invited authors. Is there a social psychologist type that is drawn to the discipline? Is there a path that personifies the great researchers and teachers? Is the attraction to the field mostly the result of happenstance and experience, perhaps a defining life event or an inspirational professor? How much of a role is played by chance?

The most obvious conclusion one takes away from these stories is how profoundly different they are. At first glance, in fact, the stories appear to be almost totally idiosyncratic. There are a few obvious surface similarities, of course—all of the authors were serious students, all spent most of their careers at universities—but the sweep of change, the beginnings and critical decision points, and the range and cadence of movement through these careers have distinct fingerprints.

The differences appear on many levels. Most obvious is that their early backgrounds span as wide a range of geography and demographics as one might expect to find in any profession or at any level of achievement. Philip Zimbardo grew up in poverty in an urban, immigrant New York neighborhood. Ed Diener grew up in comfort in rural central California. Harry Triandis and Robert Rosenthal faced the hardships of World War II, whereas Aroldo Rodrigues enjoyed relaxed Rio de Janeiro.

A few authors refer to a specific, catalyzing event in their journeys. These, too, fall into very different categories. Alice Eagly, for example, points to a report she gave in the eighth grade as awakening her to the possibility that a person could be a social scientist and that this was a career she might want. But, she notes, it was the last she saw of social science in her education until college. Robert Cialdini refers to an event when he was already a grown-up social psychologist—a self-distracted walk out of his quiet office at Ohio State University into a hysterical Saturday afternoon football crowd—that redirected his social psychology interests from isolated laboratory experiments to real-life subject matter, a shift that has profoundly affected the focus of many modern social psychologists.

The fact that such different types of people were so successful in the same discipline perhaps offers a grander lesson about social psychology: its breadth of content. Why should we expect social psychologists to come from similar backgrounds when their areas of study cover such broad ground? A more nuanced look at the data does, in fact, suggest links between early experience and adult professional content. Although we admit our N in this book is small, it seems more than chance findings that Zimbardo, who defended himself against ethnic prejudice (he was taunted with the wrong label, no less; how social psychological is that?) on the streets of New York, established his reputation studying topics such as deindividuation, power relationships in prisoners and guards, terrorists, and the psychology of evil; or that Diener, raised in a secure farm community with a mother who emphasized the importance of happiness over money, has become the foremost expert on the topic of the psychology of well-being; or that Triandis, a Greek immigrant who fondly recalls intermingling with tourists to improve his skills in foreign languages, has turned his attention to cross-cultural issues. The links also pop up in intellectual styles. Shelley Taylor believes her ability to improvise has been a key to her achievements. She traces this skill to the example of her mother, who was at one time a pop and jazz pianist.

Perhaps most notable is that most of the authors trace their early backgrounds, as disparate as they are, to their eventual curiosity in social psychology. Bertram Raven worked as a horn and saxophone player in a circus band in his youth, fully intending to become a professional musician. But at the same time he was making music, he began to notice the culture of prejudice and the virtual caste system surrounding him. Soon after, he was developing his seminal theory of social power. One of the blessings of becoming a social psychologist, as these chapters underscore, is it allows one to systematically study the very aspects of social experience that we care about.

In other words, the first lesson these stories offer students is not to be overly concerned with the questions of whether they are the right type to become a social psychologist or whether they come from a social psychology stock or have the right background. The field is broad and textured, and there are many right types. The significant issues focus on content. Students should ask themselves, Am I curious about the type of questions social psychologists ask and try to answer, questions about the psychology of people and how they interact with each another? Do I like the scientific approach that social psychologists use to answer these questions?

Another clear difference in these stories may be seen in the circuitousness of the career paths. This, too, is apparent on multiple levels. On a geographical level, for example, some seemed to be on the constant move. Rodrigues moved back and forth between Brazil and the United States throughout his career, and Harold Gerard went from graduate school at the University of Michigan to NYU to the University of Buffalo to a Fulbright fellowship in Holland to Bell Labs to the University of California, Riverside (with a stint at Stanford's Center for Advanced Studies in the Behavioral Sciences), to UCLA. Others worked from a relatively stable home base. Bernard Weiner, for example, went to UCLA in 1965 and has remained there since. Diener's first job was at the University of Illinois, where he still is.

Some began in completely different careers. Raven was working as a professional musician. Gerard was an electrical engineer in the military during World War II, intending to make that his career. (After observing firsthand the devastation created by the invasion of Europe, however, he decided after the war to become a social scientist to try to make some sense of his experience.) Rodrigues was initially a lawyer. Triandis was set to become an engineer. Rosenthal began his career as a clinical psychologist. A second message, then, is there is no singular path to success. Although the power of the situation is alive and well in these stories, what we see even more profoundly is the importance of finding a good person–environment match.

We also see how the times influenced the movement of career paths. One clear difference is the seeming informality of entering institutions in the early days. Morton Deutsch, whose story reaches furthest back into time, tells about applying to only three doctoral programs (the *only* three being the University of Chicago, with Carl Rogers and L. L. Thurstone; Yale University, with Donald Marquis and Clark Hull; and MIT, with Kurt Lewin). Being one of the first returning soldiers from World War II, he reports having "no trouble in getting interviews or admission at all three schools," eventually choosing Kurt Lewin and his newly established Research Center for Group Dynamics. Gerard recalls his graduate school path being established when his undergraduate mentor Margaret Mead casually picked up the phone and called Ronald Lippitt; a few months later he was accepted into the social psychology program at the University of Michigan. He had applied to a grand total of two programs. The next generation of our authors traces an only slightly less formal path. Weiner applied to only one graduate program—the University of Michigan—and he is convinced his acceptance was largely on account of his research connection with one of his previous mentors. He attributes his hiring in 1965 at UCLA, where he has remained until today, to an "old boy's network": His mentor—on this occasion Norman Garmezy, a senior colleague during Weiner's first academic position at the University of Minnesota—phoned a newly hired professor at UCLA who was his research collaborator, who in turn contacted the UCLA department chair, and, poof, 2 weeks later Weiner had a job offer. No awkward interviews. No sweaty colloquium. Times have obviously changed, no doubt both for better and for worse.

One similarity we see in almost all the stories is the attributions to the critical importance of luck. Rodrigues describes the "friendly spirit" who seemed to arrange the sequence of events during the many turns of his intercontinental career. Reading these chapters, we see that the friendly spirit clearly has had considerable influence in the world of social psychology. Rodrigues borrowed the spirit from no less than Fritz Heider and later lent him or her to his own mentor, Harold Kelley. Gerard looks back on the importance of "happenstance" in his career—how chance encounters with people such as Margaret Mead, William Foote Whyte, and Eliot Aronson redirected his path at critical turning points. Weiner, the attribution theorist, underscores the significance to his career of chance events, ranging from his happening to take a course in industrial psychology at the University of Chicago to that memorable occasion when his experimental rat Farfel fell to the floor. In his conclusion, Weiner attributes the successes and failures of his career to luck (along with those other three factors, of course).

The same authors are, however, ambivalent about where their luck came from. To most of these high achievers, luck is not a purely unstable, external factor. Weiner talks about good luck coming to the prepared. Taylor's final advice to students is for them to make their own luck. Achievements, she observes, emerge when mental preparedness meets opportunity. Rosenthal tells of a spooky letter that he received at the beginning of his career from his clinical supervisor, Ed Schneidman, which sketched out a hypothetical career path sending Rosenthal from North Dakota to Ohio State to Harvard. In subsequent years, Rosenthal, in a turn of events that still gives him chills, did just that, even though each move at the time seemed to be directed by chance.

Clearly, luck matters. Just as clearly, however, luck favors those who are most prepared. Some of the most interesting cases of fortuitous luck were events that had no right to make a positive difference. Taylor became a psychology major after being told to become one by a professor who, insensitively, hadn't taken the time to find out what she really wanted to do. The professor insisted even after Taylor protested and said that she wanted to become a historian. (Chalk up a point for obedience to authority.) Eagly decided to go to graduate school in social psychology largely because of its interdisciplinary promise. She soon found she was completely wrong in her assumption about the direction social psychology was taking. She turned out, however, to have made the right decision, even though it was for the wrong reasons. (Score one for the bait and switch.) Weiner tells how then-editor William McGuire of the *Journal of Personality and Social Psychology* made obsessive requests for revisions of a paper Weiner had submitted. As a result, Weiner added more and more studies to the manuscript, which eventually resulted in Weiner's famous six-experiment manuscript, one of his defining works. Diener's passion for measuring the psychology of happiness was fanned while he was an undergraduate by a professor who would not let him conduct a study on the happiness of farmworkers. The professor objected because, he said, it was an obvious fact that farmworkers were not happy, and, besides, there was no way to measure happiness. It is ironic, Diener points out, that he conducted a study on conformity instead. That professor may have contributed more to the study of the psychology of happiness than he will ever know. (Who said dogmatism always leads to no good?) Then there was the curious course of Zimbardo's acceptance into graduate school. If he had not been mistaken for a Negro, Zimbardo might never have ended up in a doctoral program at Yale, or even in social psychology. (Thank you, sloppy stereotypers.)

ADVICE TO FUTURE STUDENTS

What advice can students considering a future in social psychology take away from these chapters? Although the career paths of these social psychologists are very different, we see considerable overlap in the advice they offer to future students. Several themes stand out.

Be Open to the Unanticipated

To achieve as much creative success as the authors of these chapters have requires considerable goal orientation, what might even appear at times to be a rigid, single-mindedness of purpose. Strong hypotheses and well-planned road maps are certainly critical in the achievement process. But, to paraphrase the playwright Clifford Odets's famous observation, your most important achievements are oftentimes what happen while you are making other plans. One of the patterns we see in these success stories is an openness to the unexpected. When the unexpected illuminates a promising new path, have the courage to switch courses.

In some of the current stories, as we have seen, this translated into complete changes of career. Gerard walked away from his early success as an electrical engineer when he became more interested in studying social behavior. Rodrigues left his career as a lawyer to devote himself to social psychology, a field that barely existed at the time in his home country. Even those who went directly into psychology graduate school often dramatically changed directions. Zimbardo had his earliest successes publishing rat studies. Where would social psychology be today if he hadn't had the courage to leap into the less-precise arena of social psychology when it captured his attention?

Another variation on this theme of openness to change is what Taylor—the same Taylor who grew up listening to her mother improvise at jazz piano—calls a willingness to retool, which she continues to do even today. Taylor describes her recent turn toward genetics and neuroscience as an area of science she would never have imagined entering at the beginning of her career but one that opened new doors for her. Eagly tackled the new methodology of meta-analysis in midcareer. "It was not a move that I had anticipated in my early career," she observes, but one that carried her to a new level of accomplishment. After a stellar 40-year career conducting experiments on social influence and attitude change, Gerard entered psychoanalytic training in search of a fresh perspective on human behavior.

This openness to new paths reflects a very social psychological virtue: the courage to be an honest empiricist. Cialdini observes how the great Stanley Schachter taught him to chase the data wherever they might lead, "to get off the horse he was riding and to get on one going in the opposite direction—in midstream—because he would rather follow the data than his preconceptions." Rosenthal showed how chasing the data can spin failure into success. He describes how his apparent failures while conducting his thesis led him to research on experimenter expectancy effects, which led to his classic Pygmalion in the classroom work, which led to his achievements working on statistical programs. Cialdini grasped the wisdom of Schachter's advice that critical morning at the Ohio State football stadium when the surrounding tumult led him to conclude, "Cialdini, I think you're studying the wrong thing." Be it one's research or one's life, students are well advised to be good empiricists. As Taylor puts it, "Listen to data."

Cooperate and Collaborate

Throughout these stories we see reference to the importance of surrounding oneself with good colleagues. This advice pertains to every stage of the professional sequence.

In most of these success stories, the authors began drawing from good professionals in their student days. To begin with, they advise, find a good mentor. Weiner observes, "Students with mentors are happier, more productive, promoted more quickly during their academic careers, and overrepresented as award winners." There is not much to be afraid of on that list. Finding the right mentor, of course, requires clear thinking. You want a mentor with enough experience and standing to help you open doors. It is at least as important, however, to find a mentor who cares about you—one who is supportive, who challenges you, and who is focused on moving you forward. As Weiner also points out, if you intend to make a significant contribution to the field, you will eventually need to shed that mentor. The best mentors will prepare you for that day.

Surround yourself with good and mutually supportive students. In story after story the authors make references to fellow graduate students who have played a vital part in their careers. As Taylor points out with, we assume, tongue only partially in cheek, "My first bit of advice to graduate students, then, is to pick your cohort carefully!" Of course, this is in many ways outside of a student's control. For those of you who do have the luxury of choosing between graduate schools, however, you are well advised to speak to the current graduate students at the institution, not just the professors. You will probably get a better idea not only about how professors treat their students but also of the dynamics within the student cohort in that program. Is it an atmosphere where students support and learn from one another or one where they feel pitted against one another in a zero-sum competition? As Diener advises, the best way for graduate students to advance their career is through cooperation, not competition, with their fellow students.

Whether in graduate school or later in your career, you should also seek good collaborators. Most of the authors describe their collaborations as keys to their success. Some refer to relationships with established scholars; others underscore their collaborations with students and junior colleagues. Isn't it interesting that some of the most innovative thinkers in the field emphasize how heavily they have relied on collaboration with others?

Independent achievement and cooperation are not mutually exclusive but, under the best of circumstances, mutually reinforcing. Consider Diener's advice: "Work with excellent mentors and fellow graduate students, and your career will be enormously enhanced. When you become a professor, do everything you can to attract the most outstanding students. Don't compete with your colleagues and students; collaborate with them instead."

Listen to Others, but Judiciously

The philosopher Jacob Needleman once advised that it is good to keep an open mind but not so open that your brains fall out. Should all four reviewers of the paper you submitted to the *Journal of Personality and Social Psychology* agree that you need a control group in your study, you would be wise to listen up. But judgments about scientific work, even when they come from the most qualified of experts, can sometimes be myopic, unreliable, or just plain wrong.

These chapters are full of anecdotes recalling feedback that, had the authors accepted them uncritically, would have accomplished nothing, or worse. Rosenthal tells about two letters he received the same day about a paper he had written, one informing him that the paper had been rejected for publication in a social psychology journal, the other telling him the same paper had been awarded the AAAS socio-psychology prize for the best social science research of the year. Weiner describes how Edward Jones and Harold Kelley gave diametrically opposite criticism to an early draft of his now-classic six-author attribution paper. Jones told him it was too long and too theoretical; Kelley said it needed to be longer with more theory. The only thing they agreed on was how badly the manuscript needed these changes.

At some point in most careers it becomes important to stick to one's convictions no matter what others think. Taylor recalls a well-meaning colleague once telling her to "stop doing this health stuff; it will be the end of your career." Diener made his mark in a subject area—the psychology of happiness—that many colleagues initially told him was trivial and impossible to measure.

A career in academics requires a thick skin. Criticism and rejection are chronic events. The odds are stacked against you every step of the way: getting into gradu-ate school, obtaining a job, having a grant approved, having a paper accepted for publication. The likelihood of rejection from any particular school or journal or granting agency is well above fifty percent for all but the rarest of scholars. Taylor quotes an anonymous head of a federal granting agency who observed that "social psychology is the only field that routinely eats its young."

Some of the authors in these chapters were even turned down for tenure at their first university. They should take comfort knowing they are in good company: Several years after completing the obedience studies, which were already the most influential experiments ever conducted in social psychology, Stanley Milgram was turned down for tenure at Harvard. When he then went out on job market, Milgram received a similarly cool reception, being rejected by the universities he most preferred.

There is certainly value in listening to feedback from your critics. Listening too carefully, however, can stifle your creativity and take a terrible toll on your morale. Fortunately, one usually requires only a single acceptance to move forward—one graduate school, one tenure decision, one journal. As Taylor advises, be fearless. Accept advice, but judiciously. Have a thick skin ready to slip into when you need it. Let yourself be liberated by the assumption that no matter how well you perform, someone important will not approve. Like Diener, embrace your nonconformity. Trust the value of studying what you find interesting, even if—perhaps especially if—it has been ignored or discarded by others.

Happiness Is a Process, Not a Place

Consider form as well as content. Along with the question of whether you are attracted to the subject matter of social psychology is whether you are suited to the life of academics and research, because this is how most social psychologists spend their days (and, not uncommonly, their nights and weekends too). One question you might ask is whether you would like a career where your boss structures your days or if you prefer one where you create the structure. Most academic positions don't simply offer the opportunity to structure one's work life; they require that you create the structure. The life of a professor is, in most cases, remarkably self-determined. Except for a few required activities, you rarely answer to a boss. You create your own job. You schedule your own days. For those who focus on research, this means needing to constantly re-create. Reinvention is a way of life.

This is a blessing for some but a burden to others. If reinvention appeals to you, a career in academics may be hard to beat. There are few vocations where workers have the opportunity to adjust their priorities or switch directions, even in midstream, without needing to find a new job or even to report their decision to a supervisor. It allows creative individuals to remain fresh and passionate about their work. Reinvention is a wonderful antidote to burnout.

It is important to recognize, however, if this life of chronic reinvention is not your cup of tea. You may be a person for whom the lack of structure, the lack of "shoulds" and "musts" in the typical academic's day, simply sounds like a lot of pressure. This is a profession with no clear job description and no time to rest on one's laurels. Without reinventing oneself, an academic's career tends to turn stale.

The ability to re-create, the willingness to explore new paths, is not only critical to how successful one is as a researcher but a key to how happy one is in his or her work. Those who like to discover new paths when the old ones turn stale—like the authors in this book—tend to be most satisfied with their careers as scholars. Those who resist change and new challenges are prone to end up cynical old professors. Students thinking about a career in social psychology might want to gauge how they measure up against these two extremes. If you are a person who likes the idea of reinventing yourself, academics and research may be just the career for you. If you are not that type of person, you might want to consider a different career.

To paraphrase the advice offered by Diener—the man *Time* magazine dubbed "Dr. Happiness"—happiness as a social psychologist is a process, not a place.

Follow Your Passions

There is, of course, a strong pragmatic sensibility in these career journeys. None of the authors would have come so far had they not made shrewd decisions along the way.

But what shines through these stories more than anything is the authors' passion for their work. Here we come to perhaps the most crucial advice: Become a social psychologist because you want to study social psychology. There is an old story of a woman who always wanted to be a concert pianist but gave up the idea when she discovered it would require that she learn how to play the piano. The writers of these chapters are not like that woman. They chose their careers not because they were looking for a job title or to make lots of money (which you won't) but because it would allow them to spend their time reading, writing, talking, and thinking about social psychology. Perhaps this is the closest we come in these chapters to defining a social psychology type. It is a person with a passion for study-ing social psychology.

Love for one's work breeds persistence, which is another common element in these stories. The sculptor Clement Renzi studied under a number of modern mas-ters. When he was asked to describe the most important lesson he ever received, he told of a great sculptor who, after carefully looking over the young Renzi's work, offered three words of advice: "Keep at it." The same wisdom applies to success in social psychology.

Intelligence helps. More critical, however, is curiosity. Fortunately, there are so many interesting problems for social psychologists to choose from that we never need to bother studying anything else. The satisfaction that comes from wrestling with and occasionally even glimpsing an answer to one of life's interpersonal puzzles is, above all, what drives a successful career as a social psychologist.

Author Index

A

Abelson, R.P., 56
Adamopoulos, J., 159
Adorno, T.W., 227
Agassi, V., 183
Allport
  F.H., 202, 204
  G.W., 62, 227, xi
Armor, D.A., 45–46
Asai, M., 155
Asch, S., 118, 196
Aspinwall, L.G., 45
Atkinson, J.W., 70

B

Back, K., 193
Barrett, D.W., 25
Becker, S., 60
Berkowitz, L., 181
Berscheid, E., 181
Betancourt, H., 155
Blass, T., x
Block, J., 45
Bontempo, R., 155
Borden, R.J., 24
Bower, J.E., 46
Brannon, L.A., 59
Brehm, J.W., 56
Brown, J., 44, 221
Buss, D., 63

C

Carli, L.L., 60
Carlsmith, J.M., 203
Carnevale, P., 155–156

Catalan, J., 25
Centers, R., 183
Chaiken, S., 58–59
Chen, S., 59
Cialdini, R.B., 19, 24–26, 28
Clark, K., 140
Coelho, G., 153
Cohen, M., 189
Coleman, P.T., 238
Collins, M.E., 228
Colvin, C.R., 45
Conolley, E.S., 200
Cook, S.W., 228
Cooper, H.M., 60
Coren, S., 194
Creswell, J.D., 45
Crowley, M., 61

D

Daniels, L.R., 181
Davis, E.E., 150, 152–153
de Charms, R., 78
de Grada, E., 183
Dela Coleta, J.A., 115
Demaine, L., 25
DeNicholas, M., 24
Deutsch, M., 114, 221, 227–230,
  233–234, 238
Diekman, A.B., 62, 64
Diener, E., 1
Dunagan, M.S., 47
Dunnette, M., 154

E

Eachus, H.T., 179
Eagly, A.H., 55, 58–64

Ebbinghaus, H., 138
Eisenberger, N.I., 48–49
Erchul, W.P., 183
Evan, W.M., 229

F

Fahey, J.L., 45
Festinger, L., 56, 174, 179–180,
    193–195, 203
Fiedler, F.E., 153
Finch, J.F., 24
Fiske, S.T., 42–43
Fraser, S.C., 25
Freedman, J.L., 25
Freeman
    H.E., 183
    S., 24
French, J.R.P., Jr., 180–181
Frenkel-Brunswick, E., 227
Fritschler, A.L., 34

G

Gable, S.L., 48–49
Gelfand, M., 155–156
Gerard, H.B., 174, 189, 194–195, 200–205
Gold, G.J., 170, 183
Goldstein, N.J., 25
Gollwitzer, P.M., 45
Gonzaga, G., 48
Gouldner, A.W., 181
Greendale, G.A, 48
Greene, D., 31
Gruenberg, B.C., 138
Gruenewald, T.L., 45–48
Gurung, R.A.R., 47–48

H

Haley, R.W., 183
Harvey, J.H., 118
Heider, F., 56, 78, 105, xiii
Helgeson, V.S., 46–47
Hilmert, C.J., 48–49
Hofstede, G., 155

Hornstein, H., 114
Hough, L., 154
House
    J.S., 183
    P., 31
Hovland, C.I., 56
Hu, P., 48
Hui
    C.H., 155
    H.C., 155
Hull, C.L., 202
Hutson-Comeaux, S., 59
Hymovitch, B., 174, 194–195

I

Ickes, W., 118
Iwawaki, S., 115

J

Jahoda, M., 228
Janicki, D., 47
Jarcho, J., 47
Johannesen-Schmidt, M.C., 61, 64
Johnson
    B.T., 59, 61
    D.W., 226
    R.T., 226
Jones, E.E., 82, 212

K

Kanause, D.E., 82
Kaplan, S., 234
Karau, S., 61, 63
Kashima
    E., 155–156
    Y., 159
Kelley
    H.H., 82, 211, 213, 217
    H.W., 174, 194–195
Kelman, H.C., 153
Kemeny, M.E., 44–46
Kidd, R., 118
Kiefe, C.I., 47–48

Kim, H.S., 47
Klein, L.C., 47–48
Klonsky, B.G., 61
Koenig, A.M., 64
Koslowski, M., 181, 183
Krauss, R., 229–230
Kruglanski, A.W., 183
Kukla, A., 79, 118
Kulesa, P., 59
Kurowski, L.L., 155

L

Lambert, W.W., 149
Leff, W., 179
Lehman, B.J., 45, 47–49
Lerman, D., 118
Lerner, J.S., 45, 47
Levine, R., 241
Levinson, D.J., 227
Lewin, K., 172, 202,
    222, xii, xiii
Lewis
    B.P., 47–48
    S.K., 25
Liberman, A., 58
Lichtman, R.R., 44
Lieberman, M.D., 48–49
Lisansky, J., 155
Lobel, M., 45
Lucca, N., 155

M

Makhijani, M.G., 61
Manis, M., 45
Mann, T., 45
Marcus, E., 238
Marin, G., 155
Martin, J., 44
Massing, M., 33
Mayman, M., 45
McCusker, C., 155
McEwen, B., 47–48
McGregor, D., 182
McGuire, W.J., 56
Milgram, S., 169

Miller
    G.A., 28
    N., 201–202, 207
Mintzberg, H., 183
Mitchell, T., 153

N

Nagel, E., 189
Nassiakou, M., 152, 155
Newcomb, T.M., 115
Nisbett, R.E., 82

O

Orive, R., 201, 205
Osgood, C.E., 149

P

Paim, A., 116
Pfungst, O., 138
Pham, L.B., 46
Pierro, A., 183

R

Raven, B.H., 165, 169–170, 174–176,
    179–181, 183, 194–195
Reach, G., 154
Reed, G.M., 44, 46
Repetti, R.L., 46–47
Rhoads, K., 25
Rietsema, J., 176
Rivkin, I., 46
Robert, C., 155–156
Rodrigues, A., 105, 110–111, 115, 118, 183
Rosenberg, M.J., 56
Rosenthal, R., 129, 138–140
Rosenzweig, S., 138
Rosnow, R.L., 139
Ross, L., 31
Rotter, J.B., 75, 78
Rubin, J.Z., 169
Russell, D., 118

S

Sagarin, B.J., 25
Sage, R.M., 45, 47
Sanford, R.N., 227
Saxbe, D., 48
Schachter, S., 22, 193
Schneider, S.K., 46
Schwarzwald, J., 181, 183
Seeman
   S.E., 48
   T.E., 45–48
Segerstrom, S.C., 45
Shanmugam, A.V., 151–154
Shaw, J.I., 179
Shaw-Barnes, K., 59
Shedler, J., 45
Sherman, D.K., 45, 47
Simonich, W.L., 33
Sloan, L., 24
Steffen, V.J., 61
Suh, E.M., 155

T

Takagi, K., 47
Takezawa, S.I., 150, 152–153
Tamres, L., 47
Tanaka, Y., 151–154
Tapp, J.L., 153
Taylor, S.E., 39, 42–49
Thorne, A., 24
Trafimow, D., 155
Triandis, H.C., 145, 149–156
Triplett, N., xi

U

Updegraff, J.A., 47–48

V

Valins, S., 82
van Engen, M., 61
Vassiliou
   G., 151–154
   V., 151–155
Villareal, M.J., 155
Vincent, J.E., 25
Visscher, B.R., 44, 46

W

Walker, M., 24
Walster
   G.W., 181
   H.E., 181
Wang, H.-Y.J., 44, 46
Wasti, A., 155–156
Way, B.M., 49
Weber, M., 181
Weiner, B., 69, 75, 79–80, 82, 118
Welch, W.T., 45, 49
Wheeler, D., 25
White, G.L., 202–203
Whyte, W.F., 192
Wilhelmy, R.A., 200
Winter, P.L., 25
Wish, M., 234
Wood
   J.V., 44
   W., 58, 60, 62–63
Wright, Q., 229
Wrightsman, L., 153

Z

Zelezny, L., 241
Zimbardo, P.G., 85, 103

Subject Index

A

Abel, Theodore, 190
Abelson, Bob, 95, 100, 111
Abu Ghraib Prison, 102–103
Academic Freedom and Totalitarian Option, 116
Acme-Bolt Trucking game, research with, 229–230, 232
Adamopoulos, John, 161
Adler, Nancy, 46
Adorno, Theodor, 222
Affective Reactions of Children and Their Peers in Communities Differing in Size, 108
Albert, Rosita, 161
Allport
Floyd, 174, 204
Gordon, 56, 62, 173, 227
American Labor Party, 94
The Analysis of Subjective Culture, 152
Armor, David, 45
Aronson, Elliot, 87, 101, 122, 206, 243
Asch
Adrienne, 232
Solomon, 196–197
Assmar, Eveline Maria L., 123–124
Association for Women in Psychology, 61
Atkinson, John, 69, 73, 76, 100
"An Attempt at the Experimental Induction of the Defense Mechanism of Projection," 137
Attribution: Perceiving the Causes of Behavior, 82–83
Atzet, Jon, 200
The Authoritarian Personality, 227

B

Back, Kurt, 212, 217–218, 225
Baghat, Rabi, 161
Balet, Leo, 190
Banks, Curt, 101
Barker, Roger, 91, 108
Barry, Herbert, 90
Bass, Al, 160
Bavelas, Alex, 225, 230
Beaman, Art, 3
Beckman, Linda, 78–79, 81
Bem, Daryl, 214
Benedict, Ruth, 191
Benko, Antonius, 109
Benne, Ken, 225
Berkowitz, Leonard, 113, 122, 153
Berry, John, 159
Berscheid, Ellen, 217
Bhawuk, Darm, 161
Bion, Wilfred, 205
Birdwhistell, Ray, 134
Boardman, Susan, 231
Bok, Derek, 43
Bontempo, Robert, 161
Bower, Gordon, 90, 93, 95, 100
Bradburn, Norman, 4
Bradford, Lee, 225
Brahe, Tycho, 5
Brazilian Association of Applied Psychology, 112
Brazilian National Research Council, 115
Brehm, Jack, 90–91, 95
Brewer, Marilyn, 30
Brock, Tim, 95
Brown, J., 44, 221
Brown vs. the Board of Education, 200, 228

Bruner, Jerome, 206
Buegel, Hermann, 132
Bunker, Barbara, 231
Bush administration, 102
Buss, David, 63
Buxton, Claude, 89, 95

C

Campbell, Donald, 95, 135–136, 140, 172–173, 184–185
Cantril, Hadley, 172
Canvassing for Peace, 100
Cappello, Hector, 115
CARDIA. *See* Coronary Artery Risk Development in Young Adults
Carli, Linda, 64, 66
Carlston, Don, 161
Cartwright, Dorwin, 172–174, 225
Centers, Richard, 110–111
Chaiken, Shelly, 58, 66
Chaikin, Alan, 35
Chan, Darius, 161
Chein, Isadore, 233
Child, Irving, 95
Cialdini, Robert B., 19–37, 241, 245
Civilization and Its Discontents, 69
Clark, Kenneth, 140
A Clash of Fantasies: Cognitively Simple Self-Deceptions in Everyday Life, 150
Close Relationships, 217–218
Cochran, William, 131, 135, 141
The Cognitive Control of Motivation, 95
Cohen
    Jack, 135
    Morris, 189–190, 221, 223
    Robert, 90–91, 94–95, 174, 213
    Sheldon, 46
Cold war, 177–178
Coleman, Peter, 232, 238
Coleta, Dela, 124
Collins
    Barry, 178
    Mary Evan, 227
Conceptual Representation and Measurement of Psychological Forces, 222
Conolley, Edward, 200
Cook, Stuart, 211, 227–228, 238

Cooley, Charles Horton, 211
Cooper, Harris, 60
Copernicus, 5, 159
Coronary Artery Risk Development in Young Adults, 47
Cressey, Donald, 135
Cronbach, Lee, 135, 149
Crutchfield, Richard, 196
Cutting, James, 41

D

Dance of the Bees, 5
Darby, Joe, 102
Darley, John, 99
Darwin, Charles, 5, 239
Davidson, Andy, 161
Davis, Earl, 150, 160
de Charms, Richard, 78
Dela Coleta, Marilia Ferreira, 124
Dembo, Tamara, 225
Desiderato, Otello, 40
Deutsch, Morton, 95, 113, 122, 195, 198, 212, 221–240, 243
Diaz-Guerrero, Rogelio, 115, 154
Diekman, Amanda, 66
Diener, Ed, 1–17, 241–242, 244, 246–248
DiMatteo, Robin, 134
Distributive Justice, 235
Dollard, John, 95
Doob, Leonard, 90, 95
A Dreamer's Journey, 189
Duck, Steve, 217
Dunkel-Schetter, Christine, 44
Dunlap, Knight, 178
Durkheim, Emile, 194
Dweck, Carol, 41
A Dynamic Theory of Personality, 222

E

Eagly
    Alice H., 30, 51, 55–68, 241, 244–245
    Robert, 65
Eastwick, Paul, 66
Ebbesen, Ebbe, 96–97, 100
Echeverria, Jeri, 122
Eid, Michael, 15

Einstein, Albert, 5, 221, 239
Eisenberger, Naomi, 48
Emery, David, 225
Emmons, Robert, 10
Endresen, Karen, 3
Ettor, Joe, 191
Ewen, Robert, 160
Experimental Psychology, 149

F

Farr, Jim, 195
Faucheux, Claude, 98
Feldman, Jack, 161
Fernandes, Mervyn, 41
Festinger, Leon, 56, 90–91, 99, 113–114,
    173, 175–176, 180, 185, 190, 193–196,
    199–200, 202, 212–213, 225, 239
Fiedler, Fred, 149
Fine, Michelle, 231
Fink, Ken, 96
Fishbein, Marty, 153
Fiske, Susan, 51
Fleischer, Linda, 200
Flynn, Elizabeth Gurley, 191–192
Foa, Uriel, 152
Fode, Kermit, 133
Frank, Jerome, 233
Franz, Shepherd Ivory, 178
Fraser, Scott, 2, 97
Frederick, Chip, 102
French, John, 173–174, 176, 179–180,
    185, 225
Frenkel-Brunswick, Else, 222
Freud, Sigmund, 56, 69, 72, 92, 95,
    221, 239
Friedman
    Howard, 134
    Jon, 95
Fritz Heider: The Notebook, 111
Fromm, Erich, 222
Fujita, Frank, 10

G

García-Bouza, Jorge, 115
Garfield, Sol, 132
Garmezy, Norman, 74, 77, 243

Gelfand, Michele, 161
Gephart, Martha, 232
Gerard, Harold B., 95, 98, 110, 113,
    122, 174, 176, 178, 189–209, 228–229,
    242–243, 245
Giovanitti, Arturo, 191
Goffman, Erving, 134
Golding, William, 97
Gonzalez, Alex, 120–121
Goto, Sharon, 161
Gross, Felix, 87

H

Hall
    Edward, 134
    Robert L., 140
*Handbook of Conflict Resolution: Theory
    and Practice,* 236, 238
Handbook of Cross-Cultural Psychology,
    154, 159
*Handbook of Industrial and
    Organizational Psychology,* 154
Handbook of Social Psychology, 111
Haney, Craig, 101
Hanfmann, Eugenia, 225
Harlem Summer Project, 97–98
Harvey, John, 217–218
Hastorf, Al, 99
Head Start program, 98, 130
Hearn, Gordon, 225
Hebb, Don, 148
Heckhausen, Heinz, 79
Heider, Fritz, 56, 78, 81, 105, 111, 118,
    211, 235, 243
Heilman, Madeleine, 231
Hershkowitz, Aaron, 91
Hertzman, Max, 238
Hiroshima, bombing of, 170, 189, 226
Hitler, 130, 165, 173
HIV. *See* Human immunodeficiency virus
Hofstede, Geert, 155
Hohmann, George, 134
Holland, Paul, 135, 141
Holocaust, 88, 165
Horkheimer, Max, 222
Hornstein, Harvey, 231
Horowitz, Murray, 225

Horowtiz, Sandra, 231–232
Hovland, Carl, 94–95, 198, 212, 229–230
Hui, Harry, 161
Hull, Clark, 91, 172, 223, 243
The Human Group, 213
Human immunodeficiency virus, 46
Hunt
    Buzz, 95
    Joe, 149

I

ICCCR. *See* International Center for
    Cooperation and Conflict Resolution
Influence: Science and Practice, 29
*Influencing Attitudes and Changing
    Behavior,* 100
Insko, Chet, 19–22
International Center for Cooperation and
    Conflict Resolution, 234, 236–238
International Workers of the World, 191
Interpersonal Power Inventory, 119
Interracial Housing, 228
Interracial Marriage, 115
Irwin, Frances, 222
Iwawaki, Saburo, 115

J

Jablonski, Bernardo, 123–224
Jackson, Stonewall, 39
Jacobson, Lenore, 135
Jaffe, David, 101
Jahoda, Marie, 4, 228
James
    Henry, 21
    William, 21
Janis, Irving, 91, 95, 199, 212–213, 233
Jaspers, Joseph, 98
Jenkins
    David, 225
    Herbert, 230
Johnson
    Blair, 59, 66
    David, 226, 231, 236
    Roger, 226
Jones
    Edward, 81–82, 92, 197, 215, 247
    James, 94

*Journal of Experimental Social
    Psychology,* founding of, 22
Journal of Happiness Studies, founding
    of, 7
Joyner, Bob, 147
Judd, Charles, Jr., 231

K

Kagan, Jerry, 134
Kahneman, Daniel, 11, 15, 42, 51
Kaleuff, Alan, 90
Kanouse, Dave, 215
Kaplan, Abraham, 135
Karau, Steve, 66
Karsten, Anitra, 225
Kashima, Yoshi, 161
Katz, Daniel, 57, 69–70, 73, 83,
    173–174, 185
Katzell, Ray, 98
Kelley, Harold H., 22, 35, 74, 77–78,
    81–83, 88, 92–93, 95, 98, 105, 109–111,
    114, 122, 132, 174, 178, 185, 193,
    211–220, 243, 247
Kelman, Herbert, 56–57, 95,
    153, 233
Kemeny, Margaret, 45
Kendler, Howard, 95–96
Keniston, Kenneth, 41
Kessen, Bill, 95
Kiesler, Sara, 40
Kim-Prieto, Chu, 10
King, Laura, 5, 11
Klein
    George, 207
    Melanie, 205
Klopfer, Bruno, 134
Kluckholm, Clyde, 152
Koenig, Anne, 66
Korean War, 95
Koslowski, Meni, 183
Krauss, Bob, 229
Kraut, Robert, 41
Kressel, Kenneth, 231
Kruglanski, Arie, 214
Ku-Shu, Yang, 160
Kukla, Andy, 78–79
Kulesa, Patrick, 66
Kupaswami, Professor, 151

L

LaBarre, Weston, 134
Lambert
  Bill, 148
  Wally, 148
Langer, Ellen, 41, 96
Langfield, Herbert, 148
Lansberg, Ivan, 231
Larsen, Randy, 10, 15
Latane, Bibb, 99
Lawrence, Charles, 87, 92
Lazarsfeld, Paul, 190–191
Leavitt, Harold, 69
Lerner, Melvin J., 233
Lester, Olive, 197
Lestik, Mike, 101
Leung, Kwok, 161
Levine, Bob, 119–122
Levinger, George, 174
Lewicki, Roy, 231
Lewin, Kurt, 69, 108–109, 172–173,
  178, 184–185, 192–193, 202, 217–218,
  221–224, 231, 233, 235, 239, 243
Lichtenberg, Phil, 195
Lichtman, Rosemary, 44
Lieberman, Matt, 48
The Life of a Psychologist, 105
Lindzey, Gardner, 74
Lippitt, Ronald, 173, 192–193, 225
Lippmann, Hanns Ludwig, 106, 108
Liverant, Shep, 133
Logan, Frank, 95
Logic and the Scientific Method, 189
Loh, Wally, 160
Lonner, Walter, 149
Lord of the Flies, 97
*The Lucifer Effect: Understanding How
  Good People Turn Evil*, 103
Luck, role of, 244
Lyman, Arnie, 95
Lynd, Robert, 190
Lyubomirsky, Sonja, 5, 11

M

MacArthur, Leslie, 215
MacArthur Network on Socioeconomic
  Status and Health, 46

MacIver, Robert, 190
Mahl, George, 134
Maier, Steve, 96
Malinowski, Bronislav, 87
Maltzman, Irving, 135
Manis, Melvin, 57
Marcus, Eric, 238
The Marginal Man, 172
Marín, Gerardo, 115
Marquis, Donald, 223, 243
Marx, Karl, 112, 115, 221–222, 226,
  229, 239
Masling, Joe, 173
Maslow, Abraham, 87
Mathewson, Grover, 200
Matthews, Karen, 46
May, Mark, 95
McCarthy period, political climate
  during, 229
McClelland, David, 56
McClintock, Chuck, 216
McConahay, John, 41
McCusker, Chris, 161
McDougall, William, 165
McEwen, Bruce, 46–47
McGregor, Douglas, 182
McGuire, William, 79, 81, 83, 95, 99,
  149, 244
Mead
  George Herbert, 226
  Margaret, 134, 154, 191–192, 243
The Measurement of Meaning, 149
Medvene, Louis, 231
Meehl, Paul, 74, 135
Merton, Robert, 190, 206
Mettee, David, 40
Michalos, Alex, 6
Midwest and Its Children, 108
Milgram, Stanley, 87, 102, 169, 247
Miller
  George, 28
  Neal, 90, 94, 207
  Norman, 95, 201
Minnesota Multiphasic Personality
  Inventory, 74
Misumi, Jiujitzu, 150
Mitchell, Terry, 161
Montero, Maritza, 115
Montgomery, K.C., 89–90, 93
Morton Prince Clinic for Hypnotherapy, 96

Moscovici, Serge, 98, 113, 218
Mosteller, Fred, 111, 135, 141
Mowrer, Hobart, 132, 149
Murphy, Gardner, 173
Murray, Harry, 138
Myers, David, 11, 15

N

Nagasaki, bombing of, 170, 189, 226
Nagel, Ernest, 189, 223
Naidoo, Josie, 160
Nebraska Symposium on Motivation, 100
Needleman, Jacob, 246
Neff, Walter Scott, 221, 238
New Directions in Attribution Research, 118
Newcomb, Theodore, 56–57, 111, 114–115, 174, 178
Newton, Isaac, 5
Ng, Weiting, 10
Nielsen, Paul, 140
Nisbett, Dick, 30, 41, 215
Nuttin, Josef, 98

O

Oishi, Shigehiro, 10
Oldendorff, Tony, 176
Olds, Jim, 148
"On the Differential Effects of Some Parameters of Balance," 110
On the Psycho-logic of Interpersonal Relations, 110
Opotow, Susan, 232
Orne, Martin, 135
Osgood, Charles, 149, 152, 215, 233
Ovsiankina, Maria, 225

P

Paim, Antonio, 116
Paradigms in Transition, 139
Parsons, Talcott, 56
Pavlov, Ivan, 138
Pavot, Bill, 10

Peak, Helen, 57
Peale, Norman Vincent, 4
Pepinsky, Harold, 132, 135, 140
Pepitone, Albert, 122, 174, 176, 217, 224–225
Peplau, Anne, 178
The Person and the Situation, 217
Personal Causation, 78
Perspectives on Psychological Science, founding of, 6
Petrified Forest National Park, 25–26
Pfungst, Oskar, 138
Pierro, Antonio, 183
Planning of Experiments, 111
Platt, Gerry, 88
Plous, Scott, 101
Porter, Lyman, 95
Postman, Leo, 207
The Power of Positive Thinking, 4
Pressman, Sarah, 16
Preston, Malcolm, 222
Preventing World War III, 229, 233
Principles of Topological Psychology, 222
Prison Project Team experiment, 101–102
Prisoner's Dilemma game, research format, 228, 232
Probabilities With Statistical Applications, 111
Project for a Scientific Psychology, 194
Proshansky, Harold, 88
Pruitt, Dean, 95
Psicologia Social [Social Psychology], 115, 123
Psychological Monographs, 75
Psychological Solutions to Social Problems, 114
Psychology and Life, 92, 100
Psychology and the Social Order, 221–222
The Psychology of Attitudes, 58, 64, 66
The Psychology of Interpersonal Relations, 56, 107
Pygmalion in the Classroom, 135

R

Rabbie, Jacob, 197
Radke-Yarrow, Marian, 225
Raider, Ellen, 237
Raiffa, Howard, 213, 228

Ramallo, Luis, 115
Rappaport, David, 222
Raskin, Evelyn, 87
Raven, Bertram H., 43, 110–111,
  119–122, 165–187, 193, 197, 242–243
Ray, Gordon, 80
Reale, Miguel, 115
Reed, Geoffrey, 46
*Reflections on 100 Years of Experimental
  Social Psychology,* 122
Reich, Wilhelm, 222
Reitman, Walter, 135
Repetti, Rena, 47
Research Center for Group Dynamics,
  173–174
Research Center for Human Relations,
  227–229
*Research Methods in Social
  Relations,* 228
*The Resolution of Conflict: Constructive
  and Destructive Processes,* 232
Resolving Social Conflicts, 172
Rhine, Robert, 40, 131
Riecken, Henry, 135, 140, 176, 214, 236
Ring, Ken, 214
Rodin, Judy, 43, 99
Rodnick, Elliot, 77
Rodrigues, Aroldo, 105–127, 183,
  241–243, 245
Roediger, Henry, 41
Rogers, Carl, 147–148, 223, 243
Romero-García, Oswaldo, 115
Rommetviet, Ragnor, 98
Roosevelt
    Franklin D., 39, 170
    Theodore, 39, 125
Rorschach test, 106
Rosen, Sidney, 174
Rosenau, Norah, 229
Rosenberg
    Milton, 95, 199
    Sy, 229
Rosenthal, Robert, 129–143, 241, 243,
  245, 247
Rosnow, Ralph, 134, 139
Ross
    E.A., 165
    Lee, 99, 215
Rotter, Julian, 75, 78, 133
Rozin, Paul, 10

Rubin
    Don, 135, 141
    Jeffrey, 231
Ruch, Floyd, 100, 171
Russell, Bertrand, 139

S

Sagan, Carl, 31
Sakai, Haruki, 183
Salazar, Jose Miguel, 115
Sanchez, Euclydes, 115
Sarason
    Irwin, 2
    Seymour, 92, 95
Schachter, Stanley, 19, 22–23, 88–89, 92,
  95, 99, 176, 212–214, 218, 224–225, 245
Schatzberg, Allen, 96
Scherer, Klaus, 51, 129
Schetter, Christine Dunkel, 178
Schimmack, Ulrich, 10
Schlosberg, Harold, 148–149
Schneidman, Ed, 133–134
Schofield, William, 132
Schwartz
    Barry, 96
    Shalom, 159
Schwarzwald, Joseph, 183
Schweitzer, Albert, 13
Scodel, Al, 133
Scollon, Christie, 10
Sears, David, 41, 95, 100, 110–111, 178
Seeman
    Mef, 225
    Teresa, 47
Seligman, Martin, 11, 15
Setiadi, Bernadette, 161
Shapiro, Eli, 190
Shaver, Kelly, 215
Sheffield, Fred, 90
Shepard, Roger, 95, 100
Sherif, Muzafer, 91, 95, 150
Singer, Jerry, 214
Skinner, B.F., 235
Smith, Ronald E., 2
The Social Psychology of Groups, 22, 109
Solomon, Richard, 148
SPE. *See* Stanford prison experiment
Stahelski, Tony, 216

Stanford prison experiment, 101–102
Stanton, Annette, 44
Statistical Inference, 111
Statistical Principles in Experimental Design, 111
Statistics: A New Approach, 111
Steil, Janice, 231
Steiner, Ivan, 149
Stonequist, Everett, 172
Storms, Michae, 141
Stotland, Ezra, 174
Street Corner Society, 148, 192
Stumpf, Carl, 148
Suh, Eunkook, 10
Synder, Richard, 225

T

Tajfel, Henri, 113, 153, 239
Tamir, Maya, 10
Tanaka, Yasumasa, 150
TAT. *See* Thematic Apperception Test
Taylor, Shelley E., 39–54, 178, 244–247
Thematic Apperception Test, 74–76, 83
Theories in Social Psychology, 229
Theories of Cognitive Consistency: A Source-Book, 111
Theories of Motivation: From Mechanism to Cognition, 80
A Theory of Cognitive Dissonance, 56, 90
Thibaut, John, 19, 21–22, 35, 105, 109, 213, 216–219, 225
Through the Labyrinth: The Truth About How Women Become Leaders, 64
Thurstone, L.L., 223, 243
Timpane, Michael, 234
Tov, Will, 10
Triandis, Harry C., 145–164, 241
Tukey, John, 135

U

The Uncommitted, 41
UNESCO. *See* United Nations Educational, Scientific, and Cultural Organization
United Nations Educational, Scientific, and Cultural Organization, 157

V

Valins, Stuart, 215
Varela, Jacobo, 114–115
Vary-Szilagii, Ibolya, 159
Vassiliou, Vasso, 152
Veenhoven, Ruut, 6
Vietnam War, 13, 97, 233
Villareal, Marcelo, 161
Villegas, Julio, 115
Viteles, Morris, 222
von Frisch, Karl, 5

W

Wagner, Wolfgang, 205
Walker, Laurens, 214
Walster, Elaine, 40, 217
Wasti, Arzu, 161
Watson, Goodwin, 230–231
Watts riots, 78
Weiner
    Bernard, 69–84, 110, 118–121, 178, 215, 243–244, 246–247
    Maryann, 111
Weisenberg, Matty, 97
Weitzman, Eben, 232
Wheeler, Ladd, 214
White, Ralph, 233
Whyte, William Foote, 148, 192, 243
Wickens, Delos, 172
Wilhelmy, Roland, 200
Willerman, Ben, 176, 214, 225
Wilson, Charles, 195
Winer, Ben, 80
Wirtz, Derrick, 10
Wish, Mike, 234
Wobblies. *See* International Workers of the World
Wong, K.P., 121–122
Wood
    Joanne, 44
    Wendy, 51, 66
World War II, 39, 86, 92, 130, 146, 165, 169–171, 176, 189, 215, 221, 223, 241, 243
Wright, Herbert, 108–109

Y

Young Radicals, 41

Z

Zajonc, Robert, 98, 111, 122, 174, 195
Zander, Alvin, 91, 174, 225
Zanna, Mark, 41
Zeigarnik, Bluma, 225

Ziegler, Stan, 121
Zigler, Ed, 95
Zimbardo, Philip G., 84–104,
   122, 154, 171, 241–242,
   244–245
Ziviani, Cilio R., 124